137331487

Studies in Economic Transition

General Editors: **Jens Hölscher**, Reader in Economics, University of Brighton; and **Horst Tomann**, Professor of Economics, Free University Berlin

This series has been established in response to a growing demand for a greater understanding of the transformation of economic systems. It brings together theoretical and empirical studies on economic transition and economic development. The post-communist transition from planned to market economies is one of the main areas of applied theory because in this field the most dramatic examples of change and economic dynamics can be found. The series aims to contribute to the understanding of specific major economic changes as well as to advance the theory of economic development. The implications of economic policy will be a major point of focus.

Titles include:

Lucian Cernat
EUROPEANIZATION, VARIETIES OF CAPITALISM AND ECONOMIC PERFORMANCE IN CENTRAL AND EASTERN EUROPE

Irwin Collier, Herwig Roggemann, Oliver Scholz and Horst Tomann (*editors*)
WELFARE STATES IN TRANSITION
East and West

Bruno Dallago and Ichiro Iwasaki (*editors*)
CORPORATE RESTRUCTURING AND GOVERNANCE IN TRANSITION ECONOMIES

Bruno Dallago (*editor*)
TRANSFORMATION AND EUROPEAN INTEGRATION
The Local Dimension

Hella Engerer
PRIVATIZATION AND ITS LIMITS IN CENTRAL AND EASTERN EUROPE
Property Rights in Transition

Saul Estrin, Grzegorz W. Kolodko and Milica Uvalic (*editors*)
TRANSITION AND BEYOND

Hubert Gabrisch and Rüdiger Pohl (*editors*)
EU ENLARGEMENT AND ITS MACROECONOMIC EFFECTS IN EASTERN EUROPE
Currencies, Prices, Investment and Competitiveness

Oleh Havrylyshyn
DIVERGENT PATHS IN POST-COMMUNIST TRANSFORMATION
Capitalism for All or Capitalism for the Few?

Jens Hölscher (*editor*)
FINANCIAL TURBULENCE AND CAPITAL MARKETS IN TRANSITION COUNTRIES

Jens Hölscher and Anja Hochberg (*editors*)
EAST GERMANY'S ECONOMIC DEVELOPMENT SINCE UNIFICATION
Domestic and Global Aspects

Mihaela Kelemen and Monika Kostera (*editors*)
CRITICAL MANAGEMENT RESEARCH IN EASTERN EUROPE
Managing the Transition

Emil J. Kirchner (*editor*)
DECENTRALIZATION AND TRANSITION IN THE VISEGRAD
Poland, Hungary, the Czech Republic and Slovakia

David Lane and Martin Myant (*editors*)
VARIETIES OF CAPITALISM IN POST-COMMUNIST COUNTRIES

Tomasz Mickiewicz (*editor*)
CORPORATE GOVERNANCE AND FINANCE IN POLAND AND RUSSIA

Tomasz Mickiewicz
ECONOMIC TRANSITION IN CENTRAL EUROPE AND THE COMMONWEALTH OF
INDEPENDENT STATES

Milan Nikolic
MONETARY POLICY IN TRANSITION
Inflation Nexus Money Supply in Postcommunist Russia

Julie Pellegrin
THE POLITICAL ECONOMY OF COMPETITIVENESS AND ENLARGED EUROPE

Stanislav Poloucek (*editor*)
REFORMING THE FINANCIAL SECTOR IN CENTRAL EUROPEAN COUNTRIES

Gregg S. Robins
BANKING IN TRANSITION
East Germany after Unification

Johannes Stephan
ECONOMIC TRANSITION IN HUNGARY AND EAST GERMANY
Gradualism and Shock Therapy in Catch-up Development

Johannes Stephan (*editor*)
TECHNOLOGY TRANSFER VIA FOREIGN DIRECT INVESTMENT IN CENTRAL AND
EASTERN EUROPE

Hans van Zon
THE POLITICAL ECONOMY OF INDEPENDENT UKRAINE

Adalbert Winkler (*editor*)
BANKING AND MONETARY POLICY IN EASTERN EUROPE
The First Ten Years

Studies in Economic Transition
Series Standing Order ISBN 0–333–73353–3
(*outside North America only*)

You can receive future titles in this series as they are published by placing a standing
order. Please contact your bookseller or, in case of difficulty, write to us at the address
below with your name and address, the title of the series and the ISBN quoted above.

Customer Services Department, Macmillan Distribution Ltd, Houndmills, Basingstoke,
Hampshire RG21 6XS, England

Transition and Beyond

Essays in Honor of Mario Nuti

Edited by

Saul Estrin
London School of Economics, UK

Grzegorz W. Kolodko
Kozminski Business School, TIGER, Warsaw, Poland

Milica Uvalic
University of Perugia, Italy

First published 2007 by
PALGRAVE MACMILLAN
Houndmills, Basingstoke, Hampshire RG21 6XS and
175 Fifth Avenue, New York, N.Y. 10010
Companies and representatives throughout the world

PALGRAVE MACMILLAN is the global academic imprint of the Palgrave
Macmillan division of St. Martin's Press, LLC and of Palgrave Macmillan Ltd.
Macmillan® is a registered trademark in the United States, United Kingdom
and other countries. Palgrave is a registered trademark in the European
Union and other countries.

ISBN-13: 978–0–230–54697–4 hardback
ISBN-10: 0–230–54697–8 hardback

This book is printed on paper suitable for recycling and made from fully
managed and sustained forest sources. Logging, pulping and manufacturing
processes are expected to conform to the environmental regulations of the
country of origin.

A catalogue record for this book is available from the British Library.

Library of Congress Cataloging-in-Publication Data
Transition and beyond:essays in honour of Mario Nuti/edited by Saul Estrin,
    Grzegorz W. Kolodko, Milica Uvalic.
      p.   cm. — (Studies in economic transition)
Includes bibliographical references and index.
ISBN 0–230–54697–8 (alk. paper)
    1. Europe, Eastern—Economic policy—1989–   2. Europe, Eastern—
    Economic conditions—1989–   3. Post-communism—Europe, Eastern.
    4. Privatization—Europe, Eastern.   5. Capitalism—Europe, Eastern.
    I. Estrin, Saul.   II. Kolodko, Grzegorz W.   III. Uvalic, Milica.
    HC244.T698635 2007
    330.947—dc22   2007022297

10   9   8   7   6   5   4   3   2   1
16   15   14   13   12   11   10   09   08   07

Printed and bound in Great Britain by
Antony Rowe Ltd, Chippenham and Eastbourne

Dedicated to D. Mario Nuti

Contents

List of Tables

List of Figures

Acknowledgments

The editors gratefully acknowledge the editorial assistance of Kasia Komosa, from the Management Department at the LSE. She worked tirelessly on a manuscript containing numerous different styles, fonts and editorial conventions, sometimes in a single chapter! The fact that the book now reads as a coherent volume is due to her patience and thoroughness. The editors and the authors all thank her for her valuable contribution to this volume.

Notes on the Contributors

Marina Bakanova is the World Bank Country Economist for Belarus. Since joining the Bank in 2002 she has been involved in the preparation of major World Bank diagnostic reports on Belarus, including Public Expenditure Review, Poverty Assessment, and Country Economic Memorandum. Her research interests include economic growth, trade and competitiveness. She has also been involved in analytical and advisory work on public finance in Ukraine and Moldova. Marina has taught International Economics and International Trade at the Belarusian State University and has worked for the EU TACIS and the UNDP projects in Belarus.

Simon Commander is Director of the Centre for New and Emerging Markets (CNEM) at London Business School and Senior Adviser, European Bank for Reconstruction and Development. He holds a BA from Oxford University and a PhD from Cambridge University. He previously worked at the World Bank. He is currently an editor of the EBRD's Transition Report and has published widely on the economics of transition in both research journals and books.

László Csaba is a graduate of the Budapest University of Economics (1976) with a PhD (1984) and DSc professorial degree (1996) from the Hungarian Academy of Sciences. Since 2000 he is Professor of Economics and European Studies at the Central European University, Budapest. He serves also as full Professor at the University of Debrecen and Budapest Corvinus University and has been a visiting Professor in leading universities in Germany, Finland and Italy. He is the author of five monographs and editor of five collective volumes, about 200 articles and chapters in books published in 19 countries and is on the editorial board of 10 journals of which five are based outside Hungary. Vice President (1990–94 and 1996–98) and President (1999–2000) of European Association for Comparative Economic Studies (EACES), Co-chair (1996–2002) and Chair (2002–08) of Committee on Economics, The Hungarian Academy of Sciences. His most recent monograph is the second, revised and extended edition of *The New Political Economy of Emerging Europe* (Akadémiai/Kluwer, 2007); see website: www.csabal.com

Marcello de Cecco, BA in Economics (Cambridge, 1964), is Professor of Monetary and Financial History at the Scuola Normale Superiore di Pisa (Italy). Previously he was Professor at the University of Rome 'La Sapienza', the European University Institute (Fiesole), and the University of Siena, lecturer at the School of Social Sciences at University of East Anglia,

Professorial Fellow at St Antony's College, Oxford and at the Royal Institute of International Affairs (Chatham House). He held the Amadeo Giannini Chair of Italian culture at the University of California, Berkeley and was a visiting scholar at the IMF and Harvard University. He is Vice President of the Italian Economic Association, member of the Board of *Istituto dell'Enciclopedia Italiana*, of the Fondazione Lorenzo Valla, of the scientific advisory board of the Unicredit bank, and of Mediobanca's Ricerche & Studi, and chairs the scientific committee of the Ente Einaudi. Previously he was Executive Director of the Monte dei Paschi di Siena and of the Banca Nazionale del Lavoro, of the Italian International Bank in London and of the CREDIOP bank. From 1997 to 2000, he was a member of the Italian Prime Minister's Council of Economic Advisers. Main publications include *Money and Empire* (Blackwell, 1974), *Changing Money* (Blackwell, 1984) and other books and articles on money and finance in international journals, including entries to the New Palgrave Dictionary.

Padma Desai is Gladys and Roland Harriman Professor of Comparative Economic Systems, Director of the Center for Transition Economies at Columbia University and member of the Council on Foreign Relations. Previously President of the Association for Comparative Economic Studies (2001) and US Treasury's Advisor to the Russian Finance Ministry (1995). She holds a PhD in Economics (Harvard University) and has extensively published on economic planning in the Soviet Union, economic reforms in Russia and the emerging market economies. Main publications include *Marxism, Central Planning and the Soviet Economy* (ed.) (The MIT Press, 1983); *The Soviet Economy: Problems and Prospects* (Blackwell, 1987); *Perestroika in Perspective: The Design and Dilemmas of Soviet Reform* (Princeton University Press, 1989); *Going Global: Transition from Plan to Market in the World Economy* (ed.) (The MIT Press, 1997); and jointly with Todd Idson, *Work Without Wages: Russia's Nonpayment Crisis* (The MIT Press, 2000). Her *Financial Crisis, Contagion, and Containment: From Asia to Argentina* (Princeton University Press, 2003) was described by Paul Krugman as the 'best book yet on financial crises'. Her *Conversations on Russia* was published by Oxford University Press in April 2006, and was selected by the *Financial Times*, among several books, as 'pick of 2006'. She has combined scholarly activity with frequent writings in the *New York Times*, the *Financial Times*, and the *Wall Street Journal*, and appearances on the MacNeil-Lehrer NewsHour, CNN, BBC, Debates-Debates, Jim Lehrer NewsHour, and the Charlie Rose Show.

John Eatwell, Lord Eatwell of Stratton St Margaret (Life Peer, cr. 1992), President of Queens' College (Cambridge), Director of the Cambridge Endowment for Research in Finance, and Professor of Financial Policy in the Judge Institute of Management, University of Cambridge. Educated at Cambridge and Harvard, he has taught economics at Cambridge since 1970, and has been President of Queens' College, Cambridge, since 1997. Previously he was also Professor in the Graduate Faculty of the New School for Social Research, New York, Visiting Professor at Columbia University, New York, the University of Massachusetts, Amherst, and the University of Amsterdam. In 1997 he joined the Board of the Securities and Futures Authority (SFA), Britain's securities markets regulator (until end-2001), serving on the Enforcement Committee and the Capital Committee, where he developed his interest in securities regulation and risk management in financial institutions. His latest publications in this field include *Global Finance at Risk: The Case for International Regulation* (New York: New Press) and *Global Governance of Financial Systems: The Legal and Economic Regulation of Systemic Risk* (New York: Oxford University Press). Since the SFA ceased to operate he has been a member of the Regulatory Decisions Committee of the Financial Services Authority.

Michael Ellman, Professor of Economics at the University of Amsterdam (since 1978). Previously lecturer at the Department of Economics, Glasgow University (1967–69), research officer/senior research officer at Department of Applied Economics, Cambridge University (1969–75); and Associate Professor at University of Amsterdam (1975–78). He got his BA from Cambridge (1963), MSc in economics from London School of Economics (LSE) (1965), was a graduate student of Economics Faculty, Moscow State University (1965–67), and got his PhD from Cambridge (1972). He was awarded the 1998 Kondratieff prize for his 'contributions to the development of the social sciences'. He is honorary member (academician) of the Russian Academy of Economic Sciences and Entrepreneurship, Fellow of Tinbergen Institute, of NAKE, and of AIID. He has been Visiting Professor at ISS, the Hague (1983); New Economic School, Moscow (1997); Lecturer at Beidaihe (1996), Suzhou (1998) and Beijing (1999); Consultant to UNECE and ILO, Macdonald Commission Canada, the EU and the Dutch government. Author of numerous books and articles on the Soviet and Russian economies, on transition economics and on Soviet economic and political history. Recent publications include (ed.) *Russia's oil and natural gas: Bonanza or curse?* (London: Anthem, 2006); 'Transition: Intended and unintended processes', *Comparative Economic Studies*, 2005; 'Soviet industrialization: A remarkable success? *Slavic Review*, winter 2004.

Sergio Godoy was born in Santiago, Chile in 1969. From 1995 to 1997, he was Chief Economist of the Chilean National Chamber of Commerce, which is one of the most influential business associations in Chile, including more than 5000 firms. During his tenure, he supervised the development of retail indexes for several regions in Chile and prepared numerous press conferences, wrote several articles and gave interviews in order to convey the Chamber's policy and opinions. In 2004, he became a Senior Economist in the International Finance Group at the Central Bank of Chile, where he develops research on international events affecting the Chilean economy and on the liquidity and solvency of this economy. He currently serves as a Senior Economist in the Financial Operations Division, where his main responsibilities are developing research on the domestic and international FX and bond markets, and building models for managing foreign reserves and domestic liabilities. In addition, since 2000, he is a part-time Professor in Emerging Financial Markets at the MBA of the Universidad Católica de Chile. He is a graduate of the Universidad Católica de Chile (BS Economic and Business; MS Applied Macroeconomics, 1994) and Columbia University (MBA 1999; PhD Financial Economics, 2004).

Michael Keren, born in Germany, since 1933 in Israel. He holds a BA in Economics and Political Institutions from Keele University (UK), an MA in Development Economics from Williams College (MA, USA); and a PhD in Economics from Yale University with a dissertation on 'Central Allocation of Resources under Uncertainty'. He has been at the Department of Economics, Hebrew University, Jerusalem since 1966, first as instructor and after 1968 as Lecturer, Senior Lecturer (after 1972), Associate Professor (after 1980), and Professor (after 1986). Research interests include economics of bureaucracy: incentives, structure and efficacy; comparative economic systems; transition to the market in Eastern Europe, on which he has published extensively. He is also editor of the *European Journal of Comparative Economics*.

Gur Ofer is Harvey M. and Lyn P. Meyerhoff (Emeritus) Professor of Soviet Economics at the Departments of Economics and of Russian Studies, The Hebrew University of Jerusalem (www.economics.huji.ac.il). He was one of the founders of the New Economic School (NES) in Moscow, a graduate school of economics in the Western tradition established in 1992 (www.NES.ru). For many years he served as chair of its International Advisory Board. Gur Ofer wrote his PhD dissertation at Harvard under Simon Kuznets and Abram Bergson on *The Service Sector in Soviet Economic Growth: A Comparative Study* (Harvard UP, 1973). Among his publications are *The Soviet Household Under the Old Regime* (with Aaron Vinokur) (Cambridge University Press, 1992); 'Soviet Economic Growth: 1928–85: A Survey Article', *Journal of Economic Literature*, December 1987; *Reforming Planned Economies in the Integrating World Economy* (with Barry Bosworth) (The Brookings Institution, 1995); 'Development and Transition: Emerging but Merging?' *Revue d'économie financière* (Special Issue), 2001; *The Economic Prospects of the CIS: Sources of Long Term Growth since 1991* (co-editor, Richard Pomfret) (Elgar Books, 2004). Over the years he served as a visiting scholar, among others, in Harvard, Columbia, Yale, The Rand Corporation, the Wilson Center, the Brooking Institution, the World Bank and NES. In Israel, he worked on issues of the Welfare State and of Health Economics and is head of The Israel

National Institute for Health Policy and Health Services Research. He served as a Department Chair and President of the Israeli Economic Association.

Igor Pelipas has a MSc degree in Economics and Statistics from the Belarusian State Economic University (Minsk) and a PhD in Economics from the Belarusian Research Institute of Agricultural Economics (Minsk). Currently he is Director of the Research Center of the Institute for Privatization and Management (IPM) in Minsk. Recent research deals with macroeconomic modeling, applied econometrics, monetary policy, and transition economies. He is Chief Editor of the Belarusian quarterly economic journal *ECOWES*, and co-editor of *Economic Review: Belarus, Kazakhstan, Russia, and Ukraine*. Formerly he was Director of the Eurasia Foundation representative office in Belarus, and senior research fellow at the Institute of Economics, National Academy of Sciences. He was one of the co-founders and Deputy Director of the Independent Institute of Socio-economic and Political Studies (IISEPS), the first think-tank in Belarus. He is author of forty scientific publications, including 'Modeling the demand for money and inflation in Belarus', in L. V. de Souza and O. Havrylyshyn (eds) *Return to Growth in CIS Countries* (Springer, 2006); 'Money and prices in Belarus: information content of different monetary aggregates', and with I. Tochitskaya 'Economic Integration Between Belarus and Russia: Testing for Convergence of Monetary Policy', both in L. V. de Souza and P. De Lombaerde (eds), *Beyong the Euro Area: Monetary and Exchange Rate Policy in CIS Countries* (Ashgate, 2006); 'Money Demand and Inflation in Belarus: Evidence from Cointegrated VAR', in *Research in International Business and Finance*, 20 (2006).

Vladimir Popov, Professor at the New Economic School in Moscow, a Sector Head at the Academy of the National Economy in Moscow, and Visiting Professor at Carleton University in Ottawa. In 1996–98 he was a Senior Research Fellow in the World Institute for Development Economics Research of the United Nations University (WIDER/UNU) in Helsinki, Finland, co-directing a project 'Transition Strategies, Alternatives and Outcomes'. In the 1990s he was also teaching at the Academy of National Economy (Moscow), at Queen's University, University of Toronto and Carleton University in Canada, Helsinki School of Economics in Finland, University of Kaiserslautern in Germany and was doing research in Italy, Japan, Sweden, US. He is author of numerous books and articles, including *Political Institutions and Development* (Edward Elgar, 2007), co-edited with N. Dinello; *Three Drops of Water: Notes on China by a Non-Sinologist* (Delo Publishers, 2002, in Russian); *Transition and Institutions: The Experience of Late Reformers* (Oxford University Press, 2001), co-edited with G. A. Cornia; *The Asian Crisis Turns Global* (Institute of Southeast Asian Studies, 1999), co-authored with M. Montes; *The Turning Point: Revitalizing the Soviet Economy* (Doubleday, 1990), co-authored with N. Shmelev; and numerous articles in scientific journals (see http://www.carleton.ca/~vpopov).

Janez Prašnikar, Professor of Economics, Executive Director of the Institute for South-Eastern Europe and Associate Dean for Research, Faculty of Economics, Ljubljana (Slovenia), where he is also founder and director of the Residential Master's Program in Business and Organization. Previously he was a member of the Council for Higher Education of the Republic of Slovenia, of the Promotion Committee at the University of Ljubljana, and of the Strategic Committee of the Slovenian Government. As research fellow he is affiliated to the William Davidson Institute, University of Michigan Business School (USA) and Centre for Economic Policy Research (CEPR, London). Research interests and expertise include transition economics, enterprise behavior, entrepreneurship, managerial economics, labor relations. He holds a PhD from the University of Ljubljana (1982). Previously he was Visiting Fellow at the University of Berkeley, Cornell University, and Pittsburgh University; Visiting Professor at the University of Pittsburgh, Oxford University, and Kellogg School of Management at Northwestern. He is co-editor of the *Economic and Business Review for Central and South-Eastern Europe,* and policy advisor to companies and governments (including former Yugoslavia, China and Slovenia). Presently he is President of the Programme Committee of the Portorož Business Conference. He has also served as a president or member of Supervisory Boards in numerous Slovenian firms.

Sergei Pukovich works at the Institute of Privatization and Management, Minsk, Belarus. He has a MSc degree in Economics obtained at the Belarusian State Economic University (Minsk). Currently he is a Director of the Consulting Center of the Institute for Privatization and Management (IPM). His recent research interests are in the area of enterprise restructuring in transition economies. He participated in several projects on this topic, including the preparation of a background paper for the World Bank country economic memorandum for the Republic of Belarus. His practical activities at the IPM are focused on business consulting, marketing research and marketing strategies. He also works as a business trainer.

Joseph E. Stiglitz, Professor at Columbia University in New York and Chair of Columbia University's Committee on Global Thought. In 2001, he was awarded the Nobel Prize in Economics for his analyses of markets with asymmetric information. Stiglitz was a member of the Council of Economic Advisers from 1993–95, during the Clinton administration, and served as CEA chairman from 1995–97. He then became Chief Economist and Senior Vice-President of the World Bank from 1997–2000. His book *Globalization and Its Discontents,* was translated into 35 languages and has sold more than one million copies worldwide. His newest book, *Making Globalization Work*

(W.W. Norton: 2006) has also been translated into a number of languages (including Italian).

Jan Svejnar, Director of the International Policy Center at the Gerald R. Ford School of Public Policy, and the Everett E. Berg Professor of Business Administration, Professor of Economics and Professor of Public Policy at the University of Michigan (USA). He is Founder and Chairman of the Executive and Supervisory Committee of CERGE-EI in Prague, Chairman of the Supervisory Board of CSOB Bank, and Governing Board member of the European Economic Association. Previously (1996–2004) he was Executive Director of the William Davidson Institute at the University of Michigan Business School. Academic interests are in the areas of economic development and transition, labor economics and behavior of the firm. His research focuses on the determinants and effects of government policies on firms and labor and capital markets; corporate and national governance and performance; and entrepreneurship. He has published widely and serves as advisor to governments and firms in advanced and emerging market economies. Previously he was Professor at the University of Pittsburgh and Cornell University. He received his BS with honors from Cornell University's School of Industrial and Labor Relations and his MA and PhD in economics from Princeton University.

Vito Tanzi holds a PhD in economics from Harvard University. Currently a consultant to the Inter-American Development Bank. Previously he was Professor of Economics and Chairman of the Economics Department at the American University in Washington, DC (1967–74), Chief of the Tax Policy Division (1974–81) and Director of the Fiscal Affairs Department (1981–2000) at the International Monetary Fund; Senior Associate at Carnegie Endowment for International Peace (2000–01); and Undersecretary in the Ministry of Economy and Finance of Italy (2001–03). Over the years he has advised the Organization of American States, the World Bank, the United Nations, the European Commission, the European Central Bank, the Stanford Research Institute and other institutions. In 1990–94 he was President of the International Institute of Public Finance. He received honorary degrees from universities in Argentina, Belgium, Italy and Portugal. He is the author of many books and articles in professional journals and edited volumes. An effect in economics (the 'Tanzi effect') is named after him. Two volumes – *Macroeconomic Dimensions of Public Finance* and *Fiscal Policy and Economic Reform* (Routledge, 1997) were published in his honor.

Introduction

Saul Estrin, Grzegorz W. Kolodko, and Milica Uvalic

This volume has been prepared in honor of D. Mario Nuti on occasion of his seventieth birthday. In the light of Mario's important legacy for economists and policy-makers, we felt it appropriate to mark this event by producing a book in his honor. This introductory chapter is primarily devoted to a review of the most important features of Mario's life and work (including selected publications). We will conclude by briefly introducing the 14 contributions in the volume and outlining the themes of the book.

1 Domenico Mario Nuti

Domenico Nuti, always known as Mario, was born on 16 August 1937 in the Tuscan town of Arezzo. He was brought up in the small village of Castiglion Fibocchi in the same province, and lived there almost uninterruptedly until 1955 when, having completed his classical studies with distinction, he went to study Law at the University of Rome *La Sapienza*. His interest in economics was generated by both personal and social circumstances. His father was a small landowner financially ruined by post-War hyperinflation and by the pig cycle. As a student in Rome, Mario met Danilo Dolci, the theoretician and practitioner of self-help and non-violent action for civil rights; Danilo's 'white strike' project, with unemployed workers building roads in Sicily as volunteers, made a lasting impression on him. He wrote a dissertation on growth models and took up a research post with the Inter-Ministerial Committee for the Development of Southern Italy, with a team in charge of identifying 'growth poles'. This early personal and social background vaccinated him for good against economic theories relying on malleable capital, voluntary unemployment, and rational expectations (Nuti, 1992a).

After graduation – with the highest marks *cum laude* – Mario went to Warsaw with a fellowship of the Polish Academy of Sciences (1962–63), learned Polish, and was taught by both Oskar Lange and Michal Kalecki. Among other things, he turned a few hundred dollars into a large sum by importing from Switzerland – wholly legally – some material used to make scent and selling it to a cooperative producing for the Soviet market. 'I lived comfortably, demonstrated the twist to Polish teenagers and learned a great deal' (Nuti, 1992a).

From Warsaw Mario went to King's College, Cambridge, as a research student, and remained there for the next 17 years. His PhD thesis 'Investment planning in the socialist economies' (1970) was supervised by Nicholas Kaldor, then by Maurice Dobb. Mario's first research output – three essays on enterprise incentives (1966), investment criteria (1970a, 1971) and inflation – gained him the 1965 Stevenson Prize and a Research Fellowship at King's. Later he was to become a tutor, lecturer and Director of Studies in the College; from 1970 he held an assistant, then a full lectureship, in the Faculty of Economics.

At Cambridge then there was a lively debate between the followers of neoclassical economics and those in the Keynesian, Marxian and Ricardian traditions. A major issue was the measurement of capital and the use of aggregate production functions. Mario contributed to the critique of traditional capital theory with an article (1970b) that developed a model of 'flow input–flow output', inspired by Kalecki's investment criteria. The approach was labeled 'neo-Austrian' by John Hicks in an article published in the following issue of the *Economic Journal*. Mario made other contributions to capital theory (1969, 1973, 1974b, 1975, 1977a). This early work gained him a place in the *Who's Who in Economics* (Blaug 1983).

Mario says 'I would not renege on a single word of what I have ever written: *habent sua fata libelli* – writings have a life of their own, and are there to be judged within their context and on their own terms' (1992a); but he soon distanced himself from the Ricardian/Sraffian critique of capital theory and its developments. This is clear from the introduction to his edition of *Economic Essays on Value, Competition and Utility* by V. K. Dmitriev (1974a), which attracted exceptionally favorable reviews from Paul Samuelson in the *Journal of Economic Literature* and Maurice Dobb in the *Economic Journal*. He also wrote on Marx's transformation of labor values into production prices, in an essay published in 1977 but written much earlier, reacting to Marx's gross neglect of the importance of entrepreneurship and price adjustment. But Mario always remained a Kaleckian/Keynesian.

'Ultimately, I believe the neoclassical picture of the capitalist economy is fantasy because markets are both incomplete (where are the future markets for manufactured goods, or the contingent commodity markets?) and, most importantly, sequential. Hence resource allocation is ruled by price (and quantity) expectations as much as by actual spot prices, and therefore from [the] Arrow-Debreu [model] we instantly fall into a Keynesian world of expectations – whether self-fulfilling or false – of underemployment equilibria and economic fluctuations' (1992a; on the similarities but also substantial differences between Kalecki and Keynes, and the originality of both, see 2004a).

Mario's subsequent work was focused on comparative economic systems and, in particular, the reform of Soviet-type, socialist, centrally planned economies (CPEs) and – from 1990–92 – their transition to open market economies; the economics of participation, including cooperatives, and workers' participation in enterprise management and results; the global economic system and distribution. In recognition of his contributions to these areas he was elected President of the European Association for Comparative Economic Studies in 2001–02.

From his Polish days, Mario followed closely the repeated attempts by socialist economies first to reform the old system, then to construct a new model of market socialism. With Alec Nove, he edited a Penguin readings on socialist economics (1972), which went into several editions and translations. He was intrigued by the 1974 Polish reform attempts based on large corporations (1977c). In 1979 he published a most topical essay in which he applied Marx's own approach to the dynamics of modes of production to the conflicts and contradictions of socialist economies (see also 1978).

In 1980 he was appointed to a chair in Political Economy in the University of Birmingham and the Directorship of the Centre for Russian and East European Studies where he succeeded its founder R. W. (Bob) Davies. His inaugural lecture on 'Socialism on Earth' (1981c) is a definitive comparison and assessment of alternative socialist models, almost a sermon. At Birmingham Mario promoted research on Polish affairs, just a few months before the rise of Solidarnosc, and on the economic crisis in Eastern Europe, launching an Economic and Social Research Council project and other initiatives. He dissected the Polish crisis (1981a) and sadly but correctly predicted Polish military rule (1981b). In 1982 Mario 'retired to the ivory tower of the European University Institute at Florence, where I was able to pursue my research on the dynamics of socialism from 1982 to 1990' (Nuti, 1992a).

At the Badia (the EUI) Mario set up a lively working group on comparative economic systems, and Brussels funded research on East–West trade and financial relations, with many bright young research students – including Milica Uvalic and Renzo Daviddi who became research fellows on the project – and a stream of distinguished visitors – including Saul Estrin whom he had taught at Cambridge, and Grzegorz W. Kolodko whom he had first met in Warsaw during the World Bank mission to reconsider Poland's membership in 1986.

Mario regarded the traditional Soviet-type economy as grossly defective because of the inertia of central planners in the face of a changing world, a world of changing technology, domestic demand, and world trade opportunities and, above all, because of over-ambition, in the form of over-investment (1985c, 1986c) and other physical targets inconsistent with the maintenance of price stability (1984, 1985a, 1987b). He proposed a system of options tradable by private subjects, on state enterprise shares (owned and traded only by other state firms), so as to replicate the functioning of a capital market without private ownership (1989). Janos Kornai promptly declared him an honorary Hungarian, for this was the kind of market replication, without private ownership of capital, sought by many Hungarian economists.

Attempts to construct market socialism failed, Mario argues, because of the permanent, endemic state of excess demand at administered prices lower than market-clearing levels (Nuti, 1986b, 1988a, 1992b). 'Protracted and obtuse procrastination by communist leaders – including, indeed especially, Mikhail Gorbachev – brought about the Soviet economic catastrophe of 1990, disintegrated the Union and CMEA, freed Eastern Europe, justified the restoration of private property and the reswitching to capitalism' (1992a).

When socialism became post-socialism in Poland in 1989, soon followed by the rest of Central Eastern Europe, the European Commission lacked the expertise to deal with this momentous event, but they knew Mario well from the meetings, papers and reports generated by his EC funded project. Thus in December 1989 Mario was invited to come to Brussels as an advisor to DG-II (Economic and Monetary Affairs, as it then was), with responsibility for relations with transition economies. Mario had a grand-stand view of the transition from that position, meeting most of the protagonists and being involved in Brussels discussions. In the more general debate on stabilization, reform sequencing, the 'transformation recession', the issues of exchange rate regimes and trade opening (1991a, 1993a,b,c, 1995a, 1996c) and above all on privatization (1991b, 1993d,e,f, 1995b) he took an active part. In September 1993 Mario was able to return to Italy to take up his chair at his Alma Mater *La Sapienza*, coupled with a visiting chair at the London Business School, where he resumed his collaboration with Saul Estrin in teaching and research for the following 10 years.

In 1994 Kolodko was appointed First Deputy Premier of Poland and Minister of Finance. Mario had contributed to his economic program and, when Kolodko and his team developed the 'Strategy for Poland' Mario was appointed economic advisor, under the auspices of the European Community PHARE Program. Mario served in that capacity under Kolodko from 1994 to 1997 and Marek Belka until the end of the legislature in September 1997, and served again when Kolodko once more took office as Finance Minister in 2001–02, during the critical and final stage of the successful accession negotiations with the European Union. Kolodko and Nuti's account (1997c), with its emphasis on a market-oriented developmental role of the state rather than its demise, on competition rather than just privatization, on fiscal–monetary policy coordination, on accelerated European economic and monetary integration, is a fascinating one (Poland planned to join the Euro zone by 2006). Under Kolodko's stewardship GDP *per capita* rose by 28 percentage points, while inflation fell by 24 points, or by two-thirds (from 37 to 13 per cent by the end of 1997) and unemployment fell by 7 points (from 16.9 per cent to below 10 per cent at the end of 1997). Due to structural reforms and institutional progress in 1996 Poland joined the OECD.

In 1998–99 Mario was a World Bank and European Union consultant to the Presidential Administration of Belarus and in 2000–01 to that of Uzbekistan. He was frustrated by both assignments and described the two countries as 'command economies without central planning' (2001a, 2004b; Mario had already investigated 'post-communist mutations' in 1996b). A comprehensive assessment of the whole 17 years of transition (1990–2006) is given in Nuti 2007a (see also the earlier 2003a). The contrast with the received orthodoxy can be seen from 2003b.

Together with four colleagues – John Eatwell, Michael Ellman, Mats Karlsson and Judith Shapiro – Mario co-authored three books on post-socialist transition and European integration, commissioned by the think-tank Institute for Public Policy Research (1995c, 1997d, 2000b), all translated into several East European languages. He also wrote on the EU response to the transition (1994, 1996a, 2001b) and other aspects of European enlargement and monetary integration.

The other area of Mario's research, the economics of participation, was taken up in response to the crisis of East European socialism, in the search for alternative models based on the principles of equality and solidarity. He found that cooperatives were micro-socialist, almost monastic, institutions with defective incentives; that profit-sharing is a delusion unless it includes participation in capital gains, and in any case does not have the employment enhancement properties believed in by Martin Weitzman (Nuti, 1987a, c, 1988b); that workers' investment funds could not be the painless nationalization machines hoped for by Rudolf Meidner; that the guarantee of a basic income is a luxury that few economies could afford (1995d, 1996d). When Milica Uvalic prepared for the European Commission the first PEPPER Report – on Promotion of Employee Participation in Profits and Enterprise Results, an acronym invented by Mario to spice up European industrial relations – it was hoped that a combination of these ingredients, not so effective when used on their own, might add up to a coherent alternative model, enabling workers to transform themselves into part-entrepreneurs if they wished – a model (Nuti, 1992c, 1993g, 1995d) very close to the *Agathotopia* of James Meade, with whom Mario was in touch and whom he greatly admired. In a similar vein, Mario explored various Utopias and dis-topias (1985b, 1991c, 1992d; he also played with the idea of an employer of last resort, 1986a).

Work on the transition and on participation came to overlap with the diffusion of workers' shareholdings in their enterprises especially in the course of mass privatization, a phenomenon that Mario labeled 'Employeeism' (1997a, 1997b, 1999b, 1999c, 2000a), with the possible expropriation of other shareholders by employee-shareholders, if control was in the hands of people individually holding a smaller share in enterprise capital than in employment. A byproduct of this analysis was a critique of the notion of the stakeholder economy (1998), and more generally of the 'progressive parties' Third Way (1999a).

In developing his Roman courses on globalization, transition, and integration Mario has worked on exchange rate regimes, EU and Euro-area enlargement (2001c, 2002a, 2006), the governance of globalization (2002b, 2005), and its impact on efficiency and distribution (2007b), offering fresh thoughts on the special aspects of the 2004 and 2007 rounds of EU enlargement, the dangers of unilateral euroization, the unreasonable fiscal constraints applied to the new EU members (2006), the simultaneous need for both more globalization and for substantial re-distribution of its costs and benefits.

For all his addiction to research Mario has never been an armchair economist. Since his early fieldwork as a young man in Southern Italy, he worked for the FAO in Egypt, helped set up the research department of Italian trade union CGIL (*Confederazione Generale Italiana del Lavoro*), and worked in Zambia on the Mpongwe large-scale irrigation and resettlement scheme. In 1979 he helped the Zambian Ministry of Power regain control over its share of Kariba electricity, leading to much higher prices for electricity exports to what was then UDI Rhodesia; for his pains he was nearly napalmed in a Rhodesian raid on Lusaka and was held at gunpoint in the bush, but the price hike cost Ian Smith the equivalent of a few dozen helicopters. He has worked as a consultant for various international organizations – the World Bank, IMF, ILO, UNDP, UN-ECE, OECD – in Central Eastern Europe both before and during the transition, and elsewhere – Algeria and Vietnam, for instance. In 1989–90 he joined a task force of Soviet and Western economists under Wassily Leontief and Ivan Ivanov of the Soviet State Committee for Foreign Relations, sponsored by George Soros, on the opening up of the Soviet economy. His work in Brussels and Warsaw, Tashkent and Minsk has already been mentioned. He was Specialist Adviser to the House of Lords European Communities Committee in 1993–94 and was rebuked by landowning English lords for forgetting his wellingtons on a visit to a Hungarian pig farm.

Mario lives with Frances in his home village, visited by their children and their families from London and Florence, gardening, farming olive groves and commuting to *La Sapienza* where he holds the chair in Comparative Economic Systems. He resists environmental degradation as a member of the opposition in the local council. He regrets not having spent more time on a beach (Nuti, 1992a).

2   Contributions to this volume

The papers contributed to this book in honor of Mario Nuti depict in part the variety of areas of economics upon which Mario has worked during his rich professional career. We have grouped the papers into three sections to reflect some of Mario's most enduring intellectual concerns: the Socialist Legacy, Transition from Socialism to Capitalism, and Beyond Transition. Contributions were invited from scholars that have collaborated at different times with Mario Nuti during the last 25 years or more, from many universities, institutions and countries worldwide, from Eastern as well as Western Europe (Belarus, the Czech Republic, Hungary, Poland, Russia, Serbia, Slovenia, Italy, and the UK), Israel and the USA.

In Part I – the Socialist Legacy – we have included three papers. In 'The Rise and Fall of Socialist Planning' (Chapter 1), Michael Ellman recalls the main characteristics of planning during the different phases of its 70 years of existence, offering a fresh reading of the reasons for the discrepancy between model and outcome and also drawing some lessons from its recent replacement by capitalist 'triumphalism'. In Chapter 2, Vladimir Popov illustrates how the decade of the 1950s was the 'golden period' of Soviet economic growth and gives an explanation for the inverted U-shaped trajectory of productivity in the Soviet Union and other CPEs. Michael Keren and Gur Ofer (Chapter 3) challenge the frequent view that the transition economies should now be considered 'normal' countries; by emulating Kuznets, they define normality and explain the great divide between the new EU member states and the much less successful former Soviet Union countries, the advantages of the former being their pre-socialist history, 'softer' socialism, and benefits derived from joining the EU.

Part II includes papers on various aspects of transition from socialism to capitalism. Sergio Godoy and Joseph E. Stiglitz (Chapter 4) examine alternative hypotheses concerning the determinants of success in the transition, looking at whether speed of privatization, legal institutions or initial conditions are more important in explaining growth. The results suggest that, contrary to the earlier literature, the speed of privatization is negatively associated with growth, but it confirms the result of the few earlier studies that legal institutions are very important. Simon Commander (Chapter 5) considers existing evidence on skills and human capital in transition countries, and uses some original firm-level data to analyze two related issues in these countries: the shift in relative labor demand, and constraints deriving from the skill content of effective labor supply. Marcello de Cecco (Chapter 6) discusses the financial transition in Central and Eastern Europe in a broad historical context: by recalling the role of money and banks and attempts at reform during socialism, he reflects upon the main post-1989 features of banking reforms and possible future directions of change, also by drawing an illuminating parallel with the situation in Europe during the interwar period.

Four country case studies follow focusing on transition in two different regions – Slovenia and Serbia from the former Yugoslavia, and Russia and Belarus from the former Soviet Union. In Chapter 7, Janez Prašnikar and Jan Svejnar test various hypotheses on the determinants of and tradeoff between investment and wages using a sample of Slovenian firms with various forms of corporate governance; most of the findings are consistent with the principal theoretical models of corporate restructuring during transition, though the models underestimate the power of (elite) managers to restrain worker demands, and overestimate this power on the part of the external owners. In 'How Different Is Serbia?' (Chapter 8), Milica Uvalic analyses the case of Serbia where transition, until recently, has been substantially delayed. By taking into account the specific features of its pre-1989 economic system, negative legacy of the 1990s, and progress during the new phase of economic reforms after late 2000, she illustrates why transition has been more complex, costlier and in various ways different than in many other countries of the former socialist world.

Padma Desai's paper 'The Search for Identity: Where Is Russia Heading?' (Chapter 9) is an in-depth, very interesting analysis of today's Russia. It discusses the political and economic changes interacting with external features in Russia from Yeltsin to Putin, partly based on many recently conducted interviews, and points to some dominating features of Putin's 6 years policy record. Saul Estrin, Marina Bakanova, Igor Pelipas and Sergei Pukovich (Chapter 10) use the example of Belarus to ask whether privatization can improve economic performance in a situation where market-based institutions have not been developed. Using a new enterprise level sample they find that in Belarus privatization, and even the creation of firms under private ownership *de novo*, has no effect on company performance. They conclude that the economic environment, rather than ownership *per se*, is the primary determinant of enterprise performance in Belarus.

The third part of the book – Beyond Transition – contains four papers on issues that have been at the center of policy discussions not only in many transition and emerging economies, but also non-transition countries. Vito Tanzi's multidimensional essay on 'Complexity and Systemic Failure' (Chapter 11) is a fascinating account of the consequences of the continuously increasing complexity of today's modern world, illustrated by examples of recent technological and financial failures and its effects on monetary and financial tools. Increasing complexity today is compared to that of the once centrally planned economies, where an important cause of collapse was the growing complexity that made dirigisme more and more difficult. John Eatwell's paper 'Risk Management and Systemic Risk' (Chapter 12) discusses the evolving role of financial policy, as financial risk-taking has become a major concern of public policies due to the recent liberalization and hence internationalization of financial markets. He analyses the changing systemic characteristics of the international financial system and the effects of these changes on international regulatory developments, including the IMF move into financial regulation, the drive towards financial homogeneity, and the role of a potential World Financial Authority. László Csaba (Chapter 13) addresses the issue of whether the costs and benefits of post-communist transition can be evaluated by the most commonly used economic concept – optimality. By comparing theories and outcomes, he addresses the question of how the quality of polity and institutions determine the outcome of importing institutions from the West, and whether the EU Lisbon Agenda is a call for rethinking all existing continental European models that evolved in the first two decades of transition.

The book concludes with Grzegorz W. Kolodko's Chapter 14 on the feedback between two main processes of the contemporary world: the post-communist transformation to market and democracy, and globalization. While evaluating the merits and drawbacks of transformation, based also on his own experience as a successful policy-maker, he stresses the feedback between these two paramount features. He also draws certain important conclusions about the challenges the world economy will face in the future and the ways these challenges are supposed to be met to secure sustained growth in the long run.

References

Arestis, P. and M. C. Sawyer (1992) *A Biographical Dictionary of Dissenting Economists* (London: Elgar Publishing).

Blaug, M. (1983, 1986, 1999) *Who's Who in Economics. A Biographical Dictionary of Major Economists* (Cambridge, MA: MIT Press).

D. M. Nuti's selected publications

Nuti, D.M. (1966) 'Material incentive schemes and the choice of techniques in Soviet industry', *Australian Economic Papers*, December, 183–98.

—— (1969) 'The degree of monopoly in the Kaldor-Mirrlees growth model', *Review of Economic Studies*, 35 (2), 257–60.

—— (1970a) 'Investment reforms in Czechoslovakia', *Soviet Studies*, 21 (3), 360–70.

—— (1970b) 'Capitalism, socialism and steady growth', *Economic Journal*, 80, 32–57.

—— (1971) 'The evolution of Polish investment planning', *Jahrbuch der Wirtschaft Osteuropas*, Band 3, 395–38.

—— with A. Nove (eds) (1972, 1974, 1977) *Socialist Economics* (London: Penguin Readings in Economics).

—— (1973) 'On the truncation of production flows', *Kyklos*, 26 (3), 485–96.

—— (1974a) An edition of V. K. Dmitriev's *Ekonomicheskie Ocherki*, under the title *Economic Essays on Value, Competition and Utility*, with notes and an Introductory Essay, (Cambridge: CUP), Re-published in Russian, Moscow 2001.

—— (1974b) 'On the rates of return on investment', *Kyklos*, 27 (2), 345–69.

—— (1975) 'The wage-interest frontier', *Zeitschrift fur Nationalekonomie*, 35 (Heft 1-2), 177–86.

—— (1977a) 'Price and composition effects and the pseudo-Production Function', *Revue d'Economie Politique*, 2 (March–April), 232–43.

—— (1977b) 'The transformation of labour values into production prices and the Marxian theory of exploitation', in J. Schwartz (ed.) *The Subtle Anatomy of Capitalism* (Santa Monica, California: Goodyear).

—— (1977c) 'Large corporations and the reform of Polish industry', *Jahrbuch der Wirtschaft Osteuropas*, Band 7, 345–405.

—— (1978) 'Investment, interest and degree of centralization in Maurice Dobb's theory of the socialist economy', *Cambridge Journal of Economics*, 2 (2) (Maurice Dobb Memorial Issue), 191–202.

—— (1979) 'The contradictions of socialist economies. A Marxian interpretation', in R. Miliband and J. Saville (eds) *The Socialist Register* **1979** (London: The Merlin Press), pp. 228–73.

—— (1981a) 'The Polish crisis: economic factors and constraints', in R. Miliband and J. Saville (eds) *The Socialist Register 1981* (London: The Merlin Press), pp. 104–43.

—— (1981b) 'Poland: socialist renewal and economic collapse', *The New Left Review*, November.

—— (1981c) 'Socialism on Earth' (Inaugural lecture), *Cambridge Journal of Economics*, 5 (4).

—— (1984) 'Economic crisis in Eastern Europe: prospects and repercussions', *EUI Working Paper*, No. 26.

—— (1985a) 'Political and economic fluctuations in the socialist system', *EUI Working Paper*, No. 85/156.

—— (1985b) 'A critique of Orwell's oligarchic collectivism as an economic system', *Coexistence: A Review of East-West and Development Issues*, 22 (July), 151–63.

—— (1985c) 'Systemic aspects of investment and employment in Soviet-type economies', in D. Lane (ed.) *Labour and Employment in the USSR* (London: The Harvester Press), pp. 112–21.

—— (1986a) 'Economic planning in market economies: scope, instruments, institutions', in P. Nolan and S. Paine (eds) *Rethinking Socialist Economics* (London: Croom Helm), pp. 83–98.

—— (1986b) 'Hidden and repressed inflation in Soviet-type economies: definitions, measurements and stabilization', *Contributions to Political Economy*, 5, 37–82.

—— (1986c) 'Michal Kalecki's contributions to the theory and practice of socialist planning', *Cambridge Journal of Economics*, 10, 333–53.

—— (1987a) 'The share economy: plausibility and viability of Weitzman's model', in S. Hedlund (ed.) *Incentives and Economic Systems* (London and Sidney: Croom Helm), pp. 267–90.

—— (1987b) 'Cycles in socialist economies', in J. Eatwell, M. Milgate and P. Newman (eds) *The New Palgrave: A Dictionary of Economic Theory and Doctrine*, vol. 1, (London: Macmillan), pp. 744–46.

—— (1987c) 'Profit-sharing and employment: claims and overclaims', *Industrial Relations*, 26 (1), Berkeley, Winter, 18–29.

—— (1988a) 'Perestroika: transition between central planning and market socialism', *Economic Policy*, 3 (7), 353–89.

—— (1988b) 'Co-determination, profit-sharing and full employment', in D. Jones and J. Svejnar (eds) *Advances in the Economic Analysis of Participatory and Labor-Managed Firms*, vol. 3 (Greenwich and London: JAI Press).

—— (1989) 'Feasible financial innovation under market socialism' in C. Kessides, T. King, D. Mario Nuti and K. Sokil (eds) *Financial Reform in Socialist Economies* (Washington DC: EDI-World Bank), pp. 85–105.

—— (1991a) 'Stabilization and reform sequencing in the reform of Central Eastern Europe', in S. Commander (ed.) *Managing Inflation in Socialist Economies in Transition* (Washington DC: EDI Seminar Series, World Bank), pp. 155–74.

—— (1991b) *Privatization of Socialist Economies: General Issues and the Polish Case* (Paris: OECD).

—— (1991c) 'On Tibor Liska's entrepreneurial socialism', in M. Mendell and D. Salee (eds) *The Legacy of Karl Polanyi. Market, State and Society at the End of the Twentieth Century* (New York: St. Martin's Press), pp. 215–30.

—— (1992a) 'Domenico Mario Nuti (1937–)', in P. Arestis and M. C. Sawyer (eds) *A Biographical Dictionary of Dissenting Economists* (London: Elgar Publishing), pp. 401–09.

—— (1992b) 'Market socialism: the model that might have been but never was', in A. Aslund (ed.) *Market Socialism Or The Restoration of Capitalism?* (Cambridge: CUP), pp. 17–31.

—— (1992c) 'Traditional cooperatives and James Meade's Labour-Capital Discriminating Partnerships', in D. Jones and J. Svejnar (eds) *Advances in the Economic Analysis of Participatory and Labor-Managed Firms*, vol. 4 (Greenwich and London: JAI Press), pp. 1–26.

—— (1992d) 'On Stanislaw Lem's model of populist localism', *Economies et Sociétés*, no. 4-5-6, Série G (Economie Planifiée), no. 44, special issue on 'Transition en Europe de l'Est'.

—— (1993a) 'Economic inertia in the transitional economies of central eastern Europe', in M. Uvalic, E. Espa and J. Lorentzen (eds) *Impediments to the Transition in Eastern Europe*, European Policy Studies, no. 1 (Florence: European University Institute), pp. 25–49.

—— (1993b) 'Lessons from stabilization and reform in central and eastern Europe', in L. Somogyi (ed.) *The Political Economy of the Transition Process in Eastern Europe* (Aldershot and Brookfield: Edward Elgar), pp. 40–66.

—— (1993c) 'Socialist Banking', in J. Eatwell, M. Milgate and P. Newman (eds) *The New Palgrave Dictionary of Money and Finance*, vol. 3, (London: The Macmillan Press and New York: Stockton Press), pp. 474–479.

—— (1993d) 'Privatization of financial institutions', in J. Eatwell, M. Milgate and P. Newman (eds) *The New Palgrave Dictionary of Money and Finance*, vol. 3, (London: The Macmillan Press and New York: Stockton Press), pp. 212–14.

—— (1993e) 'The role of the banking sector in the process of privatization', in T. Clarke (ed.) *International Privatization: Strategies and Practices* (Walter de Gruyter), pp. 187–202.

—— with R. Portes (1993f) 'Central Europe: the way forward', in R. Portes (ed.) *Economic Transformation in Central Europe. A Progress Report* (London: CEPR and Brussels: EC Official Publications), pp. 1–20.

—— (1993g) 'Alternative employment and payment systems', in S. Bowles, H. Gintis and B. Gustafsson (eds) *Democracy and Markets: Participation, Accountability and Efficiency* (Cambridge: CUP), pp. 40–47.

—— (1994) 'The impact of systemic transition on the European Community', in S. Martin (ed.) *The Construction of Europe. A Festschrift in Honour of Emile Noel* (Florence and Dortrecht: European University Institute and Kluwer Academic), pp. 143–81.

—— (1995a) 'The role of the state in post-communist economies', in C. Naastepad and S. Storm (eds) *The State and the Economic Process* (London: Edward Elgar), pp. 159–76.

—— (1995b) 'Mass privatization: costs and benefits of instant capitalism', in R. Daviddi (ed.) *Property Rights and Privatization in the Transition to a Market Economy* (Maastricht: EIPA), pp. 103–32.

—— with J. Eatwell, M. Ellman, M. Karlsson and J. Shapiro (1995c) *Transformation and Integration: Shaping the Future of Central Eastern Europe* (London: IPPR).

—— (1995d)*The Economics of Participation*, IRTI-Islamic Development Bank, Eminent Scholars Lectures Series, no. 12, Jeddah.

—— (1996a) 'European Community response to the Transition: Aid, Trade Access, Enlargement', *Economics of Transition*, 4 (2), 503–11.

—— (1996b) 'Post-communist mutations', *Emergo*, 7 (Winter), pp. 7–15.

—— (1996c) 'Inflation, interest and exchange rates in the transition', *The Economics of Transition*, 4 (1), 137–58.

——— (1996d) 'Efficiency, equality and enterprise democracy', in U. Pagano and R. Rowthorn (eds) *Democracy and Efficiency in the Economic Enterprise* (London and New York: Routledge Studies in Business Organization and Networks), pp. 184–206.

——— (1997a) 'Employeeism: corporate governance and employee share ownership in transition economies', in M. I. Blejer and M. Skreb (eds) *Macroeconomic Stabilization in Transition Economies* (Cambridge: CUP), pp. 126–54.

——— (1997b) 'Employee ownership in Polish privatizations', in M. Uvalic and D. Vaughan-Whitehead (eds) *Privatization Surprises in Transition Economies. Employee Ownership in Central and Eastern Europe* (Aldershot: Edward Elgar).

——— with G. W. Kolodko (1997c) 'The Polish Alternative. Old Myths, Hard Facts and New Strategies in the Successful Polish Transformation', *UNU/WIDER Research for Action Series*, No. 33.

——— with J. Eatwell, M. Ellman, M. Karlsson and J. Shapiro (1997d) *Not Just Another Accession. The Political Economy of EU Enlargement to the East* (London: IPPR).

——— (1998) 'Stock and Stakes: the case for protecting stakeholders' interests', *Economic Analysis*, 1 (1).

——— (1999a) 'Making sense of the Third Way', *Business Strategy Review*, 10 (3), 57–67.

——— with F. FitzRoy, D. Jones, M. Klinedinst, G. Lajtai, N. Mygind, C. Rock, M. Uvalic and D. Vaughan-Whitehead (1999b) *Employee Ownership in Privatization: Lessons from Central and Eastern Europe*, Experts' Policy Report (Budapest: ILO-CEET).

——— with S. Estrin and M. Uvalic (1999c) 'The impact of privatization funds on corporate governance of enterprises in mass privatization schemes: Czech Republic, Poland, Slovenia', in M. Simoneti, S. Estrin and A. Bohm (eds) *The Governance of Privatization Funds – Experiences of the Czech Republic, Poland and Slovenia,*(Cheltenham: Edward Elgar), pp. 137–62.

——— (2000a) 'Employee Participation in Enterprise Control and Returns: Patterns, Gaps and Discontinuities', in V. Franicevic and M. Uvalic (eds) *Equality, Participation, Transition. Essays in Honour of Branko Horvat* (London and New York: Macmillan and St. Martin's Press).

——— with J. Eatwell, M. Ellman, M. Karlsson and J. Shapiro (2000b) *Hard Choices and Soft States: Social Policy in Central and Eastern Europe* (London: IPPR).

——— (2001a) 'Belarus: a command economy without central planning', in M. I. Blejer and M. Skreb (eds) *Transition. The First Decade* (Cambridge, MA: MIT Press).

——— (2001b) Not 'Just Another Accession', *Distinguished Lectures Series*, No. 3, Leon Kozminski Academy of Entrepreneurship and Management (WSPiZ), Warsaw, April 26; available at *http://www.tiger.edu.pl/publikacje/dist/nuti.pdf.*

——— (2001c) 'The Polish Zloty, 1990–99: Success and Under-Performance', *American Economic Review*, May, Papers and Proceedings, 90 (2), pp. 53–58.

——— (2002a) 'Costs and benefits of unilateral euroization in central eastern Europe', *The Economics of Transition*, 10 (2), 419–44 (Guest-Editor of Symposium on 'Exchange rate regimes in transition economies – the euroization debate', same issue).

——— (2002b) 'Governing Incomplete Globalization', *TIGER Working Papers*, no. 25, Leon Kozminski Academy of Entrepreneurship and Management (WSPiZ), Warsaw, September; available at *http://www.tiger.edu.pl/publikacje/TWPNo25.pdf.*

——— with M. Uvalic (2003a) 'Twelve years of transition to a market economy', in D. M. Nuti and M. Uvalic (eds) *Post-Communist Transition to a Market Economy. Lessons and Challenges* (Ravenna: Longo Editore).

——— (2003b) *A Comment on Leszek Balcerowicz, 'Post-Communist Transition in a Comparative Perspective',*World Bank, Washington, DC, November 18; available at *http://info.worldbank.org/etools/bspan/PresentationView.asp?PID=955&EID=328.*

—— (2004a) 'Kalecki and Keynes revisited: Two original approaches to demand-determined income – and much more besides', in Z. L. Sadowski and A. Szeworski (eds) *Kalecki's Economics Today* (London and New York: Routledge).

—— (2004b) 'The Belarus economy. Suspended animation between state and markets', in S. White, E. A. Korosteleva and J. Lowenhardt (eds) *Postcommunist Belarus*, (Rowman and Lanham, MD: Littlefield).

—— (2005) 'Governing incomplete globalization', in G. W. Kolodko (ed) *Emerging Market Economies. Globalization and Development* (Aldershot, England and Burlington, VT, USA: Ashgate Publishing Ltd).

—— (2006) 'Alternative fiscal rules for the EU new members', *TIGER Working Papers*, No. 84, Leon Kozminski Academy of Entrepreneurship and Management (WSPiZ), Warsaw, March; available at *http://www.tiger.edu.pl/publikacje/TWPNo84.pdf.*

—— (2007a) 'Managing Transition Economies', in S. White, J. Batt and P. Lewis (eds) *Developments in Central and East European Politics*, no. 4 (Duke UP: Palgrave).

—— (2007b) 'Efficiency and Distribution in the Global Economy', Lezioni Federico Caffè, University of Rome *La Sapienza,* forthcoming.

Part I
The Socialist Legacy

1
The Rise and Fall of Socialist Planning

Michael Ellman[1]

1.1 Introduction

In February 1921 Russia established a State General Planning Commission to work out and implement a unified economic plan for the national economy. For 70 years this Commission, known as Gosplan for short, played a significant, but varying role in Russian and Soviet economic life. Under the influence of the Soviet example, planning organizations spread throughout the world, to state socialist countries, to OECD countries such as France, the Netherlands and Japan, and also to third world countries such as India. In April 1991, deeply discredited by the poor performance of the Soviet economy and the ideological developments of 1985–90, Gosplan was transformed into a Ministry of Economic Affairs and Forecasting with substantially different tasks. Socialist planning had come to an end in the USSR even prior to the end of the USSR itself. What explains these dramatic developments?

1.2 The classics

Marx devoted most of his life to the analysis of capitalism and was notoriously opposed to attempts to design utopias. Nevertheless, from his scattered observations about socialism, and from those of his close comrade Engels (for example in *Anti-Duhring* and *Karl Marx*) his followers drew the idea that in a socialist economy the market mechanism would be replaced by economic planning. It came to be widely believed that the market economy was inherently inefficient, and fundamentally unsuited to coordinate large-scale industrial production. Similarly, the superiority of planning, which would enable society as a whole to coordinate production *ex ante*, became a widespread view in the international Marxist movement. These ideas became an integral part of the Marxist critique of capitalism and the Marxist conception of socialism. They were elaborated in the works of the late nineteenth century German Social Democrats and were regarded as axiomatic by the Russian Bolsheviks.

1.3   Russian discussion during the Civil War

Having come to power committed to replacing the market by planning, the Bolsheviks rapidly realized that they had no concrete ideas about how to do this. As Lenin (1918, 1929, p. 484) observed in 1918:

> We have knowledge of socialism, but as for knowledge of organization on a scale of millions, knowledge of the organization and distribution of products, etc, that we do not have. This the old Bolshevik leaders did not teach us ... Nothing has been written about this yet in Bolshevik textbooks, and there is nothing in Menshevik textbooks either.

The second Party program, adopted at its 8th Congress in March 1919, was aimed at 'the maximum centralization of production ... simultaneously striving to establish a unified economic plan'. In their commentary on this program, Bukharin and Preobrazhensky (1920, 1969, pp. 114–15), explained what lay behind this phrase. They stated that under communism, 'society will be transformed into a huge working organization for cooperative production. There will then be neither disintegration of production nor anarchy of production. In such a social order, production will be organized. No longer will one enterprise compete with another; the factories, workshops, mines and other productive institutions will all be subdivisions, as it were, of one vast people's workshop, which will embrace the entire national economy of production. It is obvious that so comprehensive an organization presupposes a general plan of production. If all the factories and workshops together with the whole of agricultural production are combined to form an immense cooperative enterprise, it is obvious that everything must be precisely calculated. We must know in advance how much labor to assign to the various branches of industry; what products are required and how much of each it is necessary to produce; how and where machines must be provided. These and similar details must be thought out beforehand, with approximate accuracy at least; and the work must be guided in uniformity with our calculations. This is how the organization of communist production will be effected. Without a general plan, without a general directive system, and without careful calculation and book-keeping, there can be no organization. But in the communist social order, there is such a plan.'

1.4   Planning in the New Economic Policy period (1921–28)

Gosplan began work in April 1921 with a staff of 34, most of them non-Party technicians and scientists, under the chairmanship of an Old Bolshevik. It grew rapidly, and by the middle of 1924 had a staff of 527. During the New Economic Policy (NEP), Gosplan was mainly engaged in giving advice on economic policy and struggling against both market forces and other bureaucratic organizations. In particular, it struggled to have control figures, which subsequently became the basis for the annual plans, accepted as the basis for current economic policy in place of the annual budget drawn up by the People's Commissariat for Finance. Similarly, it struggled to have its 5-year plan accepted as the basis for medium-term economic policy instead of the 5-year plan drawn up by the Supreme Council of the National Economy. It also undertook a variety of economic calculations.

The economic calculations and economic models which underlay the concrete figures of Gosplan and other Soviet institutions in the 1920s played a pioneering role in international economic thought. For example, the economic balances calculated and published in the USSR in the 1920s played an important role in the history of the input–output method. Input–output was developed by Leontief, a Russian economist working in the USA who was well aware of the relevant earlier Soviet work. The latter was undertaken in and published by the Central Statistical Administration. An area in which Gosplan has a better claim to priority is that of growth models. Feldman's work (1928) was a remarkable pioneering study which was published in Russian at the end of the NEP period, long before Western economics became interested in the theory of economic growth. Its influence on early Indian planning, was analyzed by Domar (1957) and translated into English in Spulber's work (1964). Feldman's model was developed as a basis for long-term planning and was originally a report to a Gosplan committee. It should be noted, however, that the concrete numerical work of Feldman and of the head of the committee to which he reported was much too optimistic. It treated as feasible entirely unrealizable goals. The attempt to realize them had disastrous effects on the economy.

It was in the 1920s that the view was developed that planning should have four essential elements; the annual plans (originally control figures); the 5-years plans; the 10, 15- or 20-year general or perspective plan; and the plans for concrete investment projects which made up the backbone of the other plans.

Gosplan's annual control figures gradually grew in importance at the expense of the annual budget. This reflected the conscious choice made by the Bolsheviks in favor of industrial expansion at the expense of financial stability. As Dzerzhinsky, chairman of the Supreme Council for the National Economy, explained in February 1926 (*Leningradskaya Pravda*, 14 February 1926): 'Therefore, when it is said that because of the shortage of resources we should halt our investment projects, or reduce them to a certain level, then I assert that I . . . will struggle against such an opinion to the end because it is fundamentally incorrect.' The results of this attitude, combined with state price control, were rising prices on the non-state market, increasing shortages of all goods and the grain crisis of the late 1920s. The latter resulted not from a *physical* shortage of grain but from an *economic* shortage resulting from the unattractive prices, and limited availability of goods, offered in return by the government. Hence, it can be seen that Gosplan and its annual control figures played an important role in undermining the NEP and in the events leading up to the collectivization of agriculture and Stalinism. Accordingly, a decisive role in overcoming the legacy of Stalinism in Central and Eastern Europe was the abolition of the planning offices and restoring the key role of the annual budget and monetary equilibrium.

After long discussions of alternative proposals, Gosplan's three volume work of more than 1700 pages *The Five-Year Plan of National Economic Construction of the USSR* was approved in its optimum variant by the 15th Party Conference in April 1929 and was published in May 1929.

1.5   The prelude to socialist planning (1929–33)

Formally the First 5-Year Plan covered the period 1928–32. By the time it was adopted, however, 1928 and part of 1929 were already over. Economic policy in 1929–30 was dominated by the bitter struggle between the state and the peasantry, and in 1931–33 the country suffered from a deep economic crisis including a major famine. Although the ambitious goals outlined in the First 5-Year Plan played an important role in generating the crisis, the pricing and agrarian policies and theories of the Bolsheviks, the bad harvests of 1931–32 and Stalin's reliance on force and repression, were the key elements in precipitating this catastrophe. The years 1929–33 were formative years, dominated by crisis, in which it is impossible to speak of a viable economic system. It was really only from about 1934 that one can speak of a stable economic system.

1.6   Socialist planning (1934–91)

In the 1930s it became a trivial orthodoxy of the international Communist movement, and came to be widely believed outside it, that the economic system realized in the USSR was a rational and equitable form of economic organization and represented a higher mode of production than capitalism. This idea was based on a comparison between the economic growth realized in the USSR (exaggerated figures which were published in the USSR and widely disseminated throughout the world) and the Great Depression in the capitalist world with its falling output, unemployment, bank failures and declining commodity prices. Both in the USSR and in the international Communist movement, the actual practice of Soviet planning came to be identified with that socialist planning about which Marx and Engels had thrown out their pregnant hints. Hence, when they came to power else-where, Communist parties naturally adopted – or in some cases had imposed on them – the Soviet model of economic planning. Accordingly, after the World War I the Soviet model was adopted throughout the state socialist world, first in Eastern Europe in 1949–53, then in China in 1953–57, and then in countries such as Vietnam and Cuba. There were naturally some differences between countries in the application of the model. Nevertheless, some important features of the model were common to all these countries. Moreover, aspects of the model (for example national economic plans, the stress on state ownership of the means of production, the restrictions on the operation of the price mechanism and a negative attitude to private enterprise) were widely copied throughout the world.

The main features of the Soviet model were: state ownership of the means of production, political dictatorship, a mono-hierarchical system, imperative planning and physical planning. The overwhelming majority of means of production were in state ownership, although in some countries some remained in the hands of individuals (for example farmers and craftsmen) and in all countries a large part of agricultural means of production were owned or managed by what were nominally cooperatives. The political dictatorship was exercised by the leadership of the Communist party, using such instruments as repression and control over appointments. As a result (Nuti, 1981b, p. 396)

> The center is out of touch with popular wishes. 'Democratic centralism' is in theory the central execution of decisions democratically reached, but in practice turns into 'voluntarism', the arbitrary pursuit of the wishes of the leadership of the day, as each new leader reveals to have been the case with his predecessor.

A mono-hierarchical system refers to the fact that although the authorities at local and central levels were both numerous and often divided, ultimately authority flowed from a small single group, often an individual, at the top of the hierarchy, to whom all other organizations and individuals were subordinate. Imperative planning refers to the fact that the plans were not forecasts, but instructions binding all participants in the economy, analogous to orders in the armed forces. As Stalin explained in the report of the Central Committee to the 15th Party Congress held in 1927: 'Our plans are not plan-forecasts, not plan-guesses, but plan-directives, which are obligatory for the directing organs and which determine the direction of our future national economic development.' Physical planning refers to the fact that the main attention of the planners was concentrated on physical flows (tons of this, cubic meters of that) and not on financial and monetary aspects of economic life. The latter were regarded as being merely a reflection of the real economic processes and of secondary importance.

A striking feature of socialist planning was the very limited correspondence between the plans and the outcomes. Although the plans were supposed to determine the outcomes, it often happened, both for individual investment projects, even high priority ones, and for major macroeconomic events, that the outcome was quite different from the plan. For example, the Chinese depression of 1959–62, the Polish depression of 1979–82, the Soviet stagnation of 1979–82 and the Soviet depression of 1989–91, were all unplanned and unexpected by the national leadership.

In view of this lack of correspondence between the plans and the outcomes, it is clear that the system of socialist planning actually introduced differs substantially from the socially rational process which Marxists had anticipated. Basing himself on a very detailed historical analysis of the actual practice of planning in the USSR, Zaleski (1980, p. 484) concluded that: 'The priority of management over planning has been the dominant feature of the Soviet economy since Stalin's time. Since management is highly centralized, this feature is characteristic of the entire model. Therefore it seems more nearly correct to call the economy "centrally managed" rather than "centrally planned"'.

The work of Zaleski and others showed how far socialist planning was from the Marxist image of planning as a socially rational system. Socialist planning was actually very wasteful, was unable to abolish the 'anarchy of production' (as shown by the existence of the second[2] and third[3] economies), and was unable to match the capitalist world with respect to technical progress. Moreover, the actual course of development often sharply diverged from the plans, and money and commodities were never abolished (except very temporarily, each time with disastrous effects, in Russia, China, Cuba and Cambodia). The relationship between plan and outcome naturally differed between sectors (the weather and the world market being notoriously 'unplannable').

The fact that there was a substantial difference between what was planned and what actually happened is easy to understand from the standpoint of systems theory. The plan was only one of the factors (and often not a very important one) in determining outcomes. Other important factors which also helped to determine outcomes were the behavior of the entities in the system (for example ministries, enterprises and households) and the economic environment. Hence, from the standpoint of systems theory, there was no reason to expect economic life to be determined solely by the plans.

Realization of these facts led in the 1970s and 1980s to the development of new terms to describe what had previously been (and still were in United Nations publications) referred to as the 'centrally planned economies'. In the USSR in the late 1980s the system was normally referred to as the 'administrative-command' economy. What was fundamental to this system was not the plan but the role of administrative hierarchies at all levels of decision making; the absence of control over decision making by the population, either through the political or economic process; the social order in which it was embedded; its economic problems in the fields of technical progress and the provision of private goods; and its successes in the fields of full employment, conservative industrialization (Brus and Kowalik, 1983) and economic growth in certain periods in certain countries (for example the USSR in the 1950s).

The difference between plan and outcome also directed attention to planning not as a means of attaining certain objectives but as a rationality ritual in the sociological or anthropological sense. As a rationality ritual it had two aspects, giving significance to human life and legitimizing the ruling group. It did the first by conveying the illusion that the waste which was 'observed' in countries with socialist planning was actually part of a rational system. It did the second by ascribing to the priests (planners, economists and other technicians) and the rulers they served, the function of bringing order out of chaos, of leading society to the glittering future.

The end of socialist planning in 1991 did not come out of the blue. It had been preceded by a sharp ideological critique. Already in July 1989, a Soviet economist, writing in the theoretical journal of the Communist party, argued in favor of abolishing 5-year plans since they were only suitable under 'conditions of a totalitarian social system' (Bim, 1989).

1.7 The theoretical explanation for the discrepancy between model and outcome

The fact that there were fundamental theoretical reasons why it would be impossible to realize the Marxist model of socialism on a national economic level was pointed out long before the Bolsheviks came to power, for example by Pierson (1902). A similar early critique is Barone (1908). Subsequently, this argument was widely repeated. Well-known criticisms after the October Revolution are those of Mises (1920) and Hayek (1935, 1937, 1945, 1988). In my opinion, the three fundamental factors which explain why the Marxist aspiration for a non-market planned national economy cannot be realized efficiently are partial ignorance, inadequate techniques for data processing and complexity (Ellman, 1978).[4] Not taking these three factors into account generates a theory of rational social decision making which is profoundly flawed and whose weaknesses are the underlying reason for the ultimate failure of socialist planning.

1.7.1 Partial ignorance

If (as in some models) the central authorities had perfect knowledge of the situation throughout the economy (and also adequate techniques for processing it and transmitting the results), then they would be able to calculate efficient plans and issue them to the periphery. In fact, the central authorities are partially ignorant of the situation throughout the economy, and this is a major factor causing such phenomena as the dictatorship over needs,[5] bureaucratization, production for plan rather than use, wasteful criteria,[6] slack plans,[7] the residual principle,[8] the instability of the plans,[9] the second and third economies, and so on.

The partial ignorance of the planners is of two types. First, ignorance which is created by the planning process. Secondly, ignorance which is unavoidable. The first type of ignorance has three causes: subordinates may transmit inaccurate information, the process of transmitting information may destroy some of it, and the addressees of information may not receive it. I will consider each in turn.

(a) *Subordinates transmit inaccurate information.* It is well known that in any bureaucracy (Downs, 1967, p. 77) 'Each official tends to distort the information he passes upwards to his superiors in the hierarchy. Specifically, all types of officials tend to exaggerate data that reflect favorably on themselves and to minimize those that reveal their own shortcomings.' This explains such phenomena as the exaggeration of agricultural output figures in the USSR, which Khrushchev and Gorbachev criticized, and in China during the Great Leap Forward. It also explains the exaggeration of input requirements and the underestimation of output possibilities that was a normal part of the process of planning and counter-planning by which the plans were drawn up.

(b) *The process of transmitting information destroys some of it.* An example of how the process of transmitting data may destroy some of it is provided by the aggregation problem. During the process of planning there was aggregation by commodities, enterprises and time periods. All three introduced errors. Aggregation errors can be reduced by following suitable aggregation criteria or by enlarging the detail of the plan, but are unlikely ever to be eliminated.

(c) *The addressees of information may not receive it.* Another example of how socialist planning can create ignorance is provided by what the cognitive theorists of decision making refer to as 'the assumption of a single outcome calculation'. This refers to the fact that the decision-making process often 'does not match the uncertain structure of the environment in which events might take a number of alternative courses. Rather, it imposes an image and works to preserve that image.' Hence, 'Pertinent information may enter the decision-making process or it may be screened out, depending on how it relates to the existing pattern of belief . . . That information which is threatening to established belief patterns is not expected to be processed in a fashion wholly dominated by the reality principle' (Steinbruner, 1974, p. 123).

The classic example, of course, is Stalin's surprise at the German invasion of 1941, despite the advance information transmitted by Sorge and others, resulting from his screening out of information that threatened an established belief pattern. Similarly, the Polish Party leader Gomulka was surprised at the outcome of his policy of self-sufficiency in grain, despite warnings by economists, such as Kalecki, of its likely adverse effects (Feiwel, 1975, Chapter 19).

A major feature of developments in the CMEA countries after the death of Stalin was a reduction in the ignorance of decision makers. The publication of statistical data was substantially increased. New, policy-related disciplines such as mathematical economics, sociology and demography grew up. Serious discussions were held on policy questions (for example, the Soviet discussions of the 1960s and 1980s about economic reform).

Nevertheless, the partial ignorance of the decision makers, which they themselves had created, still played a major role in developments. In the USSR, the distortions in economic statistics played an important part in the collapse of the whole system by giving the leadership a much too optimistic view of actual economic developments (Eydelman, 1998; Khanin, 1998). Similarly, a former colonel of Soviet military intelligence blames the Soviet defeat in the cold war on the absence in the USSR of independent research institutes studying strategic security and economic issues (Ellman and Kontorovich, 1998, p. 45). In their absence, the decisions which were made failed to reflect a good understanding of the actual situation.

Some ignorance is just unavoidable. The nature of economic life is such that the economy is continually being affected by events that were not foreseen when the plan was being drawn up. This is particularly obvious with respect to harvest outcomes, innovations (either technical or managerial/organizational), international affairs and demographic factors. This ignorance about the future can be reduced, for example by establishing institutes for research into the international conjunctural situation or demography, but it can never be eliminated.

Not only are the central decision makers unavoidably partially ignorant, but also the attempts to concentrate all relevant decision making in their hands is costly. It is costly in two ways. First, large numbers of people and considerable specialized equipment are required. Secondly, the erroneous view that social rationality can be attained by calculating a central plan which is then faithfully executed may reduce the responsiveness of the country to new information and hence generate waste. The former Soviet mathematician Lerner (1975, p. 214) argued that:

A distinguishing feature of a system with centralized control is a high degree of *rigidity* of the structure, because adaptation, to both random changes and changes caused by the evolution of the system and of the environment, does not take place in the individual parts of the system but only in the central control point. Centralized control permits stabilization of a system over a long period, suppressing both fluctuations and evolutional changes in the individual parts of the system without reconstructing them. However, in the final analysis, this may be damaging to the system because contradictions between the unchanged structure of a system and changes associated with evolution increase to global dimensions and may require such a radical and sharp reconstruction as would be impossible within the framework of the given structure and would lead to its disintegration.

Twenty-four years after the original publication of this book, the disintegration it had foreseen took place – corroborating the author's theoretical arguments against centralized control as an efficient long-term control mechanism for large complex systems.

It is because of partial ignorance that feedback mechanisms are so important in economic control. They enable the economy to respond smoothly in the event of unforeseen disturbances. Examples of what happens in the event of inadequate feedback mechanisms are the notorious shortages and queues for consumer goods which characterized the socialist countries. These partly resulted from the absence of the two feedback mechanisms, flexible prices and flexible quantities, which balance supply and demand under capitalism.

1.7.2   Inadequate techniques for data processing

The inadequacy of the techniques available to process such data was the main reason for the instability of the plans and one of the reasons for the long construction periods. The planning techniques used for socialist planning (material balances and input–output) were such that the current plans were always inconsistent (Ellman, 1973, Chapter 1). As the inconsistencies came to light during the planned period, it was necessary to alter the plans so as to allow the economy to function.

Attempts were made to overcome this problem by improving the planning techniques. It sometimes happened, however, that major innovations in planning techniques about which high hopes were held, simply failed to achieve the objectives of those who introduced them. For example, during the 1960s, input–output was widely introduced in planning in the European state socialist countries. It was the first mathematical technique to be introduced in socialist planning, and high hopes were held by many about the benefits that would flow from using it. It was widely expected that it would eliminate the problem of inconsistent plans because the use of input–output would enable consistent plans to be calculated. In fact, however, this turned out to be erroneous. Input–output, like material balances, was quite unable to resolve the problem of drawing up consistent plans for all the centrally planned commodities (Ellman, 1973, Chapter 1). This did not mean that the new technique was useless. On the contrary, it turned out to be very useful for the calculation of pre-plan variants and as a source of information. The problem it had been introduced to solve, however, remained unresolved.

Not only may new techniques fail to solve the problems they were introduced to solve, but experiments with them may simply underline the losses caused by the use of administrative methods. A well-known example was provided by the use of linear programming in the USSR in the 1960s to calculate minimum-cost transport schemes. As Belkin and Birman observed in an article in *Izvestiya* of 4 December 1964:

> This is not a complicated task. Many articles and books have been written and not a few dissertations defended, but almost no freight is shipped by the optimal schemes. Why? Simply because the transport organizations are given plans based on [maximizing] ton kilometers. One can establish computer centers, and conceive superb algorithms, but nothing will come of it as long as the transport organizations reckon plan fulfillment in ton kilometers.

1.7.3   Complexity

Complexity is used here to describe the fact that decision making is dispersed over numerous individuals and organizations. The dispersal of decision making is a normal and necessary reaction to the difficulties of collecting and processing in one spot all the data necessary for rational decision making. It creates, however, numerous problems.

One of the reasons for the inconsistency of the current plans, which in turn was a major cause of their instability, was precisely that the planning of production and supply for the entire national economy was regarded as too complicated for any one organization, and accordingly was split up among many organizations. This created numerous coordination problems (Ellman, 1973, pp. 24–25).

Similarly, numerous problems were created by the fact that in the traditional Soviet model planning, the compilation of plans and checking up on their fulfillment, was split between two organizations, Gosplan (the State Planning Committee) and TsSU (the Central Statistical Administration). For example, the introduction of input–output into Soviet planning in the 1960s was hindered by the fact that the two organizations used different commodity classifications.

The dispersal of decision making over various organizations ensures that it will be affected by what Downs (1967, p. 216) has termed the Law of Interorganizational Conflict. This states that *every large organization is in partial conflict with every other social agent it deals with.*

The traditional Marxist–Leninist theory of planning assumes that all the decision makers in an economy form a 'team', that is a group of persons working together, who have identical goals. In fact, the decision makers form a 'coalition', that is, a group of persons working together who have some, but not all, goals in common. It is because decision makers form a coalition and not a team that incentives, both negative and positive, moral and material, play an important motivating role in ensuring the necessary output of work.

The fact that decision making is dispersed among a coalition, whose members are not allowed, in many cases, to charge for their output, is one of the causes of bureaucratization. The reason for this is that it brings into operation what Downs (1967, p. 188) has termed the Law of Non-Money pricing. This states that *organizations that cannot charge money for their services must develop non-monetary costs to impose on their clients as a means of rationing their outputs.* Hence, much of the irritating behavior of bureaucrats often represents a means of rationing their limited resources so that they will be available to those truly anxious to use them. It is precisely because non-market organizations tend to breed bureaucratization that throughout the whole history of socialist planning efforts were repeatedly made – with a singular lack of success – to combat bureaucracy.

The importance of the dispersal of decision making in ensuring that even a state owned non-market economy would not necessarily be socially rational was familiar already to acute observers of War Communism. More than 80 years ago, Kritsman (1924, pp. 98–99) observed that

> If we consider the economy as a whole . . . we come to the conclusion that in our proletarian–natural economy exploitation and the market were overcome without overcoming the anarchy of economic life . . . As is well known, commodity economy is anarchic economy. It would, however, be incorrect to conclude from this that a non-commodity economy, that is a natural economy, is necessarily a non-anarchical, that is a planned, economy . . . For an economy to be anarchic it is necessary and sufficient for there to be a multiplicity of (independent) economic subjects.

With the advantage of almost a century of extra experience we can add to Kritsman's observation the twin points, that the dispersal of decision making is inevitable and permanent (because of partial ignorance and inadequate techniques for processing information) and that an economy with dispersal of decision making may be, but is not necessarily, socially irrational.

1.8   Socialist planning and a war economy

Bolshevik thinking about socialist planning began in a war situation (World War I and the Civil War) and under the influence of the German World War I war economy. Subsequently, the famous Polish economist Oskar Lange described the traditional model of socialist planning as a '*sui generis* war economy' and the British economists Ely Devons and Alec Nove drew attention to the close relationship between the traditional model of socialist planning and the British war economy during World War II. This raises the interesting question, why do capitalist countries adopt a variant of socialist planning in wartime, when maximum efficiency is required, if this system is so inefficient? The answer seems to be as follows.

First, a war economy allows the state to concentrate resources on a limited number of priority goals which it regards as the most important. Because of the three factors discussed in the Section 1.7, it will normally happen that the resources available for civilian production and consumption will not be allocated where they would produce the greatest production of civilian goods and the greatest volume of consumer satisfaction, but the state does not care much about that and the population are prepared to put up with it since their survival depends on the output of guns not butter. On the other hand, under peacetime conditions in democratic countries the population would not tolerate the government devoting the nation's resources to 'pyramids of sacrifice' (Berger, 1974) while their living standards were being squeezed.

Secondly, the waste generated by partial ignorance, inadequate techniques for data processing and complexity is offset by the additional resources obtained by the transition from a demand-constrained to a supply-constrained economy. Although in the long-run, a supply-constrained economy generates characteristic forms of waste (Kornai, 1980), in the short run it allows additional output and war reduces some of the negative effects (for example on labor morale). As Philip Hanson once observed, Soviet planning was not so much a system for allocating *given* resources as a system for *mobilizing* resources. The intermittent Russian discussion about the possibility of reintroducing a mobilization regime is a criticism of the market economic system which, in its Russian variant, has allowed substantial reserves of production capacity and labor to be unutilized and substantial potential investment resources to flee the country (capital flight).

Thirdly, complexity is of reduced importance because of the need to win the war. This is a powerful motivating force which can reduce coordination and motivation problems.

Fourthly, there is an important distributional aspect. A war economy allows the state to transfer to war purposes the normally large share of output devoted to luxury consumption under peacetime conditions. Furthermore, during a war the bargaining position of labor is strengthened. For the workers, a war economy may be beneficial because of its redistributive and anti-poverty aspects. A war economy may actually lead to an improvement in the living standards of that section of the population that was in poverty under the previous demand-constrained system (this was the case in the UK in World War II). These people benefit both from the increase in employment and from redistribution from capitalist consumption to workers' consumption. Conversely, the transition from socialist planning to capitalism in Central and Eastern Europe has been associated with an increase in inequality and poverty. Since under peacetime conditions the higher income groups normally have a disproportionate political influence, the distributive factor is an important reason why in general only in wartime do capitalist economies use socialist planning methods.

Hence, despite the general arguments against the efficiency of the *sui generis* war economy, under some conditions there are economic and social benefits from this type of organization.

1.9   Reform of socialist planning

Reform of socialist planning began in Yugoslavia in 1950, was discussed in Poland and Hungary in the mid-1950s, was discussed throughout the CMEA or Comecon in the mid-1960s and introduced in Hungary from 1968, in China from 1978, and in the USSR from 1986. These reforms, especially those in Poland, were extensively described and analyzed by Nuti (for example Nuti, 1977, 1981a, 1988). They all reflected dissatisfaction with the results of socialist planning in such key fields as agriculture, personal consumption, foreign trade, technical progress, and economic growth. In particular, the steadily declining rate of economic growth in the USSR, the homeland of the traditional model, from 1958 onwards, suggests that the model was probably not viable in the long run in a dynamic international capitalist environment (even if its death was accelerated by the unintended consequences of perestroika).

1.10   From reform to system change

Of the five main features of the traditional model of socialist planning – state ownership, political dictatorship, a mono-hierarchical system, imperative planning and physical planning – economic reform tended to abolish the last two but retain the first three. System change became possible when the Communist party lost power and politicians came to power committed to liberal democracy, predominantly private ownership, full integration into the world market and the abolition of investment planning. This happened in Central Europe in 1989 and in Russia and some of the other former Soviet republics in 1991.

System change turned out to be a painful process marked by inflation, unemployment, inequality, impoverishment, criminalization, state capture, and state collapse (in some countries). Nevertheless, it brought some concrete benefits (full shops, freedom of all kinds – from religious to travel). By the middle of the first decade of the twenty-first century, the gains already achieved, and the hope for more, seemed likely to draw all the former east European and Baltic state socialist countries in due course, although at varying speeds, along the road to an OECD type economic system, or to misuse a Chinese term, to capitalism with national characteristics. Eight of them joined the EU in 2004, and two more seem likely to join in 2007. As for the former Soviet Union (less the Baltic countries), the end point of its systemic change process varied between countries. Central Asia and the south Caucasus gradually became part of the third world. Its largest country, Russia, experienced a very difficult transformation process but its huge natural resources, in particular oil and natural gas, rescued the economy at the beginning of the twenty-first century from the depression, impoverishment, and primitivization characteristic of the Yeltsin period.

1.11 The international impact of socialist planning

The Soviet model of economic planning had an enormous impact throughout the world. Already before 1939 it influenced economic policy in countries such as Germany and Mexico. After World War II, economic planning spread to countries such as the Netherlands, France and Japan, where it acquired national characteristics and differed sharply from Soviet type planning (Ellman, 1990). After the collapse of the colonial empires it spread to many third world countries. Experience with economic planning in all these countries has been varied. In most countries economic planning has been abolished or is by now vestigial and has little impact on economic policy. In some it has found a useful niche within the policy process. In the third world, the high hopes once associated with economic planning were generally disappointed (Streeten and Lipton, 1968; Faber and Seers, 1972). On the other hand, for a long time planning in South Korea seemed to be more successful. In the former state socialist world, economic planning has been ended in the former USSR and the former Eastern Europe. In China the State Development Planning Commission ceased to exist in 2003 and was replaced by the State Development and Reform Commission. China's 10th 5-Year Plan (2001–05) was its last and was followed by the 11th 5-Year Program. These terminological changes reflected the discrediting of 'planning' and the wish to disassociate policy from it.

1.12 Capitalist triumphalism

The collapse of state socialism in 1989–91 gave rise to what has been termed 'capitalist triumphalism' (Wiles, 1992) or 'liberal optimism' (Chavance, 1994, pp. 182–84). This exalted in the collapse of an inefficient economic system, advocated a rapid transition to the rival system, and praised that system's properties. This mood lasted just a few years and was undermined by the realities of 'transition', especially in the former Soviet Union, and the realities of really existing market economies. The widespread impoverishment, criminalization, state capture, declining life expectancy, and inequality, in the former Soviet Union and some other 'transition' countries, made it clear that the abolition of state socialism was not enough to create an attractive economic and social system. Furthermore, the inequality and poverty in parts of Latin America, Africa and Asia also emphasized that markets on their own could not be relied on to generate attractive outcomes. Moreover, the last decade has demonstrated the volatility of financial markets, the risks of banking fragility, the dangers to national economies of capital surges, the costs of the demand constrained system (for example unemployment), and the growing inequality of contemporary market economies. It has also demonstrated the importance of monetary and fiscal policy, and market regulators, in ensuring the success of market economies. These developments showed that although Marx and Engels had been wrong to assume that the replacement of the market by planning would lead to an attractive economic and social system, they had been right to think that an unregulated market economy was socially undesirable.

1.13   Conclusion

The 70 years 1921–91 mark the rise and fall of socialist planning. The latter, in its traditional Soviet-type form, turned out to be an unattractive system based on an erroneous theoretical conception and probably not viable in the long run in a dynamic international capitalist environment. The idea of national economic planning has been deeply discredited. The collapse of the socialist system in Eastern Europe and the USSR gave rise to a mood of capitalist triumphalism, which lasted only a few years and was undermined by the difficulties of 'transition' and the realities of really existing market economies. Marx and Engels were right to argue that an unregulated market economy was socially and economically undesirable, but wrong to assume that the replacement of the market by planning would lead to an attractive economic and social system.

Notes

1. Earlier versions of this paper were published in Dutch and French.
2. The 'second economy' was that part of the economy relating to private production and / or (re)distribution.
3. The 'third economy' refers to transactions between state enterprises which were unplanned but were entered into in order to achieve the goals of the plan.
4. The arguments about partial ignorance and inadequate techniques for data processing can be found (in a different terminology) already in Hayek (1935, pp. 207–12). For a Soviet exposition of the view that the differences between actually existing planning and the Marxist–Leninist theory of planning were due to the theoretical defects of the latter, see Khanin (1967).
5. A term introduced by Fehér, Heller, and Márkus (1983).
6. The classic discussion is Nove (1958).
7. This is the notorious tendency of enterprises under socialist planning to strive for a plan which provides for the production of less output than is possible and/or the use of more inputs than is necessary.
8. 'The residual principle' refers to the fact that non-priority sectors (for example medical care, housing, education, retail trade) have to make do with the resources which are available after priority sectors (for example the military-industrial complex, agriculture, the space program, industry) have received what they need.
9. This refers to the fact that the plans are frequently unstable and often altered repeatedly during the 'planned' period, sometimes even retrospectively.

References

Barone, E. (1908) Italian article translated in Hayek (1935), Partial English translation in Nove and Nuti (1972).

Berger, P. (1974) *Pyramids of sacrifice* (New York: Basic Books).

Bim, A. (1989) 'Gosudarstvennyi plan: novye zadachi, novaya model', *Kommunist*, 11.

Brus, W. and T. Kowalik (1983) 'Socialism and development', *Cambridge Journal of Economics*, 7 (3–4), 243–55.

Bukharin, N. and E. Preobrazhensky (1920, 1969) *The ABC of Communism* (Harmondsworth: Penguin).

Chavance, B. (1994) *La fin des systèmes socialistes* (Paris: L'Harmattan).

Domar, E. (1957) 'A Soviet model of growth', in E. Domar *Essays in the theory of economic growth* (New York: Oxford University Press).

Downs, A. (1967) *Inside bureaucracy* (Boston: Little, Brown and Co).

Ellman, M. (1973) *Planning problems in the USSR* (Cambridge: Cambridge University Press).

Ellman, M. (1978) 'The fundamental problem of socialist planning', *Oxford Economic Papers*, 30 (2), 249–62.

Ellman, M. (1990) 'Socialist planning', in J. Eatwell, M. Milgate, and P. Newman (eds) *Problems of the planned economy* (London: Macmillan).

Ellman, M. and V. Kontorovich (eds) (1998) *The destruction of the Soviet economic system* (New York: M.E. Sharpe).

Eydelman, M. (1998) 'Monopolized statistics under a totalitarian regime', in M. Ellman and V. Kontorovich (eds) *The destruction of the Soviet economic system: an insiders' history* (London: M.E. Sharpe).

Faber, M. and D. Seers (eds) (1972) *The crisis in planning* (London: Chatto and Windus for Sussex University Press).

Fehér, F., A. Heller, and G. Márkus (1983) *Dictatorship over needs* (Oxford: Blackwell).

Feiwel, G.R. (1975) *The intellectual capital of Michal Kalecki* (Knoxville, Tenn.: University of Tennessee Press).

Feldman, G.A. (1928) 'K teorii tempov narodnogo khozyaistvo', *Planovoe khozyaistvo*, no. 11 and 12.

Hayek, F.A. (ed.) (1935) *Collectivist economic planning* (London: Routledge and Kegan Paul).

Hayek, F.A. (1937) 'Economics and knowledge', *Economica*, 4 (13), 33–54.

Hayek, F.A. (1945) 'The use of knowledge in society', *American Economic Review*, 35 (4), 519–30.

Hayek, F.A. (1988) *The fatal conceit* (London: Routledge).

Khanin, G. (1967) *Nekotorye metodologicheskie voprosy tsentral'nogo planirovaniya sotsialisticheskoi ekonomiki* (mimeo, *avtoreferat*, Novosibirsk).

Khanin, G. (1998) 'An uninvited advisor', in M. Ellman and V. Kontorovich (eds) *The destruction of the Soviet economic system: an insiders' history* (London: M.E. Sharpe).

Kornai, J. (1980) *Economics of shortage* vols A and B (Amsterdam: North Holland).

Kritsman, L. (1924) 'Geroicheskii period Velikoi Russkoi Revolyutsii', *Vestnik kommunisticheskoi akademii*, 9.

Lenin,V.I. (1918, 1929) *Sochineniya* (Moscow: Politizdat) 2nd edition, vol. 22.

Lerner, A.Y. (1975) *Fundamentals of cybernetics* (New York: Plenum).

Mises, L. von (1920) German article translated in Hayek (1935), Partial translation in Nove and Nuti (1972).

Nove, A. (1958) 'The problem of success indicators in Soviet industry', *Economica*, 25 (97), 1–13.

Nove, A. and D.M. Nuti (eds) (1972) *Socialist economics* (Harmondsworth: Penguin).

Nuti, D.M. (1977) 'Large corporations and the reform of Polish industry', *Jahrbuch der Wirtschaft Osteuropas*, 7.

Nuti, D.M. (1981a) 'The Polish crisis: economic factors and constraints', *The socialist register 1981* (London: Merlin Press).

Nuti, D.M. (1981b) 'Socialism on earth', *Cambridge Journal of Economics*, 5 (4), 391.

Nuti, D.M. (1988) 'Perestroika: transition from central planning to market socialism', *Economic Policy*, October.

Pierson, N.G. (1902) Dutch article translated in Hayek (1935).

Spulber, N. (ed.) (1964) *Foundations of Soviet strategy for economic growth* (Bloomington: Indiana University Press).

Steinbruner, J.D. (1974) *The cybernetic theory of decisions* (Princeton: Princeton University Press).

Streeten, P. and M. Lipton (eds) (1968) *The crisis of Indian planning* (London: Oxford University Press for RIIA).

Wiles, P. (1992) 'Capitalist triumphalism in Eastern Europe, or the Economics of Transition: an interim report', in A. Clesse and R. Tokes (eds) *Preventing a new East-West divide: the economic and social imperatives of the future Europe* (Baden-Baden: Nomos).

Zaleski, E. (1980) *Stalinist planning for economic growth, 1933–52* (Chapel Hill, NC: University of North Carolina Press).

2
Life Cycle of the Centrally Planned Economy: Why Soviet Growth Rates Peaked in the 1950s[1]

Vladimir Popov

2.1 Introduction

In the second half of the twentieth century the Soviet Union experienced the most dramatic shift in economic growth patterns. High post-war growth rates of the 1950s gave way to the slowdown of growth in the 1960s–80s and later – to the unprecedented depression of the 1990s associated with the transition from a centrally planned economy (CPE) to a market one. Productivity growth rates (output per worker, Western data) fell from an exceptionally high 6 per cent a year in the 1950s to 3 per cent in the 1960s, 2 per cent in the 1970s and 1 per cent in the 1980s. In 1989 transformational recession started and continued for almost a decade: output was constantly falling until 1999 with the exception of one single year – 1997, when GDP increased by a barely noticeable 0.8 per cent. If viewed as an inevitable and logical result of the Soviet growth model, this transformational recession substantially worsens the general record of Soviet economic growth.

The nature of Soviet economic decline from the 1950s to 1980s does not fit completely into the standard growth theory. If this decline was caused by the over-accumulation of capital (investment share doubled in 1950–85 from 15 per cent to over 30 per cent), how could it be that Asian countries were able to maintain high growth rates with even higher share of investment in GDP and higher growth of capital–labor ratios?[2] Why in the 1980s, as the conventional saying held it, the Soviet Union maintained the Japanese share of investment in GDP with very 'un-Japanese' results? If, on the contrary, the Soviet growth decline was caused by the specific inefficiencies of the CPE, why had CPE been so efficient in the 1950s, ensuring high growth rates of output, labor productivity and total factor productivity (TFP)? In the 1950s Soviet defense spending was already very high and rising (from an estimated 9 per cent in 1950 to 10–13 per cent by the end of the decade), whereas Soviet investment spending, although increased markedly, was still below

25 per cent by 1960. Medium–high share of investment spending and very high share of defense expenditure is not exactly the kind of combination that could account for high productivity growth rates even in market economies.

2.2   Growth accounting for the USSR

For decades Soviet experience with economic growth was textbook proof of the 'disease of over-investment' resulting in declining factor productivity. It was even referred to as the best application of the Solow model ever seen. Most estimates of Soviet economic growth found low and declining TFP (in the 1970s–80s TFP was even negative) suggesting that growth was mostly due to large capital and labor inputs and in this sense was extremely costly.

More recently, parallels have been made between East Asian and Soviet growth. Krugman (1994), referring to the calculations by Young (1994), has argued that there is no puzzle to Asian growth; that it was due mostly to the accelerated accumulation of factor inputs – capital and labor, whereas TFP growth was quite weak (lower than in Western countries). The logical outcome was the prediction that East Asian growth is going to end in the same way the Soviet growth did – over-accumulation of capital resources, if continued, sooner or later would undermine capital productivity. It may have happened already in Japan in the 1970s–90s (where growth rates declined despite the high share of investment in GDP) and may be happening in Korea, Taiwan and ASEAN countries after the currency crises of 1997. The only other alternative for high growth countries would be to reduce the rates of capital accumulation (growth of investment), which should lead to the same result – slowdown in the growth of output. Radelet and Sachs (1997), however, challenged this view, arguing that East Asian growth is likely to resume in 2–3 years after the 1997 currency crises.

A different approach (based on endogenous growth models and treating investment in human capital as a separate source of growth) would be that in theory rapid growth can continue endlessly, if investments in physical and human capital are high. According to this approach, all cases of 'high growth failures' – from USSR to Japan – are explained by special circumstances and do not refute the theoretical possibility of maintaining high growth rates 'forever'. The logical 'special' explanation for the Soviet economic decline would be of course the nature of the CPE itself that precluded it from using investment as efficiently as in market economies.

To what extent the Soviet economic slowdown was caused by the specific CPE factors and to what extent it reflected the more general process of TPF decline due to the over-accumulation of capital? Gomulka (1977), Bergson (1983), Ofer (1987) and others using the Cobb–Douglas production function attributed the slowdown in growth rates to the very nature of the extensive growth model, where the contribution of technical progress to growth was small and falling in line with the accumulation of capital.

Weitzman (1970), Desai (1976), however, pointed out that another explanation is also consistent with the stylized facts, namely constant rates of technical progress, but low capital/labor substitution (CES – constant elasticity substitution – production function) leading to declining marginal product of capital. The debate about the most appropriate form of the production function is summarized in Ofer (1987), Easterly and Fischer (1995), Schroeder (1995), Guriev and Ickes (2000).

Easterly and Fischer (1995) argue that Soviet 1950–87 growth performance can be accounted for by a declining marginal capital productivity with a *constant* rate of growth of TFP. They show that the increase in capital–output ratio in the USSR was no higher than in fast growing market economies, such as Japan, Taiwan, Korea (Table 2.1). The reason for poorer Soviet performance is seen in low elasticity of substitution between capital and labor that caused a greater decline in returns to capital than in market economies. In this case, however, the question of interest would be why exactly the elasticity of substitution was low and whether this low level is related to the nature of the planning system. The recent endogenous growth models suggest that physical, human and organizational capital can substitute for labor virtually without limits.

Besides, there is still no exhaustive explanation for the 'golden period' of Soviet growth of the 1950s, when output per worker was growing at about 6 per cent a year both in industry and in the economy overall, while capital per worker was increasing by 3.9 per cent and 7.4 per cent respectively. An

Table 2.1 Growth in the USSR and Asian economies, Western data, 1928–87 (average annual per cent)

Period/country	Output per worker	Capital per worker	Capital– output ratio	TPF growth (unit elasticity of substitution)	TPF growth assuming 0.4 elasticity of substitution
USSR (1928–39)	2.9	5.7	2.8	0.6	
USSR (1940–49)	1.9	1.5	−0.4	1.3	
USSR (1950–59)	5.8	7.4	1.6	2.8	1.1
USSR (1960–69)	3.0	5.4	2.4	0.8	1.1
USSR (1970–79)	2.1	5.0	2.9	0.1	1.2
USSR (1980–87)	1.4	4.0	2.6	−0.2	1.1
Japan (1950/57/ 65–85/88/90)			2.3–3.2	1.7–2.5	
Korea (1950/60/ 65–85/88/90)			2.8–3.7	1.7–2.8	
Taiwan (1950/53/ 65–85/88/90)			2.6–3.1	1.9–2.4	

Source: Easterly, Fischer (1995).

explanation of Soviet economic growth based on low elasticity of capital–labor substitution, has to point to factors that accounted for the dramatic decline in returns to capital from the 1950s to the 1980s.

2.3 Why was the elasticity of capital–labor substitution low in centrally planned economies?

A plausible explanation for low capital–labor substitution may be associated with the inability of the centrally planned economy (CPE) to renovate obsolete capital stock as quickly as the market economy does. It is well documented that in CPEs actual service life of fixed capital stock was long, retirement of machinery and equipment and buildings and structures was slow and the average age of equipment was high and growing (Shmelev and Popov, 1989).

Typically in the USSR the service lives of machinery and equipment, buildings and structures were very high, and the retirement rate, respectively, very low. In industry in the 1980s it was just 2–3 per cent, as compared to 4–5 per cent in US manufacturing for all capital stock, and 3–4 per cent, as compared to 5–6 per cent in US manufacturing for machinery and equipment. Consequently, the major part of gross investment was used not to replace the retiring capital stock (since retirement was low), but to expand it. While in the US manufacturing 50–60 per cent of all investment was replacing retirement, and only 40–50 per cent contributed to the expansion of capital stock, in Soviet industry the proportion was reversed: replacing the retirement required about 30 per cent of gross investment, while over 70 per cent contributed to the expansion of capital stock or to the unfinished construction.

The production capacities were brought into operation mostly through the construction of new and the expansion of existing plants, not through reconstruction of old capacities: of 16 types of capacities on which data are available, in 15 cases the share of those capacities brought into operation through reconstruction of the old ones was lower than 50 per cent over the whole period of 1971–89; the unweighted average indicator of the share of reconstructed capacities was just 23 per cent (Narkhoz, various years).

The reason for massive investment in the expansion of capital stock at the expense of investment to replace retirement was the permanent concern of Soviet planners about expanding output and meeting production quotas. Replacing worn-out aged machinery and equipment usually required technical reconstruction and was associated with temporary work stoppage and reduction in output. Even if the replacement could have been carried out instantly, the resulting increase in output (because of greater productivity of new equipment) was smaller than in the case of the construction of new capacities or the expansion of existing capacities: in the latter case there was a hope that the new capacities would have been added to the existing ones that will somehow manage to operate several more years.

Aged and worn-out equipment and structures were thus normally repaired endlessly, until they were falling apart physically; capital repair expenditure amounted to over one-third of annual investment. The capital stock meanwhile was getting older and was wearing out, the average age of equipment and structures increased constantly.

The official statistics suggest that the share of investment into the reconstruction of enterprises (as opposed to the expansion of existing and construction of new enterprises) increased from 33 per cent in 1980 to 39 per cent in 1985 to 50 per cent in 1989 (Narkhoz, 1989, p. 280), but this is not very consistent with the other official data. For instance, the retirement ratio in Soviet industry was not only very low (below 2 per cent and about 3 per cent respectively for the retirement of physically obsolete and retirement of all assets), but mostly falling or stable in 1967–85 (Figure 2.1). Only in 1965–67 (right after the economic reform of 1965), and in 1986–87 (acceleration and restructuring policy) was there a noticeable increase in the retirement rate.

The share of investment to replace retirement in total gross investment also stayed at an extremely low level of below 20 per cent for the most part of the 1960s–80s; only in 1965–67 and in 1985–87 were there short-lived increases in this ratio – up to 30 per cent (Figure 2.2).

Besides, accumulated depreciation as a percentage of gross value of fixed capital stock (gross value minus net value, divided by gross value) grew from 26 per cent in 1970 to 45 per cent in 1989, and in some industries, such as steel, chemicals and petrochemicals, exceeded 50 per cent by the end of

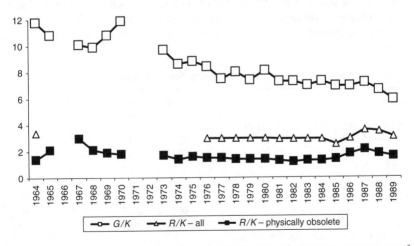

Figure 2.1 Gross investment and retirement in Soviet industry, as a percentage of fixed capital stock

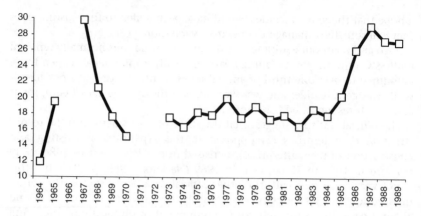

Figure 2.2 Share of investment to replace retirement in total gross investment in Soviet industry, %

the 1980s. The average age of industrial equipment increased from 8.3 to 10.3 years in the 1970s–80s, and actual average service life was 24–28 years (as compared to a 13 years period, established by norms for depreciation accounting). The share of equipment over 11 years old increased from 29 per cent in 1970 to 35 per cent in 1980 and to 40 per cent in 1989, while the share of the equipment used for 20 years and over – from 8 to 14 per cent (Table 2.2).

The planners' reluctance to modernize existing plants and heavy emphasis on new construction – a policy that was supposed to increase output as much as possible, in the long run led to declining capital productivity. Capacity utilization rate in Soviet industry was falling rapidly, although official statistics registered only a marginal decrease (Faltsman, 1985; Valtukh and

Table 2.2 Age characteristics of equipment in Soviet industry

Years	1970	1980	1985	1989
Share of equipment with an age of:				
– less than 5 years	41.1	36.0	33.7	31.6
– 6–10 years	29.9	28.9	28.5	28.6
– 11–20 years	20.9	24.8	25.5	26.2
– over 20 years	7.8	10.3	12.3	13.7
Average age of equipment, years	8.3	9.31	9.91	10.32
Average service life, years	24.0	26.9	27.9	26.2
Accumulated depreciation as a % of gross (initial) value of capital stock	26.0	36.0	41.0	45.0

Source: Narkhoz, for various years.

Lavrovskyi, 1986; Shmelev and Popov, 1989). Growing 'shortages' of labor force during the 1970s–80s may be regarded as a sign of an increasing share of unloaded production capacities. On the whole, as was estimated by a *Gosplan* specialist, the excess capacities, not equipped with labor force, constituted in late 1980s about one-fourth of all capital stock in industry and one-fifth of capital stock in the entire economy. In the mainstream production of all industrial plants 25 per cent of jobs were vacant, while in machine-building plants – up to 45 per cent. In machine-building there were only 63 workers per 100 machines. The number of these machines exceeded that in the US by a fraction of 2.5, yet each Soviet machine was actually operating for twice less time in the course of a year than the American one (Shmelev and Popov, 1989; IMF *et al*, 1991). Meanwhile, the shift coefficient (number of shifts a day) in Soviet industry declined from 1.54 in 1960 to 1.42 in 1970, to 1.37 in 1980, and to 1.35 in 1985 (Narkhoz, various years).

It may seem that the whole problem of under-loaded production capacities, or rather 'the shortage of the labor force', as it was usually referred to by Soviet planners, had a simple and feasible solution, especially in the CPE. To resolve the whole issue of labor shortage, it was necessary to cut the investment in new plants and equipment, increasing the investment in the replacement of obsolete capital stock. Because this type of structural maneuver involved a change of macroeconomic (not microeconomic) proportions, it may seem that it could have been carried out quite easily in a planned economy.

However, as was already mentioned, excess investment in new construction resulted not from mismanagement, but from the very idea of directive planning carried out through setting production quotas and oriented towards constant increases in output. Shortages were inevitable in such a system and resulted from disproportions created through central planning almost by definition, while capital investment was regarded as a major means of eliminating the bottlenecks resulting from shortages. So capital investment was diverted to create new production capacities that would have allowed expanding production of scarce goods. The whole planning procedure looked like an endless chain of urgent decisions forced by emergency shortages of different goods that manifested themselves quicker than the planners were able to liquidate them.

This was a sort of a vicious circle, a permanent race, in which decisions to make capital investment were predetermined by existing and newly emerging shortages. It turned out, therefore, that any attempts to cut the investment in new plant and equipment led to increased distortions and bottlenecks, resulting, among other things, in the lower capacity utilization rate, while the increased investment in the construction of new production facilities contributed to the widening of the gap between job vacancies and the limited supply of the labor force, also causing the decline in the capacity utilization. Under central planning, unfortunately, there was no third option.

As a result, the CPE with the inherent and unavoidable low capital–labor elasticity trap was doomed to survive through a life cycle linked to the service life of fixed capital stock. Assuming the service life of capital stock is about 20 years, in the first 20 years of the existence of the CPE the construction of new modern production capacities led to rapid increases of labor productivity even though the capital–output ratio rose. In the next 10 years production capacities put into operation 20 years earlier started to retire physically, which contributed to the slow down of the growth rates, but was compensated by the continuing expansion of fixed capital stock. After 30 years of the existence of the CPE, it entered the stage of decline: over half of the capital stock was worn-out and falling apart (but not completely replaced), while the newly created production capacities were just barely enough to compensate for the decline in output resulting from aging of the capital stock.

To summarize, low elasticity of capital–labor substitution is the intrinsic feature of the CPE because it is oriented towards the expansion of capital stock at the expense of the replacement of the retirement. Such an investment strategy can produce best results in the first 30 years (a period equivalent to one and a half times service life of capital stock), but later inevitably leads to a rapid decline in capital productivity. Viewed in such a way, CPEs, despite all their inefficiencies and high costs of growth, can support reasonable growth rates, but only in the first several decades of their existence – for the Soviet Union, where the CPE emerged in the early 1930s after the roll back of NEP, this was probably a period until the 1960s. Later the CPE is doomed to witness a severe decline in capital productivity associated with the aging of fixed capital stock.

There are papers that consider the low ability of the CPE to replace retirement as the important stylized fact; it is used in the theoretical models of the CPEs to explain particular features of their performance. Ickes and Ryterman (1997) demonstrate that in the absence of the mechanism of exits of firms inefficient enterprises will tend to be allocated less resources than efficient ones and that this will generate an industrial structure that is bi-modal in nature, one in which inefficient enterprises agglomerate at one end of the size spectrum and efficient enterprises agglomerate at the other end. Iacopetta (2004) explains the gap between high level of research and inventions in the CPEs and poor innovation activity and performance by the perverse Soviet managerial compensation system, which generated incentives for the managers to perform only a modest retooling activity out of fear of breaking the production norm that the planner imposed upon the firm.

In this paper the same stylized fact (inability of the CPE to properly replace retiring elements of capital stock) is used to explain cyclical patterns of growth of TFP in a planned economy and the life cycle of CPE.

2.4   Effects of low investment to replace retirement: numerical example

Consider an economy with growing gross investment, $G(t)$, that exceeds the retirement of fixed capital stock, $R(t)$, and so is partly used to expand the existing capital stock by the amount equal to net investment, $I(t)$. Retirement of fixed capital stock, in turn, is equal to investment made m years ago, where m is the service life of capital equipment:

$$G(t) = R(t) + I(t)$$

$$R(t) = G(t - m)$$

This is a set up of the Domar model (Domar, 1957) that assumes constant rates of growth of gross investment and shows that in the growing economy depreciation, equal to capital stock divided by the average service life, $D(t) = K(t)/m$, is larger than retirement, $R(t) = G(t - m)$, so that the future growth of capital stock can be financed from the part of depreciation that exceeds retirement, that is future growth can build up on the previous growth, so that the economy can remain in the growth equilibrium, even if all profits are consumed and are not used to finance investment. Gross investment, $G(t)$, is equal to the sum of investment that goes to replace retiring elements of capital stock, $R(t)$, and net investment, $I(t)$, that contribute to the expansion of capital stock:

$$K(t) = K(t - 1) + G(t) - R(t)$$

$$I(t) = \Delta K(t) = K(t) - K(t - 1) = G(t) - R(t)$$

The Domar model explicitly demonstrates that in fast growing economies the share of investment in replacing retirement, $R(t)/G(t)$, is low, whereas the share of investment in the expansion of capital stock, $I(t)/G(t)$, is high, so that there is a cumulative mechanism to promote growth – the faster economic growth, the smaller portion of gross investment is needed to replace retirement, so the larger portion is used for the expansion of capital stock, that leads to the expansion of output (assuming constant Capital–Output Ratio, COR).

But the Domar model can also be used to demonstrate the effect of the big push. If the economy is in a no-growth equilibrium, so that gross investment is equal to retirement, $G(t) = R(t) = G(t-m)$, but at a certain point experiences a 'big push', so that investment starts to exceed annual retirement of fixed capital stock, then growth can be maintained indefinitely even if all profits are consumed and are not used to finance investment. In this paper the basic setup of the Domar model is used to demonstrate another effect: the impact of the 'big push' on the growth rates of an economy is not sustainable, if the ability of the system to invest into the replacement of the retirement of fixed capital stock is constrained.

Unlike investment into the expansion of capital stock (construction of new production capacities), investment in the replacement of the retirement does not create new jobs. Let us make a distinction between the actual retirement of capital equipment due to the end of its service life, $G(t-m)$, and annual investment into the replacement of retirement, $R(t)$. The reasonable assumption for the market economy would be that investment in the replacement of retirement (reconstruction of existing production capacities) is higher than the actual retirement of capital equipment (wear and tear of capital stock), $R(t) > G(t-m)$, because machinery and equipment, buildings and structures become not only physically obsolete, but also technologically obsolete: it may pay off to replace a piece of machinery before its actual physical retirement by a more technically advanced one. Suppose, therefore, that investment into the replacement of the retirement is equal to actual retirement, $G(t-m)$, plus an additional 10 per cent of gross investment, $G(t)$:

$$R(t) = G(t-m) + 0.1G(t) \tag{2.1}$$

Capital stock this year is equal to capital stock in the previous year, plus net investment, equal to the difference between gross investment and investment into the replacement of retirement:

$$K(t) = K(t-1) + I(t) = K(t-1) + G(t) - R(t) \tag{2.2}$$

Gross investment is a constant share of income, $Y(t)$:

$$G(t) = aY(t) \tag{2.3}$$

(later it is assumed that a is equal to 5 per cent before the 'big push' and 10 per cent afterwards).

Finally, the most important equation is the one that describes the increase in income. The assumption here is that this increase is proportional to the increase in the fixed capital stock, $\Delta K = I(t) = G(t) - R(t)$, but also depends on the share of investment into the replacement of retirement in total gross investment, $R(t)/G(t)$:

$$\Delta Y = b[G(t) - R(t)] \times R(t)/G(t) \tag{2.4}$$

The rationale for such a relationship is twofold. First, if the growth of the labor force is limited, then productivity of the investment into the expansion of capital stock (creation of new production capacities, that is new jobs, requiring new employees) is constrained by the labor force shortage: the increase in output of newly created production capacities would be accompanied by the decline in output in the old plants, from where workers will have to leave in order to take new jobs at the newly created plants. On the contrary, if all gross investment is used to replace retirement (to reconstruct the existing production capacities without creating new jobs), so that $R(t) = G(t)$, then $R(t)/G(t)$ is equal to 1 (maximum) and the productivity of new investment is the highest.

Second, if the speed of structural change is high enough as compared to the rate of retirement of capital stock due to physical wear and tear, so that it requires the re-allocation of capital and labor from old industries/regions/plants to new ones and this re-allocation is associated with adjustment costs (re-training of employees, shut down of physically non-obsolete capacities), the productivity of new investment in the expansion of production capacities may be lower as compared to investment into the reconstruction of the old capacities. A certain pace of structural change is necessary in any economy for the technical progress to proceed. But this pace may be so high that it requires the shut down of physically non-obsolete enterprises, if the country is catching up rapidly with the technological leader and/or changes its specialization in the international trade. Imagine, for example, that a country switches from export of agricultural output to export of industrial goods and has to reallocate labor and capital from agriculture to industry. Even if private returns from investment in industry are greater than from investment into agriculture, social returns (taking into account adjustment costs) can be lower. Hence, the productivity of investment into the expansion of fixed capital stock is assumed to be proportional to the share of investment into the replacement of retirement in total gross investment, $R(t)/G(t)$.

The last equation is the one that links output in the current year to output in the preceding year:

$$Y(t) = Y(t-1) + \Delta Y(t-1) \tag{2.5}$$

Assume now that in the initial year capital stock is equal to 20, output is equal to 20, gross investment is equal to 1 (the share of gross investment in income is thus 5 per cent), retirement is also equal to 1, and service life of capital stock is 20. So the system is not growing, and maintains stable no-growth equilibrium (growth rates of output are defined as $\Delta (t)/Y(t)$). After the first 20 years the 'big push' occurs – investment in year 21 increases to 2, so that the share of investment in income rises to 10 per cent. The trajectory of the growth rates, assuming b, the productivity of new investment is equal to 10, is shown in Figure 2.3 (the trajectory in the middle) – growth rates increase to 31 per cent a year right away, then gradually decline in the course of the next 20 years to 13 per cent and then after some fluctuations stabilize at a level of 16 per cent.[3]

Growth rates could be better than that, if we change the rule for the investment into the replacement of retirement, given by Equation (2.1). To

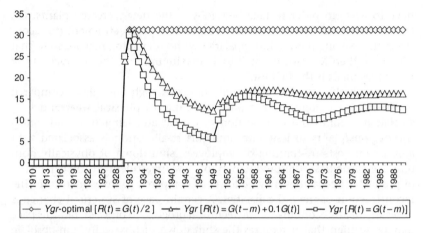

Figure 2.3   Growth rates after the 'big push' in a market economy (with investment to replace higher than actual physical retirement of capital stock), %

get the maximum possible growth rates, it is necessary to find the optimal investment into the replacement of the retirement of fixed capital stock, $R^*(t)$, by taking the first order condition (FOC) of Equation (2.4). Differentiating (2.4) and equating it to zero, we get:

$$R^*(t) = G(t)/2 \qquad (2.6)$$

Using this Expression (2.6) instead of the Equation (2.1), namely assuming that investment into the replacement of retirement are equal exactly to half of the gross investment, we get the best possible trajectory for the growth rate – it shoots to 31 per cent a year right away and stays at this level thereafter (upper trajectory at Figure 2.3).

The other extreme case is the lowest possible investment into the replacement of retirement: it is assumed that this investment is equal to the actual retirement of the fixed capital stock due to the expiration of its service life, $R(t) = G(t-m)$, and this expression is used instead of Equation (2.1). The result is that the growth rate shoots up to 30 per cent right after the 'big push', gradually declines to 5 per cent in the course of the next 20 years, and then stabilizes after some fluctuations at a level of 12 per cent – the lower trajectory at the chart (Figure 2.3).

The point of these simulations is to show that in all cases the growth rates after the 'big push' stabilize at a positive level. This is not the case, however, if the assumptions are slightly modified, so as to allow for the investment into the replacement of retirement of the fixed capital stock, $R(t)$, to be below the actual physical retirement, $G(t-m)$. Equation (2.2) will then have to be modified, so that the increase in capital stock is equal to gross investment minus actual retirement, $G(t-m)$, and not the investment into the replacement of retirement, $R(t)$:

$$K(t) = K(t-1) + G(t) - G(t-m) \qquad (2.2')$$

Equation (2.4) will have to be modified as well, so that the increase in the fixed capital stock is defined accordingly:

$$\Delta Y = b[G(t) - G(t-m)] \times R(t)/G(t) \qquad (2.4')$$

Finally, for describing investment into the replacement of retirement, let us use the simplest rule – a constant fraction of gross investment, c, small enough to make investment to replace retirement lower than the actual physical retirement of fixed capital stock:

$$R(t) = cG(t) \qquad (2.1')$$

This Equation (2.1') replaces the Equation (2.1). As a result, the new trajectories of growth rates, shown at the chart (Figure 2.4), are very different from the ones that were obtained previously under the assumption that investment into the replacement of the retirement is higher than actual retirement.

If c is equal to 0.1, that is investment into the replacement of the retirement of fixed capital stock are only 10 per cent of total gross capital investment, then growth rates after the 'big push' increase immediately to 5 per cent, then gradually grow to 9 per cent in the course of the next 20 years, but afterwards fall and converge after some fluctuations to a level of 8 per

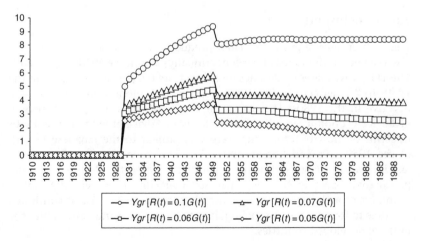

Figure 2.4 Growth rates after the 'big push' in a CPE (with constraints on investment to replace retirement of capital stock), %

cent (the upper trajectory on Figure 2.4). The next two trajectories (assuming c equal to 0.07 and 0.06 respectively) are similar – growth rates converge to 3.6 and 1.8 per cent respectively, but the last trajectory ($c = 0.05$) does not produce any convergence to a positive growth rate – it falls constantly and in the long run approaches zero.

The results of the simulation therefore demonstrate more rigorously the intuitively clear effect of the impact of the constraints on investment into the replacement of the retiring elements of the capital stock: in the presence of such constraints, the 'big push' can lead to a temporary increase in the growth rates, but later, after a period equal to the service life of the fixed capital stock, they fall and converge to a low positive level or even to zero (if the investment into the replacement of retirement are low enough).

The fact that growth rates in the USSR started to fall in the 1960s, 30 years after the 'big push', and not 20 years after, as the simulation exercise suggests, should be explained probably by the impact of the World War II that resulted in the destruction of a large portion of fixed capital stock. For 10 years (1940–50) capital stock, in fact, did not increase (first it was destroyed during the war, then it increased to the pre-war level during reconstruction), so 10 years should be added to the life cycle of 20 years. Besides, the average service life of capital stock is a very statistically uncertain indicator. In the 1970s–80s for machinery and equipment the service life was about 25 years (implying a retirement ratio of 4 per cent) – see Table 2.2, but for the earlier period the statistics are absent. If the service life in the 1930s–50s was about 30 years, the peak of the growth rates in the 1950s could be explained even without the impact of the war.

2.5   Conclusions

The highest rates of growth of labor productivity in the Soviet Union were observed not in the 1930s (3 per cent annually), but in the 1950s (6 per cent). The TFP growth rates by decades increased from 0.6 per cent annually in the 1930s to 2.8 per cent in the 1950s and then fell monotonously becoming negative in the 1980s. The decade of 1950s was thus the 'golden period' of Soviet economic growth. The patterns of Soviet growth of the 1950s in terms of growth accounting were very similar to the Japanese growth of the 1950s–70s and Korean and Taiwanese growth in the 1960s–80s – fast increases in labor productivity counterweighted the decline in capital productivity, so that the TFP increased markedly. However, high Soviet economic growth lasted only for a decade, whereas in East Asia it continued for three to four decades, propelling Japan, South Korea and Taiwan into the ranks of developed countries.

This paper offers an explanation for the inverted U-shaped trajectory of labor productivity and TFP in CPEs. It is argued that CPEs under-invested into the replacement of the retiring elements of fixed capital stock and over-invested into the expansion of production capacities. The task of renovating physical capital contradicted the short-run goal of fulfilling planned targets, and, therefore, Soviet planners preferred to invest in new capacities instead of upgrading the old ones. Hence, after the massive investment of the 1930s in the USSR, the highest productivity was achieved after the period equal to the service life of capital stock (about 20 years) – before there emerged a need for massive investment into replacing retirement. Afterwards, the capital stock started to age rapidly, sharply reducing capital productivity and lowering labor productivity and TFP growth rates.

The simulation exercise allows to demonstrate clearly that under very reasonable assumptions (that the productivity of new investment is proportional to the share of investment into the reconstruction of existing production capacities in total investment, and that investment into the reconstruction of these capacities is lower than the actual retirement due to physical wear and tear), growth rates first increase and then fall to a very low level or even zero after the 'big push' – the initial increase in the share of investment in GDP.

Among many reasons for the decline of the growth rates in the USSR in the 1960s–80s, the discussed inability of the CPE to ensure adequate flow of investment into the replacement of retirement of fixed capital stock appears to be most crucial. What is more important, even if these retirement constraints were not the only reason of the decline in growth rates, they are sufficient to explain the inevitable gradual decline after 30 years of relatively successful development. To put it differently, the CPE is doomed to experience a growth slowdown after three decades of high growth following the 'big push'. In this respect, Chinese relatively short experience with the CPE (1949–79) looks superior to the Soviet excessively long experience (1929–91). This is another reason to believe that the transition to the market economy in the Soviet Union would have been more successful, if it had started in the 1960s.

Appendix

Table 2A 1 Market economy after the 'big push' (with investment to replace retirement equal to actual physical retirement of capital stock plus another 10% of gross investment), %

Years	$G(t)$	$G(t-m)$	$R(t) = G(t-m) + 0.1G(t)$	$K(t)$	$\Delta Y(t)$	$Y(t)$	$Ygr [R(t) = G(t-m) + 0.1G(t)]$, %	G/Y	R/K
1929	1	1	1	20	0	20	0	0,05	0,05
1930	2	1	1,2	20,8	4,8	20	24	0,1	0,057692
1931	2,48	1	1,248	22,032	6,199742	24,8	30,99871	0,1	0,056645
1932	3,099974	1	1,3099974	23,82198	7,564143	30,99974	30,500579	0,1	0,054991
1933	3,856389	1	1,3856389	26,29273	8,87765	38,56389	28,637819	0,1	0,0527
1934	4,744154	1	1,4744154	29,56246	10,16188	47,44154	26,35077	0,1	0,049875
1935	5,760342	1	1,5760342	33,74677	11,4483	57,60342	24,131384	0,1	0,046702
1936	6,905172	1	1,6905172	38,96143	12,76646	69,05172	22,162686	0,1	0,04339
1937	8,181818	1	1,8181818	45,32506	14,14141	81,81818	20,479453	0,1	0,040114
1938	9,595959	1	1,9595959	52,96143	15,59426	95,95959	19,059649	0,1	0,037
1939	11,15539	1	2,1155385	62,00127	17,14342	111,5539	17,865247	0,1	0,034121
1940	12,86973	1	2,2869727	72,58403	18,80574	128,6973	16,85799	0,1	0,031508
1941	14,7503	1	2,4750301	84,8593	20,59732	147,503	16,004472	0,1	0,029166
1942	16,81003	1	2,6810033	98,98833	22,53415	168,1003	15,277076	0,1	0,027084
1943	19,06345	1	2,9063447	115,1454	24,63254	190,6345	14,653475	0,1	0,025241
1944	21,5267	1	3,1526701	133,5195	26,90949	215,267	14,115753	0,1	0,023612
1945	24,21765	1	3,421765	154,3153	29,38296	242,1765	13,649543	0,1	0,022174
1946	27,15595	1	3,7155947	177,7557	32,07211	271,5595	13,243278	0,1	0,020903
1947	30,36316	1	4,0363157	204,0825	34,9975	303,6316	12,887599	0,1	0,019778
1948	33,86291	1	4,3862907	233,5592	38,18131	338,6291	12,574881	0,1	0,01878
1949	37,68104	1	4,7681038	266,4721	41,64755	376,8104	12,29887	0,1	0,017893
1950	41,84579	2	6,1845793	302,1333	52,70532	418,4579	13,987227	0,1	0,02047

Table 2A 1 (Continued)

Years	G(t)	G(t-m)	[R(t) = G(t-m) + 0.1G(t)]	K(t)	ΔY(t)	Y(t)	Ygr [R(t) = G(t-m) + 0.1G(t)], %	G/Y	R/K
1951	47,11632	2,48	7,1916325	342,058	60,93933	471,1632	14,562833	0,1	0,021025
1952	53,21026	3,099974	8,4209999	386,8473	70,88301	532,1026	15,044258	0,1	0,021768
1953	60,29856	3,856389	9,8862444	437,2596	82,65346	602,9856	15,53337	0,1	0,02261
1954	68,5639	4,744154	11,600544	494,2229	96,37811	685,639	15,983485	0,1	0,023472
1955	78,20172	5,760342	13,580513	558,8441	112,2212	782,0172	16,367389	0,1	0,024301
1956	89,42384	6,905172	15,847555	632,4204	130,3908	894,2384	16,673644	0,1	0,025059
1957	102,4629	8,181818	18,428109	716,4552	151,1379	1024,629	16,901294	0,1	0,025721
1958	117,5767	9,595959	21,353629	812,6783	174,755	1175,767	17,055441	0,1	0,026276
1959	135,0522	11,15539	24,660605	923,0699	201,5757	1350,522	17,144184	0,1	0,026716
1960	155,2098	12,86973	28,390704	1049,889	231,9752	1552,098	17,17671	0,1	0,027042
1961	178,4073	14,7503	32,59103	1195,705	266,2738	1784,073	17,162178	0,1	0,027257
1962	205,0447	16,81003	37,314499	1363,435	305,2392	2050,447	17,109122	0,1	0,027368
1963	235,5686	19,06345	42,620306	1556,384	349,0922	2355,686	17,025177	0,1	0,027384
1964	270,4778	21,5267	48,574481	1778,287	398,511	2704,778	16,916985	0,1	0,027315
1965	310,3289	24,21765	55,250541	2033,365	454,1381	3103,289	16,790217	0,1	0,027172
1966	355,7427	27,15595	62,730218	2326,378	516,6863	3557,427	16,649634	0,1	0,026965
1967	407,4113	30,36316	71,104292	2662,685	586,9467	4074,113	16,499191	0,1	0,026704
1968	466,106	33,86291	80,473508	3048,317	665,797	4661,06	16,342133	0,1	0,026399
1969	532,6857	37,68104	90,94961	3490,054	754,2107	5326,857	16,181098	0,1	0,02606
1970	608,1068	41,84579	102,65647	3995,504	853,267	6081,068	16,018207	0,1	0,025693
1971	693,4335	47,11632	116,45967	4572,478	969,0069	6934,335	15,934814	0,1	0,02547
1972	790,3342	53,21026	132,24368	5230,568	1101,158	7903,342	15,879797	0,1	0,025283
1973	900,45	60,29856	150,34356	5980,675	1252,415	9004,5	15,846646	0,1	0,025138

Table 2A 1 (Continued)

Years	G(t)	G(t−m)	[R(t) = G(t−m) + 0.1G(t)	K(t)	ΔY(t)	Y(t)	Ygr [R(t) = G(t−m) + 0.1G(t)], %	G/Y	R/K
1974	1025,691	68,5639	171,13305	6835,233	1425,801	10256,91	15,834316	0,1	0,025037
1975	1168,272	78,20172	195,02887	7808,476	1624,712	11682,72	15,840158	0,1	0,024977
1976	1330,743	89,42384	222,49811	8916,72	1852,968	13307,43	15,860762	0,1	0,024953
1977	1516,039	102,4629	254,06686	10178,69	2114,888	15160,39	15,892541	0,1	0,024961
1978	1727,528	117,5767	290,32953	11615,89	2415,366	17275,28	15,932076	0,1	0,024994
1979	1969,065	135,0522	331,95869	13253	2759,948	19690,65	15,976281	0,1	0,025048
1980	2245,06	155,2098	379,71573	15118,34	3154,929	22450,6	16,022475	0,1	0,025116
1981	2560,553	178,4073	434,46255	17244,43	3607,45	25605,53	16,068392	0,1	0,025194
1982	2921,298	205,0447	497,17442	19668,56	4125,605	29212,98	16,112167	0,1	0,025278
1983	3333,858	235,5686	568,9544	22433,46	4718,57	33338,58	16,152307	0,1	0,025362
1984	3805,715	270,4778	651,04931	25588,12	5396,733	38057,15	16,187652	0,1	0,025443
1985	4345,388	310,3289	744,86774	29188,65	6171,857	43453,88	16,217339	0,1	0,025519
1986	4962,574	355,7427	852,00013	33299,22	7057,244	49625,74	16,240767	0,1	0,025586
1987	5668,298	407,4113	974,24119	37993,28	8067,931	56682,98	16,257552	0,1	0,025642
1988	6475,092	466,106	1113,6152	43354,75	9220,907	64750,92	16,267504	0,1	0,025686
1989	7397,182	532,6857	1272,4039	49479,53	10535,35	73971,82	16,270584	0,1	0,025716
1990	8450,717	608,1068	1453,1785	56477,07	12032,91	84507,17	16,266885	0,1	0,02573

Table 2A 2 CPE after the 'big push' (with investment to replace retirement equal to 5% of gross investment), %

Years	G(t)	G(t−m)	R(t)= 0.05G(t)	K(t)	ΔY(t)	Y(t)	Ygr [R(t)= 0.05G(t)], %	G/Y	R/K
1929	1	1	1	20	0	20	0	0,05	0,05
1930	2	1	0,1	21	0,5	20	2,5	0,1	0,004762
1931	2,05	1	0,1025	22,05	0,525	20,5	2,625	0,1	0,004649
1932	2,1025	1	0,105125	23,1525	0,55125	21,025	2,6890244	0,1	0,004541
1933	2,157625	1	0,107813	24,31013	0,578813	21,57625	2,7529727	0,1	0,004438
1934	2,215506	1	0,110753	25,52563	0,607753	22,15506	2,816769	0,1	0,00434
1935	2,276282	1	0,113814	26,80191	0,638141	22,76282	2,8803384	0,1	0,004246
1936	2,340096	1	0,117005	28,14201	0,670048	23,40096	2,9436069	0,1	0,004158
1937	2,4071	1	0,120355	29,54911	0,70355	24,071	3,006502	0,1	0,004073
1938	2,477455	1	0,123873	31,02656	0,738728	24,77455	3,0689526	0,1	0,003992
1939	2,551328	1	0,127566	32,57789	0,775664	25,51328	3,1308902	0,1	0,003916
1940	2,628895	1	0,131445	34,20679	0,814447	26,28895	3,1922483	0,1	0,003843
1941	2,710339	1	0,135517	35,91713	0,85517	27,10339	3,2529629	0,1	0,003773
1942	2,795856	1	0,139793	37,71298	0,897928	27,95856	3,3129732	0,1	0,003707
1943	2,885649	1	0,144283	39,59863	0,942825	28,85649	3,3722211	0,1	0,003644
1944	2,979932	1	0,148997	41,57856	0,989966	29,79932	3,430652	0,1	0,003583
1945	3,078928	1	0,153946	43,65749	1,039464	30,78928	3,4882146	0,1	0,003526
1946	3,182875	1	0,159144	45,84037	1,091437	31,82875	3,5448612	0,1	0,003472
1947	3,292018	1	0,164602	48,13238	1,146009	32,92018	3,6005476	0,1	0,00342
1948	3,406619	1	0,170331	50,539	1,20331	34,06619	3,6552337	0,1	0,00337
1949	3,52695	1	0,176348	53,06595	1,263475	35,2695	3,7088827	0,1	0,003323
1950	3,653298	2	0,182665	54,71925	0,826649	36,53298	2,3438064	0,1	0,003338

Table 2A 2 (Continued)

Years	G(t)	G(t−m)	R(t)= 0.05G(t)	K(t)	ΔY(t)	Y(t)	Ygr [R(t)= 0.05G(t)], %	G/Y	R/K
1951	3,735963	2,05	0,1867981	56,40521	0,842981	37,35963	2,3074531	0,1	0,003312
1952	3,820261	2,1025	0,191013	58,12298	0,85888	38,20261	2,2989533	0,1	0,003286
1953	3,906149	2,157625	0,1953074	59,8715	0,874262	39,06149	2,2884875	0,1	0,003262
1954	3,993575	2,215506	0,1996787	61,64957	0,889034	39,93575	2,2759869	0,1	0,003239
1955	4,082478	2,276282	0,2041239	63,45576	0,903098	40,82478	2,2613784	0,1	0,003217
1956	4,172788	2,340096	0,2086394	65,28846	0,916346	41,72788	2,2445833	0,1	0,003196
1957	4,264423	2,4071	0,2132211	67,14578	0,928661	42,64423	2,2255172	0,1	0,003175
1958	4,357289	2,477455	0,2178644	69,02561	0,939917	43,57289	2,204089	0,1	0,003156
1959	4,451281	2,551328	0,222564	70,92557	0,949976	44,51281	2,1802002	0,1	0,003138
1960	4,546278	2,628895	0,2273139	72,84295	0,958692	45,46278	2,1537438	0,1	0,003121
1961	4,642147	2,710339	0,2321074	74,77476	0,965904	46,42147	2,1246039	0,1	0,003104
1962	4,738738	2,795856	0,2369369	76,71764	0,971441	47,38738	2,0926538	0,1	0,003088
1963	4,835882	2,885649	0,2417941	78,66787	0,975116	48,35882	2,0577555	0,1	0,003074
1964	4,933394	2,979932	0,2466697	80,62133	0,976731	49,33394	2,0197577	0,1	0,00306
1965	5,031067	3,078928	0,2515533	82,57347	0,976069	50,31067	1,9784946	0,1	0,003046
1966	5,128674	3,182875	0,2564337	84,51927	0,9729	51,28674	1,9337838	0,1	0,003034
1967	5,225964	3,292018	0,2612982	86,45322	0,966973	52,25964	1,8854244	0,1	0,003022
1968	5,322661	3,406619	0,266133	88,36926	0,958021	53,22661	1,8331945	0,1	0,003012
1969	5,418463	3,52695	0,2709231	90,26077	0,945756	54,18463	1,7768488	0,1	0,003002
1970	5,513039	3,653298	0,2756519	92,12051	0,92987	55,13039	1,7161147	0,1	0,002992
1971	5,606026	3,735963	0,2803013	93,99057	0,935031	56,06026	1,6960366	0,1	0,002982
1972	5,699529	3,820261	0,2849764	95,86984	0,939634	56,99529	1,6761144	0,1	0,002973

Table 2A 2 (Continued)

Years	G(t)	G(t−m)	[R(t) = G(t−m) + 0.1G(t)]	K(t)	ΔY(t)	Y(t)	Ygr [R(t) = G(t−m) + 0.1G(t)], %	G/Y	R/K
1973	5,793492	3,906149	0,2896746	97,75719	0,943672	57,93492	1,6557012	0,1	0,002963
1974	5,887859	3,993575	0,294393	99,65147	0,947142	58,87859	1,6348381	0,1	0,002954
1975	5,982573	4,082478	0,2991287	101,5516	0,950048	59,82573	1,6135704	0,1	0,002946
1976	6,077578	4,172788	0,3038789	103,4564	0,952395	60,77578	1,5919487	0,1	0,002937
1977	6,172818	4,264423	0,3086409	105,3647	0,954197	61,72818	1,5700291	0,1	0,002929
1978	6,268237	4,357289	0,3134119	107,2757	0,955474	62,68237	1,5478738	0,1	0,002922
1979	6,363785	4,451281	0,3181892	109,1882	0,956252	63,63785	1,5255519	0,1	0,002914
1980	6,45941	4,546278	0,3229705	111,1013	0,956566	64,5941	1,5031399	0,1	0,002907
1981	6,55067	4,642147	0,3277533	113,0143	0,95646	65,55067	1,4807229	0,1	0,0029
1982	6,650713	4,738738	0,3325356	114,9262	0,955987	66,50713	1,4583946	0,1	0,002893
1983	6,746311	4,835882	0,3373156	116,8367	0,955215	67,46311	1,4362592	0,1	0,002887
1984	6,841833	4,933394	0,3420916	118,7451	0,95422	68,41833	1,4144317	0,1	0,002881
1985	6,937255	5,031067	0,3468627	120,6513	0,953094	69,37255	1,3930391	0,1	0,002875
1986	7,032564	5,128674	0,3516282	122,5552	0,951945	70,32564	1,372222	0,1	0,002869
1987	7,127759	5,225964	0,3563879	124,457	0,950898	71,27759	1,352135	0,1	0,002864
1988	7,222849	5,322661	0,3611424	126,3572	0,950094	72,22849	1,332949	0,1	0,002858
1989	7,317858	5,418463	0,3658929	128,2566	0,949698	73,17858	1,3148518	0,1	0,002853
1990	7,412828	5,513039	0,3706414	130,1563	0,949895	74,12828	1,2980501	0,1	0,002848

Notes

1. This paper was initially presented at the American Economic Association conference in Boston in January 2006.
2. In China and some Southeast Asian countries high growth still coexists with high investment/GDP ratios. Chinese growth rates stayed at close to 10 per cent a year for nearly three decades (1978–2005); the share of investment in GDP during this period increased from 30 per cent in 1970–75 to nearly 50 per cent in 2005 (Wang *et al.*, 2001; China Statistical Yearbook).
3. For the purpose of illustration the year of the 'big push' is set as 1930. The assumption that the system was in the no growth equilibrium in 1910–30 is not that far from reality: even though Russian/Soviet output fell from 100 per cent in 1913 to about 30 per cent in 1920 and then recovered to about 130 per cent by 1930, fixed capital stock in this period most probably did not change much – investment were generally enough only to replace retirement, not to expand the capital stock.

References

Bergson, A. (1983) 'Technological progress', in A. Bergson and H. Levine (eds) *The Soviet Economy Towards the Year 2000* (London, UK: George Allen and Unwin).

Desai, P. (1976) 'The Production Function and Technical Change in Postwar Soviet Industry', *American Economic Review*, 60 (3), 372–81.

Domar, E. (1957) *Essays in the Theory of Economic Growth* (New York: Oxford University Press).

Easterly, W. and S. Fischer (1995) 'The Soviet Economic Decline', *The World Bank Economic Review*, 9 (3), 341–71.

Faltsman, V. (1985) 'Proizvodstvenniye Moschnosty (Production Facilities)', *Voprosy Economiki*, 3, 47.

Gomulka, S. (1977) 'Slowdown in Soviet Industrial Growth, 1947–1985 Reconsidered', *European Economic Review*, 10 (1), 37–49.

Guriev, S. and B. Ickes (2000) 'Microeconomic Aspects of Economic Growth in Eastern Europe and the Former Soviet Union, 1950–2000', *William Davidson Institute Working Paper*, No. 348.

Iacopetta, M. (2004) 'Dissemination of Technology in Market and Planned Economies', *Contributions to Macroeconomics*, 4 (1), 1–30.

Ickes, B. and R. Ryterman (1997) *Entry Without Exit: Economic Selection Under Socialism*, Department of Economics. The Pennsylvania State University, Mimeo.

IMF, WB, OECD, EBRD (1991) *A Study of the Soviet Economy*, 1,2,3, February.

Krugman, P. (1994) 'The Myth of Asia's Miracle', *Foreign Affairs*, November/December, 62–78.

Narkhoz, *Narodnoye Khosyaistvo SSSR (National Economy of the USSR)*, Moscow, Goskomstat, various years.

Ofer, G. (1987) 'Soviet economic Growth: 1928–85', *Journal of Economic Literature*, 25 (4), 1767–833.

Radelet, S. and J. D. Sachs (1997) 'Asia's Reemergence', *Foreign Affairs*, November/December, 44–59.

Schroeder, G. (1995) 'Reflections on Economic Sovietology', *Post-Soviet Affairs*, 11 (3), 197–234.

Shmelev, N. and V. Popov (1989) *The Turning Point: Revitalizing the Soviet Economy* (New York: Doubleday).

Wang, Y. and Y. Yudong (2001) *Sources of China's Economic Growth, 1952–99* (The World Bank, World Bank Institute, Economic Policy and Poverty Reduction Division).

Weitzman, M. (1970) 'Soviet Postwar Economic Growth and Capital-Labor Substitution', *American Economic Review*, 60 (5), 676–92.

Young, A. (1994) 'Lessons from the East Asian NICs: A Contrarian View', *European Economic Review*, 38 (4), 964–73.

Valtukh, K. and B. Lavrovskyi (1986) 'Proizvodstvennyi Apparat Strany: Ispol'zovaniye i Rekonstruktsiya (Production Facilities of a Country: Utilization and Reconstruction)', *EKO*, N2, 17–32.

3
Are Transition Economies Normal Developing Countries? The Burden of the Socialist Past

Michael Keren and Gur Ofer

3.1 Introduction: What is normalcy

The view that the socialist past of the transition economies (TEs) is irrelevant and that these economies should now be considered as just another group of developing, low or middle income countries, has been gaining many adherents. This overlooks, so we believe, the fact that transition is path dependent and that the process of transition cannot be understood without regard to the socialist heritage. This heritage is relevant in many aspects of the transition process, but it is probably most important in the transformation of the institutional infrastructure from that of the old regime to institutions of a market economy and a democratic society. This paper focuses on the transition of this institutional infrastructure. In it we first summarize, on the basis of previous literature, the stylized characteristics of the two sets of institutions, the dissonance between them and the problems involved in moving from one to the other. This discussion in based to a large extent on Ofer (2001, 2003, 2004) and on references therein. We then estimate the institutional diversion of different groups of TEs from 'normal' patterns at comparable levels of development (à la Kuznets). The empirical analysis is based mostly but not exclusively on the database of the Governance and Anti-Corruption project of the World Bank Institute (WBI; Kaufmann *et al.*, 2005). In the analysis that follows we relate the gaps to the specific socialist institutional heritage and underline the differences in the nature of the problems and solutions of building new institutions that stem from this heritage.

The claim that Russia is a normal country (Shleifer and Treisman, 2003; Shleifer, 2005) is a case in point. Is Russia really 'normal'? In order to determine this we employ a Kuznets-type normality: that is, we follow Simon Kuznets' method and look for regularities in the relations between the development level of countries and various attributes of state and institutional base.

Kuznets conducted his analysis within the framework of a more or less uniform, even if evolving institutional framework. He could therefore assume that there was a normal path of development taken by all non-socialist countries, excluding the latter on the basis of differences in their institutional structure (see below). With the collapse of socialism and the long-drawn-out process of transition the focus shifted to the study of the process of change in institutions across systems and with it also to a deeper study of the dynamics of institutional change as a determinant and part of economic development, both within and across systems. These interrelations are the topic of this paper, and it is the change in institutions that we are trying to chart. Luckily transition has led to a search for databases that may describe, if not define, economic, social and political institutions. These databases make our task feasible.

In his classical study on *Modern Economic Growth* (1966) Kuznets excluded from the analysis all countries whose institutional framework differed, that is, the then socialist countries, stating that 'differences in institutional and political structure ... were so large that [these countries] had to be excluded from the comparative analysis aimed at the common characteristics of modern economic growth' (p. 508). A few sentences lower down Kuznets continues:

> ... if within three to five decades the Communist countries progressed to the point where their basic capital framework is completed ... At that stage – of a typical welfare state with a broad democratic frame-work – it might become necessary to include [these states] in our sample of developed countries ... differing in the character of their transition phases but converging toward the others as they mature. (p. 508)

We follow him by tracing first the path of institutional development of the non-socialist countries – which we then term the relevant Kuznets curve – and only then add the various sets of transition countries. In this manner we include the TEs in the analysis of modern economic growth, and also follow the transition and evolution of their institutions as they join the rest of the world, using Kuznets' methods.

Let us add here a word of caution or clarification: the title of our paper obviously owes to Shleifer and Treisman (2003) and Shleifer (2005), and it is important to clarify the different aims of ours with those of the cited contributions. Shleifer and Treisman are concerned with Russia alone, and often use the comparison of its performance with that of other TEs as evidence for its normalcy. We, on the other hand, are interested in the ex-socialist countries *in toto* and in their institutional transition. We believe that there are institutional elements in all these countries that distinguish them from the 'normal' countries. This will become clearer when we get to the discussion of Russia's performance, to which Section 3.10 is devoted.

The paper has the following structure. Section 3.2 outlines the differences between the institutions of socialism and those of market economies, that is, charts the task of institutional transition. Section 3.3. discusses the variables that should represent the level of development, and Section 3.4 – the regression model used to map the Kuznets curve. The findings are presented in the following three sections: Section 3.5 charts the basic Kuznets curve, the relation between the level of development and the effectiveness of government, Section 3.6 does the same for corruption and Section 3.7 for all other indicators. How growth is affected by governance is the subject of Section 3.8. The discussion of the Great Divide between the Former Soviet Union (FSU) and Eastern Europe, which concludes the main empirical part, is in Section 3.9 while the special case of Russia is analyzed in Section 3.10. Section 3.11 concludes.

3.2   The institutions of socialism and their transition

The institutions that define the state, the economy and society stand at the center of our paper. The significant difference that transition has taken in the Former Soviet Union (FSU)[1] and some of the countries of Eastern Europe, the new EU accession countries (NEU[2]) below can be ascribed to these differences, so we believe. There have been several explanations of the differences of the paths of transition, and most explanations put the onus on historical factors. These refer either to recent history, that is, to the longer time that FSU countries have spent under socialist rule, and others to farther history, that is, to the fact that whereas considerable parts of the East European countries were under Hapsburg rule, the FSU was under the suzerainty of the Czars. And the differences may also be rooted in the different manner in which transition was initiated. These matters are discussed in depth later, on the basis of the empirical findings.

The fundamental nature of a socialist state is very different from that of a capitalist market state. This is because the essence of socialism is the prohibition of private ownership of capital, and this molds the institutions of socialism, both the political and the economic ones. A socialist economy has never been run except by a centralized bureaucracy, and it is arguable that it cannot be run as a decentralized market, that is, that the socialist market is not feasible (Keren, 1993). Instead, socialism turns the whole productive sphere into one huge bureaucratic monofirm, with enormous authority and discretion to the bureaucrats who run it, open to abuse. The well-known dysfunctions of the Soviet-type economy are rooted in bureaucratic allocation and the incentives that it entails.

The implications for the political institutions are no less severe. The whole apparatus of the party and the state that it owns is geared toward the elimination of any buds of non-state entrepreneurship. The bureaucracies of both the party and the internal intelligence had to oversee the economic apparatus, with hardly any constraints on their decisions. Corruption was all but unavoidable in a huge bureaucracy with extensive authority and almost unlimited discretion.

The well-known characteristics of the socialist economies in Eastern Europe have grown out of the economic and political institutions:

- Structure: absence of small and medium-sized firms.
- Over-industrialization, too high a share of heavy industry, low share of services.
- Low quality and high cost of output.
- Insufficient infrastructure, given the high degree of industrialization.
- A high level of corruption.

These characteristics differed markedly from those of developing economies. Markets in the latter were integral parts of the economy. They also suffered from corruption, but this tended to decline with the advance of development. Protection of property, private as well as public, also progressed in tandem with development. Thus socialist economies possessed many characteristics of advanced developed countries, mixed in with traits of countries at early stages of development. The path of transition was conditioned, almost warped, by these characteristics. In particular, it was affected by the political structure, whose evolution differed: in some countries of Eastern Europe new national movements replaced the top of the state apparatus and tried to speed up transition, while in others the old hierarchies kept their position, albeit in a new guise. As for the FSU, here the old state was dissolved, replaced by a score of new, mostly weak, states and statelets. Where the state was weakened, the previous limits on corruption all but disappeared. The corrupt state in effect put brakes on economic transition. As a result the path of transition could not converge toward that of developing countries. It retains its own character and its own obstacles to growth and convergence toward the rich west.

There is little need to discuss the contradiction, indeed orthogonality between the type of economic and political institutions that serve central planning and authoritarian regimes and those that support market economies and democratic states. While the former are focused on making people follow and obey government orders, the latter are composed mostly of a set of laws and regulations that guide private actions and initiatives of people and firms and establish boundaries to these actions and tools to enforce the laws and to negotiate conflicts. Under authoritarian communism the state is above the law and the responsibility of courts is to uphold the state, whereas under a free market system law is supreme. The differences in the definition and protection of private property under the two systems are probably among the most extreme and crucial.

The shift from one set of institutions to the other under such conditions must be long and arduous, and face many unexpected hurdles on the way. There are a number of key difficulties here. First, legislation and the creation of new institutions, mostly imported from the outside, resulting in a multitude of misconceptions and misunderstanding of concepts. Second, the new and foreign formal institutions clash with the established culture and the perceptions of the rules of the game and the informal institutions by the population, officialdom included. It takes a long time to make the informal consistent with the formal. Third, under communism, especially during its latest phase, the prevailing norm among firms and people alike was to disobey orders and circumvent the system. The essence of the market system is the close conformity between informal and formal institutions. Due to all these and other difficulties the new governments tend to be weak and inefficient in implementing the desired policies.

The six indexes compiled by the World Bank Institute (WBI; Kaufmann *et al.*, 2005) cover the institutional requirements of modern democracies with market systems. They illustrate the inherited weaknesses of the transition process in TEs. The quality of the democratic institutions – represented in the database by 'Voice and accountability' is weak and inefficient, not only for the reasons mentioned above but also because many, both inside government institutions and the public, interpret democracy as anarchy. 'Political Stability', another index, can only be achieved, even if we ignore internal ethnic strife, if the laws governing the exercise, and even more so, the transition of power are well understood, accepted and enforced. This was not the case under communism. The key indicator, we believe, is 'government effectiveness', because on it depends the ability to lead reforms in all walks of life. It not only depends on the acceptance of the legitimacy of the rulers by the public, on the skills which the leaders of the government chart and carry out their policies, but also on the training of the bureaucracy with the new laws, the methods of operation and the internalization of the new behavioral culture. 'Regulatory quality' is at the heart of institutional transition: this is the ability to direct and oversee economic activity through arms-length regulation and the leverage of incentives, rather than by arm twisting through direct orders. The 'rule of law' is no less complex: it involves having proper laws, proper enforcement, and the understanding and readiness to observe the law by the government, the officialdom, the business community and the public. Corruption is the outcome of failures to build new efficient institutions in all the above spheres to adhere to the law and enforce it. In this way corruption is the mirror image of the weakness of all the above. 'Control of corruption' is a summary index of the level of success in limiting corruption.

The above may create the impression or the expectation that one should expect a more or less uniform institutional transition for TEs, and with relatively limited diversity. As is well known this is not the case. The 'great divide' between the much better performance of Eastern and Central European TEs as compared with the FSU states is notorious. This means that other factors have to be taken into account: the duration of the communist phase, the pre-communist history of the different TEs, the manner in which transition took off in different countries, and current supporting and disrupting factors. We come back to the diversity and the other factors in the empirical part of the paper.

3.3   Kuznets normalcy: the development variables

There is a close relation between the development of an economy and its political and economic institutions. The set of organizations that is the modern state cannot grow up in an economy that lacks human capital and the economic resources that only economic development can supply; but the latter is hampered by the lack of protection of property and the freedom of entry. In other words, the efficacy of the state and the level of economic development are closely related. This relation we label the Institutional Kuznets Curve. We have calculated six governance dimensions of the Kuznets curve, but we discuss in detail only those dimensions which we believe are the most important, namely the 'effectiveness of government' and the 'control of corruption'.

There are many factors besides the level of development that determine the quality of the institutions of governance. These factors, which differ for each polity, lead countries to diverge from the Kuznets curve. We call all countries, or groups of countries, the quality of whose institutions does not diverge too far from the Kuznets curve, normal countries. It is very likely that different groups of countries, for example, those of Latin America, may exhibit common characteristics and diverge as a group. We, however, are concerned with merely one grouping, that is, with countries that have been through a socialist era. We show below that some of those countries, namely the FSU, diverge significantly from most dimensions of the curve.[3]

As we said in Section 3.2, we focus on two sets of ex-socialist countries, those that used to make up the Soviet Union, and the new accession countries of the EU (NEU). The Baltic countries belong to both these sets, but various statistical tests showed that their institutions behaved very similarly to those of the other accession countries and very differently from those of the other members of the FSU set. We discuss the possible reasons in Section 3.9. We therefore include them among the NEU. As for the non-European FSUs, the countries of the Caucasus and central Asia, they were usually very similar to the other FSU countries, that is, their institutions were of poorer quality than those of non-socialist countries of a similar development level, often poorer than those of other FSU countries. We saw no reason to separate them out of the FSU.

The institutional Kuznets curve, like the original relations charted by Kuznets, is based on the experience of non-socialist economies. It is a relation between the level of economic development and the governance indicators. While the choice of an indicator for income for the normal Kuznets curve is straightforward – the per-capita GDP, based on Purchasing Power Parity (PPP) is mostly used – the appropriate comparators for TEs is more problematic and requires further consideration. The levels of per-capita GDP of most TEs in 1996 and even in 2004 are lower than those achieved during the last years of the socialist system. So while the latter may be considered somewhat exaggerated, it may well be that the estimated levels during the transition period do not reflect a true 'potential' and that the existing levels are underestimates. These transition levels can also be considered as underestimates of the potential levels due to the many inefficiencies inherited from the old regime. In other words, the existing levels of input can produce higher output when these inefficiencies are removed. A fuller discussion of the contending parameters and the biases they lead to can be found in the Appendix. In what follows we use the 2003 per-capita GDP as the indicator of development, and compare the results a couple of times with estimates based on 2003 Human Development Index (HDI). Our choice of the 2003 level of income biases our results in favor of the TEs because it predicts a lower quality of governance for them.

The analysis covers the period 1996–2004, which is very short for 'normal' countries but may be of greater moment for the TEs. Yet, even for the latter, time is the crucial dimension of change rather than changes in income levels.[4] Another element that may affect institutional development is the endowment with human capital. The relatively greater endowment of TEs with human capital should improve their institutions, in addition to making them more productive, both directly and indirectly, by improving the quality of governance. And if it does not – this may be a justified indicator of inefficiency.

There is one aspect inherited from the 'old regime' that demands a higher level of institutional infrastructure. This is the 'modern' and 'advanced' structure of the economies of TEs. All of them, in particular the more advanced among them, are more industrialized and urbanized, more 'modernized' in the sense that a larger part of the economy is made up of large firms with demand for modern finance, business and government services. This is quite unlike the multitude of small firms, mostly family-owned and managed and more self-supporting in most of the countries which, like the TEs, do not belong to the 'higher income' group. This point can be illustrated by comparing the list of countries classified by per capita GDP that belong to the same 'Lower Middle Income' group as Russia and other FSU – the Philippines, Morocco, Bolivia, Jamaica and the like; or to Malaysia, South Korea, Lebanon, Mexico, and Brazil that belong to the 'Higher Middle Income' together with most NEU countries. Clearly these countries have much smaller requirements for modern market institutions than the TEs classified along with them. This problem arises from the asymmetry between the modern structure of the production sector in TEs, and the lack of market institutions, both characteristics inherited from the old regime. This is why the TEs need better institutions and faster than the comparators at a similar level of income or development.

3.4 Institutions and Kuznets normalcy: the empirical framework

In the remainder of this paper we use Kuznets' concepts as interpreted by us in the introduction, to compute the normal pattern of modern economic growth and the place of the TEs in it. True to Kuznets, we first compute the model, excluding all ex-socialist countries, and then examine where the TEs are to be found with regard to this basic structure of 'normality'. We trace the process of institutional building among the TEs by checking their standing in 2004 against 1996 (unfortunately the first observation extant). The dependent governance variables for the analysis are five of the six institutional indexes compiled by WBI: 'voice and accountability', 'government effectiveness', 'regulatory quality', 'rule of law' and 'control of corruption'.[5] An additional dependent institutional variable is the 'corruption perception index' of Transparency International (2006).[6]

The equations estimated are of the following form:[7]

$$y_t = \text{const.} + b_y \cdot y\_PPP\_2003 + b_y{}^\wedge 2 \cdot Sq\_y\_PPP + b_z \cdot z_t \qquad (3.1)$$

where $t = 1996, 2004, y_t$ is one of the WBI governance indicators or CPI, and z_t are other explanatory variables that may affect y_t.

As we said in the introduction, the institutional Kuznets curve charts the relation between the level of economic development and the governance indicators. Of the three available candidate indicators of the development level, we have chosen the 2003 PPP per capita income level.

The remaining right-hand side variables, those labeled z_t in Equation (3.1), include:

- The number of R&D researchers per million people, 1990–2003 (source: HDI). This variable represents educated human capital. As mentioned above, this variable also pushes the level of development of most TEs upward in the comparison.
- 'Government effectiveness', 1996, was used in the regressions of all other 2004 governance indicators, because we assume that this is a key variable that determines the polity's ability to reform and transform the economy and the state.
- FSU – a dummy variable that ascribes the value of 1 to members of FSU and 0 to all others.[8]
- NEU – a dummy variable, equals 1 for new EU members, 0 for the remainder.[9]

3.5   The 'government effectiveness' Kuznets curve

The results for the key indicator of 'government effectiveness' for 1996 and 2004 are reported in Tables 3.1 and 3.2.

Column (1) of the table is the 'government effectiveness' Kuznets curve for 1996. This curve is drawn in Figure 3.1. Although all ex-communist countries were excluded from the regression of the Kuznets curve itself, several groups of these countries were added to the figure, using the estimated parameters of Column (1). The thick red line is the Kuznets curve, and the light blue and purple lines – the boundaries of the 95 per cent confidence limits. The black dots represent the FSU countries, most of which lie – Georgia, Armenia and Kyrgyzstan are the exceptions – below the curve, close or even below the light blue lower confidence boundary. The same is true for the new EU countries, but these lie very close to the curve. This is an indication of the non-normality of the ex-communist countries as a whole and the FSUs in particular. In Columns (2) and (3) the ex-communist countries have been added to the regression, and the dummies, FSU and NEU, indicate the degree by which they differ from the 'normal' countries: the parameters of the

Table 3.1   Government effectiveness – 1996

Regression	(1)	(2)	(3)
Dependent variable: Gov_Effectiveness_1996			
Constant	3.23***	3.34***	3.44***
	21.98	23.42	15.53
y_PPP_2003/1000	0.27***	0.24***	0.23***
	9.29	8.59	6.38
Sq_y_PPP	$-2.93E-09$**	$-2.10E-09$*	$-2.24E-09$*
	-3.31	-2.45	-2.24
FSU		-0.88**	-0.85**
		-3.35	-2.65
NEU		-0.38	-0.48
		-1.15	-1.47
R&D_Researchers_per_m_1990–2003			9.02E–05
			0.96
R Square	0.84	0.82	0.86
Durbin-Watson	2.45	2.09	1.84
N	112	140	86

t-values below estimates; *significant at 0.05; **significant at 0.01; ***significant at 0.001.

Table 3.2 Government effectiveness – 2004

Regression	(1)	(2)	(3)	(4)
Dependent variable: Gov_Effectiveness_2004				
Constant	3.01***	3.06***	3.32***	1.04***
	21.44	23.73	16.92	3.97
Gov_Effectiveness_1996				0.66***
				9.96
Y_PPP_2003/1000	0.30***	0.29***	0.24***	0.09**
	10.86	11.37	7.41	3.23
Sq_y_PPP	$-3.90E-09$***	-3.55***	$-3.28E-09$***	$-1.80E-09$**
	-4.66	-4.62	-3.71	-2.95
FSU		-0.74**	-1.03***	-0.47*
		-3.10	-3.63	-2.36
NEU		0.10	-0.00	0.31
		0.33	-0.02	1.59
R&D_Researchers_per_m_1990–2003/1000			0.26**	0.20***
			3.19	3.67
R Square	0.85	0.85	0.88	0.95
Durbin-Watson	2.12	2.08	1.73	1.74
N	113	141	86	86

t-values below estimators; *significant at 0.05; **significant at 0.01; ***significant at 0.001.

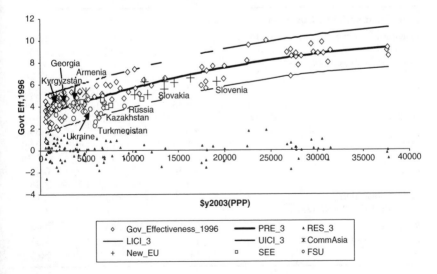

Figure 3.1 The 'government effectiveness' Kuznets curve, 1996

two dummies are negative, though the NEU dummy is much smaller, and only the FSU dummy is significant. Equation (3.3) adds the human capital variable, which is of no significance here.

Table 3.2 presents the same findings for 2004. There is little difference between the parameters of the first three columns of Table 3.1 and Table 3.2. An exception is the human capital variable, R&D researchers per million inhabitants, which is highly significant: human capital that is higher than the average raises the Kuznets curve. The significantly negative FSU dummy is unaffected, which is surprising, but NEU becomes more negative, that is, the higher level of human capital should have led to a higher 'government effectiveness'. Column (4), which includes the 1996 value of 'government effectiveness' in the set of explanatory variables, z_{2004}, casts a new perspective. Let $\Delta y \equiv y_{2004} - y_{1996}$, the change in the given governance indicator between 1996 and 2004. Then the indicator of convergence or divergence along the Kuznets curve is $1 - b_y$: if b_y is smaller (greater) than 1, we have an indicator of convergence (divergence). The parameter of the 1996 value of the right-hand variable, b_y, is 0.66. Thus by this finding the Kuznets curve has a tendency toward convergence: low 'government effectiveness' countries in 1996 tend to have a larger improvement than

Table 3.3   Government effectiveness – 2004 and HDI – 2003

Regression	(1)	(2)	(3)	(4)
Dependent variable: Gov_Effectiveness_2004				
Constant	8.33***	8.29***	9.61***	1.59
	7.61	7.97	4.93	1.15
Gov_Effectiveness_1996				0.70***
				11.49
HDI_2003	−21.55***	−21.37***	−23.02***	−2.41
	−6.15	−6.43	−3.90	−0.60
HDI03_sq	22.69***	22.53***	21.73***	2.66
	8.62	9.03	4.93	0.84
FSU		−1.33***	−1.36***	−0.50*
		−4.63	−4.19	−2.36
NEU		−0.16	−0.03	0.46*
		−0.47	−0.11	2.38
R&D_Researchers_ per_m_1990–2003/1000			0.33***	0.19**
			3.61	3.37
R Square	0.78	0.79	0.84	0.94
Durbin-Watson	2.03	1.99	2.24	1.55
N	121	141	86	86

t-values below estimators; *significant at 0.05; **significant at 0.01; ***significant at 0.001.

high performers. The human capital variable continues to be significant, that is, the existence of a well-educated population improves the effectiveness of government. Both dummies, FSU and NEU, become more positive: some of the poor governance is already explained by the 1996 value of 'government effectiveness' and less is left for the dummies to explain in 2004.

We have also run this regression with HDI-2003 serving as the development level indicator (see Table 3.3). The difference between this table and Table 3.2 is small, but, unsurprisingly, the negative parameter of the FSU dummy is 50 per cent higher in Table 3.3: the relative position of the ex-socialist countries is higher in terms of HDI, which take into account the high investment in human capital, as predicted by the discussion in Section 3.6 and the Appendix. In spite of the inclusion of human capital in the very definition of the development level, R&D researchers raise the Kuznets curve yet further, and are a significant aid in improving the effectiveness of government and its change. The effects on the two dummies are similar to those of Table 3.2, and their discussion above carries over.

3.6 Corruption as a mirror image of governance

The only other governance indicator whose Kuznets curve we present in full in this paper is the 'control of corruption'. As mentioned above the extent of corruption in a country is to a large extent a reflection of weakness in all other governance indicators put together. It may also be interpreted as a wide gap or conflict between the newly established formal institutions and the norms of behavior, the informal institutions á la Douglas North, of the officialdom and public alike.

The two tables that report the 'control of corruption' for 1996 and 2004, Table 3.4 and Table 3.5, and the Transparency International 'Corruption Perception Index' (CPI) in Table 3.6, carry a very similar message: corruption in FSU countries is significantly higher than their level of development would signify, and the situation in 2004 with this respect is worse than back in 1996. Again, while the NEU dummy is not (negatively) significant in either 1996 or 2004 (Tables 3.4 and 3.5), it becomes negative and (moderately) significant when the R&D variable is added in the CPI equation. The R&D variable acts as an income enhancing factor for both NEU and FSU states, thus widening the negative gap of corruption also for the FSU group, most significantly in 2004 (Table 3.5) and 2005 (Table 3.6). Finally, when controlling for earlier (1996) levels of 'control of corruption' and of 'government effectiveness' the FSU coefficient is still negative (though naturally smaller), while the impact on NEU is very small; another manifestation of the great divide.

Table 3.4 Control of corruption – 1996

Regression	(1)	(2)	(3)
Dependent variable: Control_Corruption_1996			
Constant	3.32***	3.36***	3.44***
	17.75	19.20	13.14
Y_PPP_2003/1000	0.23***	0.21***	0.20***
	6.30	6.15	4.57
Sq_y_PPP/109	−1.81#	−1.16	−1.51
	−1.69	−1.16	−1.29
FSU		−1.01**	−1.056**
		−3.31	−2.82
NEU		−0.36	−0.51
		−0.93	−1.35
R&D_Researchers_per_m_1990–2003/1000			0.15
			1.40
R Square	0.77	0.77	0.81
Durbin-Watson	2.29	2.19	1.87
N	103.00	131	85

t-values below estimators; #significant at 0.10; *significant at 0.05; **significant at 0.01; ***significant at 0.001.

Table 3.5 Control of corruption – 2004 and 'government effectiveness'

Regression	(1)	(2)	(3)	(4)	(5)
Dependent variable: Control_Corruption_2004					
Constant	3.03***	3.05***	3.36***	1.12***	0.67*
	21.22	23.26	15.22	4.17	2.33
Control_Corruption_1996				0.64***	0.45***
				9.85	5.50
y_PPP_2003/1000	0.27***	0.26***	0.20***	0.08**	0.04
	9.64	9.95	5.43	2.87	1.32
Sq_y_PPP	−2.70E−09**	−2.23**	−1.96E−09#	−1.13E−09#	−6.4E−10
	−3.16	−2.85	−1.97	−1.67	−0.97
FSU		−0.98***	−1.46***	−0.75**	−0.69**
		−4.07	−4.56	−3.35	−3.23
NEU		−0.19	−0.33	0.002	0.06
		−0.61	−1.00	0.008	0.29
R&D_Researchers_per_m_1990–2003/1000			0.33***	0.24***	0.23***
			3.566158	3.730694	3.95148
Gov_Effectiveness_1996					0.32**
					3.342986
R Square	0.86	0.858367	0.870527	0.94348	0.950643
Durbin-Watson	2.11	1.897134	1.684041	2.129057	2.133026
N	113.00	141	86	85	85

t-values below estimators; #significant at 0.10; *significant at 0.05; **significant at 0.01; ***significant at 0.001.

Table 3.6 Corruption perception index – 2005

Regression	(1)	(2)	(3)	(4)
Dependent Variable: CPI_2005				
Constant	2.12***	2.17***	2.29***	−0.57
	12.04	13.39	8.63	−1.49
y_PPP_2003/1000	0.25***	0.23***	0.20***	0.00
	7.26	7.22	4.54	0.12
Sq_y_PPP/1000	−1.65E−06	−9.95E−07	−1.88E−06	0.00
	−1.57	−1.03	−1.57	−0.01
FSU		−0.68*	−1.29**	−0.58#
		−2.25	−3.35	−1.99
NEU		−0.31	−0.66#	−0.26
		−0.82	−1.68	−0.90
R&D_Researchers_			0.45***	0.37***
per_m_1990–2003/1000			4.00	4.57
Gov_Effectiveness_1996				0.83***
				8.59
R Square	0.81	0.81	0.85	0.92
Durbin-Watson	2.01	1.94	1.78	1.98
N	116.00	144	86	86

t-values below estimators; #significant at 0.10; *significant at 0.05; **significant at 0.01; ***significant at 0.001.

3.7 Findings: the other governance indicators

The first finding is that all five institutional quality indicators improve with income per capita, that is, with economic development, when the TEs are excluded. This is also true when HDI replaces GDP per capita. This, and the fact that these single explanatory variable regressions have a high explanatory value, with R^2 usually over 0.80 and never below 0.65, is an indication that our Kuznets curves do indeed serve as efficient descriptions of the institutional dimensions of the development process. We have reproduced above only Table 3.1. and Table 3.2, the tables for 'government effectiveness' – in which Column (1) displays the Kuznets curve – and the chart of Figure 3.1, but the corresponding tables for all other indicators carry a very similar message. By construction, upheld by the estimates, institutional improvement is increasing at a declining rate as income rises and the fitted curve in Figure 3.1 (as well as all the others where income per-capita is the measure of development) is convex.

A brief explanation of the provenance of the parameters reported in Table 3.7 below is in place. They come from regressions of Equations (3.1), run for all governance indicators, of which only two are reported in full (in

Table 3.7　The estimates of the FSU and new EU dummy variables

Governance index	FSU dummy			New EU dummy		
	1996	2004	Change	1996	2004	Change
Voice&Acc	−1.00**	−1.36***	−0.36	0.74	1.32**	0.58
Gov_Effectiveness	−0.88**	−0.74**	0.14	−0.38	0.10	0.48
Regul_Qual	−1.49***	−1.12***	0.37	−0.02	0.99*	1.01
Rule_of_Law	−0.99**	−0.97***	0.02	−0.55	0.25	0.81
Control_Corruption	−1.01**	−0.98***	0.02	−0.36	−0.19	0.17

Source: Column (2) in Regression Tables (for example, Table 3.1 and Table 3.2); see text for explanation. Legend: t-values below estimators; *significant at 0.05; **significant at 0.01; ***significant at 0.001.

Tables 3.1, 3.2, 3.3 and 3.4) in this paper.[10] They report the levels (and the statistical significance) of the FSU and NEU dummies for all six institutional variables and for both 1996 and 2004.

As can be seen from the table, all FSU dummies for both years are negative and quite large, and all are significant at 1 per cent or better. The changes over the period are very modest, but all show deterioration, albeit slight. But the coefficients for NEU, while mostly negative in 1996, are smaller than those for FSU, and none is significant. Moreover all but one, 'control of corruption', have become positive by 2004, and two, 'regulatory control' and 'voice and accountability', have become significantly positive. This is in a nutshell our portrait of the 'great divide' between these two groups of countries.

Before reviewing the conventional explanations for the great divide in Section 3.9, let us point out that the FSU and the NEU dummies decline, that is, become more negative or less positive when HDI replaces GDP per capita as the development indicator. The same result is obtained when the level of income in 2003 is replaced by the highest level of income since 1975. This is so since most TEs, in particular FSU countries, have not reached by 2004 their highest past income level.

3.8　'Government effectiveness' and growth

Finally, does the quality of state governance affect growth, or, in particular, does 'government effectiveness' affect growth? The result of two sets of regressions is displayed in Table 3.8. The regressions of the first two columns were run on the sample of non-communist countries, the second two — on the full sample, including 23 socialist states and ex-socialist TEs. In both groups of equations it is 'government effectiveness' that provides the strongest effect on growth: the alternative explanatory variable, per capita

Table 3.8 Growth and 'government effectiveness'

	(1)	(2)	(3)	(4)
	Non-socialist sample		Full sample	
Dependent variable: Gy_1990–2003				
Constant	0.46	−1.61*	0.47	−1.45[#]
	1.24	−2.13	1.29	−1.94
y_PPP_2003/1000	0.19**	−0.07	0.20**	−0.03
	2.65	−0.87	2.78	−0.39
Sq_y2003_PPP/1000	−4.14E−09[#]	−2.53E−10	−4.30E−09*	−1.16E−09
	−1.86	−0.13	−1.98	−0.58
FSU			−3.16***	−2.66***
			−4.51	−4.25
NEU			0.14	0.64
			0.15	0.84
Gov_Effectiveness_1996		0.73***		0.67***
		3.56		3.37
R Square	0.09	0.17	0.21	0.31
Durbin-Watson	1.84	1.76	1.92	1.77
N	136	114	159	137

t-values below estimators; [#]significant at 0.10; *significant at 0.05; **significant at 0.01; ***significant at 0.001.

income, which itself is closely related to 'government effectiveness', loses all significance once the latter variable is added to the regression. An additional point of government effectiveness adds between 2/3 and 3/4 per cent of growth per annum. Once the socialist and ex-socialist countries are added, we get the highly significant FSU dummy, which reduces annual growth rates over the period of 1990–2003 by over 2.5 to 3 per cent, an enormous degree. The NEU dummy is not significant.

Thus the burden of the socialist past in those countries that have not managed to reform their governance explains the slow growth we have witnessed in the FSU. We should remember that these data do not include the recent few years of extremely high oil prices, which have accelerated the growth of Russia and a couple of other FSU countries. But then this growth does not owe to reforms and economic and political transformation and is not likely to be sustainable.

3.9 FSU vs. NEU: the great divide and 'normalcy'

The data presented in the previous sections demonstrates the large gap in institutional development between the group of NEU and those of the FSU states. While the first group seems to have reached near normality by 2004, the FSU states as a group and Russia in particular have not. The quality and performance of their evolving institutions are not up to the level of other countries of the same level of development measured by income, albeit that most of the latter are far behind in terms of creating a modern economy. This gap, called in the literature 'the great divide' (see for example, Berglöf and Bolton, 2002) has been explained by a number of factors. First, while most NEU states could turn to their relatively recent past and even to the more distant past for helpful experience and traditions, most FSU states had to start almost from scratch. While most NEUs belonged to relatively well-governed empires in Europe since the nineteenth century, Russia could only go back to its less modernized Czarist regime. Likewise, NEUs had enjoyed periods of some democracy and buds of market economy and its institutions for over a generation before the advent of socialism, for Russia and the FSU such a period, if it did at all exist, was much shorter and farther away in the past.

Turning to the socialist period, this was not only shorter for all NEU states but in a number of cases also 'softer'. Poland had a sizable private agriculture, Hungary had embarked on reforms much earlier, Slovenia was a part of Yugoslavia that toyed with market socialism, and some of the NEUs had a fairly developed semiprivate service sector and, as a rule, were more open to the West. They also suffered less from the burden of the military sector. Transition itself was for the NEUs an essential element of the strategy of attaining national independence from the Soviet yoke. It therefore unleashed the positive energies that go along with such a change. Finally, the very prospect of joining the EU, an aspiration which was widely shared in the countries that have just been freed from the yoke of communism, imposed a regime which was capable of enforcing the reforms that were the conditions for admission to the club.[11] All these helped to accelerate the institutional transition, much beyond what could be achieved by the FSU states.

On the other side of the divide, the FSU, Russia included, lacked most of these advantages. The next section goes into greater detail of the Russian case. Let us point our here, first, that for Russia, for most of its population and leadership alike, the demise of the Soviet Empire, the Soviet Union and the socialist system must have been a major blow to their national pride that colored all changes with a deep tinge of ambivalence. Second, the breakdown of the Soviet Union left 11 newly created states lost in search of their national identity and the proper tools of governance.

The process of breakdown of the old Soviet Union, a highly central-ized state with a strong central government (of which the CPSU was an important part), even though it proceeded with hardly any bloodshed, was accompanied by political struggles between the old communist leaderships and weak reformist groups, between those trying to keep alive the union and those fighting for its disintegration. It weakened and corrupted the state, and strengthened the corrupt local potentates who were courted by both sides.

The FSU governments were both corrupt and weak, unable to enforce the rule of law, which was privatized to local mafias with political and economic agendas. The next section reports on the effects of the weakening of the Russian state.

3.10   The Russian case

The development of new economic and political institutions in Russia deserves special attention, both because it is of special interest for a number of reasons and because the most influential contributions to the normalcy thesis referred explicitly to Russia.[12] Russia does not only have twice the population and economy of all other FSU countries put together, but also continues to possess significant influence over most of them and is still a major world power. As the senior heir to the Soviet Union, the founder of the socialist system and the leader of the old regime, Russia is considered by many as the showcase and symbol of the transition process. Yet the transition process in Russia is also influenced by idiosyncratic Russian features, ranging from its long Russian historical heritage, strong military orientation, and the abundance of its natural resources.

As can be seen from Tables 3.9 and 3.10 and Figure 3.2, in 1996 all institutional indicators for Russia were ranked at the range of 20–30 percentiles (out of 100 – relative to the best-performing country), and most of them were at the same level in 2004, although there were ups and downs in the interim years. In 2004, with one exception, Russia remained in the same range with relatively minor changes of the individual indicators. The absolute levels of all the indicators (whose range is −2.5 – +2.5) stayed in the negative territory until 2004, also with minor changes over time, none of which reached the boundaries of the confidence interval. The same outcome can be also seen in Table 3.9 where the Russian residuals from the 'Kuznets Tables' are shown.[13] The one exception is 'government effectiveness', which we discuss below.

The pattern of change in the level of the indicators during the sub-periods follows quite consistently the economic history of the transition period. During 1996–98 there was a process of some stabilization and consolidation from the stormy early 1990s, but then came the sharp retreat caused by the financial crisis of 1998. A period of improvement of (almost) all indicators followed, till 2002, reflecting among others the replacement of Yeltsin by Putin. Then, however, the trend started to diverge again following the change of course by Putin, who seemed to shift away from market reforms in favor of more centralization and government control, in both the economic and political spheres. The observed rise in the indicator of 'government efficiency' following the 1998 crisis, proceeded throughout and until 2004 despite the above mentioned oscillations in the other indicators (see chart): it seems that while between 1998 and 2002 the rise in 'government effectiveness' depended more on improved 'regulatory control' (since 2000), better

Table 3.9 Russia: governance indicators and residuals

WBI governance index	WBI estimate, transformed			Kuznets residual		
	Estimate[a]		Change	Residual = Actual − predicted Change		
	(1)	(2)	(3)=(2)–(1)	(4)	(5)	(6)=(5)–(4)
	1996	2004	1996→2004	1996	2004	1996→2004
Government effectiveness	4.00	4.58	0.58	−1.93	−0.88	1.05
Voice and accountability	4.28	3.38	−0.89	−1.01	−1.82	−0.81
Regulatory quality	4.18	3.98	−0.20	−1.90	−1.46	0.44
Rule of law	3.32	3.60	0.29	−2.22	−1.68	0.53
Control of corruption	3.52	3.56	0.03	−1.74	−1.76	−0.02
CPI 2005					−1.88	

[a] Transformed estimates = original estimate (Table 3.1)×2 + 5.

Table 3.10 Russia: the six governance indicators, 1996 and 2004

Governance indicator	Year	Percentile rank (0–100)	Estimate (−2.5 to + 2.5)	Standard deviation
Voice and accountability	2004	25.7	−0.81	0.11
	1996	39.8	−0.36	0.17
Political stability	2004	21.8	−0.85	0.19
	1996	17.1	−0.93	0.27
Government effectiveness	2004	48.1	−0.21	0.13
	1996	31.3	−0.50	0.17
Regulatory quality	2004	30.5	−0.51	0.17
	1996	31.5	−0.41	0.20
Rule of law	2004	29.5	−0.70	0.11
	1996	19.9	−0.84	0.14
Control of corruption	2004	29.1	−0.72	0.12
	1996	26.7	−0.74	0.17

Source: Kaufmann D., A. Kraay, and M. Mastruzzi (2005): Governance Matters IV: Governance Indicators for 1996–2004.

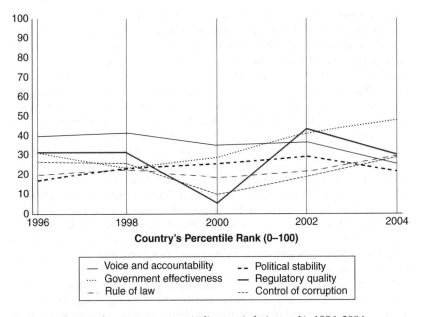

Figure 3.2 Russia: the six governance indicators (relative rank), 1996–2004
Source: D. Kaufmann, A. Kraay, and M. Mastruzzi (2005), Governance Matters IV: Governance Indicators for 1996–2004

'control of corruption' and some increase in 'political stability', since 2002 it continued to improve mostly on the basis of greater authoritarianism that goes along with a better rule of law, law which still requires improvement. Since 2002 we see retreats in the quality of regulation, 'voice and accountability' (that is, democracy and freedom), and, 'political stability', probably due to the events in Chechnya.

The events of Yukos signaled that the main task of government in a market economy, the protection of property, private as well as public, depends in Russia to a greater degree on the whim of the rulers than on legal institutions. Rather than the rule of law we find the imposition of the law of the ruler. Recent growth, impressive though it is, owes to the steep rise in the price of oil and gas, still the mainstays of Russia's exports. This same boom in energy prices is also hiding, for the time being, the need for further market reforms. This separates Russia from other TEs that must face high energy and raw material prices as buyers, not sellers.

While improved government efficiency during the early Putin years was consistent with needed reforms, the trend during the recent period resembles the institutional patterns of the old regime rather than that of earlier transition trends.[14] It is also worth observing that despite increasing authoritarian tendencies and rising government efficiency, there is no significant improvement in Russia's level of corruption, which continues to be exceptionally high even when the level of development is taken into account. This is confirmed by both the WBI data and the CPI (see Columns (1) and (2) of Table 3.9). A recent World Bank report singles out Russia, as one of the few transition countries with a rise in corruption in recent years (Anderson and Gray, 2006, pp. xii, 9–11). Finally, a Russian think-tank, InDem, specializing in the study of corruption, reports a sharp rise during the last years in the volume and cost of corruption related to doing business, in spite of a decline in corruption frequency related to citizens (InDem, 2006).

Russia in comparison: In all the 'Kuznets equations' discussed above the observations on Russia are below the estimated lines and at distances very close to the lower bound of the 5 per cent confidence level. This finding is also consistent with the direct comparison of Russia's institutional indicators in 2004 with the averages for the group of 'lower middle income' countries where Russia belongs (see Figure 3.3a). As can be seen Russia performs slightly better only with respect to 'government effectiveness', and as we have mentioned above this has to do to some extent with old rather than new institutions.

Figure 3.3b underscores what we have already seen with respect to FSU as a group vs. NEU, the EU accession countries: the institutional profile and achievements of Poland (representing the latter group) are much better than those of Russia. Figure 3.3d presents a comparison between Russia on the one side, and Mexico on the other: Mexico and Argentina are the two countries brought up by Shleifer and Treisman as comparators that demonstrate the 'normality' of Russia. As can be seen, Russia is deeply inferior, even in 2004. The same applies to Argentina.[15]

Finally, as could be expected, Russia's institutional infrastructure is superior in all indicators but one to the average of the FSU group of countries (Figure 3.3c). The exception is 'political stability', which is below the FSU average, possibly because of the Chechen events. There could be many explanations for Russia's leading position, some working in different directions, but the dominant factor here seem to be that while all FSU countries suffered from the negative influence of the old regime on their emerging new institutions, in contrast with Russia, they had even less of a 'state' to speak of under the Soviet rule. We see also the Putin effect: 'government effectiveness' is far better in Russia, twice the average. But the rule-of-law and 'control of corruption' in Russia, by far the most developed of all FSU countries, are merely marginally above the FSU average (Figure 3.3c). This signifies that in all of these important dimensions Putin's effect has not been significantly positive.

3.11   Summary and conclusions: not normal states

We have shown that the TEs, especially the FSU states, are not normal countries. We have taken the concept of normalcy from late Simon Kuznets, who

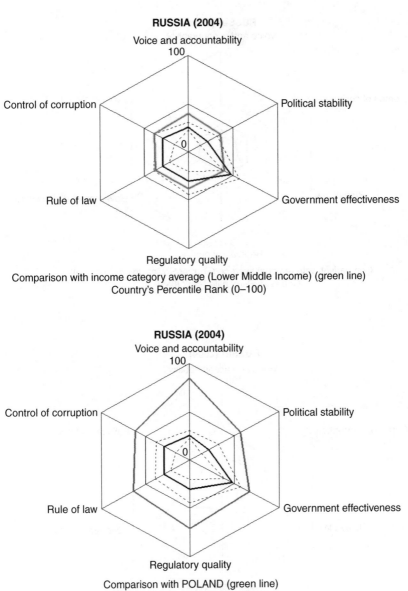

Figure 3.3 (a) Russia (blue) and low middle-income countries (green); (b) Russia (blue) compared to Poland (green); (c) Russia (blue) compared to average of FSU countries (green); (d) Russia (blue) compared to Mexico (green)

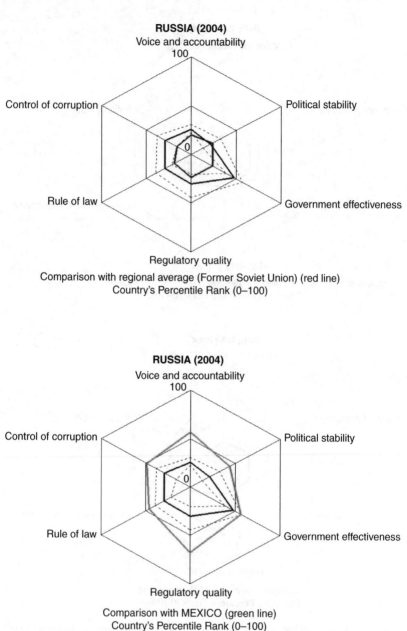

RUSSIA (2004)
Comparison with regional average (Former Soviet Union) (red line)
Country's Percentile Rank (0–100)

RUSSIA (2004)
Comparison with MEXICO (green line)
Country's Percentile Rank (0–100)

Figure 3.3 (Continued)

has taught us how normal structural evolution that countries undergo in their development and growth process can be charted, and therefore how countries that follow this well-trodden path can be distinguished from those that do not. We have used the Kuznetsian recipe to chart the path of institutional development, in order to check whether the ex-socialist countries were normal, were becoming normal, or have already become normal.

The six-dimensional Kuznets curve, constructed by regressing the relevant WBI governance criterion and Transparency International's CPI, have shown that the deviations of TEs, particularly those of Russia and the FSUs, from the common institutional Kuznets path are too extreme and persistent to be classified as 'normal'. In particular, their governments were less effective than their development level would suggest when they embarked upon their transition, and they were steeped in deeper corruption than was justified by it, and all other WBI governance indicators were far enough from their Kuznets curve to justify the sobriquet of abnormality.

The governance indicators of Russia, the largest country of the group, the initiator of the Soviet economic experiment and the country that led the socialist bloc, all of them, lay below the Kuznets curve. Its institutional performance was worse than that of the NEUs, worse than Latin American countries of a similar development level, and not much better than that of the FSU group at large, even though Russia is far more developed than the other members of the group. In other words, Russia can certainly not be called a 'normal country'.

The governance of the NEUs was much closer to the Kuznets curve, and has improved in recent years. The Great Divide between the FSUs and the NEUs has been discussed by many in the field, and its historical roots are well known. All we can add is a greater stress that we can put on the direct causes that nudged the NEUs onto the path and kept Russia and the FSUs off it. The manner by which the communist regime collapsed is an important force that influenced the institutional development path (Keren, 2000; Ickes and Ofer, 2006). For the East European NEUs the collapse of socialism signaled a return to independence and liberation from the communist yoke. The lure of the EU and its promise of assurance of independence provided the governments with the authority to transform institutions and prepare the country for accession. The fate of Russia and the FSU was quite different. The Soviet Union collapsed and with it the central authority. It collapsed amid a struggle that led directly to the breakdown of the rule of law and its takeover by mafias. And although this was reversed when Putin came to power, he imposed authority, but not the rule of law.

What can we learn from this exercise about the future? It is clear that institutions improve with internally bred growth. They do not necessarily improve with growth that is the outcome of natural wealth, as is the case now with Russia. Therefore the outlook for the laggards is not too bright; they will stumble ahead, but it may take a long time before they start to achieve the level that their natural and human resources justify. The EU's new accession countries may also start stumbling now that they have achieved their great goal, and there are indications that once inside the EU, their governance has started to stumble.[16] Hopefully the pressure of growth and the environment will lead to a continuous improvement of institutions.

A number of questions remain for further investigation. For example, is Kuznetsian normalcy really 'normal'? Specifically, have those NEU countries that reached the line by 2004 become fully independent of the institutional burden and legacy of the socialist system? We doubt it. Or consider another question: what is the interaction between the six governance indicators? Which one is more difficult to improve, given the socialist legacy? Finally for now, how do different groups of countries that we have not separated out in this paper, fare with institutional building during the transition? The group of least-developed FSU states in Central Asia? The TEs in the Balkans? And above all there is still much to learn about what makes governance institutions 'normal' and how exactly they interact with the process of economic development.

Appendix

Choice for indicators of the development level:

- *GDP per capita*, at a given date, for example, the 2003 level of income at US \$PPP. The advantage of this indicator is that it is as up-to-date as possible. Its disadvantage is that it is based on a single year's GDP, and the level of development is a state variable that does not move with, say, the cyclical variations of income. The use of a single income level for every country for the entire period 1996–2004 is justified by the consideration that institutional evolution is a long-term process, and short-term changes in it are too minuscule to count.
- The maximum per-capita income level of the country over a relevant recent period. The indicator we have is the maximum per-capita GDP level over the period of 1975–2003, and this was the indicator we first used. Its disadvantage is that it often ascribes to ex-communist countries the possibly inflated income level of a pre-transition, 1989 or 1990, which would bias our measures against these countries.
- The UN's HDI, which takes account of the health and educational level of a country as well as its per-capita income. One of the dimensions of 'abnormality' of the socialist countries has been their significantly higher investment in human capital, including health and education, than non-socialist countries of the same level of development. While in the longer run this should benefit them in covering the productivity gap caused by the socialist system, in the short term it raises their income level in comparison with the other countries and thus reflects the considerations

listed above. We therefore include for comparison a few regressions in which HDI-2003 is the main explanatory variable.

The choice is important, because it determines to which countries the TE is compared. If we use the maximum per capita income, 1975–2003, we ascribe to the TEs a relatively high income, which is linked to a high governance index, and their performance per force looks worse, as it indeed did when we made our first run of analysis using the maximum income. The choice of HDI instead of 2003 income does also raise the relative position of the TEs, even though to a lesser extent. We have used the first variable as our indicator of development, supplementing it once or twice with the third, HDI.

Notes

1. The term FSU covers all the countries that used to compose the Soviet Union, except the Baltic states of Estonia, Latvia and Lithuania. The reasons why the latter have been shifted into the NEU group are explained in Section 3.0.
2. NEU comprises the Baltic countries (see Note[1]) as well as the Czech Republic, Slovakia, Hungary, Poland and Slovenia.
3. It is important to see that our definition of normality is more stringent than that of Djankov *et al.* (2006). They define normalcy as a common development paradigm, and claim that a similar vector of determinants affects similarly development in all countries. But since they do not specify these determinants, they cannot be tested empiricaly. Our claim is specific, that is, that the level of development is closely related to institutional development, a proposition that can be empirically confirmed or invalidated.
4. We estimated a quadratic function (that is, included the square of y_PPP_2003) to allow for the fact that the relation need not be linear.
5. The indicators are explained in Section 3.3.
6. The WBI governance estimates lie in the range of –2.5 to +2.5, and the CPI ones in 0–10. To equalize the range we transformed the former to lie in the range of CPI, by multiplying them by 2 and adding 5. Namely, denoting the former by b and the latter by c, $c = b*2 + 5$.
7. This may be the place to recall that Kuznets never used equations and regression analysis in his work. His main tools were tables and he possessed the ability to penetrate them and extract the proper results. We confess that our weakness in this respect forces us to turn to regression analysis.
8. See note[1] for the definition of FSU.
9. See note[2] for the list of NEUs.
10. The remainder can be obtained from the authors.
11. But it seems that some of the positive impetus has disappeared once these countries have joined the EU (Economist, 2006a, 2006b).
12. See Shleifer and Treisman (2003) and Shleifer (2005), and our comments at the end of the Introduction, Section 3.1.
13. See Columns (4) and (5) in the table. They report the vertical difference between the actual level of the indicator *minus* the computed level at which Russia would have been, using the coefficients of Column (1) in Table 3.1 and Table 3.2 (for

84 The Socialist Legacy

government efficiency) and Table 3.4 and Table 3.5 (for corruption), and similar regressions for the other indicators.

14. The sharp oscillations in institutional qualities observed in Figure 3.2, while reflecting to some extent extreme economic and political changes in Russia, like the crisis of 1998 and the ascendance of Putin, may also be somewhat exaggerated by the views of some of the observers that participated in the various surveys, particularly the high esteem toward Putin when he replaced Yeltsin (in 2000) and the disappointment from him when he 'turned his back' on reforms and democracy. For example, it is unlikely that regulation deteriorated so much by 2000 and recovered so drastically by 2002 to fall again afterwards. This is the type of a problem that more objective statistics are free of.

15. Likewise Russia is inferior in all indicators to the group average of Latin America. Similar results, even more extreme, are obtained in the comparisons between Russia and Greece, Portugal, even Turkey.

16. See the *Economist* articles cited in note 11.

References

Anderson, J. H. and C. W. Gray (2006) *Unticorruption in Transition 3: Who is succeeding . . . and Why?* (Washington DC: The World Bank).

Berglöf, E. and P. Bolton (2002) 'The Great Divide and Beyond: Financial Architecture in Transition', *Journal of Economic Perspectives*, 16 (1), 77–100.

Djankov, S., Y. Qian, G. Roland, and E. Zhuravskaya (2006) *Entrepreneurship in Brazil, China, and Russia*, paper presented at the 9th Bi-Annual Conference of the European Association for Comparative Economics Studies (EACES), (Development Strategies – A Comparative View).

[Economist, 2006a] 'Central Europe, The Shoelace Handicap: Central Europe Risks becoming a Bad Advertisement for the Further Expansion of the European Union', *The Economist*, July 22.

[Economist, 2006b] 'Central and Eastern Europe – Shadows at Europe's Heart: The Ex-communist Countries have been an Economic Success – but Risk becoming Political Failures', *The Economist*, October 14.

Ickes, B. W. and G. Ofer (2006) 'The political economy of structural change in Russia', *European Journal of Political Economy*, 22, 409–34.

InDem (2006) *Corruption Process in Russia: Level, Structure, Trends* (Preliminary Report) Moscow, available at http://www.indem.ru/en/publicat/2005diag_engV.htm.

Kaufmann, D., A. Kraay, and M. Mastruzzi (2005) *Governance Matters IV: Governance Indicators for 1996–2004*, available at www.worldbank.org/wbi/governance/pubs/govmatters4.html.

Keren, M. (1993) 'On the (Im)Possibility of Market Socialism', *Eastern Economic Journal*, 19 (3), 333–44.

Keren, M. (2000) 'An Essay on the Political Economy of Transition: How the Collapse of the Russian State Led to Russian Non-Transition', *The Soviet and Post-Soviet Review*, 27 (1), 7–16.

Kuznets, S. (1966) *Modern Economic Growth: Rate, Structure and Spread* (New Haven and London: Yale University Press).

Mohacsi, N. P. (2000) *The Meltdown of the Russian State: The Deformation and Collapse of the State in Russia* (Cheltenham, UK: Edward Elgar).

Nivet, J. F. (2006) *Institutions, Governances and Development: the Chinese Puzzle*, Paper presented at the 9th Bi-Annual Conference of the European Association for Comparative Economics Studies (EACES), (Development Strategies – A Comparative View).

Ofer, G. (2001) 'Development and transition: emerging but merging', *Revue d'économie financière*, Special issue, 107–46.

Ofer, G. (2003) 'Transition and Developing Economies: Comparing the Quality of Governments' in N. F. Campos and J. Fidrmuc (eds) *Political Economy in Transition and Development* (Boston: Kluwer Academic publishers) pp. 69–95.

Ofer, G. (2004) *Switching Development Strategies and the Costs of Transition: the Case of the Soviet Union and Russia*, paper presented at the AEA meetings, San Diego, 3–5 January.

Rosefielde, S. (2005) 'Russia: An Abnormal Country', *European Journal of Comparative Economics*, 2 (1), 3–16.

Shleifer, A. (2005) *A Normal Country: Russia After Communism* (Cambridge: Harvard University Press).

Shleifer, A. and D. Treisman (2003) 'A Normal Country', *NBER Working Paper*, 10057, available at http://www.nber.org/papers/w10057.

Part II

Transition: From Socialism to Capitalism

4
Growth, Initial Conditions, Law and Speed of Privatization in Transition Countries: 11 Years Later

Sergio Godoy and Joseph E. Stiglitz[1]

4.1 Introduction

The end of the communist era brought much optimism over the growth possibilities of the economies that are now referred to as the transition countries. An inefficient system, rife with distortions and without incentives, was to be replaced by the market. Privatization, liberalization, and decentralization would bring unprecedented prosperity. To be sure, there were some worries about a short transition recession. But the only real issue was how best to secure the transition.

Two schools of thought developed, one advocating shock therapy[2] and the other supporting gradual change. The former contended that the faster these countries achieved an economic structure similar to market economies the better off the population would be, and that the best way of doing so was to liberalize and privatize as quickly as possible. This school tended either not to emphasize the importance of institutions, including the legal and financial infrastructure, or to argue that the best way to achieve the requisite institutions was to privatize quickly in order to create a political and economic demand for these institutions.[3] The gradualists worried that without the institutional infrastructure, which could only be gradually created, privatization might lead to asset stripping rather than wealth creation. They also were concerned that not only would the dynamics of the economy be undermined, but rapid privatization might lead to large concentrations of wealth, and those with wealth might use their wealth to advance political institutions and policies which would maintain their wealth and monopoly. Today, the record of those economies that pursued shock therapy has been at best mixed; several countries have shown a dismal growth performance (see Table 4A1 in Appendix 4A).

The most successful transition economies by far have been China and Vietnam,[4] both of which pursued gradualist policies. There are, however, some major problems in interpreting these experiences. First, each of the countries in transition differs from the others in initial conditions. Some[5] argue, for instance, that China and Vietnam have an advantage because they are *less* developed. But the least developed countries have, in general, not done well over the past 20 years; it is not obvious why compounding one difficult problem, development, with another, transition, should make life easier. Moreover, the countries of the FSU that were the least developed, like Kyrgyz Republic, did not fare particularly well. By the same token, some have argued that countries, like China, that were more agrarian should have had an easier time in transition, simply because that sector is less complex than the industry (Blanchard, 1997). But some of the countries, like Moldova, that were most agrarian were among those that performed the poorest, and the agrarian sector in Russia and in other countries has not performed particularly stellar.

At the same time, others have argued that in some respects, China's transition was not gradual. The transition from the communal agricultural system to the individual responsibility system was, in fact, done remarkably rapidly. But the gradualists nonetheless claim China as a case on their side: even this change was not forced all of a sudden from the top; there was an experiment, first in one province, then in others; the repeated successes led to the demand for this reform by successive provinces. Moreover, in contrast to the countries that followed the shock therapy model, land was not privatized; the farmers were given only long-term use rights. Finally, other reforms were introduced only gradually. But the debate about whether transition in China was or was not gradual serves to highlight the multidimensional nature of these transition strategies that are hard to summarize in a single descriptor such as 'shock therapy' or 'gradualism'.[6]

Economic theory provided less guidance on this subject than one might have hoped. Economic theories are better at analyzing equilibrium than they are at analyzing change, and especially changes of the magnitudes involved in the transition. And there were relatively few historical experiences that seemed similar enough to provide much guidance. In light of this, it is remarkable how strongly the shock therapists argued for their views.

Still, economic theory did have some things to say about the transition, and what it said did not provide much support for the advocates of shock therapy. It was remarkable how they were able to ignore these lessons: incentives matter, but if there are wrong incentives in place, individuals will be motivated to strip assets rather than create wealth. Without good corporate governance laws, for instance, those who had control of assets had an incentive to divert those assets to their own benefit. Capital market liberalization enhanced the ease with which these individuals could move their assets abroad – taking advantage of the security of property rights outside the country at the same time they took advantage of the absence of a good legal framework at home to amass fortunes. The illegitimacy of the privatization process meant that their property rights were inherently insecure at home (unless the oligarchs who seized this wealth could somehow short circuit democratic processes that might naturally question these asset claims), and the subsequent events under Putin confirmed such worries. The oligarchs thus had an incentive to take as much of their money out of the country as they could; and as they all did this, the economy weakened, reinforcing both the judgment that, say, Russia was not a good place in which to invest one's money, and weakening further the security of those property rights. The claims of those who said it made little difference how the state's assets were privatized – it only mattered that they be privatized quickly, if Russia was to make a quick and successful transition – increasingly lacked credibility: how, ordinary Russians asked, could an oligarch's investment in a British football club help Russia's development?[7]

In the end, the advocates of shock therapy often seemed to bolster a simplistic theoretical argument – markets are the most efficient economic system, and therefore, the more rapidly one establishes a market economy the better off one will be[8] – with an empirical claim: those countries that privatized and liberalized most rapidly did better.

In the mid-1990s, cross-sectional studies attempted to sort out the relative importance of policies[9] and initial conditions[10] in determining the success in transition. There are many aspects of economic policy that might, in principle, affect success – not only privatization and liberalization, but also, for instance, inflation and macro-stability. Moreover, different aspects of initial conditions – institutional initial conditions and economic institutions' conditions – might affect success differently. Many of the studies concluded that policies, in particular, fast liberalization and privatization, combined with macro-stability were the key to success.

But as in Aesop's fable, the tortoise may have overtaken the hare. These studies were conducted at an early stage in the transition. Countries like Poland and Slovenia that pursued gradualist policies appear far more successful than those under shock therapy. In some cases, they may have even advanced further in privatization or liberalization. With the additional data of five years – doubling the span of time of the earlier studies – we can at last begin to ask the question: 'does speed help?' Of two countries, both by 2001 having privatized most of their enterprises, did the country that did so rapidly outperform the country that did so more gradually? The results confirm casual impressions: shock therapy was not conducive to success.

In answering this question, as well as identifying the relative role of initial conditions, policies, and institutions, we should be clear: cross-section analysis can at best be only suggestive. We do not have a full set of data that would enable us, for instance, to quantify precisely all of the relevant initial conditions, which would include not only the level of per capita income (a measure of development), and the economic structure (for example the fraction of the economy in agriculture or the fraction of output in commodities which are easily marketed internationally), but also the implicit tax or subsidy leveled on the country as a whole by Russia (for example whether the prices they received for their sales were below international prices, or the prices they paid for, say, oil were below international prices), or the degree of dependence on Russia (determining the extent to which the country's decline was related to the decline in the Russian economy).

Moreover, with so many variables, and only a limited number of countries, it is not easy to sort out the relative role played by each factor. Making matters worse, there is a high level of multicollinearity, and there are multiple interpretations of the coefficients on particular variables. Those countries that were nearer Western Europe might not only have greater access to Western European markets, but also be more influenced by Western European ideas. The countries of Western Europe had a geographical advantage *and* a difference in history. Furthermore, the prospect of accession to the EU provided some spur for faster institutional change. Policies and institutions may both be endogenous.[11] Most of the earlier studies not only ignored the problem of endogeneity and paid insufficient attention to multicollinearity but they also lumped institutional and economic initial conditions together in a single index. In this paper, we not only look at what insights the past half-decade can provide on the transition, but also try to deal explicitly with each of these other problems. Most importantly, with the additional data we can begin to sort out the effect of the *level* of 'reform' (the extent of liberalization) from the *speed* of reform. Of two countries that, say, by 2001 had achieved comparable levels of liberalization, did the countries that rush to liberalize do better? On the whole, does the evidence support shock therapy or gradualism?[12]

This paper is organized as follows. The next section covers the literature review. Section 4.3 describes the data and methodology used in this paper. Section 4.4 describes the results using both Ordinary Least Squares (OLS) and Two-Stage Least Square (TSLS) regressions. Section 4.5 presents our conclusions.

4.2   Literature review[13]

Our paper relates to the cross-country empirical literature on growth in transition countries, trying to sort out the roles of:

a) Policies, more specifically, liberalization and privatization, and the speed with which they were implemented (including using instrumental variables to correct for endogeneity of policy indexes);
b) Initial conditions, and especially the 'burden' left by the Communist era;
c) Institutions and, more specifically, legal institutions.

Most of the studies described below related to the first years of transition. A scatter diagram of performance during these years and subsequent periods shows that performance during the first period was not a good indicator of good performance during the second. This means that we need to be extremely cautious in interpreting these earlier studies, no matter how well conducted they were. There are many reasons, in particular, to be suspicious about relying on studies based on performance in the first few years of transition. Growth strategies might, for instance, have been neither economically nor politically sustainable. Some countries borrowed heavily, and invested their money poorly; the borrowings could have supported a consumption binge,[14] or at least prevented an even greater fall in consumption; but such strategies were clearly not sustainable.[15] Increases in inequality and poverty associated with some of the reform strategies made those strategies politically unsustainable within a democratic context. The longer time series now available at least give us a somewhat better perspective on long-term performance; and it is, of course, this long-term performance in which we are interested.

4.2.1 Liberalization policies

De Melo *et al.* (1996) first identified the positive relationship between indexes of liberalization and economic growth for (26) countries in transition. They calculated annual indexes of liberalization. They employed a cumulative measure: the Cumulative Index of Liberalization (CLI).[16] Though one might have wanted separate indices for, for example, trade liberalization and privatization, the variables were sufficiently correlated that it made sense to use an aggregate index. Controlling for initial income per capita and a dummy for regional tensions, they found that the liberalization index has a positive significant effect on 1989–94 average growth.

Subsequently, Selowsky and Martin (1997) used indexes from De Melo *et al.* (1996) for a panel data of 25 transition economies. They attempted to adjust growth rates for under-reporting and to control for 'war' using a war dummy. They also obtained results similar to De Melo *et al.* (1996). Sachs (1996) provided a similar regression analysis for 1989–95 average growth without controlling for any other variables and obtained a similar positive relationship.[17]

Fischer, Sahay and Vegh (1996a, 1996b) performed Generalized Least Square on a pooled panel data of 25 transition countries for 1992–94 growth rates and De Melo *et al.* (1996) liberalization indexes, controlling for country effects. In the first paper they included as controlling variables inflation, fiscal deficit as percentage of GDP and official external aid as percentage of GDP. In their second paper they only controlled for fiscal deficit and a dummy for fixed/flexible exchange rate. In both cases, they found a positive relationship between growth and liberalization policies.

The papers described so far were widely viewed as supporting the hypothesis that the faster the rate of liberalization, the faster the growth. But further work suggested that these results were not robust. Aslund, Boone and

Johnson (1996) also used CLI for explaining cross-sectional 1989–95 cumulative growth rate of 24 transition countries. In addition, they included a dummy for ruble zone and war-torn countries. When these variables were added to the regression, the effect of CLI vanished. As Fidrmuc (2001) pointed out, these variables could be interpreted as capturing the distinctive negative legacy of the communist regime. In this sense, FSU countries received a worse legacy than Eastern European countries. This issue of legacy draws attention to a different and competitive explanation for explaining the cross-sectional growth of transition countries, that is, initial conditions related to the 'burden' left by the communist era.

4.2.2   Role of initial conditions and instrumental variables

De Melo *et al.* (1997) provided the first comprehensive analysis of the effect of initial conditions on growth in 28 transition countries. Moreover, they introduced the principal components methodology to this literature. Just as earlier studies had been forced by limitations on data points and problems of multicollinearity to resort to an index of liberalization, so too with initial conditions. They included in their estimation the first two principal components of 11 initial conditions.[18] Based on a panel data growth regression, they concluded that both liberalization policies and initial conditions are important to explaining growth. However, in their cross-sectional regression the liberalization index had a negative but insignificant coefficient.

Popov (2000) too found that after controlling for initial conditions, the liberalization index becomes insignificant. This author ran several regressions using 1990–96 growth rates and 1990–98 growth rates for a cross section of 28 transition countries. In his regressions he included an aggregate measure of distortions,[19] a FSU dummy,[20] a War dummy, 1987 Purchasing Power Parity (PPP) GDP per capita as a percentage of the US level and log of average inflation. He found that the CLI is insignificant for both cases of growth rates. In the second step he replaced the FSU dummy with the fall of government revenues as a percentage of GDP and shadow economy as a percentage of GDP in 1994, finding again that CLI was insignificant. Finally, and more important for our paper, he included a measure of rule of law, which is marginally significant.

Krueger and Ciolko (1998) found results similar to that of De Melo *et al.* (1997). This paper was among the first to recognize that the speed of liberalization should be viewed as an endogenous variable, affected, for instance, by many of the same initial conditions that might affect growth directly. They used an instrumental variables approach to output growth from 1989–95 for 18 transition countries. The instruments used are share of export in 1989 Gross National Product (GNP) and 1988 GNP per capita. These authors ran first a regression of CLI on the instrument and obtained a predicted CLI. In the second regression (growth regression) the coefficient on predicted CLI was negative but not very significant.[21]

Heybey and Murrell (1999) dealt with several potentially significant methodological issues existing in the cross-country empirical literature on growth in transition countries besides the endogeneity of the speed of reform:

1) The failure to include some key initial conditions causes an omitted variable bias;
2) The use of cumulative liberalization indexes (or annual indexes) does not allow distinguishing between the effect of the *level* of the policy variable and the *speed* with which it was implemented;
3) Different countries began their transition in different years.

They performed a three-stage least square (THSLS) on growth rate for 26 transition countries. Among their results were: (1) initial conditions are significant but (2) the coefficient of speed of liberalization and the coefficient of policy level are insignificant; while (3) results adjusting for differences in starting dates are very similar to those using the same starting point.

4.2.3   Role of institutions

Until recently, differences in the strength of legal institutions as a possible explanation for dissimilar growth performance was largely ignored in the empirical literature on transition countries, probably because of a lack of data for the first half of the decade. Since 1997 several organizations started to collect data. In addition, Campos (1999) provides an index for institutional variables from 1989 to 1997[22] which we make use of in this paper.

Brunetti *et al.* (1997) were the first to estimate OLS regressions using legal and political institutional variables as explanatory variables. These variables were obtained from a survey that quantified *perceptions* of companies in different countries around the world.[23] They considered only variables pertaining to 20 transition countries and ran regressions using 1990–95 per capita growth rates for those countries as dependent variables.[24] They found that in a cross-section analysis, these institutional measures affect growth positively. In addition, they used instrumental variables for correcting some endogeneity problems of these institutional variables and showed that their results stand.

Moers (1999) and Grogan and Moers (2001) ran four cross-sectional growth regressions for 25 transition countries in 1990–95 using four institutional measures[25] and two controlling variables (inflation and war dummy). They found that in all cases these measures are positively associated with growth but are not very significant. In addition, they checked for endogeneity of the institutional measures and they found similar results to the OLS results.

Havrylyshyn and Rooden (2000) ran the same panel data as De Melo *et al.* (1997) but only for 25 transition countries. They employed the same measures of initial conditions and liberalization indexes, but they included lagged values of the latter measure. Moreover, they included the inflation rate and, more importantly, institutional variables. These consisted of the first principal component of nine institutional variables from diverse sources. In addition, they split them into legal and political variables. They found a significant positive relation between growth and liberalization indexes and between growth and the principal components of institutional variables; the latter relationship is especially strong for legal variables.

Stiglitz (2001) provides another attempt to include an institutional variable in explaining cross-sectional growth among transition countries. He ran an OLS regression on 1990–98 growth rates of 25 countries. The explanatory variables are 1997 EBRD indices of privatization of large and small-scale enterprises (policy measure), 1997 EBRD index of governance and enterprise restructuring (institutional measure), and a variable that measures the interaction of the two former variables. He found that the privatization index is insignificant, but the index of governance and enterprise restructuring and the interaction variable are highly significant.[26]

4.2.4 Summary

The main conclusions coming out of this review of the literature are: (a) the earlier studies, which failed to deal adequately with institutional and initial conditions and a range of statistical problems, were not robust; in particular, the finding that the speed of liberalization has a significantly positive effect on growth was not supported robustly by the data; and (b) there are plausible grounds for arguing that institutional variables and initial conditions did have a significant effect on performance.

The main contribution of this paper is to re-examine these questions within a somewhat longer time series. With this longer time series, we can begin to ask, in a meaningful way, did those countries that privatized rapidly do better? Of two countries, say, that began with the same initial conditions, and ended up with the same degree of privatization (liberalization), did the country that got there more quickly do better? Or worse? Of course, as we ask that question, we must simultaneously control for initial conditions, institutions, and other policy variables.

4.3 Data description

In this section we describe the variables used in our empirical analysis. The tables in Appendix 4A show the complete data exploited in this paper. We employ as a dependent variable the total growth rate for 1990 through 2001 for 23 transition countries.[27] Because the variability among countries' growth rates is relatively high,[28] there is some hope of identifying critical determinants of growth in spite of the relatively small size of the sample. Still, the small number of countries and the large number of possible explanatory variables suggests that the task of cleanly defining the relative importance of different variables may not be easy.

We measure the strength of legal institutions employing data from a survey conducted by the World Bank and EBRD. They surveyed more than 4000 firms in 23 transition countries on several areas such as business environment, corruption and legal system. Specifically, we consider positive answers related to the strength of the legal system and enforcement of property rights (see Table 4.1: Panel 1).[29] The expected sign of this variable in the growth regressions is positive.

The effect of policy on growth is quantified by two different variables. In order to measure the effect of policy speed we use the absolute difference between 1991 and 2000 EBRD small-scale and large-scale privatization indexes (see Table 4.1: Panel 1). The effect of policy level is captured by the 2000 level of the same index.

Table 4.1 Data description

Variable	Definition	Source
Panel 1: Regressions Data		
Growth	Logarithm of the ratio of 2001 GDP and 1989 GDP	United Nations Economic Commission for Europe Common Database
Enf	Proportion of firms in the countries of the sample that agree in 1997 to the following question: To what degree do you agree that the legal system will uphold contract and property rights?	Business Environment and Enterprise Performance Survey. World Bank and the European Bank for Reconstruction and Development (EBRD).
Dp00p91	One-tenth of the difference between the 2000 average of the indexes of small-scale and large-scale privatization and the 1991 average of the same indexes.	EBRD
Privi00	2000 average of indexes of small-scale and large-scale privatization.	EBRD
PC1inst	First principal component of the institutional initial conditions.	Based on variables obtained from Campos (1999).
Panel 2: Institutional Initial Conditions		
Transacc8991	Indicator from 0 to 10 that measures both transparency of policy-making and accountability of the executive.	Campos (1999)
Rulelaw8991	Indicator from 0 to 10 that measures both quality of law enforcement and 'substance' of law itself.	Campos (1999)
Buroqual8991	Indicator from 0 to 10 that measures the quality of local bureaucracy.	Campos (1999)
Civsoc8991	Indicator from 0 to 10 that measures civil liberties, political rights and influence of civic organizations.	Campos (1999)

Table 4.1   (Continued)

Variable	Definition	Source
Panel 3: Instruments		
Years	Years under communist rule.	De Melo *et al.* (1997)
Blkpr	1990 per cent difference between black market exchange rate and official exchange rate.	De Melo *et al.* (1997)
Def	Late 1980s defense expenditure as percentage of GDP.	Popov (2000)
Indst	Late 1980s sum of the absolute value of deviations of the share in GDP of each three sectors (agriculture, industry, services) from the 'normal' level. 'Normal' was defined as the average for the group of market economies with comparable PPP GDP per capita. These values are 1990.	Popov (2000)
Trdist	Late 1980s sum of the three trade distortion measures calculated by Popov (2000). These are the following: trade openness, which is the 'normal' share of external trade in GDP (defined in a similar way as before) minus the actual share; external trade within FSU as share of GDP; and external trade with socialist countries as share of GDP. These values are 1990.	Popov (2000)

Note: For East European countries we used the 1989 score, and for FSU republics we used the 1991 score.

As Heybey and Murrell (1999) so forcefully explained, it is important to discriminate the effect of policy *level* from policy change on growth. Much of the empirical literature has incorrectly used empirical results suggesting a positive effect of the level of privatization to argue for fast privatization. The two schools of thought on transition differ strongly on their prior beliefs about the coefficient of the *speed* of privatization. The shock therapists believe that, 10 years out, the countries that privatized most quickly would be ahead of the game – their growth rates would be higher. The gradualists argue that the coefficient on the speed variable should be negative.

The initial conditions are gauged by a set of institutional variables, using principal component analysis.[30] This analysis provides two important pieces of information that give some intuition as to what exactly the components are measuring. They are the degree of correlation among components and the original variables, as represented by an eigenvector decomposition of the covariance matrix of standardized variables (that is, a variable x that has been normalized dividing by its standard deviation), and the percentage of variance explained by i^{th} principal component. The latter measure is computed by dividing the eigenvalue associated to the corresponding principal component by the total sum of the eigenvalues. Intuitively, the first output tells us about the nature of the component and possible interpretations of it, that is, which variables have influenced it the most. The second output gives a sense of the importance of the component in terms of the overall variability of the original system of variables.

Initial conditions are calculated using the 1989 observation of institutional variables for East European countries and the 1991 observation for FSU countries from Campos (1999).[31] Table 4.1: Panel 2 explains the nature of these data. We employed the 1991 observation for the former Soviet Union republics because the actual transition started approximately that year. In the case of East European countries the transition began after the Berlin Wall fell in 1989.

Table 4.2 shows that the first principal component is strongly correlated with each of the institutional variables. In addition, this component explains a good portion of the variability of the original variables. In consequence, this component can be thought of as a measure of the initial institutional strength and, thus, its expected sign in the growth regressions is positive (the higher the score in these indexes the better the institutions and the faster expected growth).

Finally, Table 4.1: Panel 3 shows the detail of the instruments for the policy variables used in the TSLS regressions. These instruments are selected based on the two traditional econometric criteria used for choosing instrumental variables.

First, our instruments are clearly correlated with our measures of policy. They reflect the amount of distortions left by the communist policies: the greater these distortions, the greater the extent of policy reform. (This relationship is confirmed in the statistical analysis.)

For instance, the variable that captures years under communist rule reflects the fact that East European countries were communist for a much shorter

Table 4.2 Principal component analysis

Principal Component of the Institutional Initial Conditions			
	Correlations	Percentage of variance explained	
	1PC		
Transacc8991	0.8021	1PC	0.4908
Rulelaw8991	0.8844	2PC	0.2874
Buroqual8991	0.6398	3PC	0.1206
Civsoc8991	0.3117	4PC	0.1013

span than FSU countries, except for the Baltic countries and Moldova. The black market foreign exchange premium reflects the fact that, generally speaking, East European official rates were closer to market exchange rates. Defense spending, industrial structure and trade distortions are also lower on average for East European countries than for FSU republics.

Moreover, our instruments also reflect an important variability within our sample. For example, in the case of industrial structure and trade distortions, former Yugoslav countries were much less distorted than other East European countries. The other important criterion for selecting instruments is that these instruments may be correlated with the other explanatory variables, but, like the dependent variable, the instruments are orthogonal to the errors of the growth regressions. To be sure, we ran the test of overidentifying restrictions and we found that they are effectively uncorrelated with the errors of the growth regressions.[32]

4.4   Econometric analysis

4.4.1   Ordinary least square regressions

We first estimated OLS regressions using the variables described in the Section 4.3. The R square is reasonably high considering the size of the sample.

The first regression is a simple regression with our institutional variable, the property rights enforcement variable described before (see Table 4.3). The coefficient has the expected sign (positive) and is highly significant. The adjusted R square is also fairly high, above 40. Note that this is consistent with the gradualist view, which highlighted the importance of the institutional infrastructure.

In the second regression we only include the variables that measure policy level and policy speed. The adjusted R square is also high. The coefficient for

Table 4.3   OLS regressions (Dependent variable is the 1990–2001 GDP growth rate)

Variable	Regression 1		Regression 2		Regression 3		Regression 4	
	Beta	Tstat	Beta	Tstat	Beta	Tstat	Beta	Tstat
Constant	−0.91	−5.57	−0.78	−2.15	−1.00	−3.20	−1.33	−3.42
Enf	1.44	4.23			1.10	3.04	1.14	3.22
Dp00p91			−4.34	−3.06	−2.72	−2.08	−3.00	−2.32
Privi00			0.42	2.96	0.24	1.81	0.27	2.07
PC1inst							0.03	1.37
R-Squared (%)		46.0		35.1		56.4		60.5
Adj R-Squared (%)		43.5		28.6		49.5		51.7
N		23		23		23		23

policy speed (Dp00p91) is significant and negative. The coefficient of level of policy (Privi00) is positive and significant.[33]

In the third regression we put together the two sets of variables. The privatization speed preserves its significant negative effect. The privatization level maintains its sign but decreases its significance to only 10 per cent. The property rights enforcement still has a positive and significant effect on cross-sectional growth. In addition, the adjusted R square has a noticeable increase, from 35 per cent to 56 per cent.[34]

In the fourth and final regression we add the principal component that captures the institutional initial conditions. It has the expected sign but it is not significant. Other authors[35] have found that these variables are very significant in explaining growth among transition countries. One possible interpretation is that initial conditions have decreased its importance since the beginning of the transition.

In summary, the most important result of our study, based on a longer period of analysis than earlier studies and including variables capturing institutional variables, initial conditions, and measures of both policy level and change is *that privatization speed has a negative effect on growth*. The study, one of the first that explicitly attempts to assess the role of speed, lends cautious support to gradualism versus shock therapy. A second result, consistent with earlier literature, is that property rights enforcement has a positive and very significant effect. A third result provides mild support for earlier findings on the level of privatization: the coefficient is positive but only marginally significant.

Finally, unlike earlier studies, initial conditions seem to have little effect on growth after 10 years of transition.[36] In the next section, we will see whether these 'new' facts are able to stand the check for endogeneity.

4.4.2 Two-Stage least square regressions

In this section we perform a simultaneous equation approach. Both policy measures (speed and level) may themselves depend on economic growth.[37] For instance, in successful countries it may be possible to build political support for reforms such as privatization and, thus, faster growing countries may be able to privatize more and faster. One of the major sources of opposition to privatization is a worry about lay-offs, and normally, faster growth is associated with faster growth of employment – and therefore less worries about lay-offs.

Table 4.4 provides the OLS and TSLS regressions. In the first regression we only include the property rights enforcement and policy variables. In the second regression we add the institutional initial conditions variable.

The most noticeable difference between the OLS and TSLS estimation is that the coefficient of the variable that measures level of privatization becomes less significant (in the first regression, it is insignificant though it is still positive; in the second, it is significant only at the 10 per cent level). The

Table 4.4 TSLS regressions (Dependent variable is the 1990–2001 GDP growth rate)

	OLS		TSLS		OLS		TSLS	
	Beta	Tstat	Beta	Tstat	Beta	Tstat	Beta	Tstat
Constant	−1.00	−3.20	−0.95	−2.30	−1.33	−3.42	−1.33	−2.79
Enf	1.10	3.04	1.07	2.87	1.14	3.22	1.13	3.12
Dp00p91	−2.72	−2.08	−3.12	−2.05	−3.00	−2.32	−3.10	−2.09
Privi00	0.24	1.81	0.25	1.64	0.27	2.07	0.28	1.82
PC1inst					0.03	1.37	0.03	1.38
R-Squared (%)		56.4		56.1		60.5		60.5
Adj R-Squared (%)		49.5		49.2		51.7		51.7
N		23		23		23		23

Note: Instruments: Years, Blkpr, Indst, Def and Trdist.

sign and significance of the coefficient on the property rights enforcement and speed variables is unchanged. In addition the R-squares are practically the same. The results obtained from the previous section are still valid.[38]

One might ask: how is it that the level of privatization does not matter, but the speed does? One could understand the opposite result – that the level matters but the speed does not – as saying that it just does not matter how you get there, what matters is where you get. One could understand the result of a positive effect on the level and a negative effect on speed as supporting the gradualist argument for privatization. This result is consistent with the view that rapid privatizations had a very disruptive effect on the economy; they were associated with asset stripping (tunneling) and huge increases in inequality, which undermined subsequent and more meaningful reform efforts. In some cases, countries that did not privatize worked to strengthen public institutions (good management of government-run enterprises, public pension funds, and so on). The statistical analyses suggest that (controlling for other variables) the countries that ended up with a lower level of privatization did just as well as countries that ended up with a higher level of privatization.

Hoff and Stiglitz (2004a, 2004b, 2005) argue that the institutional infrastructure itself should be viewed as endogenous, and a fuller analysis would clearly seek to explain why different countries differed in the quality of their institutions.

On the other hand, failure to take account of the endogeneity of institutions may not result in a significant bias in the estimated parameters. This is partly because the speed of adjustment of institutions is relatively slow, because while institutional development is endogenous, it is not likely to be highly dependent on growth itself. Hoff and Stiglitz argue that tight monetary policy may contribute negatively to institutional development; and tight monetary policy also might contribute negatively to growth, so institutional development might be picking up the effects of an omitted variable (tight monetary policy). But as we noted, when we introduced macro-economic variables explicitly into the analysis (proxied by inflation), it appeared to have an insignificant effect.

4.5 Conclusions

At the beginning of the 1990s the Eastern European and FSU countries started a massive process of political and economic reform. The hope was that they would achieve living standards similar to developed countries.

Two strategies were offered. One argued that the process of liberalization and privatization should be done as quickly as possible.[39] The advocates of this position believed that the faster a transition country became a market economy, in particular, the faster it privatized, the quicker this country would be able to avail itself of the growth opportunities that the market provided.[40]

Others proposed a more gradual process of reform. The sale of government assets needed to be done slower and the economy had to be liberalized more gradually. This school argued that there are large costs associated with very rapid adjustments, and that there were large risks associated with, for instance, privatization before certain institutional changes (the creation of a legal infrastructure, including corporate governance laws, and of a financial infrastructure, including an effective and well regulated banking system) have been put into place.

In the mid-1990s a growing empirical literature started to develop in support of the 'faster' position. This literature claimed that the evidence supported the view that the faster transition countries liberalize and privatize the more they would grow. This important conclusion was attacked in several directions, in terms of model specification and econometrics. First, the above assertion disregarded the role of initial conditions. Second, important questions were raised about the exogeneity of these policies. Third, institutional differences could also be important in explaining the uneven performance of transition countries. Fourth, this literature did not distinguish between the level of reform and *speed*, and thus did not really address the question at issue.[41]

The conclusion that the more rapid the transition the better played an important advocacy role – it supported the position advocated by the IMF and (at the time) the World Bank; much of this research was conducted by these institutions and/or supported by them. The most important critique was that there simply were insufficient data to come to a strong conclusion. These institutions should have, accordingly, been less confident and more cautious in the advice they gave.

In this paper we extend the period of analysis and at the same time consider all these concerns in our estimations. The clearest and most important result is that privatization speed has a negative effect on growth, reinforcing the growing anecdotal support for the gradualists and against shock therapy. On the other hand, perhaps the most striking (though perhaps not surprising) result is the importance of our measure of institutional strength. This result is similar to what other authors have found. Third, we found that initial conditions have an insignificant effect on cross-sectional growth. One possible explanation for the insignificance of initial conditions (which previous studies have emphasized) is that we are using a longer period of analysis.

While we believe our paper has made some advances over earlier literature in untangling the various factors affecting success in transition, much remains to be done.

First, it is important to disentangle the effect of privatization itself from related policy decisions that also influence long-term growth. For instance, the method chosen to privatize state-owned enterprises is an important policy decision that actually differed greatly across transition countries. Each country used some distinctive combination of three privatization methods: direct sale (sometimes to foreigners), mass privatization programs (often through vouchers) and management–employee buy-outs. These choices certainly affected the ownership structure, corporate governance and restructuring process of the privatized companies.[42] The impact of privatization (including the speed of privatization) almost surely depended on the form of privatization.[43]

Regulatory and competition policies are other important policies that help to determine how privatization would affect country growth performance.[44] A country that simultaneously privatized and established a regulatory framework that promotes competition may boost its growth potential compared to a country that only privatizes and leaves unchanged the old business environment or allows the emergence of unregulated monopolies. As Stiglitz (2000) emphasized, the legal framework affecting corporate governance too can be an important determinant of the success of privatization. Policies that affect the development of the financial sector can also be critical, not only in determining overall growth (for example, as a result of the creation of new enterprises), but also in the success of privatization. Without access to finance, those who obtain the privatized assets are more likely to engage in asset stripping.[45]

Macro and monetary policies and conditions too play a role, since they can affect the terms at which finance is made available. Factors external to each of the countries play an important role in determining their growth. As we have already noted, Russia's weakness contributed to the weakness of its trading partners. But oil and commodity prices have played an important role in Russia's performance. Weak oil prices in 1997–98 almost surely contributed to the crisis of 1998; and strong oil prices after 2003 almost surely contributed to its recovery.

Moreover, even the legal structure could be viewed as endogenous, as Hoff and Stiglitz (2004a, 2004, 2005) point out. Policies that affected the desirability of asset stripping versus wealth creation (macro-policies, liberalization policies, such as those relating to capital outflows, and financial policies) affect the likelihood of the development of the 'rule of law', of institutional variables that are critical for success in growth.

One challenge is to find good proxies for many of these potentially important variables (for example privatization method, ownership structure, corporate governance, and quality of regulation and competition policies). Given the relatively limited number of countries, the high collinearity among many of the important variables and the complex interdependencies among them, cross-section empirical studies may never be able to resolve fully some of the critical controversies. Would it, for instance, have been possible that fast privatization would have had less adverse effects had alternative privatization methods been employed, if monetary policy had been less tight, or if greater efforts had been made to create domestic financial institutions providing credit to the newly privatized companies? To what extent should we blame some of these policies for the failure of appropriate legal institutions to develop?

This paper has at least helped to resolve one controversy: there is no evidence that, controlling for other relevant variables, fast privatization contributed to medium-term growth (that is, over a 10-year period). On the contrary, the weight of evidence – both the cross-section study reported here as well as more detailed anecdotal evidence concerning the successful countries – appears to support the worries of the critics of shock therapy: fast privatization adversely affected decadal growth.

Studies such as this will need to be repeated as the transition continues. It is possible that 10 years from now, we may say that all of this was a tempest in a teapot: the speed of privatization may have made a difference in the short or medium-term, but in the long run, as countries become more deeply rooted into the market economy, how they got there will not matter much, just as our study suggests the effects of initial conditions are taking on less importance than earlier. On the other hand, it is possible that history matters, and the countries that undertook rapid privatizations, which resulted in large inequalities in wealth ownership and which undermined confidence in markets and resulted in widespread perceptions of a lack of legitimacy of property rights, may fare less well[46] even in the long run. We each can conjecture, but only time will provide the answer.

Given the overconfidence exhibited by the early advocates of shock therapy, a confidence not warranted by economic theory and not justified by the empirical studies to which they often referred, we should, perhaps, end on a note of caution. Given the paucity of 'experiments', the small number of countries, and the large set of potential explanatory variables, it is unlikely that even a much longer time series will fully resolve the controversies. A more textured analysis of what happened – case studies, detailed analyses of firms, industries, and sectors in different countries, a careful look at the impact on how resources were mobilized and deployed – supported by theoretical analyses of why individuals, firms, and governments behaved in the way that they did, will need to supplement these statistical studies. The comparisons between the successes of China and Vietnam, and the failures especially in so many countries of the FSU, are also informative. We believe that at the end of the day, the conclusion that will emerge may be a simple one: that incentives matter; that one of the reasons why shock therapy in the way that it was done in much of the FSU and the other countries in transition (other than China and Vietnam) failed is that so often it did not get incentives right; that without good laws on corporate governance, and in the absence of financial institutions and macro-economic policies that make resources available at reasonable terms for wealth creation, incentives are in place for asset stripping rather than wealth creation; and that these natural incentives played themselves out in country after country.[47] Political institutions themselves are endogenous, and in many of the countries, shock therapy created conditions that were adverse to the creation of institutions that would themselves in the long run be conducive to wealth creation. The costs of shock therapy may, in this sense, be far greater than its critics realized at the time: it was not only that the economies did not perform as well as might have been hoped or expected, but, in some cases at least, the institutional legacy – as well as the legacy of inequality – has imposed long-term costs to society that are hard to calculate. History matters, and the consequences of shock therapy may be as long lived as the effects of the Communist regime itself.

Mario Nuti is the master of this kind of careful and thoughtful work in comparative economic systems that would have warned against the risks of shock therapy and that would have enhanced the prospects of a successful transition. Such analyses contribute to our understanding of economic processes and structures. They are as essential for deriving good policies now as they were then, at the beginning of the transition. It is a pleasure to present this paper in his honor.

Appendix 4A: Data

Table 4A 1   Regressions data

Countries	Growth	Enf	Dp00p91	Privi00	PC1inst
Albania	0.0908	0.358	0.15	3.0	10.6
Armenia	−0.3524	0.512	0.215	3.15	9.6
Azerbaijan	−0.5604	0.449	0.15	2.5	11.5
Belarus	−0.1098	0.413	0.05	1.5	7.5
Bulgaria	−0.2446	0.512	0.27	3.7	9.1
Croatia	−0.1720	0.627	0.165	3.65	9.4
Czech Republic	0.0218	0.401	0.215	4.15	8.6

Table 4A 1   (Continued)

Estonia	−0.1076	0.614	0.315	4.15	9.2
Georgia	−1.0996	0.305	0.265	3.65	5.3
Hungary	0.0797	0.772	0.265	4.15	5.6
Kazakhstan	−0.2510	0.32	0.25	3.5	11.7
Kyrgyz Republic	−0.3079	0.295	0.25	3.5	11.3
Latvia	−0.3696	0.354	0.265	3.65	10.4
Lithuania	−0.3581	0.333	0.265	3.65	8.9
Macedonia	−0.2459	0.485	0.15	3.5	8.1
Moldova	−1.0217	0.181	0.215	3.15	6.6
Poland	0.2476	0.617	0.13	3.8	6.2
Romania	−0.1803	0.432	0.2	3.35	7.4
Russia	−0.3960	0.208	0.265	3.65	4.8
Slovak Republic	0.0602	0.558	0.215	4.15	5.1
Slovenia	0.1284	0.634	0.18	3.8	5.1
Ukraine	−0.7897	0.254	0.2	3.0	5.4
Uzbekistan	0.0198	0.744	0.185	2.85	5.4

Note: For definitions and sources see Table 4.1 in the text.

Table 4A 2   Institutional initial conditions

Countries	Transacc8991	Rulelaw8991	Buroqual8991	Civsoc8991
Albania	8.00	7.00	3.33	0.00
Armenia	7.70	7.00	1.67	0.00
Azerbaijan	7.50	7.00	5.00	1.67
Belarus	5.00	7.00	0.83	0.00
Bulgaria	6.50	6.67	2.50	0.00
Croatia	6.00	6.00	3.33	3.33
Czech Republic	7.50	4.00	3.33	0.00
Estonia	8.00	3.00	5.00	0.00
Georgia	4.50	3.00	1.67	0.00
Hungary	6.50	2.00	0.83	0.00
Kazakhstan	7.70	8.33	2.50	5.00
Kyrgyz Republic	7.70	8.33	1.67	5.00
Latvia	7.70	6.70	1.67	5.00
Lithuania	7.00	6.70	0.83	1.67
Macedonia	6.75	5.00	0.83	3.33
Moldova	5.00	4.17	1.67	1.67
Poland	5.00	4.17	0.83	1.67
Romania	8.00	3.00	0.83	1.67
Russia	5.25	2.00	0.83	0.00
Slovak Republic	5.25	2.00	0.83	1.67
Slovenia	5.25	2.00	0.83	1.67
Ukraine	5.25	2.00	0.83	3.33
Uzbekistan	5.25	2.00	0.83	3.33

Note: For definitions and sources see Table 4.1 in the text.

Table 4A 3   Instruments

Countries	Years under central planning	Defense spending (percentage of GDP)	Industrial structure distortion	Trade distortions	Black market premium
Albania	47	5.3	12.3	27.3	43.4
Armenia	71	14.6	23.3	42.8	182.8
Azerbaijan	70	4.3	23.3	25.2	182.8
Belarus	72	11.2	28.3	24.2	182.8
Bulgaria	43	14.1	27.3	13.0	92.1
Croatia	46	3.7	12.3	19.5	2.7
Czech Republic	42	8.2	19.2	8.5	18.5
Estonia	51	1.9	21.3	52.8	182.8
Georgia	70	4.1	6.1	33.2	182.8
Hungary	42	7.2	7.3	2.6	4.67
Kazakhstan	71	5.2	20.3	28.8	182.8
Kyrgyz Republic	71	8.9	19.4	33.0	182.8
Latvia	51	9.5	21.3	41.4	182.8
Lithuania	51	7.5	23.9	42	182.8
Macedonia	47	3.7	12.3	7.5	2.7
Moldova	51	4.4	26.3	42.2	182.8
Poland	41	8.1	22.3	20.8	27.7
Romania	42	4.5	30.3	16.1	72.8
Russia	74	15.3	14.9	17.8	182.8
Slovak Republic	42	8.2	19.2	36.3	18.5
Slovenia	46	3.7	4.2	17.3	2.7
Ukraine	74	14.8	22.3	29.7	182.8
Uzbekistan	71	5.6	21.4	28.7	182.8

Note: For definitions and sources see Table 4.1 in the text.

Appendix 4B: Three-Stage Least Squares Estimates

The results of THSLS estimations for our model are the following

Table 4B 1   THSLS regressions

	Panel 1: Dependent variable is Gr				
	Constant	Enf	Dp00p91	Privi00	PC1inst
Beta	−1.3291	1.0959	−3.1961	0.2920	0.0307
Tstat	−3.86	3.50	−2.80	2.52	1.49
R-Squared	0.6044				
Adj R-Squared	0.5164				

Table 4B 1 (Continued)

Panel 2: Dependent variable is Dp00p91

	Constant	Gr	Privi00	Years	Blkpr	Def	Indst	Trdist
Beta	−0.1255	−0.0069	0.1004	−0.0012	0.0008	0.0004	−0.0008	−0.0010
Tstat	−2.20	−0.46	13.97	−1.64	5.32	0.39	−0.96	−2.20
R-Squared	0.8985							
Adj R-Squared	0.8511							

Panel 3: Dependent variable is Privi00

	Constant	Gr	Dp00p91	Years	Blkpr	Def	Indst	Trdist
Beta	1.3183	0.0713	9.8275	0.0108	−0.0079	−0.0038	0.0073	0.0103
Tstat	2.65	0.49	13.97	1.45	−4.62	−0.33	0.84	2.20
R-Squared	0.8985							
Adj R-Squared	0.8511							

Panel 4: Correlation Matrix of Errors of the Above Regressions

	Gr-reg	Dp00p91-reg	Privi00-reg
Gr-reg	1		
Dp00p91-reg	0.0726	1	
Privi00-reg	−0.0776	−0.8897	1

Notes

1. This paper was presented at the 2004 American Economics Association meetings at San Diego and at the conference 'Comparative Transitions: A Critical Review' at London Business School (11–12 June 2004). We would like to thank Karla Hoff, Charles Himmelberg, Rajeev Dehejia and participants from both conferences for helpful comments, and Giselle Guzman for her research assistance. However, any error remaining is our responsibility. The views expressed in this paper are ours and do not reflect those of the Central Bank of Chile.
2. Shock therapy referred both to policies attempting to rapidly bring down the hyperinflation that afflicted many of the countries (especially after they engaged in 'shock' liberalization) and to the policies attempting to change rapidly the structure of the economy through privatization and liberalization. In this paper, we focus on the latter. Poland, for instance, engaged in shock therapy to bring inflation under control (though it did not bring inflation down to single-digit levels rapidly) but employed a gradualist strategy for privatization. In our taxonomy, Poland is a gradualist.
3. This was sometimes referred to as the political Coase theorem. There was neither theory nor historical experience to support this perspective; as Hoff and Stiglitz (2004a, 2004b, 2005) argue elsewhere, there are strong reasons why an illegitimate privatization might impede the creation of the rule of law. The evidence (included that cited in Hoff and Stiglitz, 2005) supports that conclusion.

4. Interestingly, the World Bank (1996) and most of the other studies of the economies in transition do not include China and Vietnam, even though they represent more than 75 per cent of the people making the transition. The obvious suggestion is that the results would have been markedly different were these to have been included (in an appropriately weighted way) in the statistical analyses. To make our results comparable to the earlier studies, we too exclude China and Vietnam.

5. See, for instance, Sachs and Woo (1997).

6. Poland provides another example: while it engaged in 'shock' macro-therapy, its privatization process, and other institutional reforms, were more gradual.

7. Corruption in the privatization process – in which some of the advocates of rapid privatization were themselves not only implicated but convicted – also contributed to the loss of credibility.

8. This simplistic argument elides some of the critical questions, for example concerning what are the most relevant aspects of a market economy. China emphasized competition, as opposed to property rights; in many of the transition economies, more emphasis was placed on assigning control rights (in the absence of good laws on corporate governance and clear restrictions on permissible actions of sub-national actors, these control rights were not tantamount to a clear assignment of property rights), rather than competition.

9. See for example De Melo *et al.* (1996), Sachs (1996) and Fischer *et al.* (1996b). We talk more about these papers and others when we review this literature in Section 4.2.

10. See, for instance, De Melo *et al.* (1997) and Krueger and Ciolko (1998). More generally, economic historians like North (1990) have also emphasized the importance of institutions.

11. Krueger and Ciolko (1998) and Heybey and Murrell (1999) also explore the issue of endogeneity. Fidrmuc (2001) performed an instrumental variable analysis in order to consider the possibility of endogeneity and also included an institutional variable (a democracy index). However, his methodology had important pitfalls. See more on this in Section 4.2.

12. As it turns out, when one controls appropriately for the level and speed of liberalization and institutional variables, some of the other econometric problems turn out to be less significant than seemed to be the case earlier.

13. This literature has been reviewed in several other papers. See, by example, Campos and Coricelli (2002) and World Bank (2001, 16–20). Therefore, it is not our intention to go over the whole literature again. Instead we plan to review the papers that, based on our judgment, have been more influential in shaping or mis-shaping the perceptions on the lessons that can be obtained from the cross-country empirical studies on growth in transition countries. We also do not touch the country-specific studies (see for example Berkowitz and DeJong, 2003).

14. As happened in Argentina and many other countries in Latin America in the early 1990s.

15. In that sense, Russia's performance – as dismal as it was – was higher during the first years of transition than the sustainable levels, that is, a true estimate of Russia's performance during this shock therapy era would have been even more pessimistic.

16. This index is a weighted average of liberalization in three areas: internal markets, external markets and private-sector entry.

17. Sachs (1996) employed liberalization indexes calculated by the European Bank for Reconstruction and Development (EBRD). These indexes are an extended version of De Melo *et al.*, (1996) indexes. The EBRD expanded these indexes in both policy

areas and years covered. Sachs (1996), Sachs and Woo (1997), Fidrmuc (2001) and others have used the EBRD extended version of these indexes. We employ these indexes in this paper and discuss them further in Section 4.3.

18. They are the following: (1) Location (measured using a dummy and not distance from somewhere, usually some city in Western Europe; see Fidrmuc, 2001); (2) Previous economic growth rates; (3) Categorical variable for differentiating states that were independent or not before 1989; (4) Richness of natural resources (dummy); (5) Over-industrialization; (6) Urbanization; (7) 1989 PPP income per capita; (8) Repressed inflation; (9) Trade dependence among communist area; (10) Black market exchange rate premium (11) Number of years under Communism. These variables capture mostly economic, structural and, indirectly, institutional conditions but are not direct measures of institutional variables. In our estimation we employ variables that gauge direct initial institutional weaknesses. In addition, we use the last two variables as instruments in our TSLS estimations. In addition, they performed a simultaneous equation approach but they asserted that there is no difference with the OLS approach, so they stayed with OLS.

19. We use more disaggregated measures of distortions in our empirical analysis as instruments in our TSLS estimation; see Section 4.3.

20. Such a variable may be important for several reasons. The countries of the FSU may have performed poorly partly because Russia performed poorly; most of the countries of the region were highly dependent on Russia, not least as a market for their goods. Just as a slowdown in the US economy leads to a slowdown in economies which export to the US, such as Mexico, so too would one expect a marked decline in Russia to adversely affect these countries. Their performance thus could have more to do with Russia's decline than with any policies that they instituted. The FSU dummy could be capturing this effect. Because the FSU countries also liberalized less, earlier studies (which had not used an FSU dummy) which suggested that liberalization had a significant effect were essentially picking up a spurious correlation.

21. In addition, they employed as controls a tension dummy and FSU dummy in the growth regression; see Regression 5 in Table 4.2. While this paper was the first attempt in the literature to make CLI endogenous, it has one problem. The estimators of the coefficients in the second equation are potentially inconsistent (Wooldridge, 2002, Chapter 5). The omission is that in the first regression of this two-step procedure it is necessary to include all the (exogenous) variables and not only the instruments. In our work we included all the other (exogenous) variables in the estimation of the first equation. (As we shall see, it turns out that the problem of endogeneity does not appear to be as important as we originally thought; we had worried that, for instance, countries that were closer to Brussels liberalized faster, because of the prospect of joining the EU. And these countries were more successful. But it was not liberalization itself which drove the success, but the proximity to Western Europe, with all of the advantages that it brought.) Besides, consistency of estimates may not be an important problem when (as here) there is a small sample.

22. We use in our estimation the data on these indexes as a measure of initial institutional conditions.

23. Perception variables play an important role in much of this literature. They have to be used with caution. It is possible, for instance, that when the economy is performing poorly, individuals would *perceive* institutional failures as more serious than when the economy is performing well, even though more objective measures show little difference.

24. Their control variables are 1992 GNP per capita, trade openness (sum of export and import over GDP), secondary enrollment rate in the initial year, average rate of government consumption, and average rate of inflation. (They use these variables one a time. They do not try to explore the idea that these variables might measure different kinds of initial conditions.)

25. These variables are obtained from *The Wall Street Journal Europe's Central European Economic Review, Nation in Transit 1997* and *Euromoney*.

26. There is a related literature that tried to measure the empirical influence of social culture institutions on cross-sectional growth among transition countries; see Raiser *et al.* (2001) and Katchanovski (2000).

27. These countries are Albania, Armenia, Azerbaijan, Belarus, Bulgaria, Croatia, Czech Republic, Estonia, Georgia, Hungary, Kazakhstan, Kyrgyz Republic, Latvia, Lithuania, Macedonia, Moldova, Poland, Romania, Russia, Slovak Republic, Slovenia, Ukraine and Uzbekistan.

28. The simple mean growth rate is 26 per cent and the standard deviation was 34 per cent.

29. For details on this survey see the website of the World Bank: http://info.world-bank.org/governance/beeps.

30. The principal component analysis is a statistical method used frequently for reducing the dimensionality of a given data set of correlated variables while maintaining as much of the variables' variability as possible. This efficient reduction of the number of variables is achieved by obtaining orthogonal linear combinations of the original variables – the so-called principal components. The first principal component preserves most of the variability existing in the original variables, the second component preserves the second most variability existing in the original variables, and so on. Each component is a linear combination of the eigenvector of the variance–covariance matrix of the original variables. For a discussion of the principal component analysis, see for example Flury (1988) and Jolliffe (2000). In addition, see Fuentes and Godoy (2005) for a more abridged but more economic discussion of principal component analysis. In order to obtain these components we normally need to use the variance–covariance matrix of the original variables. However, this procedure is sensitive to the units in which the original variables are measured. In order to avoid this problem we calculate the components using the correlation matrix of the original variables. This method allows us to obtain principal components that are independent of the unit of measure of the original variables. See Jolliffe (2000, Chapter 2) for an extensive discussion of the advantages and disadvantages of either method. Fuentes and Godoy (2005) also provide a brief discussion of these issues.

31. This author was very kind in providing these data.

32. One referee of an earlier version of this paper pointed out that this is not a powerful test. It is clearly conceivable that some of these instruments might have a direct effect on growth (and not just an effect through their effect on the policy variable). For instance, even apart from policy, in the process of moving to a market economy, black market premia might be reduced, and this reduction would have an effect on growth (as a result of eliminating a distortion in the economy). We shall discuss later the possible bias that this imparts to the estimates.

33. These results differ from Heybey and Murrell (1999), who found that speed has a positive sign but was insignificant and that their measure of policy level was not significant. There are several possible reasons for the differences. This difference in sign can be attributed to the fact that their measure of growth is shorter (only the

first four years of transition), that they do not control for institutional variables and that they used De Melo *et al.* (1996) liberalization measures.

34. It is possible to argue that since (1) we are controlling for the end point and (2) the countries with a higher level of privatization index in 1991 were mostly East European countries and these countries had a high rate of growth, it is not surprising that the coefficient of speed is negative. In order to address this concern we ran two additional regressions: first, we only included speed of privatization. Second, we added to the third regression in Table 4.3 the level of privatization in 1991, and we replaced the final level of privatization with the level in 1995. This last variable is a compromise between being a good proxy for final level privatization (the correlation is 76.67 per cent) and avoiding the problem of collinearity (including the variables that measure level of privatization closer in time to 2000 makes all coefficients insignificant because of collinearity). The results are the following:

Additional regressions (Dependent variable is the 1990–2001 GDP growth rate)

	Constant	Dp00p91			
Beta	0.06	−1.49			
Tstat	(0.21)	(−1.22)			
R-Squared	0.0664				
Adj R-Squared	0.0220				

	Constant	Enf	Dp00p91	Privi91	Privi95
Beta	−0.925	1.073	−2.177	0.005	0.214
Tstat	(−3.17)	(3.21)	(−1.73)	(0.03)	(2.04)
R-Squared	0.6458				
Adj R-Squared	0.5671				

In the first regression the coefficient of speed is still negative. This shows that the variable that measures speed of privatization has a negative sign *without controlling for the end point*. It is not just a statistical artifice. In the second regression the coefficient of the initial level of privatization is insignificant and the other variables essentially maintain their signs and significance. The results suggest: (a) of two countries that made the same change in the degree of liberalization, there was a *slight* advantage in growth to the country that did relatively more of the change initially; but (b) of countries with the same degree of privatization in 1991, those who had adjusted more slowly did better. In the subsequent analysis we do not include the level of privatization in 1991. (These results are consistent with the view that, the longer the time period since the beginning of the transition, the less important are at least some of the initial conditions.) We attempted other ways of identifying the role of speed, for example looking effectively at the fraction of the change that occurred in the first 5 years. The results are consistent with those reported here: the countries that privatized faster did more poorly.

35. De Melo *et al.* (1997), Krueger and Ciolko (1998) and Havrylyshyn and Rooden (2000).

36. An additional important variable that we include in our analysis as a proxy of macroeconomic stability is inflation (see Popov, 2000, for another paper using a similar variable). Specifically, we use the logarithm of accumulated change

in Consumer Price Index between 1990 and 1994. We exclude later years to minimize the obvious possibility of endogeneity of this variable. The results are the following:

Additional regressions with inflation as independent variable (Dependent variable is the 1990–2001 GDP growth rate)

	Constant	Inf9094
Beta	−0.14	−0.02
Tstat	(−0.95)	(−0.92)
R-Squared	0.0391	
Adj R-Squared	−0.0067	

	Constant	Enf	Dp00p91	Privi00	PCIinst	Inf9094
Beta	−1.24	1.11	−2.90	0.28	0.02	−0.01
Tstat	(−2.66)	2.99	(−2.14)	2.05	0.73	(−0.38)
R-Squared	0.6084					
Adj R-Squared	0.4933					

Because the coefficient on the inflation variable is insignificant, we excluded it from the regression analysis reported in the text. (The result implies that those countries that were more successful in quickly bringing down inflation in the early years of the transition fared no better over the long run than those that did not.)

37. Heybey and Murrell (1999) mentioned another problem. There is a chance that there are extra variables omitted in the estimation that drive both speed and level of privatization. For example, distance to Brussels is an interesting possible omitted variable. Countries closer to Brussels might be reforming faster and growing faster because they have a better chance to become members of the European Union (EU; this accession to the EU indeed happened for some of the countries included in our sample). In order to test for the presence of this problem, it is necessary to perform THSLS estimations. These estimations are shown in Appendix 4B. Based on these results, we find no evidence of this source of endogeneity. In both policy speed and policy level regressions the coefficient of growth is insignificant (see Panel 2 and 3 of Table 4B1 in Appendix 4B). In addition, the THSLS estimators of the growth regression are extremely similar to the OLS and TSLS counterparts (compare Table 4B1 Panel 1 with Tables 4.3 and 4.4 in the text). Moreover, the correlation among the errors of the Growth regressions and Dp00p91 and Privi00 regressions (policy variables) are very low (see Table 4B1: Panel 4 in Appendix B). A strong correlation among the errors is a symptom of an omitted third variable problem. (The correlation among the errors of Dp00p91 and Privi00 regressions is high because of the way these variables are constructed.) Our results seem to differ from those of Heybey and Murrell (1999). They found that correlation among the errors was high and the coefficient of the growth variable is significant in the policy variable regression. As we explained before, this difference can be attributed to a shorter sample, to their no control for institutional variables and to their use of De Melo *et al.* (1996) liberalization measures.

38. As we noted earlier, some of the instruments may themselves have a direct effect on growth. If it were true, it would imply that we are capturing in the policy variable some of the 'direct' effect of the instrument, so that the policy variable is biased. For instance, if years under communist rule leads to more growth (the

longer the country was under Communist rule, the more its growth was depressed, so the greater the growth potential in the movement away from Communism) and more reform (for the same reason), then the coefficient on change in the degree of privatization (speed) will have a positive bias. Thus, our analysis underestimates the adverse effects of speed.

39. There were, of course, also political arguments (on both sides); advocates of shock therapy worried that unless privatization was done quickly, there might be backsliding. Critics argued that, because quick privatization was more likely to be done poorly, quick privatization would lead to an undermining of support for reform. In the elections in Russia in the early years of this decade, the reform parties were resoundingly defeated, partly because of the almost universal feeling that privatization was done poorly. The countries that have subsequently elected governments that appear most closely aligned with the old Communist parties have been shock therapy countries; while some of the non-reforming countries have retained authoritarian regimes, none of the gradualist countries have had a reversion. These experiences lend support to the gradualist critique.

40. Shock-therapy would also undermine the domestic opposition to reform. Because of entrenched interests, slow privatization was likely (in this perspective) to lead to (close to) no privatization.

41. In our opinion, Heybey and Murrell (1999) are the only ones that so far have measured policy speed correctly.

42. Another complicated issue in the transition countries' privatizations was the participation of private investment funds; see Cadogan Financial (2003) and Castater (2002).

43. For details on privatization methods see Castater (2002) and his references. In addition, Castater (2002) provides some preliminary results on the effect on growth rate of the different privatization methods. Stiglitz (2001) provided a review of the corporate governance and restructuring issues in transition countries. Dutz and Vagliasindi (2000) related corporate governance and restructuring with privatization methods.

44. See Vickers and Yarrow (1995).

45. But the development of the financial sector may itself be endogenous to privatization (both the extent of privatization and its form). For instance, if privatized companies' securities are traded publicly, they can be the backbone for a more sophisticated financial market. Thus, privatization can influence growth not only through expected efficiency gains within private companies but also through other channels. Another indirect channel through which privatization may affect growth is that privatization may possibly release physical and human assets that can be employed in *de novo* companies; see Earle and Estrin (1997) and Havrylyshyn and McGettigan (1999). In many economies in transition, however, there is extensive disguised unemployment, both for skilled and unskilled labor. The absence of opportunity is evidenced by massive emigration. Thus, in these countries, there is little reason to believe that this channel plays an important role. A more complete analysis would look too at *what* was privatized. A standard argument for privatization is that it improves the efficiency of resource allocation. In Czech Republic, banks were not privatized, implying that the government could continue to play an important role in determining who got access to resources.

46. Accounting, of course, for other differences, such as natural resource wealth.

47. Shock therapy failed because in the rush to privatize and liberalize, typically they did not get incentives right. It takes time to design institutions right and to create appropriate legal structures. But there is another argument for gradualism: it takes time to change, to adapt, and to learn.

References

Aslund, A., P. Boone and S. Johnson (1996) 'How to Stabilize: Lessons from Post-communist Countries', *Brookings Papers on Economic Activity*, 1, 217–313.

Berkowitz, D. and D. N. DeJong (2003) 'Policy Reform and Growth in Post-Soviet Russia', *European Economic Review*, 47 (2), 337–52.

Blanchard, O. J. (1997) *The Economics of Post-Communist Transition* (Oxford, UK: Oxford University Press, Clarendon Lectures).

Brunetti, A., G. Kisunko and B. Weder (1997) 'Institutions in Transition: Reliability of Rules and Economic Performance in Former Socialist Countries', *World Bank Working Paper*, no. 1809.

Cadogan Financial (2003) 'Countries Summaries', Cadogan Financial; available at http://www.cadoganfinancial.co.uk/Cadogan/default.htm.

Campos, N. F. (1999) 'Context Is Everything: Measuring Institutional Change in Transition Economies', *World Bank Working Paper*, no. 2269.

Campos, N. F. and F. Coricelli (2002) 'Growth in Transition: What We Know, What We Don't, and What We Should', *Journal of Economic Literature*, 40 (3), 793–836.

Castater, N. M. (2002) 'Privatization as a Mean to Societal Transformation: An Empirical Study of Privatization in Central and Eastern Europe and the Former Soviet Union', *FEEM Working Paper*, no. 76, September.

Chenery, H. B. and M. Syrquin (1989) 'Patterns of Development: 1950–1986', *World Bank Discussion Papers*, no. 41.

De Melo, M., C. Denizer and A. Gelb (1996) 'Patterns of Transition from Plan to Market', *World Bank Economic Review*, 10 (3), 397–424.

De Melo, M., C. Denizer, A. Gelb and S. Tenev (1997) 'Circumstance and Choice: The Role of Initial Conditions and Policies in Transition Economies', *World Bank, Working Papers – Transition Economies. Current and former socialist economies*, no. 1866.

Dutz, M. and M. Vagliasindi (2000) 'Corporate Governance and Restructuring: Policy Lessons from Transition Economies', in *Privatization and Regulation in Developing Countries and Economies in Transition* (New York: United Nations).

Earle, J. S. and S. Estrin (1997) 'Voucher Privatization: The Structure of Corporate Ownership in Russian Manufacturing Industry', *CEPR Discussion Paper*, no. 1736.

Fidrmuc, J. (2001) 'Economic Reform, Democracy and Growth During Post-Communist Transition', *CEPR Discussion Paper*, no. 2759.

Fischer, S., R. Sahay and C. Vegh (1996a) 'Economies in Transition: The Beginnings of Growth', *American Economic Review*, 86 (2), 229–33.

—— (1996b) 'Stabilization and Growth in Transition Economies: The Early Experience', *Journal of Economic Perspectives*, 10 (2), 45–66.

—— (1998) 'How Far is Eastern Europe from Brussels?', *International Monetary Fund Working Paper*, WP/98/53.

Flury, B. (1988) *Common Principal Components and Related Multivariate Models* (New York: Wiley).

Fuentes, M. and S. Godoy (2005) 'Co-movements in Emerging Market Spreads: A Principal Component Analysis', *Central Bank of Chile Working Paper*, 333.

Grogan, L. and L. A. M. Moers (2001) 'Growth Empirics with Institutional Measures for Transition Countries', *Economic Systems*, 25 (4), 323–44.

Havrylyshyn, O. and D. McGettigan (1999) 'Privatization in Transition Countries: A Sampling of the Literature', *International Monetary Fund Working Paper*, WP/99/6.

Havrylyshyn, O. and R. van Rooden (2000) 'Institutions Matter in Transition, but so do Policies', *International Monetary Fund Working Paper*, WP/00/70.

Heybey, B. and P. Murrell (1999) 'The Relationship between Economic Growth and the Speed of Liberalization During Transition', *Journal of Policy Reform*, 3 (2), 121–37.

Hoff, K. and J. E. Stiglitz (2004a) 'After the Big Bang? Obstacles to the Emergence of the Rule of Law in Post-Communist Societies', *American Economic Review*, 94 (3), 753–63.

—— (2004b) 'The Transition Process in Post-Communist Societies: Towards a Political Economy of Property Rights', in B. Tungodden, N. Stern and I. Kolstad (eds) *Toward Pro-Poor Policies: Aid, Institutions and Globalization* (World Bank/Oxford University Press), pp. 231–45.

—— (2005) 'The Creation of the Rule of Law and the Legitimacy of Property Rights: The Political and Economic Consequences of a Corrupt Privatization', *NBER Working Paper*, no. 11772.

Katchanovski, I. (2000) 'Divergence in Growth in Post-Communist Countries', *Journal of Public Policy*, 20 (1), 55–81.

Krueger, G. and M. Ciolko (1998) 'A Note on Initial Conditions and Liberalization during Transition', *Journal of Comparative Economics*, 26, 718–34.

Jolliffe, I. T. (2000) *Principal Component Analysis* (New York: Springer-Verlag) Springer Series in Statistics, Second Edition.

Moers, L. A. M. (1999) 'How important are Institutions for Growth in Transition Countries', *Tinbergen Institute Discussion Papers*, No. 99-004/2.

North, D. C. (1990) *Institutions, Institutional Change, and Economic Performance* (New York: Cambridge University Press).

Popov, V. (2000) 'Shock Therapy Versus Gradualism: The End of the Debate (Explaining The Magnitude Of Transformational Recession)', *Comparative Economic Studies*, 42 (1), 1–57.

Raiser, M., C. Haerpfer, T. Nowotny and C. Wallace (2001) 'Social Capital in Transition: A First Look at the Evidence', *EBRD Working Paper*, No. 61.

Sachs, J. D. (1996) 'The Transition at Mid Decade', *American Economic Review*, 86 (2), 128–33.

Sachs, J. D. and W. T. Woo (1997) 'Understanding China's Economic Performance', *NBER Working Paper*, No. 5935.

Selowsky, M. and R. Martin (1997) 'Policy Performance and Output Growth in Transition Economies', *American Economic Review*, 87 (2), 349–53.

Stiglitz, J. E. (2000) 'Whither Reform? Ten Years of the Transition', *Proceedings of the Annual Bank Conference on Development Economics 1999* (Washington DC: World Bank), pp. 27–56.

—— (2001) 'Quis Custodiet Ipsos Custodes? Corporate Governance Failures in the Transition', in J. E. Stiglitz and P-A. Muet (eds) *Governance, Equity, and Global Markets: The Annual Bank Conference on Development Economics in Europe* (New York: Oxford University Press), pp. 22–54.

Vickers, J. and G. Yarrow (1995) *Privatization: An Economic Analysis* (Cambridge MA: MIT Press).

Wooldridge, J. (2002) *Econometric Analysis of Cross Section and Panel Data* (Cambridge MA: MIT Press).

World Bank (1996) *World Development Report 1996: From Plan to Market* (New York: Oxford University Press).

World Bank (2001) *Transition–The First Ten Years: Analysis and Lessons for Eastern Europe and the Former Soviet Union* (New York: Oxford University Press).

5
Skills and the Transition

Simon Commander

5.1 Introduction

The empirical evidence of the link from human capital to growth has at times seemed elusive. Yet recent work suggests that the effect of schooling on the level of output can be quite substantial – Bassanini and Scarpetta (2001) estimate approximately 6 per cent for each additional year of schooling. Other work has explored whether there is an association between output growth and the mean stock of human capital per worker. This direction of work finds a robust link from years of schooling to total factor productivity (TFP) growth (see Benhabib and Spiegel, 1994; Dowrick, 2002). In other words, a more educated labor force can use ideas more productively.

The evidence for transition and developing countries is – not surprisingly – much weaker, hampered by questionable data, institutional aspects and other factors. However, in the case of the transition countries, it has commonly been assumed that they did have one important and positive inheritance from the epoch of central planning: namely, the level of human capital. This inheritance could have been assumed to have positive consequences for growth. This paper takes a look at whether the assumption about human capital has been appropriate and then uses some original firm-level data to look at two related aspects. The first is the shift in relative labor demand. The second is to look at whether firms are constrained in terms of the skill content of effective labor supply. The evidence suggests that the assumption that these countries are still rich in human capital has to be questioned. Indeed, it seems, rather, that the legacy has been far more ambiguous with asset-specific skills and a corresponding lack of labor-market flexibility being important factors behind the persistence in unemployment and the sharp rise in non-participation. At the same time, the inadequacies of the educational system have required substantial reforms which in many transition countries have been implemented slowly and often incompletely. Given the secular trend towards the use of more skilled labor in production and the associated shift in relative labor demand, these features have the potential to hold back productivity and employment growth in many of the transition countries.

5.2   Education and skills in transition countries

The first broad point to establish is that many of the transition countries have relatively poor education levels and skills. For example, comparative data on expected years of schooling in the Organization for Economic Cooperation and Development (OECD) for two points in time – 1995 and 2002 – show that four of the leading reform countries (as measured by European Bank for Reconstruction and Development (EBRD) transition indicators) – Czech Republic, Hungary, Poland and Slovakia – have expected years of schooling below the sample mean. Although, there is clear evidence of a major relative improvement over the period, relatively poor scores were reported at both points in time.[1] This information suggests that the adult population's level of schooling at the start of transition was quite low – contrary to many priors. Indeed, the share of the population in tertiary education was actually quite small at the start of transition. Hungarian Labor Force Survey data, for example, suggest that under 14.5 per cent of 20–24 year olds were in tertiary education in 1992.[2] If anything, this problem is likely to have been accentuated in the Commonwealth of Independent States (CIS) countries and in South Eastern Europe (viz, Bulgaria, Romania and the Balkans).

Results from the International Adult Literacy Survey (IALS) – an international skills survey conducted in 1994–98 – reported in Table 5.1 for the Czech Republic, Hungary, Poland and Slovenia show (with the exception of the Czech numbers) that the transition countries scored relatively poorly. The picture that emerges is certainly not one of high proficiency. Table 5.2 also gives education-specific employment ratios for some transition countries that have comparable data as well as some EU countries with similar educational composition. The differences between the mean employment ratios and those of low-educated people have become much larger in transition countries. This is particularly the case in Hungary – one of the leading reformers – where the skill-specific difference amounts to 32 percentage points for men, and 22 percentage points for women (despite a relatively high share of the population – a third – having been classed as 'low-educated'). Kollo (2006a) also uses data from the IALS, and applies multiple choice models to study how educational groups and jobs requiring literacy and numeracy were matched in the four Central European countries (Czech Republic, Hungary, Poland and Slovenia) and two groups of comparator West-European countries. His results show that selection for skill-intensive jobs was more severely biased against the less-educated in Central Europe than in the rest of Europe, including countries hit by high unskilled unemployment at the time of the survey.

In short, it appears that the skill deficiencies of workers with primary and apprentice-based vocational qualification contribute significantly to the problem of unskilled unemployment in the transition countries and to a greater extent than in the comparator Western European economies.

Table 5.1   Direct measures of skills in recent surveys of literacy and related proficiencies

Total Population

	Czech Republic	Hungary	Poland	Slovenia	Survey mean
All adults					
Prose	−2	−13	−17	−17	0
Document	8	−13	−15	−18	0
Quantitative	16	−8	−15	−18	0
Adults, primary					
Prose	13	−13	−15	−21	0
Document	17	−17	−19	−21	0
Quantitative	17	−11	−17	−18	0
Adults, secondary					
Prose	9	−17	−15	−21	0
Document	19	−15	−17	−19	0
Quantitative	21	−13	−17	−19	0
Adults, tertiary					
Prose	−7	−21	−19	−15	0
Document	13	−17	−19	−15	0
Quantitative	21	−9	−19	−17	0
Per cent at Level 1 (prose)	15.7	33.8	42.6	42.2	22.1
(ii) 15-year-olds					
International Survey of Student Assessment (PISA, 2000)					
Reading proficiency	492	480	479		500
(iii) 10-year-olds					
Study of Reading Literacy Achievement in Primary Schools (PIRLS, 2002)					
Reading proficiency	537	543		518	529

Note: The scores are based on pair-wise comparison of the country with 21 other countries in the survey: better = 1, equal = 0, worse = −1. Zero means the country is in median position. The range is −21 to +21.
Source: Second International Adult Literacy Survey (IALS, 1998).

Commander *et al.* (2005) provide evidence that the unemployment rate of low-educated workers is high in Central Europe in both absolute and relative terms.[3] (The same picture emerges when looking at labor force participation data). The education-specific differential is mostly stronger in Central Europe than for the other OECD countries in the sample. Whereas in relatively low income OECD countries such as Mexico, Greece or Spain and Portugal, the pattern is for low-educated workers to flow in and out of low-wage unstable jobs with relatively short mean unemployment spells between jobs, in Central Europe the large majority of the low-educated remain in unemployment for protracted periods of time or drop out of employment

Table 5.2 Employment ratios of the population aged 25–62 by level of educational attainment in 1998

| | Share of ISCED 0/1 and 2 | Employment ratios (per cent) | | | | | |
| | | Men | | | Women | | |
		All levels	ISCED 0/1 and 2	Difference	All levels	ISCED 0/1 and 2	Difference
Hungary	33	69.1	37.1	32.0	53.9	31.6	22.3
Poland	24	75.9	57.4	18.5	60.5	40.7	19.9
Comparators							
Austria	28	80.7	65.3	15.4	60.3	45.1	15.2
Finland	28	76.2	61.6	10.9	69.8	57.8	12.0
Czech Republic	16	82.9	57.6	25.3	63.4	41.8	21.6
Comparators							
Denmark	20	84.0	69.0	15.0	73.2	55.7	17.5
Germany	19	76.9	62.5	14.4	59.7	40.4	19.3

Notes: ISCED categories: 1 = primary education; 2 and 3 = first and second stages of secondary education; 5 = tertiary education without a first university degree; 6 and 7 = tertiary education with a university degree.
Source: OECD (Paris, 2000).

either permanently or for extended periods. The continuing absence of a small-firm sector reliant largely upon low-wage labor – as opposed to sole proprietorships and family labor firms – appears to be an important part of the reason.

Moving further east, the picture appears to have many common features with that in Central Europe. Consider the case of Russia. To get a reasonable set of benchmarks against which to compare the Russian educational system and its outputs is difficult, not least because of institutional and other differences that make such comparisons problematic. However, the OECD's Program for International Student Assessment (PISA) surveys now allows for comparisons across a number of dimensions with a sustained attempt to measure comparables. While the recent PISA report relates to 2003, information on the educational attributes of parents allow for some historical evidence to emerge. What is evident is that when converted into years of schooling, the Russian mean for primary education for parents was 4 years, putting it on an equivalent plane to Brazil, Hungary or Serbia. By contrast, the bulk of OECD countries had mean years of primary schooling in excess of 6 years. While there was still a gap for those with secondary and tertiary education, the gap was much smaller.

Turning to the current generation of students, the PISA data also allow cross-country comparison with respect to reading and science attainments.

Distinguishing six proficiency levels for reading, Russian students score relatively poorly. For example, students with skills below Level 1 generally have serious difficulty in using reading literacy as an effective tool. In Russia, nearly 13 per cent of students scored below Level 1, as against 7 per cent for the OECD as a whole. Indeed, in Russia over 51 per cent of students fell into Levels 1 or 2. In the OECD the comparable share was 35 per cent. Only 11 per cent of Russian students were grouped at the top end of the scale (Levels 4 and 5), as against 30 per cent in the OECD. The mean score for all Russian students for reading was roughly 11 percentage points below the OECD mean. In the case of science, the Russian mean score was far closer to the OECD average (being only 2 percentage points below). As regards the distribution nearly 19 per cent of Russian students recorded low (<400 points) science scores (as against 18 per cent in OECD) while around 13 per cent had high (>600 points) scores (as against 18 per cent in OECD). In the specific case of mathematical proficiency, the PISA survey found that over a quarter of Russian students failed to reach the baseline level of proficiency (Level 2). In short, by 2002–03 Russian students did relatively poorly in reading scores. Indeed, the Russian scores are better – but not substantially better – than either Thailand or Brazil. By contrast, it appears that science scores are little off the OECD average and clearly better than developing countries, like Thailand or Brazil.

What should be concluded from the above summary? In the first place, it appears that these countries entered transition with relatively weak education and skills profiles, at least when compared with advanced market economies. However, when compared with many developing countries the opposite tends to hold. Second, a high share of workers lacking adequate skills – alongside a weak or absent low-wage sector – has resulted in very large numbers over time being effectively excluded from work. Significant long-term unemployment and non-participation has resulted. One plausible conjecture is because prior work histories may not be viewed as carrying adequate information for employers, the latter may have turned to education (possibly in combination with age) as a key screening mechanism. Education is an easy-to-observe proxy, so that a likely outcome will indeed be high education-specific differences, relatively small skill-specific differences, and poor matching of actual skills and jobs. Third, evidence from a wider group of transition countries suggests that problems associated with the educational system may actually have been magnified over time as expenditures have contracted and poor incentives and high variation in quality within national educational systems have emerged. With these features in mind, we now turn directly to try and see what evidence exists regarding, first, the presence of shifts in labor demand disaggregated by skill, and then the impact of the supply of skills on firms.

5.3   The changing demand for skills

There is now a body of robust analytical and empirical work that explains and chronicles the shift in labor demand in advanced market economies. The shift in labor demand has been mostly across-the-board, and not just restricted to tradables sectors. If traded goods were largely inputs – rather than final goods – then it might be possible to argue that they could be substitutes for unskilled labor. But this looks like an implausible explanation for the widespread shift within industries in the skill component of labor demand. An alternative – and widely accepted – argument concerns the impact of a General Purpose Technology (GPT, principally computers and their extensions) that affects an entire economy. By requiring different skill and educational levels, the new GPT shifts relative labor demand, in this case raising the skill content of employment. Crudely speaking, the losers in the process are those workers with low education/skills. This shift has in turn been associated with a large increase in wage inequality.

What to date has been the impact of these changes on the transition countries and with what implications for labor demand and wages? Transition provides an interesting laboratory. These countries have been undergoing massive reallocation of resources and restructuring, albeit at different speeds. As such, they provide a way of seeing what shifts in the skill distribution are likely to occur when large order change or reform occurs. Given the substantive reforms that countries such as Brazil, India and China have pushed through in the last decade and more, the wider relevance may be considerable.

A good starting point is some evidence from a large firm survey – the Business Environment and Enterprise Performance Survey (BEEPS) implemented by EBRD and the World Bank in 2002. It provides evidence for 26 transition economies and a total of more than 5600 firms on: (a) the education and skill composition (as measured by three broad categories – unskilled, skilled and managerial/professional) of the firms' labor force, and (b) changes between 1998–2002 in the skill composition of firms. Limiting the analysis to Central and Eastern Europe and the Baltic States (CEB), Bulgaria, Croatia and Romania and the CIS (and hence a sample size of nearly 4400 firms), it emerges that there is a clear tendency for firms to increase the share of skilled employees in total employment.[4] This has been common across regions for both manufacturing and services. In CEB it is also the case that nearly half the firms had increased the share of workers with at least secondary education. Table 5.3 reports simple probit estimations relating the increase in the share of skilled workers and workers with at least secondary education to a set of explanatory variables as well as region dummies. In both specifications, we find that the coefficient on the state ownership was negative and significant. Having some foreign ownership share enters positively but insignificantly. The restructuring variable – an index of actions weighted by

Table 5.3   Changes in skill shares, 1999–2002

	Probit Estimation	
	Increasing share of skilled workers	Increasing share of workers with at least secondary education
State Ownership	−0.503(0.061)***	−0.472(0.069)***
Log employment	0.161(0.013)***	0.178(0.147)***
Foreign ownership share	−0.001(0.001)	0.001(0.001)
Restructuring index	0.092(0.011)***	0.104(0.011)***
Services sector	−0.043(0.042)	0.049(0.046)
Decreasing unskilled share	0.295(0.047)***	−0.008(0.052)
Region dummies	√	√
N	4372	4371

Note: Standard errors in brackets: *** significant at 1 per cent level.
Source: Business Environment and Economic Performance Survey, 2002 round.

perceived importance – is positive and highly significant in both equations. The size of the firm – as measured by employment – enters positively and significantly. In sum, the evidence from the survey suggests that there has been widespread up-skilling in firms and that this has been true across the different regions. It appears to be positively associated with restructuring. It also appears more pronounced in firms experiencing increased sales.

In addition to the BEEPS, a dataset collected by the EBRD allows a more quantitative and detailed look at the changing structure of skills and work.[5] A survey of 921 firms in the three countries – Hungary, Romania and Russia – was implemented in mid-2000. For each country, the sample was stratified both by employment size and sector. Farms and rural firms were excluded from the sample. Sampling occurred over a wide regional base. In Russia, firms were interviewed in 25 oblasts or regions, in Romania in eight regions and in Hungary in six districts. For the majority of the quantitative questions, the reference period covered the period from 1997 to 2000 thereby yielding a maximum of four data points. With restructuring and reallocation of resources, there has obviously been large-scale job destruction. While this has affected all skill types, it appears that it has fallen disproportionately on the relatively unskilled. Further, with regard to the demand for skills, the shift towards the employment of educated white-collar workers has been a marked feature in all three countries. Firms with new vintage capital and relatively high ICT adoption had notably larger net job creation rates for more educated workers. Table 5.4 provides some measure of the net changes in employment disaggregated by skill and educational types. It shows unequivocally that the biggest net losers in terms of employment have been manual/low education categories. There has been an equally

Table 5.4 The net relative change of employment 1997–2000: Hungary, Romania and Russia (net change as a percentage of the mid-period stock)

Education:	Primary	Vocational	Secondary	Higher	Total
Hungary					
Unskilled blue collar	−7.6	19.2	14.4		−1.7
Skilled blue collar	−9.7	−4.0	9.3		−1.7
White collar	−41.3	7.7	4.3	8.7	4.8
Manager		−9.8	1.6	4.9	2.0
Total	−8.2	−1.0	6.3	6.6	−0.4
Romania					
Unskilled blue collar	−53.5	12.6	45.9		−39.1
Skilled blue collar	−22.0	−20.0	6.4	−1.4	−10.4
White collar	−71.9	−20.4	−9.1	6.1	−3.5
Manager			−9.3	15.3	12.8
Total	−35.3	−19.5	2.1	8.0	−9.3
Russia					
Unskilled blue collar	−14.1	−19.8	−10.8	1.4	−11.7
Skilled blue collar	−12.0	8.5	3.0	9.7	2.8
White collar	3.6	−0.5	11.0	9.4	6.1
Manager	−34.1	−4.5	−11.6	6.0	1.5
Total	−12.7	2.9	1.9	7.6	1.0

Source: EBRD Survey.

unambiguous shift from less to more educated blue-collar workers. Further, the presence of education-specific wage differentials within blue-collar skill grades also suggests that the skill content of blue-collar work has itself been changing substantially. This transformation seems to be as important as the increased bias toward employment of more highly educated workers. There is also the issue of the role of within and intra-firm effects. Table 5.5 provides three measures: (1) overall: the sum of net changes/stock; (2) firm-specific: the sum of firm-specific net changes/stock; and (3) intra-firm: the sum of

Table 5.5 Net rates of employment change by education category

	Hungary			Romania			Russia		
	Overall	Firm-specific	Intra-firm	Overall	Firm-specific	Intra-firm	Overall	Firm-specific	Intra-firm
Primary	−8.2	−3.6	−4.6	−35.3	−22.9	−12.4	−12.7	−7.7	−5.0
Vocational	−1.0	−5.8	4.8	−19.5	−28.3	8.8	2.9	−3.9	6.8
Secondary	6.3	2.7	9.0	2.1	−15.1	17.2	1.9	−6.0	7.9
Higher	6.6	7.1	−0.5	8.0	−15.7	23.7	7.6	−4.9	12.5

Source: EBRD Survey.

skill-specific, intra-firm changes/stock. These are calculated as follows. The firm-specific change of employment (n) of a given educational group is defined as $-\Delta n^F = n^0(N^1/N^0) - n^0$, where N stands for total employment in the firm. This is the change that would have occurred in the case of skill-neutral expansion or contraction. Intra-firm, skill-specific change is defined as $\Delta n^I = \Delta n - \Delta n^F$. The overall or net measure is the sum of net changes/stock.

Table 5.5 demonstrates very clearly that workers with low education are at far higher risk of job loss not only because their firms are likely to contract, but because intra-firm demand has also been biased against them. For both Romania and Russia all groups would have lost in the case of skill-neutral changes of employment but skill-specific changes maintained a strong relative demand for highly educated workers. However, in Hungary growing demand for highly educated workers was fully explained by the skill-neutral expansion of firms employing high-skilled workers.

The change in the demand for skills emerging from the analysis of these three countries carries some important, broader implications.

- Workers with limited education have lost their jobs disproportionately and their relative wages have also been falling.
- This is not just about the elimination of labor hoarding. New firms and sectors have also, in the net, destroyed rather than created low-skill jobs.
- There have been clear shifts from the employment of relatively low to high-educated labor within the blue-collar category.
- These findings point to a bleak future for the employment prospects of those with low skills or education. While incentive problems may be a serious part of the unemployment problem in this segment of the labor market, demand-side developments look to be critical.
- Further, cross-country evidence on the evolution of educational spending since the start of transition shows that most countries have experienced substantial declines in education spending with associated falls in the quality of educational services.

Additional detailed evidence that looks at the evolution of employment among workers with low education is also available for Hungary. Kollo (2006a) shows that while high-skilled employment was stabilized at levels comparable to OECD means, it has been the employment of low-skilled labor that has suffered. In Hungary, the employment ratios of people with primary education fell by two-digit percentage after 1995 at a time when employment of this category was actually growing slightly in the OECD and when the worst of the initial recession was passed. What appears to have happened is that less-educated workers have been effectively excluded from work through skill-biased technological change and the substitution of workers with primary education by those with more education.

These findings have a number of wider implications. They suggest, inter alia, that aside from raising the share of resources devoted to education, there is a need to change the content of education in the transition countries. In particular, the reform of vocational training and certification and the relationship with other educational streams remains a priority. Without such initiatives, the longer-run implications for employment and inequality will be adverse. For example, evidence from the OECD suggests that the diffusion of a GPT has been associated with significant increase in pre-tax earning inequality. The change can be broken down into three main strands: (a) an increase in educational wage differences; (b) an increase in age related wage differences; and (c) an increase in within-group wage inequality. For the transition countries, it appears that there has been some shift in relative wages in favor of the skilled. In principle, this could be consistent with both an increase in within-industry earnings inequality and between-industry inequality. There are also good reasons for supposing that the diffusion of a GPT (within and between firms/sectors as well as countries) is unlikely to be linear on account of strategic complementarities, social learning and so on. Different speeds of adoption – allied to adaptability constraints on the part of workers (for example, through labor-market frictions or inadequacy of training, etc.) – can result in a technological gap between new technology and old technology sectors. The impact on wage inequality will critically depend on the ability to move from the old to the new technology and the extent to which that ability is constrained. For example, an adverse shock to the educational system – as in many transition countries – will likely tighten any adaptability constraint, reducing the share of workers who can move to the new technology and raising the equilibrium level of within-cohort inequality.[6]

5.4 Supply of labor: how constrained are firms?

Given the apparent shortcoming in the education systems of the transition countries, what have been the consequences for firms? From the firm perspective, a key consideration is the availability of appropriate skills. For example, skills imbalances may be present in the labor market, not least because of workers' lack of adaptability, lack of knowledge of information technology (IT) and other inadequacies of the educational systems. Table 5.6 allows a better understanding of whether this is indeed the case in Russia, while also permitting comparison with two other transition countries, Hungary and Romania. The responses are also drawn from the EBRD survey of skills in three countries. For each country, responses to whether the availability of types of labor or particular skills was a barrier to growth of the firm are given. These are then related to a restructuring index constructed for each firm.[7]

Table 5.6 The perceived availability of labor as an obstacle to growth: Hungary, Romania and Russia, 2002

	Hungary	Romania	Russia
Availability of unskilled labor			
1 – is not an obstacle	71.19	91.35	79.60
2	11.26	6.92	16.39
3	10.93	1.38	3.68
4 – is a major obstacle	6.62	0.35	0.33
Total	100.00	100.00	100.00
Mean score	1.53	1.11	1.25
Effect of the restructuring index[a]	0.44	−0.06	0.01
	(2.8)	(0.3)	(0.1)
Availability of skilled labor			
1 – is not an obstacle	47.35	67.91	43.48
2	7.28	9.12	24.75
3	16.23	11.82	21.74
4 – is a major obstacle	29.14	11.15	10.03
Total	100.00	100.00	100.00
Mean score	2.27	1.66	1.25
Effect of the restructuring index	0.40	0.29	0.10
	(2.9)	(2.2)	(0.5)
Workers adaptability			
1 – is not an obstacle	45.03	51.01	56.19
2	18.87	21.28	32.11
3	23.18	18.92	9.70
4 – is a major obstacle	12.91	8.78	2.01
Total	100.00	100.00	100.00
Mean score	2.03	1.86	1.58
Effect of the restructuring index	0.44	0.21	0.19
	(3.9)	(1.7)	(0.7)
Workers IT knowledge			
1 – is not an obstacle	49.83	43.24	53.51
2	18.94	26.69	29.77
3	20.27	21.96	15.05
4 – is a major obstacle	10.96	8.11	1.67
Total	100.00	100.00	100.00
Mean score	1.92	1.94	1.64
Effect of the restructuring index	0.62	0.43	0.51
	(4.5)	(3.5)	(2.0)

a – Coefficients and Z-values from univariate ordered probits with the scores (1,2,3,4) on the left hand and a restructuring index on the right hand.
Source: EBRD Survey.

In all three countries, in the case of unskilled labor there is little evidence of problems of availability. However, the availability of skilled labor was viewed as a moderate or major problem (Responses 3 and 4) by around a third of Russian firms, as against 45 per cent of Hungarian firms and 23 per cent of

Romanian firms. There was, however, no significant relationship with the restructuring measure in Russia, unlike in Hungary or Romania. In the latter two, perceived shortages of skilled workers were positively related to restructuring in the firm, suggesting that it is better firms that perceive or experience such shortages. With respect to worker adaptability, it is interesting to note that over 35 per cent of Hungarian firms viewed this as a significant problem, a share notably higher than in either Romania or Russia. This clearly points to some of the adverse consequences of an educational system that was historically quite narrow in terms of the skills it imparted, particularly for those in vocational streams. In terms of IT knowledge, around 30 per cent of both Hungarian and Romanian firms viewed this as a moderate or major obstacle. In sum, the evidence does suggest that in the more advanced reform country – Hungary – firms have found difficulty in securing the services of skilled workers with appropriate skills.

The descriptive statistics of the perceptions data contained in Table 5.6 while suggestive, do not allow for identifying the actual impact on firm performance. To do that requires recourse to another dataset. The Business Environment and Enterprise Performance Survey (BEEPS) for 2005 has information not only on performance variables but also on perceived constraints, including for skills. The BEEPS data are stratified random samples of firms. With regard to ownership, most firms were privatized or had always been private from the start of their operations. However, quota sampling was imposed for foreign-owned companies (defined as having a foreign stake of at least 50 per cent) and state-owned companies (defined as the state owning more than 50 per cent). These quotas were set at 10 per cent of the total sample for each category. The distribution of the sample between manufacturing and service sectors was determined according to these sectors' relative contribution to GDP in each country. Firms that operated in sectors subject to government price regulation and prudential supervision, such as banking, electric power, rail transport, and water were excluded from the sample. As regards size, firms that had 10,000 employees or more were excluded from the sample, as were firms that had started operations in 2002, 2003 or 2004. Around 90 per cent of the BEEPS sample in 2005 comprised small and medium enterprises. The 2005 round covered nearly 9100 firms in 26 transition countries.

Table 5.7 provides results from a set of estimations relating performance – as measured by TFP, value added or labor productivity – to factors, education shares and two constraints terms. The first constraints term measures how problematic the perceived constraint was to the firm with respect to the growth of the business. Rather than using individual responses – given likely endogeneity – average responses at the two-digit industry level by year and country are used. The same procedure is used for the second constraints term which is an average of a range of other constraints, including corruption, taxation and labor regulation. For the education variables, lagged values for

Table 5.7   Productivity estimates

	(1) Total Factor Productivity (Logs)	(2) Value Added (Logs)	(3) Labor Productivity (Logs)
Log employment	0.202***	0.908***	−0.074***
	(0.010)	(0.018)	(0.013)
Log fixed assets	0.015***	0.114***	0.132***
	(0.003)	(0.015)	(0.019)
Log material inputs	0.787***		
	(0.010)		
Skills constraint	−0.005	−0.017	−0.038
	(0.011)	(0.052)	(0.061)
Other constraints (mean)	0.015	0.048	0.065
	(0.015)	(0.062)	(0.089)
Log education – some university	0.114***	0.611***	0.675***
	(0.029)	(0.087)	(0.099)
Log education – secondary	0.069*	0.276***	0.236*
	(0.034)	(0.096)	(0.120)
Log education – vocational	0.057*	0.227**	0.121
	(0.031)	(0.099)	(0.117)
Observations	4062	3912	4094
R-squared	0.99	0.89	0.64

Note: Robust standard errors in parentheses; *significant at 10%; **significant at 5%; ***significant at 1%.
Source: Business Environment and Economic Performance Survey, 2005 round.

2002 are applied. In addition, sector and country dummies are used in the estimation. Table 5.7 shows that the education shares variables enter positively and mostly significantly. Interestingly, the coefficients on the higher skill categories – university and secondary – are larger than for vocational. The omitted variable is primary education. With respect to the constraints variables, the skills availability term enters consistently negatively. However, the coefficient is never significant. In short, this evidence suggests a strong link from education shares to performance. There is some limited evidence that skill constraints may exert an adverse impact on performance. However, the fact that the coefficient is insignificant may suggest that firms have been able to deal with such constraints by strategies involving shifts in factor shares as well as in terms of the educational structure of employment. Certainly, the evidence from unemployment and participation data indicates that workers with low educational attainment have disproportionately lost their jobs as well as not being hired.

5.5   Conclusion

For transition countries the legacy of central planning in terms of human capital appears to be less positive than had been supposed. What emerges is that not only was the quality of education generally lower than many assumed – at least when using OECD countries as the benchmark – but that the ability to improve the quality of education over time has been relatively poor. Many countries have indeed reduced public spending on education while failing to address the persistent problems connected with curricula, management and pricing of educational services. In particular, the problem of low quality and overly-specific vocational education – hence, low adaptability – has persisted, especially – but not exclusively – in the CIS countries.

The paper has also argued that – in common with the advanced market economies – there has been a secular shift in relative labor demand away from unskilled labor. This appears to have been driven largely by technology. The resulting skill bias has had important ramifications for those with low skills as well as in terms of wage inequality. Not only do low-skill categories have relatively low employment rates but they also have far higher probabilities of being in unemployment than other groups. Indeed, it seems that much of the persistence of high unemployment in many transition countries can be traced to this weak ability to match low-skill workers to jobs.

Finally, firm-level perceptions evidence suggests that the availability of appropriate skills is indeed viewed as a problem – particularly in the more advanced reformers, such as Hungary. Moreover, it seems likely that such constraints exert a negative impact on firm performance. The same estimations also show that the level of productivity tends to be positively and significantly associated with the share of more skilled workers in the firm. In sum, the combination of a secular shift in technology associated with higher skill requirements, the legacy of the educational systems and their faltering reform has had severely adverse consequences for the employment prospects of the low-skilled.

Notes

1. OECD (2003).
2. The share of 20–24 year-olds in education in Hungary, Poland, Czech Republic and Slovakia continued to be relatively low in 2001 (see OECD, 2003).
3. For a more extended discussion of the issue, see Commander *et al.* (2005) and Kollo (2006a,b).
4. Unfortunately, the survey does not provide information on the change in employment mix by education.
5. This section draws on Commander and Kollo (2007).
6. See Aghion and Commander (1999).

7. The index was defined as the first principal component of ten variables indicating changes in technology, networks and types of investment that might have affected labor use.

References

Aghion, P. and S. Commander (1999) 'On the dynamics of inequality in the transition', *Economics of Transition*, 7 (2), 275–98.

Bassanini, A. and S. Scarpetta (2001) 'The drivers of growth in the OECD countries: empirical analysis on panel data', *OECD Economic Review*, 33 (11).

Benhabib, J. and M. Spiegel (1994) 'The role of human capital in economic development: evidence from aggregate cross-country data', *Journal of Monetary Economics*, 34(2), 143–73.

Dowrick, S. (2002) *The Contribution of Innovation and Education to Economic Growth*, paper presented at Melbourne Institute Economic and Social Outlook Conference, April, mimeo.

Commander, S. and J. Kollo (2007) 'The changing demand for skills: evidence from the transition', *Economics of Transition*, forthcoming.

Commander, S., J. Kollo and A. Tolstopiatenko (2005) *Explaining Unemployment and its Persistence in the Transition Countries: Some Conjectures* (London: London Business School), mimeo.

IALS (International Adult Literacy Study) (1998) OECD and Statistics, Canada.

Kollo, J. (2006a) *Workplace Literacy Requirements and Unskilled Employment in East-Central and Western Europe: Evidence from the International Adult Literacy Survey* (Budapest: Institute of Economics), mimeo.

Kollo, J. (2006b) *Effects of Upskilling Versus Crowding-out on the Employment of Primary Degree Holders – Evidence from Hungary* (Budapest: Institute of Economics), mimeo.

OECD (2003) *Education at a Glance* (Paris: OECD).

PIRLS (Progress in International Reading Literacy) (2002) IEA and Boston College.

PISA (Programme for International Student Assessment) (2000) OECD.

6
Financial Transition in Central and Eastern Europe. A Note

Marcello de Cecco

6.1 Introduction

The 5 years following the terrorist attack on the World Trade Center have witnessed what may be called the initiation and pursuit of a war-time monetary policy on the part of the main world monetary authorities, in particular those of the United States (US), Japan and the European Monetary Union (EMU). The very day the terrorist attack was perpetrated, the Federal Reserve put into action a strategy of flooding markets with very cheap liquidity, and persevered in it for almost 5 years, in order to allay any fear of implosion of the US and the international financial and monetary system. The Central Bank of Japan and the European Central Bank (ECB) followed suit. This created extremely expansionary conditions from which the US and other Pacific Basin countries particularly benefited. The easy money atmosphere, however, especially helped other countries too, like those of Latin America, and the ones which are now called 'New Europe', the transition economies of Central and Eastern Europe (CEE; in what follows I do not include the former Soviet Union countries in my definition of CEE).

Their transition from Socialism to Capitalism had taken place initially in the fast growth atmosphere of the 1990s, including, for the CEE area, the early economic consequences of German re-unification. When that faded, the easy money policy which began in September 2001 intervened and the joint effect of the two phenomena allowed the countries of CEE to get back into the fold of capitalism without paying too high a price for the rather serious mistakes many of them had made in sequencing transition.

Looking at the banking scene in CEE today we would not imagine that about a decade ago many CEE countries were plagued with problems stemming from excessively close relations between banks and industry, which were the result of the way the so-called two-tier banking systems had been carved out of the socialist monobank system.

In the CEE area today, there is an absolute prevalence of private banks. Banking markets in CEE countries are dominated by foreign-owned banks which in the majority of countries own more than 75 per cent of total banking assets. In some countries, like the Czech republic and others, this rises to 90 per cent and over. Yet, only 10 years ago this phenomenon was still in its early infancy, and few guessed it would receive a boost strong enough to bring about the present-day situation in the following 5 years. In fact, cross border mergers and acquisitions involving CEE banks as targets began in earnest between around 1997 and surged until 2001, with a peak in 1999 and 2000. Today, Western, especially EU, banks can be said to have almost completely overhauled the very large chunk of CEE banking system they now own.

If we compare foreign-owned banks in that area with banks in the EU, the formers' balance sheets do not appear to be of inferior quality. Most standard indicators of banking efficiency give very similar readings in the two areas. Credit to firms seems to have lost importance in both areas with respect to credit to individuals and families, especially under the form of house financing mortgages. Satisfactory profit margins, in the CEE countries, are still achieved mainly by charging private borrowers interest rates that are much higher than those bank customers are charged in Western Europe, although most of this differential is explained by higher country risk. In spite of its rapid growth the banking market is still very small in CEE countries, if compared to that of Western Europe. It is much smaller, by a factor of four, than the share of European GNP that CEE countries represent today (2 per cent against 8 per cent). Yet, the overall picture the CEE credit market presents today is a healthy one.

In 1987, when socialist countries in CEE were still trying to reform their economic and political systems, but still fully within the context of the planned economy, I helped Mario Nuti finance a joint World Bank European University Institute (EUI) conference on the reform of socialist financial systems. We were both still at the EUI, he as a full-time professor while I, having done my stint already, lingered on, in a part-time capacity, to finish some research projects I had initiated there. I directed some of my residual research funds towards the organization of the conference.

The book that came out of it is,[1] in my opinion, a fascinating document to read. It shows what in 1987 the profession thought the future of socialist countries would be, only 2 years before the Berlin Wall actually fell and the postwar world abruptly ended. We did not show much explicit foreboding of the sudden collapse that was soon to come about.

At that conference I presented a paper on modes of financial development, one of my favorite subjects. It dealt with the capitalist economy. The 1980s had been a decade of slow growth in the US and the United Kingdom (UK), and economists and politicians, in both those countries, were busy studying what was considered the more successful financial model, prevailing in countries like Germany and Japan. As late as 1992, President Clinton's electoral platform contained explicit references to the continental European model as one worth imitating on the part of the US to get out of its low-growth performance. In my paper I tried to show the economic consequences of financial systems based on universal banks. One of the points I made – as I will try to show in the following pages – was to be of relevance in the transition process, which had not yet started and which – I repeat – we did not expect to happen so soon and so fast and to take the course it did, from Socialism back to full-fledged Capitalism.

In short, the point I made in the paper was that universal banks, far from being a limited species of financial system, only successful in Japan and Germany, were going to prevail in the US and UK too. They had, after all, characterized the US financial system before the crisis of the early 1930s and were forcibly repressed by legislation which prevented their reappearance until the late 1990s. They had already reappeared, nevertheless, as a natural consequence of banking concentration in the UK, and I predicted that the trend towards concentration would lead to their reappearance in the US, too.

Large international financial markets, like the Euro-dollar market, I maintained, had been the direct consequence of US legislation trying to prevent the further growth of large commercial banks in the US mainland and to perpetuate the banking localism which had been inflicted on the US by almost a century of legislation.

If, as it seemed, universal banking was proving to be the rule rather than the exception, in most developed countries, it would be useful to spell out – so my reasoning went – what its prevalence would mean for financial markets, for industry and for central banks.

The most important consequence was that the special relationship which universal banks established and maintained with large-scale industry wherever they prevailed meant a substantial softening of budget constraints for industry, as banks would provide their industrial clients with the 'patient money' necessary to finance new capacity through fixed investment. This made the emergence of excess capacity very likely in the countries where universal banks prevailed; a phenomenon which would entail difficulties for both banks and industry unless some of the additional production generated by excess capacity would be absorbed by countries where universal banks had not created a similar problem.

A financial system where universal banks prevailed also required, to be stable, that its central bank would be prepared to provide universal banks with enough liquidity to prevent firms from becoming insolvent, when demand for their products flagged or new fixed investment temporarily created excess capacity. A universal bank system thus required either that individual banks be equipped with vast branch networks to provide them with enough liquidity at all times or that the central bank be prepared to act quite often as lender of last resort, in cases like the ones I just quoted.

Alternatively, the umbilical cord tying large-scale industrial firms to banks should be cut and firms compelled to go to the market to look for investment finance, in order to permanently relieve bank balance sheets of long-term industrial loans, more akin to equity than to credit.

As I read what I wrote in 1987, it occurred to me that it could also be used to understand financial transition in former socialist countries. What follows here is an attempt to do that. Like most of what I have written, it will take the form more of sketches than of systematic analysis. Some of my friends find this method rather irritating. I know Mario Nuti is not one of them. He has always treated my sketches with more benevolence than they deserve. That is why I dare to contribute what follows to a Festschrift in his honor.

6.2   Money and banking under socialism

The sequencing of transition from actual socialist banking systems as they existed in CEE countries in the 1980s followed a common pattern. A small digression to briefly recall what was the role of money and banking under socialism may be useful at this point.

After the Bolshevik Revolution, it was Lenin's intention to establish a type of state capitalism largely borrowed from what he thought to be the most advanced form of capitalism, which had come about in Germany. Large industrial trusts were formed in the Soviet Union in the 1920s, owned by banks, which in turn were owned by the State. This mimicked the German system, with the State replacing banks at the head of the corporate ownership and governance structure. Banks were, like in Germany, assigned the role of governing the production trusts. This was the NEP, to which all reform-minded but still orthodox communists in Gorbachev's Russia dreamed of going back to. It was a phase of socialist development considered positively and favorably, if compared with the Physical Planning phase which replaced it in Stalin's time and at his behest.

In the latter phase, the role of money and banks was reduced almost to insignificance. Banks were still linked to industry, but their only task was to provide the various plants with the funds necessary to mobilize the resources assigned to the banks by the Plan. All the functions that banking performed vis-à-vis production were concentrated in the central bank, thus giving rise to the monobank system (an expression coined by George Garvy and used universally ever since). A completely separate circuit was established to pay wages in currency. Ideally, the supply of consumer goods, multiplied by their prices, had to be just equal to the total wage-fund paid to the workers. Every now and again, signally in times of economic pressure, workers would receive higher money wages, while consumer goods did not increase, They would be then allowed to accumulate money savings at the Sberbank (or its equivalent in other socialist countries). Only in Poland and Hungary, the more reform-minded countries, did the Savings banks give housing loans to individuals, at very low interest rates.

Savings were thus used to accommodate repressed inflation when it was deemed necessary not to decrease money wages nor to raise prices to accommodate shortfalls in production.

The only sector of banking that vaguely resembled Western banking was the one concerned with foreign-trade financing. This was because the people working in it had to learn Western banking methods to sell exports and buy imports. The segregation of this sector from the rest of Socialist banking prevented this knowledge from spreading to other parts of the banking system. Domestic trade, therefore, remained wed to central planning, with banks playing the part of socialist accountants. They enforced the practical application of 'planning by the Ruble', but did not use any of the financial instruments which in the West are employed to finance domestic trade. The central bank played the part of clearing house for all the paper equivalents of physical balances which moved through the system from plant to plant. This total equivalence between physical balances and their paper representations suggested the comparison between socialist banking and the 'real bills doctrine'. It was a completely idle comparison, however, as real bills moved in actual markets and received their valuation in them. The paper equivalents of physical balances, on the contrary, were shuffled about by so-called bankers at values which not only were fixed, but fixed by the Central Planning Office.

6.3   Money and banking in socialist reforms

As Kornai warned us several years ago, there is a great danger implicit in the nominal resemblance of socialist institutions to capitalist ones. The fact that banks and markets had existed in Tsarist Russia and that Lenin wanted to establish bank-dominated German-style capitalism in the USSR, with the variant of state ownership, meant that entities called banks and central banks remained in operation even after the transition to physical planning. Thus, whenever the socialist countries' political authorities agreed to some measure of reform and liberalization, bankers and central bankers would initiate contacts with bankers and central bankers in the West. Those contacts would lead some Western bankers to conclude that they were dealing with people involved in a type of profession not too different from their own, as if they had been doctors or mathematicians, or military officers. This was however completely removed from reality, as we have already noted.

When Socialism tried to reform itself, before its final demise, Soviet and CEE bankers and central bankers were immediately marked for a much bigger role. They were told to perform functions similar to those their namesakes perform in Western economies. Accordingly, the separation of the central bank from commercial banks began to take shape in several socialist countries, giving place to the so-called two-tier banking systems. But the newly created commercial banks could in no way refuse to give credit to firms.

Credit was administered according to the credit plan which accompanied the cash plan and the material balances plan. The accumulation points of the economy were thus still determined by the planning authority and the attempt to create a central bank and banks similar to the western ones only resulted in further confusion in the division of functions in the socialist economies. The new monetary and banking system could be seen as an exercise in superstructure building, which left the structure of governance of the socialist economy largely intact. Since firms could not go bankrupt, banks had no reason to grade loans according to relative risk and to either ration credit or to make it more expensive accordingly. Firms were, on the other hand, in no way liquidity constrained. Late payments would certainly arrive at some date, and there was even no reason to delay payments, if receipts were delayed. Time was not money even in the late socialist financial system.

The transition process of the former socialist countries did not take place 'in vacuo'. Powerful forces of imitation were present in the transition countries themselves. Moreover, most developed countries and international economic institutions soon got busy giving advice to them.

Transition took place not as an ungoverned phenomenon but, as it were, from top to bottom and it was thus likely that model-copying would occur. Institutions were in fact established more because they seemed to be essential to the functioning of systems that were the object of imitation than because an immediate need for them was felt in the transition countries. This was not an unknown phenomenon. It seemed to be a perquisite of the whole modernization process, starting with the Navigation Act of Queen Elisabeth the First, and proceeding with the unification of Italy and Germany, and the spread of modernization to the Third World.

We must, however, heed Kornai's warning: when importing an institution the danger exists of mixing up causes with consequences, as well as only reproducing the outward appearances of that institution.

A further problem is that of 'appropriate technology'. Given the fact that developed countries went through various stages in their growth, does it follow from it that it was necessary to reproduce the same stages in succession in the transition countries? Might not transition countries take some short cuts?

Above all, the nonuniqueness of the financial growth path in capitalist countries, on which I dwelt in my 1987 paper, should have been kept in mind, when transition countries went over developed countries' financial experiences with the intention of borrowing from them.

The heterogeneity of financial development paths presented a problem. Transition countries might try to get their new financial systems as it were 'à la carte'. They could and did easily fall prey to the desire to get the best, taking institutions from countries, without paying enough attention to the mutual compatibility of different institutions, when taken out of their natural context.

Worse, it often happened that transition countries just took what help was offered to them. And the 'missionaries' from some national and international financial institutions were generous with human and financial resources.

To be more to the point, if a transition country wanted to borrow institutions judging by their superficially successful appearance and by their world renown, it would 'import' large universal banks from Germany, the Stock Exchange and Mutual Funds from Britain or the US, and the central bank again from Germany. Legislation would accordingly be passed to give a very high level of independence from political power to the central bank, to encourage citizens to own shares, to license mutual funds and to start up a stock exchange overseen by some equivalent of the US SEC. Finally, a banking law would be passed allowing banks to engage in all sorts of banking business, like German universal banks did. In many transition countries, all these laws were actually promulgated.

In what follows I shall consider the implications of mutually inconsistent institutions being set up, because of imitation or unsound foreign consulting, focusing on the implications of the choice of traditional universal banking for central banking.

6.4   Late socialist financial reforms

Before doing that, however, it might be useful to retrace the last steps socialist reformers trod in the field of financial engineering. Late socialist financial reforms usually split the monobank into multiple self-styled 'commercial banks'. In some cases this was done several years before the demise of Socialism, but the reconstruction of true capitalist financial systems was in most cases hindered rather than helped by these late socialist reforms. The financial structure of CEE countries was transformed into a needlessly more intricate one which only mimicked a capitalist financial structure. While institutions multiplied, their management philosophy did not seem to change appreciably. To many observers, the financial engineering abilities displayed by last generation socialist reformers seemed directed more than anything else at providing some sort of respite from growing macroeconomic imbalances which beleaguered their systems. In particular, while banking reforms looked more or less cosmetic in their nature, the need to find some remedy to supply constraints induced socialist authorities to resort to the printing press to provide more money, which was used to calm the growing restlessness of workers. On the eve of socialism's demise, therefore, a considerable monetization of socialist economies had occurred, which coexisted with the essentially unchanged production and distribution systems. This monetary overhang could have been absorbed by a change of currency, as many countries, including Stalin's USSR and Germany, had done just after the end of World War II. It could be more or less confiscatory in nature according to political will. Alternatively, a post-socialist government with no direct ties to its predecessors could unleash open inflation by freeing prices, as the Italian post-fascist government had done in 1946–47, before administering traditional monetary stabilization and devaluation.

The skewed monetization of the economy had in any case created a contradiction with the planned economy. Individuals had been given the chance of accumulating monetary inventories. Now the authorities had to decide whether to confiscate them and go back to full-fledged physical planning or to truly monetize the production process and give up central planning in favor of decentralized price-setting and accumulation by firms.

Barring a return to central planning, which no one had the political power to enforce, all solutions implied some form of financial liberalization, in order to smooth the macroeconomic imbalance created by monetization not accompanied by removal of supply constraints. Most experts knew, however, that freeing prices would have solved the overhang problem for one period only, as firms which found themselves in credit to the rest of the economy would have been severely harmed by price liberalization, in many cases so severely as to become insolvent. Meanwhile, the allocative system would remain at least partially in bureaucratic hands, as even the newly created 'ersatz' commercial banks could not invent out of the blue a resource allocation system not based on queues and rationing.

Moreover, the long-term relationships, forged by the monobank with enterprises under socialism, would not be swept away just because the monobank had been split into several commercial banks. Some of the old monobankers had been assigned as personnel to the new commercial banks, which had been created either on regional or sectoral lines of division. They would as a matter of course try to maintain the old links they had formed with firms' managers, and the latter would try to hold on to them even more.

The persistence of old managerial ways both in newly created banks and in reformed enterprises thus gave very little chance of success to a liberalization policy based on an open inflation followed by stabilization through budgetary and banking squeezes and devaluation. Freeing prices would have not meant higher supply of commodities, as managers, being monopolists and supply-constrained by lack of inputs and credit, would have reacted as medieval guild members had, by producing less while raising prices to obtain an unproblematic increase in total revenues. Commercial banks could not be relied upon to administer a credit squeeze by saving the most efficient firms while letting the worse ones go under. Moreover, pre-existing credit–debt relations not at all based on relative efficiency made price liberalization totally haphazard as a selector of efficient firms.

The money overhang could have been disposed of by selling state-owned houses to their own occupants. This was either not done or done too late, thus losing a chance to give the new system a solid base of owner occupiers, a social and economic stabilizer common to all developed countries, as house ownership absorbs the largest part of family savings for most income categories.

Had that been done, further monetization of the economy would have been then possible, by letting the cash circuit and the credit circuit of the old financial system overlap. When the two monetary circuits were allowed to overlap, it was essential to make sure that cash would function as an even keel for the new monetary and financial system. There was a risk that the old managers, in financial, industrial and commercial institutions, would operate the new cash economy as they had operated the old credit economy, that is by building on the available amount of cash, a credit structure exactly necessary for the maintenance of the production status quo. This would have meant complete failure of both price and financial liberalization.

The solution was therefore attempted to keep cash separate from credit but to extend cash transactions to cover many of the transactions where credit was hitherto used. This ought to have kept repressed inflation from becoming open. But the commercial and industrial firms reacted to cash starvation by developing trade credit. As a result, credit migrated from the banking system to the enterprise system. The early exercise of going from an economy with a passive financial system to one with active banks thus ended up with credit migrating from banks to firms and general deflation.

In addition, the sequencing of financial system reforms saw, in the large majority of cases in CEE, new central bank laws being passed very early in the transition process, that is to say between 1991 and 1992. The monobank had been a kind of central bank, so it was easy to start from what already existed. In addition, open inflation was the prime threat of early transition, and reining in the actions of those who controlled the money supply was taken to be of paramount importance.

A careful study of these laws shows how most of them took the Bundesbank as their ideal type. The independence of the central bank from political power was therefore powerfully asserted, and its main feature was, as could be expected, that the central bank could not directly provide the government with financial resources.

As I noted earlier, the *à la carte* reform process thus unfolded as expected, and yielded the consequences which were feared. Financial reform preceded reform of the productive sector. Within this financial reform, the central bank was the first to be westernized, often with the help of western advisors. It will be fascinating, when archival sources covering those years become available, to reconstruct the details of this process, specifying the role of foreign advisers, as some of us have already done for the interwar period in CEE. Until then (and I will not be there to take part in the research effort), we have to be content with studying the visible process, and its results. The establishment of a westernized central bank, whose Law, however, was generally much stronger on independence than on banking supervision, preceded other parts of the financial system's reform. It was rapidly followed by the creation of pseudo-universal banks, which resembled the German original only because of their close links to industrial firms. Attempts to transform the large industrial kombinats of Socialism into firms resembling their western counterparts began soon after that, but had scant success, because they involved rationalization and that meant massive open unemployment, which was still a political dynamite.

The independent central bank which resulted from reform was thus prevented from providing the government with new finance, while banks and firms coexisted uneasily, each of them really unable to match its new western style clothes with genuinely western behavior. Deflation was the obvious result of this early bungled attempt to reform the financial system.

6.5   Money and banking reforms in later transition

The ultimate way out has been for both finance and industry to follow what at the start was considered an unicum, economic and financial reform in what had been the DDR. It had been considered as an unicum because something which was thought to be unavailable to other former socialist countries was used: new managers, coming from West Germany, to replace those working in socialist times and take the former DDR back to capitalism. The DDR economic system was destroyed and reconstructed by this army of West German managers, who closed old firms or sold them to mostly West German companies and operated the new ones which emerged from this veritable revolution. West German banks simply went back and reopened their old branches, sometimes even reclaiming the original buildings. The Bundesbank took over the functions of central bank for the new Laender, too. The Deutsche mark became the currency for the whole of re-united Germany.

This process could not be completely repeated in the other CEE countries. However, after early financial reforms not accompanied by industrial reforms ended up in a stalemate and in financial crisis, the large international crisis which raged between 1997 and 1998 precipitated a semi-German solution even in the CEE countries. Commercial banks were privatised, stripped of their bad loans (which were often stored in 'bad banks') and then sold to big western commercial banks. Large companies were also privatized and often sold to foreigners. In the most recent years, moreover, a very impressive process of industrial relocation from Germany to the CEE countries has taken off, which has integrated CEE and German industry to an extent even greater than that which existed in the original pre-1914 version of Mittel Europa or in its forced second coming in the late 1930s and early 1940s. The German relocation example has been followed by other western European countries, like Austria and Italy.

In this process, the use of foreign managers has been massive, even if local managers at lower levels in the hierarchical ladder are much more numerous and in the end essential. What emerges is the failure of financial and industrial transition as a process governed at national level.

6.6 Money and banking in CEE countries, today and tomorrow

Governments and central banks have remained local, nevertheless. Is this going to be in future a source of disequilibrium in CEE economies?

As far as the central bank is concerned, the coincidence of CEE transition with the birth of the European Monetary Union (EMU) and of the Euro has meant that CEE central bankers look to the ECB rather than to the Bundesbank for inspiration and advice. This has, however, not meant as yet a complete alignment of CEE monetary (and exchange rate) policies with that of the ECB. Inflation rates in CEE countries still differ considerably from one another and are often higher than those prevailing in the EMU.

Banking supervision seems to have been, with notable exceptions, superseded as a monetary authorities' problem in CEE. Foreign-owned banks can and do look after themselves and their group headquarters in Western countries take the place of CEE supervisors. As lending rates in CEE are still much higher than in the West, allegedly because of country risk, foreign banks conduct a sort of carry trade between the source of their funds, which is often the international money market, and CEE credit markets. The independent central banks of CEE have thus seen the original contradiction that had resulted from *à la carte* financial reforms, an independent central bank facing a very undercapitalized and fragile group of pseudo-universal banks saddled with liquidity-strapped former socialist firms, resolved by the intervention of foreign ownership in the most important part of the banking system. Central banks can thus play their role as independent wardens of national currencies without having to worry about the consequences their behavior may have on national economies. The CEE banking system's liquidity does not depend on CEE central banks' monetary policies, but on that of the home central banks of the foreign owned banks' group headquarters, which mostly means the ECB's monetary policy.

This is proved by the fact that lending, especially retail lending to families, has increased in CEE countries, in the years since 2002, at much faster rates than deposits have in the same period. Since banking penetration rates are still much lower than in Western Europe, the expectation is that the trend will continue in the near future, barring exogenous or endogenous shocks that might intervene.

It remains to be seen, however, whether banking systems as unbalanced as the CEE ones have recently become, tilted towards lending much more than home deposits growth would warrant, are to be considered to be in a state of dynamic equilibrium. Are they completely similar to regional banking systems? If they are, one has to remember that shifts in loans and deposits between regions are normally much bigger than those occurring between countries because regional factor mobility is higher than that occurring between countries. In other words, if a shift to a more restrictive monetary policy occurs in the EMU, and is followed by a serious decrease in lending in CEE countries, how will the CEE governments react to this sudden dearth of financial resources? Will they take the ensuing fall in aggregate demand as an inevitable fact of life, even if it means large-scale unemployment, while the regional solution, much higher emigration to Western Europe, remains unavailable? We have seen that for new members free labor mobility inside the EU does not mean exactly that. We must also remember that even for old EU members an integrated labor market is by no means a fact of life even today. Perhaps as a consequence of this, new members and new accession countries do not seem at all eager to join the EMU and to adopt the Euro. Obviously, they think that, with almost completely foreign-owned banking systems where banks' loan dynamics far exceeds that of deposits, and with an industrial system mainly producing parts and components for Western European firms, they cannot do without the possibility of devaluing exchange rates if, for instance, reduced lending by foreign-owned banks induces a fall in aggregate demand, in the hope that foreign trade elasticities will be favorable and let them export their goods since they could not export all their unemployed labor to the rest of Europe.

Economists have known for centuries that capital moves much more rapidly than labor and even commodities. This seems to have happened and still to be happening in the transition from Socialism to Capitalism in CEE. The problem, as economists have also known for just as long, is that fast advance also implies the possibility of equally fast retreat. This collides with the difference between international and inter-regional mobility of goods and factors. Recent events in CEE banking and finance have shown how fast the advance can be. Let us hope that we are not to witness an equally fast retreat.

6.7   Financial transition in the interwar period, a reminder

This note ends with a brief comparison of the transition from socialist to capitalist money and finance in CEE with what we may call the transition from Imperial and Global to National capitalist money and finance, which occurred in the 1920s and 1930s in the same area. It is an instructive, if somewhat sobering, comparison.

When the Austrian Russian and German Empires dissolved, during and after the Great War, successor states in Danubian Europe strove to furnish their newly won political independence with what they thought were the necessary instruments of economic sovereignty, national currencies, central banks to govern them, and firms and banks owned by citizens of the new nations. Imperial and regional economic integration, which had proceeded unfettered for close to 30 years, was thus rolled back, and most existing economic institutions, like industrial companies and banks, were subjected to what in Czechoslovakia was called 'nostrification', an expression which became widely used to indicate a process of forced sale of banks and companies operating in a country to its citizens. There was little economic rationale in these changes of ownership, while the political rationale was clear, and nationalist politics was in those decades rampant everywhere in Europe. Successor countries were often very small and made little economic sense. Still, each of them strove to get all the appurtenances of economic power.

The creation of national central banks was deemed to be of prime importance in the sequencing of the transition to national capitalism. This was a feeling shared by both the authorities in the new countries and by monetary and financial experts of the Great Powers. It is fascinating to see how the concept of central bank independence was hatched in the early twenties, as the intellectual product of Montagu Norman's fertile mind. Norman was the powerful governor of the Bank of England, which he steered on, mostly dangerous, courses in the 1920s and 1930s. He thought the gold standard, the international monetary standard which had prevailed in most European countries in the 15 years before 1914, had in the last pre-war years worked against the permanence of Britain at the center of the world financial system. Britain just did not have enough gold to manage the world monetary system before the war, as other fast-growing countries started to accumulate huge gold reserves which they were loath to even temporarily losing, as it implied deflation and credit crunch for their gold-based monetary systems. An unfettered gold market was at the core of the international settlements system centered in London and it was prevented from working properly by national central banks because they would not release again the gold they had accumulated when the Bank of England raised interest rates. After the enormous stock of British foreign investment, which still existed in 1914 and yielded enough income to allow British merchant banks to dominate the new issues markets, had been sold to finance the World War, and most gold had migrated to the US to pay for essential primary commodities and raw material imports, Norman understood a new world monetary system had to be devised, which would allow London to remain the prime financial center of the world, fighting off what New York bankers thought was their city's manifest destiny to replace it. It was in order to achieve that difficult goal that Norman devised what he called independent central banks, to be established in each country. Independence meant freedom from political subjection. Politicians had already shown in the last decade before the war that they could use gold reserves to play power politics. Central bankers had to be insulated from that danger by their legal independence from governments.

Norman, in order to maximize the scant gold reserves present in Europe just after the war, urged on central bankers the need to have exclusive relations with one another. That meant that international payments had to be effected only from one central bank to another, and that central banks should not have branches in foreign financial centers, so that they would not bypass those centers' central banks, dispersing scarce gold through the free market. Norman thus wanted an international reserves circuit to be established among central banks, immune from leakages. New European countries, as well as old ones, had to stabilize their currencies after most of them had adopted paper standards during the war. If they all tried to go back to gold and to do it at the same time, the London free gold market would have to be closed as soon as it was reopened, as the meager gold reserves of the Bank of England would be exhausted in almost no time. Norman thought it essential that the London gold market be re-opened, as this was the only way of getting new gold to be shipped there from producing countries like South Africa. Without new gold flowing to London, the gold market would be totally dominated by the United States, which had accumulated an enormous gold reserve at Fort Knox. The US were as eager to see the world monetary system back on gold as Norman and the British Treasury were eager to see it on what they called the gold exchange standard, a system which had been used to manage the British colonies' monetary systems before the war. The British deluded themselves they would be able to convince France, Italy, Belgium and the successor countries in CEE to go back to convertible currencies in an orderly queue, each of them in turn using the same gold, which they were to borrow to stabilize their currency from countries like Britain, and immediately redeposit in London, or even in Paris, using Sterling or Franc short-term deposits as reserves. The network of independent central banks Norman hoped to establish in Europe would allow currency stabilization to be effected with a minimum of actual gold being used and sterilized in central banks' vaults.

The Bank of England and the Treasury thus developed an articulate strategy to bring the gold exchange standard to life in as many countries as was possible. They used the Economic Section of the League of Nations to effectively promote this scheme and tried first of all to stabilize the currencies of the defeated countries, in order to bring back monetary order in central Europe, because the Allies held sway with those countries' governments and central banks. Thus Austria and Hungary were urged to establish independent central banks and so was Weimar Germany.

The US economic and political authorities were furthering another agenda, one which would promote the return to a full fledged gold standard. If currencies went back to gold with the help of American stabilization loans, they would stabilize their currencies at rates which did not overvalue the dollar excessively. The US agriculture had gotten used to, during the war, producing for the whole western world and farmers in the US tried to keep their produce competitive even after local agriculture started recovering from war dislocation. If the whole of Europe went back to a pure gold standard this would be easier. If Norman and the Treasury, helped along by the League of Nations, succeeded in their attempt to establish the gold exchange standard, the chances of European countries jointly stabilizing their currencies at low-dollar rates were very high.

Thus the US government and central bank successfully convinced Germany to go back to gold in 1924, earlier than any of the European victors. The story of the Dawes and Young Plans need not be told here again. After that had happened, no effort on the part of the British would be enough to turn the tables again in favor of Norman's scheme. In the successor states, however, independent central banks were established, although a careful study of their statutes reveals that, although financing the government was prohibited and in many cases central banks were established, as Norman advised, as limited companies, some measure of political control was more or less openly inserted into central bank laws in several countries and independence did not prevent central banks from being required to foster their countries' economic growth.

Excluding government financing through the purchase of public debt, was a generally asserted clause in those laws. This made open-market operations very difficult and lending of last resort even harder.

At the same time as independent central banks were established in the successor countries of CEE, national authorities promoted the creation of universal banks, either as green-field operations or by 'nostrification' of pre-existing banks. Successor countries being rather small, those universal banks were also small, and tended by their nature not to have a solidly territorial deposit base. They specialized, like the German banks they imitated, in the promotion of industrial companies, either by deposit transformation or by owning part of the equity of industrial companies.

Those banks, in the 1920s, obtained a large part of their loanable funds from the international financial market. Most of them thus showed a marked financial fragility, and a dangerous proneness to contagion from disturbances originating in the international financial market. They would have required the continuous assistance by central banks free to intervene as lenders of last resort in case the international market withdrew funds from the semi-peripheral countries. But the independent central banks Norman, the British Treasury, and the League of Nations had fostered upon them were not designed to perform that function. Moreover, since commercial bank supervision was not among the functions the Bank of England performed, it did not try to see it performed in the central banks it helped to establish in CEE countries. Central banks were therefore left without effective instruments to know in what state of health the accounts of their private banks were at any time, and so could not prepare in time to face possible national and international financial emergencies. The Federal Reserve, on the contrary, was given by law the function of supervising banks. Accordingly, Governor Strong tried to export this model to CEE, as it was clearly shown by the contrasting advice his emissary, Professor Edwin Kemmerer and British advisers gave the National Bank of Poland in the 1920s.

This contrast between the central bank's 'mission' and the actual needs of universal banks became evident at the beginning of the 1930s, when the age of large US capital exports came to a close and this unleashed a financial crisis in Europe. Universal banks collapsed almost everywhere, and in particular in the successor states, as central banks were prevented by their laws from coming to their rescue or were unable to help them because they were not used to having close relations with them.

The collapse of universal banks in the early 1930s ushered in a new financial age, one of wide financial repression in the whole of Europe, with financial nationalism becoming even more marked in the successor countries. New banking laws were promulgated in most countries, which transformed banking into an activity of national interest, institutionalized banking supervision, and turned the banking system into a hierarchical structure dominated by the central bank. CEE countries this time did not look to London for advise. They more often imitated the corporatist financial and economic reforms passed in Fascist Italy and Nazi Germany, after the financial systems in both those countries had been ravaged by the international crisis of the early 1930s.

Note

1. Kessides, C., T. King, M. Nuti and C. Sokil (eds) (1989), *Financial Reform in Socialist Economies* (Washington, DC: Economic Development Institute of the World Bank and Florence: European University Institute, EDI Seminar Series).

7
Investment, Wages and Corporate Governance during the Transition: Evidence from Slovenian Firms[1]

Janez Prašnikar and Jan Svejnar

7.1 Introduction

As the transition to a market economy unfolded, investment and wage determination became important issues in virtually all the post-communist economies. The Soviet bloc countries as well as Yugoslavia displayed high rates of investment until the 1980s, when economic slowdown and popular pressure for higher consumption forced the authorities to reduce the rate of investment and allow wages to rise (EBRD, 1995, 1996). As both the Soviet bloc and former Yugoslavia disintegrated, analysts and policy-makers started worrying about the fact that the rate of investment declined further, principally as a result of declining enterprise saving (EBRD, 1995).[2] At the same time, investment has been identified as a principal indicator of *strategic* or *deep* restructuring in the microeconomic models of transition (for example, Blanchard, 1997; Grosfeld and Roland, 1997) and a number of theoretical papers have examined conditions, such as managerial ownership stake, under which managers would restructure firms prior to privatization (for example, Aghion *et al.*, 1994a; Blanchard, 1997).

Concomitantly, there was considerable concern that the loosening of central controls in the absence of developed markets and competitive pressures would result in excessive wage increases (for example, Blanchard, 1991; Burda, 1993). One reason for this concern was the fact that real wages, after falling together with output in the early 1990s, started rising from about 1992–93 in most Central and East European countries (EBRD, 1996, pp. 113–19). Another cause of the concern was the fact that insiders (workers and managers) often seized control of firms and many transition countries took on features of labor-managed economies (for example, Hinds, 1990; Prašnikar and Svejnar, 1991; Commander and Coricelli, 1995; Earle, *et al.* 1995).

The literature on labor-managed firms has for a long time debated the seriousness of the so-called 'under-investment problem,' allegedly brought

149

about by the short time horizon of individual workers in these firms. The basic argument is that worker-insiders, unlike diversified capital owners (outsiders), would prefer to distribute enterprise surplus as labor income and fringe benefits rather than reinvesting it in the firm for future growth (see for example, Furubotn and Pejovich, 1970; Vanek, 1970; Uvalic, 1992). More recently, Blanchard and Aghion (1995) argued that insider-dominated firms might neither generate resources needed for restructuring activities such as investment, nor have an incentive to sell the firm to outsiders who have such resources.

In the context of a transition to a market economy, the investment-wage issue is especially important. The lifting of central controls gave workers significant powers in enterprises, a phenomenon that has been enhanced by insider privatization in countries such as Russia, Ukraine and some other newly independent states (NIS). Moreover, with the inability of many firms in the transition economies to pay wages, the tradeoff between using the firm's value added for financing investment versus paying wages and fringe benefits has become particularly acute.

In this paper, we analyze the investment and wage (labor cost per worker) behavior of a panel of 458 Slovenian firms during the 1991–95 period. The data are of high quality and they are also unique in terms of the corporate governance characteristics of the firms. The first important characteristic is that we examine the behavior of firms while they were going through the transition-related restructuring but before they were privatized in the late 1990s – a situation that corresponds to the focus of many theoretical models of enterprise restructuring.[3] Yet, during the period of our analysis, the managers, workers and the general public knew how the firms would ultimately be privatized – through the sale of the majority of shares to either insiders or outsiders ('internal vs. external' privatization). This information and sequence of events permit us to focus on the insider–outsider aspect of governance that is at the heart of theoretical modeling and test whether the pre-privatization investment and wage behavior differed for firms that were approved for privatization to insiders versus outsiders. Second, among the 458 firms we identified 82 firms whose chief executive officers (CEOs) established their own private (so-called 'bypass') companies in the early 1990s.[4] These CEOs have been perceived in Slovenia as being very capable managers, but there is also the question of whether these CEOs siphoned off enterprise profit and otherwise looted (tunneled) the firms for their own benefit. We hence check if firms headed by these CEOs displayed significantly different investment and wage behavior than other firms and if this behavior is consistent with the problem of looting by managers. Third, since 1991 or earlier, 108 of the 458 firms in our sample were partly owned by other companies and institutions, such as banks and government agencies, rather than being fully socially owned.[5] We use this information to assess if this more tangible ownership, frequently connected with a potential source of financing, affected the investment and wage behavior of firms. In sum, we carry out the analysis in a way that permits us to examine the wage-investment tradeoff in several categories of firms that are of interest from the policy standpoint in many transition countries.

Our analysis is also of interest because the environment and behavior of Slovenian firms have traditionally displayed a number of similarities to those in the Soviet bloc. Like firms in the Soviet bloc countries, the Slovenian firms traditionally exhibited high rates of investment as a result of government pressure and easy credit (soft budget constraint) policies of the banks.[6] The Slovenian firms were traditionally socially-owned, which meant that the society at large owned them but in practice government officials, managers and workers shared control (Prašnikar *et al.*, 1994). In this sense the Slovenian firms resembled those in Poland, Hungary and several other countries just before and after the fall of communism (Hinds, 1990). Between 1989 and 1991, the Slovenian government greatly relaxed its traditional influence over firms and decision-making power devolved to a significant extent to managers and workers. In this respect, the Slovenian firms exemplified the greater autonomy observed in Russia, Ukraine and several other NIS after their insider privatization. As we show below, the Slovenian wage setting system, like the systems in the other transition economies, was flexible enough so that within a given year wages varied considerably across firms and with firm-specific performance.

Finally, while our study is of obvious interest to the analysts of the transition process, the fact that we use a relatively large panel of annual firm-level data makes our work relevant in the context of the investment literature in general. In particular, by using the micro panel data we are able to eliminate bias introduced by aggregation (for example, Abel and Blanchard, 1986), reduce measurement error and take into account the heterogeneity across firms and over time (for example, Bond and Meghir, 1994).

7.2 The model

Our empirical model consists of an investment equation and a wage (labor cost per worker) equation. In the investment equation, we extend the usual approach that examines the relative importance of firm's output demand (demand side) and internal funds (supply side) by adding labor cost as a determinant of investment.[7] Our basic hypothesis is that labor cost should have a negative effect on investment, *ceteris paribus*, in firms where workers appropriate part of value added that would otherwise be used for investment. We complement the investment equation with a wage equation that is based on a bargaining model in which workers may appropriate part of the surplus. We estimate the two equations independently as well as jointly in order to check efficiency gains obtained from joint estimation.

7.2.1   The investment equation

On the demand side we start with a basic investment equation used in the transition context by Lizal and Svejnar (2002). The equation corresponds to the neoclassical and accelerator models of investment demand (see for example, Jorgenson, 1971). These models are internally consistent and have been widely used in the western context. They allow us to check if the behavior of firms in the transition is consistent with the profit maximization hypothesis embedded in these models. The two models are based on somewhat restrictive assumptions about input substitutability (the accelerator model) or speed of adjustment (the neoclassical model), but they do not suffer from the problems of convergence and counter-intuitive parameter values encountered in some Euler equation estimations (compare for example, Bond and Meghir, 1994 and Lizal and Svejnar, 2002). Moreover, we do not employ the Tobin Q approach since in the 1990s the Slovenian financial markets were still severely underdeveloped and reliable data hence do not exist to construct an adequate measure of Q. On the supply side, we use a specification that allows us to test whether the firm's availability of internal funds affects its investment decisions.

In terms of actual specification, on the demand side we start with the accelerator and neoclassical models, as developed and used by Koyck (1954), Jorgenson (1971), Kopcke (1985) and others. Letting I_t denote gross investment in period t, K_t the stock of capital at time t, δ the depreciation rate, and Y_t output in period t, the gross investment equation may in the accelerator framework be expressed as

$$I_t = K_t - (1 - \delta)K_{t-1} = \lambda \mu Y_t + (\delta - \lambda)K_{t-1} \qquad (7.1)$$

where λ is the proportion of the gap between actual and optimal level of capital closed in each period.[8] Since the specification in Equation (7.1) requires the adjustment process to be a distributed lag, we follow the literature and relax this restriction to estimate an investment equation of the form:

$$I_t = \text{const} + \Sigma b_i \, Y_{t-i} + cK_{t-1} + e_t$$

$$i = 0, 1, 2, \ldots, m \qquad (7.2)$$

where e is the error term; Equation (7.2) may also be viewed as a special case of Jorgenson's rational lag function.

In a neoclassical model we arrive at an equation such as (7.2) by assuming that the firm maximizes a profit function $\pi_t = p_t Y_t - w_t L_t - c_t K_t$ subject to a neoclassical production function $Y_t = f(K_t, L_t)$, where capital K_t and labor L_t are substitutable, p is the output price, w is the wage (labor cost per worker), and c is the user cost of capital. The maximization results in the standard first order conditions equating the marginal product of labor to the wage and the marginal product of capital to its user cost. This approach requires one to specify the production function and define the user cost of capital c. Depending on the production function, a general form of the estimating investment equation is of the form

$$I_t = \text{const} + \Sigma b_i (p/c)_{t-i} Y_{t-i} - \Sigma d_i (p/c)_{t-i} Y_{t-i-1} + \delta K_{t-1} + e_t$$

$$i = 0, 1, 2, \ldots m$$

If one considers a one-period investment ordering in the context of a Cobb–Douglas production function $Y = K^\alpha L^{1-\alpha}$, one obtains $\alpha(Y_t/K_t) = c_t/p_t$, $K_t^* = \alpha(p/c)_t Y_t$ and the investment equation is of the same form as Equation (7.2):

$$I_t = \alpha(p/c)_{t-i} Y_{t-i} + \delta K_{t-1} + e_t$$

$$i = 0, 1, 2, \ldots m \tag{7.3}$$

The neoclassical and accelerator models embedded in equations (7.2) and (7.3) are usually operationalized by relating a firm's investment/capital ratio to its output/capital ratio:[9]

$$\frac{I_t}{K_{t-1}} = \alpha + \sum_{k=1}^{m} \gamma_k \frac{Y_{t-k}}{K_{t-1}} + \varepsilon_t \tag{7.4}$$

where the interpretation of γ's depends on whether the underlying theory refers to the neoclassical or accelerator models and m is the number of lags in the specification. The practice of standardizing variables by the capital stock reflects the fact that the Euler equations corresponding to intertemporal profit maximization with cost of capital adjustment have been formulated in a per-unit-of-capital form (see for example, Bond and Meghir, 1994; Lizal and Svejnar, 2002) and equations such as (7.4) are taken to be approximations to these Euler equations. The power of workers in many transition economies of course calls into question the usefulness of profit as the goal of the firm. Note that when one carries out the dynamic maximization of income per worker in the presence of cost of capital adjustment (the dynamic analog to the traditional objective function in the static literature on labor-managed firms), one obtains an Euler equation that is analogous to the one obtained from profit maximization except that it is scaled by labor rather than capital. In a linearized approximation form, the per-worker specification then provides an alternative specification to the per-unit-of-capital investment Equation (7.4). In view of the lack of previous literature to provide clear guidance about the relative merits of the two specifications, we have estimated both. They provide broadly similar findings and the per-worker form fits the data better more frequently than the per-unit-of-capital form. As a result, in what follows we report estimates based on the per-worker specification.

Equation (7.4) reflects the firm's demand for investment and it implicitly assumes that the supply of investment funds is perfectly elastic. In

accounting for the possibility that the firm faces transaction costs or restrictions in obtaining external financing (imperfect capital market), the usual
approach in the investment literature is to augment these types of equation
with measures of internally available funds, such as profit.[10] Let value added
VA be defined as $VA = R - H$, where R is revenue and H is non-labor cost,
and let yL be the actual labor cost, where y is the income per worker and
L is the total number of workers.[11] The traditional approach can then be
viewed as augmenting the basic investment equation with profit, defined as
$\pi = VA - yL = R - H - yL$.

Unlike the existing literature, we are interested in analyzing the possible
tradeoff between investment and wages. As a result, we need to include a
broader measure of internally generated funds than profit, namely funds
that may be used by the firm for paying higher wages or internally financing
investment. The measure that we use for internal funds (π^a) is profit net of
best alternative labor cost, defined as value added minus reservation labor
cost – $\pi^a = VA - y^a L = R - H - y^a L$, where y^a is the reservation (best alternative) income per worker. The augmented profit variable π^a gives the firm's
maximum surplus (over and above the threat point of labor) that could be
used for payments to owners, internal financing of investment, or higher
wages of workers.

In order to capture bargaining between workers and management over the
allocation of π^a between investment and worker compensation, we include
as an additional regressor the actual labor cost, yL, minus the reservation cost
of labor, $y^a L$. Controlling for π^a, a negative coefficient on surplus labor cost
($yL - y^a L$) implies that workers appropriate as wages part of internal funds
that would have been used for investment.

Finally, we also include revenues R as an explanatory variable in order to
assess the investment effect of output demand that underlies the neoclassical
and accelerator models of investment outlined above. While the inclusion of
sales revenue conforms to the practice in studies of the market economies, it
might be argued that π^a captures some or all of the output demand effect that
is normally picked up by the sales variable. We test and reject this hypothesis.

Suppressing time subscripts on variables for simplicity of exposition,
our basic firm-specific investment equation in a per-worker form may be
written as

$$I/L = \alpha_0 + \alpha_1(\pi^a/L) + \alpha_2(y - y^a) + \alpha_3(R/L) + (YEAR)\alpha_{4'}$$
$$+ (INDUSTRY)\alpha_{5'} + \varepsilon_1 \tag{7.5}$$

where primes denote column vectors and we control for data heterogeneity
in level estimates by including a vector of annual dummy variables (*YEAR*)
and industry dummy variables (*INDUSTRY*). These variables also control for
the ratio of output price to user cost of capital that one may want to control
for in view of the theoretical derivation above. Finally, ε_1 is the error term.

In terms of our conceptual framework, the capital market imperfection (internal funds) hypothesis implies $\alpha_1 > 0$, while the neoclassical and accelerator models based on output demand are consistent with the hypothesis $\alpha_3 > 0$. The latter hypothesis may be formulated more strictly by testing the condition $\alpha_3 > 0$ in the presence of $\alpha_1 = 0$, that is, the effect of sales revenue being positive when net profit π^a is excluded from the regression. Finally, if workers are able to appropriate part of the firm's investable surplus as wages and fringe benefits (labor cost), one should find support for the hypothesis $\alpha_2 < 0$.

In order to capture the effects of the interesting aspects of corporate governance that we discussed earlier, we extend the basic estimating equation as follows:

$$I/L = \beta_0 + (FIRM)\beta_{1'} + \beta_2(\pi^a/L) + [FIRM(\pi^a/L)]\beta_{3'} + \beta_4(y - y^a)$$

$$+ [FIRM(y - y^a)]\beta_{5'} + \beta_6(R/L) + [FIRM(R/L)]\beta_{7'} + (YEAR)\beta_{8'}$$

$$+ (INDUSTRY)\beta_{9'} + \varepsilon_2 \tag{7.6}$$

where the coefficients β_0, β_2, β_4, and β_6 correspond to the firms that we use as the base, namely firms that would be eventually privatized to insiders, had CEOs without bypass companies, and were historically fully in social ownership. We then measure the effects of the other corporate forms as differentials over and above these basic coefficients. In particular, $FIRM = (EXTERNAL, BYPASS, PREVIOUS)$ is a row vector of dummy variables capturing the following categories of corporate governance: (i) the firm would be eventually privatized to outsiders (external privatization dummy $EXTERNAL = 1$), (ii) the CEO owns a bypass company (CEO bypass dummy $BYPASS = 1$), and (iii) the firm had since the early 1990s a tangible, partial owner (previous owner dummy $PREVIOUS = 1$).

In most investment studies, the issue of endogeneity of regressors is traditionally handled by including the lagged rather than current values of variables on the right-hand side of equations such as (7.4). Unfortunately, to the extent that the error term contains a fixed component, this approach does not eliminate the correlation of the regressors with the error term. In order to assess the sensitivity of our results to this problem, we report in the main tables estimates based on this approach as well as three other econometric methods: instrumental variable (IV) estimation with instrumented regressors being current values of explanatory variables (IV levels), IV estimation with instrumented regressors being lagged values of explanatory variables (IV lagged levels) and IV estimation applied to the first difference specification of the equation (IV first difference). By design, the first difference model eliminates the problem of the fixed component of the error term and it also avoids the problem of data heterogeneity across firms. We combine this approach with the IV procedure since the first difference regressors may still be endogenous. Similarly, if one selects appropriate instrumental variables in the levels specification, one also eliminates the problem of the fixed component in the error term. Depending on the particular specification, we use lagged values or lagged first differences of the principal variables in addition to dummy variables as instruments. Our principle is that for specifications in levels, we use current and lagged levels of strongly exogenous variables and lagged first differences of weak exogenous variables as instruments. For the first difference specifications, we use as instruments current and lagged first differences of strongly exogenous variables and twice lagged levels of weak exogenous variables. The lists of instrumental variables used in the various specifications are given in notes to Tables 7.2 and 7.3.

We have also checked if the above four sets of estimates are sensitive to additional econometric extensions. In particular, we have explored the determinants of EXT (whether a firm would eventually be privatized to outsiders as opposed to insiders) and used the predicted values from a probit equation and a Heckman selection model in estimating investment Equation (7.6). As we show in Appendix B, the principal results reported in the text are not materially affected when using these procedures.

Our approach is to estimate Equation (7.6) first in order to obtain parameter estimates that may be compared to the existing literature on firms in market economies. We next draw on the bargaining and labor–management literatures and complement Equation (7.6) with a wage (labor cost per worker) equation.

7.2.2 The wage equation

The wage equation illuminates further the extent to which workers share in value added and possibly even appropriate funds that the Slovenian firms were required to set aside by law for depreciation (replacement investment). The equation is based on the Nash non-symmetric bargaining solution and represents an extension of the models of Svejnar (1982, 1986) and Prašnikar *et al.* (1994) to the transition setting of the Slovenian firms. It predicts that the actual income per worker y equals the best alternative income per worker y^a plus a share γ_2 of the net surplus per worker $(R - H - y^a L)/L$, where as before the surplus is defined as revenue R net of the non-labor cost H and workers' reservation income $y^a L$:

$$y = y^a + \gamma_2[(R - H - y^a L)/L] \tag{7.7}$$

The share γ_2 reflects workers' bargaining power relative to managers and any other party that has a claim on the firm's surplus. At one extreme, $\gamma_2 = 0$, workers obtain just their reservation-level income y^a and appropriate no surplus. This case corresponds to a competitive labor market or a situation where the government sets the wage at a market clearing level. At the other extreme is a pure labor-managed firm, with $\gamma_2 = 1$ and workers appropriating all surplus $[y = (R - H)/L]$. In practice, one expects $0 < \gamma_2 < 1$, as workers share the surplus with managers and other parties.

For estimation purposes it is convenient to rearrange the bargaining Equation (7.7) as

$$y = (1 - \gamma_2)y^a + \gamma_2[(R - H)/L] \qquad (7.8)$$

where $R - H$ is the value added of the firm. Moreover, an interesting empirical and policy question is whether the relatively low rate of investment discussed in the introduction is in part brought about by workers appropriating funds that the firm should set aside for depreciation DEPR. Since the allocation of funds for depreciation is required by Slovenian law, it may be hypothesized that it is more difficult for workers to appropriate the depreciation funds DEPR than to share in the surplus that the firm generates over and above this amount (that is, $R - H - \text{DEPR}$). This hypothesis may be tested by subtracting DEPR from $R - H$ and entering $(R - H - DEPR)/L$ and $DEPR/L$ as two separate terms on the right-hand side of the basic estimating equation, in which we also include regional, annual, and industry dummy variables:

$$y = \gamma_0 + \gamma_1 y^a + \gamma_2[(R - H - DEPR)/L] + \gamma_3(DEPR/L)$$
$$+ (REGION)\gamma_{4'} + (YEAR)\gamma_{5'} + (INDUSTRY)\gamma_{6'} + \varepsilon_3 \qquad (7.9)$$

Equation (7.9) permits us to test the hypothesis $\gamma_2 = \gamma_3$ (workers appropriate depreciation funds as easily as surplus over and above depreciation) against the alternative hypothesis $\gamma_2 > \gamma_3$ (surplus may be appropriated easier than depreciation funds). In addition, we can test whether $\gamma_1 = 1 - \gamma_2$, as implied by Condition (7.8) of the bargaining model. Finally, combining the basic investment model of Equation (7.5) with the bargaining model of Equation (7.9), note that if workers appropriate part of the surplus and/or depreciation funds, and do so at the expense of investment, we should observe simultaneously $\alpha_2 < 0$ and $\gamma_2 > 0$ and/or $\gamma_3 > 0$.

As in the case of investment, we capture the effects of the three important forms of corporate governance by adding the vector FIRM to the basic estimating Equation (7.9) as follows:

$$y = \delta_0 + (FIRM)\delta_{1'} + \delta_2 y^a + [FIRM(y^a)]\delta_{3'} + \delta_4[(R - H - DEPR)/L]$$
$$+ [FIRM(R - H - DEPR)/L]\delta_{5'} + \delta_6(DEPR/L) + [FIRM(DEPR/L)]\delta_{7'}$$
$$+ (REGION)\delta_{8'} + (YEAR)\delta_{9'} + (INDUSTRY)\delta_{10'} + \varepsilon_4 \qquad (7.10)$$

where coefficients δ_0, δ_2, δ_4, and δ_6 correspond to the firms that we use as the base, namely firms that would be eventually privatized to insiders, had CEOs without bypass companies, and were historically fully in social ownership. The effects of the three other corporate forms, captured by vector $FIRM = (EXTERNAL, BYPASS, PREVIOUS)$, are estimated as differentials over and above these basic coefficients.

7.3   Slovenian transition and enterprise data

In this section we describe the main institutional developments that are relevant for our analysis and discuss the data that we use in our empirical work.

7.3.1   Slovenian transition to a market economy[12]

The Slovenian transition of the 1990s was a process consisting of macro-stabilization in imperfectly developed markets, relatively slow ownership transformation and a gradual change of the legal system (Mencinger, 1991; Bole, 1997; OECD, 1997). In 1991, Slovenia declared independence from Yugoslavia, created its own currency (Tolar) and the (central) Bank of Slovenia started pursuing floating exchange rate policy together with sterilization of capital inflows as a strategy for macro-stabilization.

At the micro level, the government in 1993 rehabilitated the commercial bank sector, bringing the two largest banks into state ownership and inducing them and the other smaller commercial banks to meet regulatory conditions, improve evaluation of loan applications, reduce operating costs, and increase profitability. In its attempt to maintain macro stability in the presence of low domestic savings, the Bank of Slovenia kept interest rates high and it also limited competition in the banking sector.[13] These policies, together with the problem of asymmetric information between bankers and managers are believed by some analysts to have generated credit rationing at the firm-level.[14] Moreover, profitable firms could be expected to rely more on internal funds or funds from abroad in financing investment, even if the domestic supply of credit remained positively related to profitability and other performance criteria.[15] In fact, the extent of financing of firms by domestic banks throughout the early-to-mid 1990s was limited. In 1994, for instance, Slovenian commercial bank credit amounted to a mere 23.2 per cent of GDP and it declined to 14.5 per cent by 1996.[16]

The part played by the newly established Ljubljana Stock Market in capital supply and allocation was also limited. With very few new issues and transactions, the primary and secondary capital markets were almost non-existent throughout the 1990s. The information provided by the capital markets was also very limited as a result of insufficient regulation, high volatility and insider trading.

The corporate ownership and governance issues that we explore in this paper were very much conditioned by the 1993 Privatization Law. The law applied to firms in virtually all sectors of the economy and required them to allocate 20 per cent of their shares to insiders (employees), 20 per cent to a Development Fund that auctioned the shares to investment funds, 10 per cent to a National Pension Fund, and 10 per cent to a Restitution Fund.[17] In addition, in each enterprise the workers council or the board of directors (if it existed) was empowered to allocate the remaining 40 per cent of shares for sale to insiders (employees) or outsiders (through a public tender). Based on the decision of how to allocate these remaining 40 per cent of shares, we classify the firms in our sample as being eventually privatized to insiders (the internal method) or outsiders (the external method).

In terms of wage setting, Slovenia has since 1990 had a layered system of agreements that permitted wages to vary across firms and defy government attempts to reign in real wage growth. In August 1990 an 'umbrella' general collective agreement was signed between the Slovenian Chamber of Commerce (representing all employers) and Trade Union Organization (representing all workers). This agreement set initial wages for each category of workers and it was supplemented by industry-specific agreements that effectively converted the initial wages in the umbrella agreement into minimum wages at the level of industries. Moreover, at the level of each firm the union and management bargained in the context of the firm's annual plan to adjust further the industry-level wages. The multi-layer bargaining structure resulted in wage dispersion, rapid wage growth and attempts by the government to limit these tendencies. Overall, the early-to-mid 1990s was a period of relatively rapid wage growth that allowed insiders to influence wages significantly at the firm level.

In this context, Slovenia's economic performance during the 1990s was relatively successful. Mirroring the situation in the other transition economies, Slovenia experienced a period of economic decline in 1990–92. Thereafter growth resumed, with annual percentage GDP increase reaching 0.9 in 1993, 4.9 in 1994, 4.1 in 1995, 3.5 in 1996, 4.6 in 1997, 3.8 in 1998 and 5.0 in 1999. After experiencing hyperinflation while being part of Yugoslavia in the late 1980s and early 1990s, Slovenia reduced inflation below 10 per cent, but has not been able to bring the rate below 5 per cent. Hence, while retail prices increased by 104.6 per cent in 1991, the annual percentage increases declined to 92.9, 22.9, 18.3, 8.6, 9.7, 9.1, 7.9, and 6.1 in 1992, 1993, 1994, 1995, 1996, 1997, 1998, and 1999, respectively. As in most other transition economies, the registered unemployment rate rose dramatically, starting at 2 per cent in 1989 and reaching the highest point at 14.5 per cent in 1998.[18]

7.3.2 Data and summary statistics

The main data source for our research is the Slovenian Agency for Privatization, to which all Slovenian firms had to provide their privatization plans. We use data on 458 firms that were given permission by the Agency in the early 1990s to start implementing privatization by January 1997 and whose data were internally consistent for the period 1989–95. The enterprises are from 12 industries, comprising all areas of the Slovenian economy. Each firm's privatization plan indicates whether the government permits workers and managers to use enterprise profits to buy the residual 40 per cent of shares at a discount price over a 5-year period (internal privatization) or prescribes that the residual 40 per cent of shares be sold to outsiders (external privatization). The privatization plan also provides information on whether the firm was already partially owned by a domestic or foreign institution (usually a bank or a government agency) in or before 1991. The data set for the 458 firms also includes balance sheets and income statements that the Slovenian firms were required by law to provide to the government.

The second data set comes from the Slovenian National Office of Statistics and contains annual enterprise-level investment data during the 1990–95 period. These data were supplied by firms in their annual reports on investment spending in fixed capital. The third data source is the 1992–93 Directory of Slovenian Legal Entities, which provides data on private enterprises and their founders and owners. By comparing the names and addresses of CEOs of the fully or partly socially-owned firms with the names and addresses of founders and owners of private firms, we are able to identify CEOs who own or are partners in private bypass firms.

In Table 7.1, we present the means and standard deviations of the principal variables that we use in our analysis. The values are averages for the 1991–95 period and they are presented for the entire sample of 458 firms as well as for the four principal categories of firms that we analyze:

   (i) 303 firms that were subsequently privatized to insiders (internal privatization firms),
  (ii) 155 firms that were subsequently privatized to outsiders (external privatization firms),
 (iii) 82 firms whose CEOs established private bypass firms (CEO bypass firms), and
  (iv) 108 firms that were since the early 1990s less than 100 per cent in social ownership (previous owner firms).

The internal and external ownership categories are mutually exclusive and they span the 458 firms. The bypass and previous owner firm categories are not mutually exclusive and firms with these characteristics were subsequently privatized by either the internal or external method.

As may be seen from column 1 of Table 7.1, during the 1991–95 period the average firm employed 301 workers, generated 51 million Tolars (US $4.7 million) in value added, paid 38.5 million Tolars (US $3.7 million) in wages and fringe benefits, and reported 0.57 million Tolars (US $54,000) in profit. The average level of gross investment was 11.8 million Tolars (US $1.1 million), with the average level of capital stock[19] being reported at 140 million Tolars (US $13.3 million).[20] All variables show sizable standard deviations, reflecting significant cross-sectional as well as temporal variations in the values of the relevant variables. Interestingly, during the 1991–95 period the mean value of gross investment fell slightly short of the (legally prescribed) mean level of depreciation investment. This shortfall was in part

Table 7.1 Means and standard deviations of selected variables during the 1991–95 period

	Entire sample	Internal privatization	External privatization	Bypass firm	Previous owner
No. of workers	301 (546)	252 (475)	397 (652)	206 (298)	411 (663)
Value added	50957 (129013)	36876 (73539)	78482 (193646)	36408 (76959)	80373 (209137)
Labor cost	38491 (79751)	30058 (56666)	54977 (110078)	26242 (42114)	56013 (118159)
Profit	566 (38985)	1016 (19362)	−313 (61321)	2406 (30510)	2431 (29781)
Revenue	205362 (463857)	142609 (262476)	328033 (691940)	149627 (262588)	332074 (777043)
Investment	11822 (55397)	6333 (17846)	22553 (90986)	9439 (29187)	25292 (105437)
Capital	140066 (478726)	69441 (116646)	278126 (788861)	120619 (425447)	268407 (788959)
Alternative wage	94.377 (16.807)	94.384 (17.185)	94.365 (16.054)	94.627 (17.217)	93.466 (16.603)
Profit+labor cost	39057 (95551)	31074 (63714)	54664 (136717)	28649 (61017)	58444 (138912)
Profit/value added	0.111 (0.765)	0.027 (0.525)	−0.004 (0.781)	0.066 (0.837)	0.030 (0.370)
Labor cost/worker	127.47 (264.11)	119.00 (224.35)	138.47 (277.25)	126.86 (203.58)	136.26 (287.43)
Value added/worker	168.75 (427.25)	146.00 (291.15)	197.67 (487.73)	176.00 (372.02)	195.51 (508.74)
Profit/worker	1.875 (129.11)	4.023 (76.66)	−0.788 (154.45)	11.634 (147.49)	5.913 (72.45)
Revenue/worker	680.10 (1536.16)	564.62 (1039.19)	826.20 (1742.76)	723.30 (1269.35)	807.79 (1890.21)
Investment/worker	39.15 (183.460)	25.07 (70.66)	56.80 (229.16)	45.63 (141.09)	61.53 (256.48)
Capital/worker	463.86 (1585.40)	274.93 (461.82)	700.51 (1986.87)	583.07 (2056.61)	652.92 (1919.20)
No. of workers/capital	0.002 (0.003)	0.003 (0.006)	0.001 (0.002)	0.001 (0.002)	0.001 (0.002)
Value added/capital	0.363 (0.921)	0.531 (1.059)	0.282 (0.696)	0.301 (0.638)	0.299 (0.779)
Labor cost/capital	0.274 (0.569)	0.432 (0.816)	0.197 (0.395)	0.217 (0.349)	0.208 (0.440)
Profit/capital	0.004 (0.278)	0.014 (0.278)	−0.001 (0.220)	0.019 (0.252)	0.009 (0.110)
Revenue/capital	1.466 (3.311)	2.053 (3.779)	1.179 (2.487)	1.240 (2.177)	1.237 (2.895)
Investment/capital	0.084 (0.395)	0.091 (0.257)	0.081 (0.327)	0.078 (0.241)	0.094 (0.392)
No. of firms	458	303	155	82	108
No. of observations	2290	1515	775	410	540

Notes:

• Numbers are in thousand of Tolars in constant 1991 prices.

• Numbers in parentheses are standard deviations.

• Means and standard deviations for ratios are calculated by dividing the numerator of each observation by the mean value of the denominator (taking into account the different sample means) and calculating the mean and standard deviation for each of these created variables.

brought about by the fact that loss-making firms paid wages and fringe benefits out of funds that were earmarked for depreciation.

In examining the variable values across types of firms in Table 7.1, one observes that firms that have been privatized to insiders were on average smaller and less capital-intensive than firms that have sold residual shares to outsiders. Since the Slovene capital market was underdeveloped throughout the 1990s, the finding that insiders bought smaller and less capital-intensive firms is in accordance with expectations.[21] The insider-privatized firms were on average also more profitable, a finding that is consistent with (a) the hypothesis that insiders had been able to cherry-pick the firms that they subsequently privatized and (b) the fact that insiders were legally allowed to use the profits generated by their firms during the 1990s to pay for their private purchase of shares of their companies. Correspondingly, the fact that the group of outsider-privatized firms contains a number of firms with sizable losses accounts for the finding that investment on average fell short of depreciation in all firms taken together. Moreover, the insiders were obviously less able to bid on and privatize internally the large firms. Finally, the negative value of average profit among the outsider-privatized firms probably reflects the fact that insiders would be less interested in (a) obtaining majority ownership of loss-making firms and (b) generating profit in firms that would be majority-owned by outsiders.

Enterprises run by CEOs with bypass firms were on average relatively capital-intensive and displayed high value added and profit, as well as high profit/value added ratio. They reported high rates of investment per worker but low investment per unit of capital in comparison to the other types of firms. Finally, firms with previous owners were on average larger than the other types of firms. They were relatively capital-intensive, reported positive profit, and displayed high rate of investment in relation to the size of their capital as well as labor.

7.4   Empirical results

The estimated parameters are reported in Tables 7.2 and 7.3. In Table 7.2 we present the estimates of Equation (7.6), while in Table 7.3 we report the estimated parameters of Equation (7.10). In all specifications, firms that were eventually privatized to insiders and had neither previous owners nor CEOs with bypass companies serve as the base. The coefficients for the three other types of firms hence measure the effects relative to the coefficients of this base group rather than relative to zero.

7.4.1   The investment equation

In all four specifications of the investment equation, we found the coefficient on sales revenues per worker R/L to be very small and statistically insignificant for all types of firms. While traditionally this finding would be

Table 7.2 Determinants of investment/worker

Model: variable:	OLS lagged levels	IV Levels	IV Lagged levels	IV First difference
π^a/L	0.399^a (0.041)	0.602^a (0.094)	0.934^a (0.145)	0.285^a (0.120)
$Y - y^a$	-0.383^a (0.049)	-0.600^a (0.113)	-0.995^a (0.168)	-0.324^b (0.171)
(π^a/L)* External	-0.319^a (0.051)	-0.508^a (0.093)	-0.734^a (0.126)	-0.281^a (0.118)
$(y - y^a)$* External	0.516^a (0.092)	0.574^a (0.183)	0.615^a (0.201)	0.353^c (0.215)
(π^a/L)* Previous	0.350^a (0.052)	0.560^a (0.085)	0.214^b (0.109)	0.411^a (0.112)
$(y - y^a)$* Previous	0.172^c (0.099)	-0.346^c (0.185)	0.507^a (0.209)	-0.329 (0.223)
(π^a/L)* Bypass	-0.182^a (0.057)	-0.388^a (0.077)	-0.827^a (0.148)	-0.037 (0.097)
$(y - y^a)$* Bypass	0.346^a (0.100)	0.761^a (0.161)	1.271^a (0.219)	-0.027 (0.191)
External dummy	-10.287 (8.292)	7.666 (16.026)	40.144^a (15.763)	–
Previous dummy	-19.587^b (9.002)	-37.868^b (17.657)	-80.165^a (16.772)	–
Bypass dummy	-12.382 (9.055)	-39.144^b (17.755)	-27.327 (17.109)	
Constant	-2.486 (5.624)	3.765 (7.462)	9.160 (7.649)	1.859 (3.831)
Year dummies	Yes	Yes	Yes	Yes
Industry dummies	Yes	Yes	Yes	No
Adjusted R-squared	0.198	0.255	0.114	0.007
No. of observations	2290	1832	1832	1832

Notes:

1) Values in parentheses are standard errors.

2) a, b, c = statistically significant at 1 per cent, 5 per cent and 10 per cent on a two-tail test, respectively.

3) In the level estimates, the constant term reflects the year 1991, firms in manufacturing industry and firms that (a) had CEOs with bypass firms, (b) were not in part owned by external institutions and (c) were eventually privatized by the internal method.

4) In the IV Levels model we used the following instruments: dummy variables for industry, region, time and firm types, lagged first difference of value added/worker, lagged first difference of revenue/worker, lagged capital/worker, lagged first difference of capital/worker, lagged first difference of the alternative wage, first difference of the alternative wage, lagged first difference of depreciation/worker, and lagged first difference of (profit + labor cost)/worker.

5) In the IV Lagged Levels model we used the following instruments: dummy variables for industry, region, time and firm types, lagged first difference of value added/worker, lagged first difference of revenue/worker, lagged first difference of capital/worker, lagged capital/worker, lagged first difference of the alternative wage, lagged alternative wage, lagged first difference of profit plus labor cost per worker.

6) In the IV First Difference model we used the following instruments: dummy variables for industry, region, time and firm types, twice lagged value added/worker, twice lagged revenue/worker, lagged first difference of capital/worker, lagged first difference of the alternative wage, first difference of the alternative wage, twice lagged depreciation/worker, twice lagged (profit + labor cost)/worker, lagged first difference of the revenue/worker, lagged first difference of value added/worker, lagged first difference of depreciation/worker, and lagged first difference of (profit + labor cost)/worker.

interpreted as a lack of support for the neoclassical and accelerator models, in most other studies the sales revenue variable competes against a regressor (for example, profit or cash flow) that constitutes a narrower measure of internal funds than our augmented profit per worker π^a/L.[22] A possible interpretation of our insignificant coefficients on the sales revenue variable could therefore be that the output demand effect of the neoclassical and accelerator models is already being captured by the augmented profit variable. To check this conjecture, we re-estimated the investment equation without the augmented profit variable, but we again found the resulting estimated coefficients on sales revenue per worker to be very small and insignificant. The two sets of results hence suggest that the investment behavior of Slovenian firms was principally determined by the availability of internal funds (that is, supply-side factors) rather than by demand side considerations (as implied by the neoclassical and accelerator models).[23] In view of these findings, we have constrained the estimated coefficients on sales revenue to zero so as to increase the efficiency of our estimates.

The investment equation estimates in Table 7.2 show that our results are quite robust. The different estimation methods yield similar estimates of the coefficients on augmented profit and surplus labor cost, respectively. The only difference across specifications is that few coefficients in the first-difference specifications are statistically insignificant, which is normal when there is limited inter-temporal (within) variation in variable values.

Firms that serve as the base (those scheduled to be privatized to insiders and having no previous non-state owner or CEO with a bypass firm) register a strong positive relationship between augmented profit and investment, as well as a negative relationship between surplus labor cost and investment in all four econometric specifications. The positive coefficient on augmented profit is consistent with the internal funds (credit rationing) hypotheses, suggesting that the availability of internal funds is an important determinant of investment in firms slated for insider privatization. As we discussed earlier, the Slovenian capital markets were undeveloped during the period of our study, thus providing an institutional setting that is consistent with this empirical finding. The negative estimated coefficients on surplus labor cost per worker indicate that in firms slated for insider privatization there is a trade-off between worker compensation and the amount of investment, *ceteris paribus*, with a 100 Tolar increase in the labor cost per worker resulting in a 32–100 Tolar decrease in investment per worker.

The corresponding coefficients on firms that were to be privatized externally (that is, to outsiders) and, like the base firms, did not have previous ownership nor CEOs with bypass firms, are similar in size but go in the opposite direction of the respective base coefficients. They hence show a much weaker (usually insignificant) relationship between both internal funds and investment and between surplus labor cost and investment. In this second category of firms one hence observes investment behavior that is virtually unrelated to firm's internal funds and to the ability of workers to obtain higher wages. From a corporate governance perspective, this finding is not surprising. In the pre-privatization period that we study, these large and on average loss-making firms had close ties with suppliers and banks, and hence could more easily obtain capital by delaying payments to suppliers (arrears) or by receiving supplier or bank credit.

The effect of a CEO owning a bypass company is similar in that it mitigates or offsets the effects observed for the base category of firms slated for insider privatization. In particular, while the coefficients in the first difference specification are statistically insignificant, the coefficients in the three-level estimations are significant and suggest that firms whose CEOs own bypass companies have a weak or non-existent link between both internal funds and investment and surplus labor cost and investment. These elite CEOs may hence be able to secure external investment funds and thus weaken or eliminate any positive link between investment and internal funds. These CEOs also appear to be able to resist wage increases at the expense of investment. These findings are consistent with a number of other types of behavior, however, including the view that the elite CEOs siphon off (loot) investment funds that they prevent the workers from appropriating.

Finally, previous ownership by an external institution has a positive effect on the coefficient of augmented profit in all specifications, while the coefficient on surplus labor cost varies across specifications. Contrary to what might be expected, previous ownership by an external institution hence strengthens rather than reduces the dependence of investment on the availability of internal funds, while its effect on the surplus labor cost-investment relationship is sensitive to model selection.

7.4.2 The wage equation

Estimates of the labor cost per worker equation are reported in Table 7.3. As may be seen from the table, firms in the base category (those with internal privatization and no previous ownership or bypass firm) show a uniformly positive set of coefficients γ_2 on surplus per worker. With the γ_2 coefficients ranging from 0.676 to 0.854, the results suggest that workers in these firms appropriate a very significant part of their firm's surplus. The corresponding γ_1 coefficients on the alternative wage are between zero and unity, as expected.[24] In these specifications, we cannot reject the null hypothesis of the bargaining model that $\gamma_1 = 1 - \gamma_2$ in three of the four specifications (see Note (7) to Table 7.3). Interestingly, in the base category of firms one finds no support for the hypothesis that workers appropriate part of the funds allocated by law for depreciation investment ($\gamma_3 > 0$). As a result, as may be seen from Note (6) to Table 7.3, in all specifications we reject the hypothesis ($\gamma_2 = \gamma_3$) that workers appropriate depreciation funds as easily as surplus in favor of the hypothesis ($\gamma_2 > \gamma_3$) that workers appropriate surplus much more readily than depreciation funds. These findings are quite logical,

Table 7.3 Determinants of labor cost/worker

Model: Variable:	OLS lagged levels	IV levels	IV lagged levels	IV first difference
y^a	0.475^a (0.123)	0.332 (0.257)	0.691^a (0.171)	−0.063 (0.316)
$(R-H-DEPR)/L$	0.676^a (0.018)	0.854^a (0.016)	0.696^a (0.024)	0.766^a (0.032)
$DEPR/L$	0.083 (0.090)	0.011 (0.095)	0.107 (0.149)	−0.141 (0.129)
y^a. External	0.216 (0.198)	0.523^a (0.163)	0.193 (0.312)	1.511^a (0.356)
$[(R-H-DEPR)/L]$· External	−0.334^a (0.034)	−0.435^a (0.034)	−0.312^a (0.067)	−0.429^a (0.045)
$(DEPR/L)$· External	0.476^a (0.101)	0.575^a (0.094)	0.471^a (0.162)	0.592^a (0.145)
y^a. Previous	0.029 (0.223)	0.189 (0.189)	0.158 (0.363)	0.855^b (0.399)
$[(R-H-DEPR)/L]$· Previous	0.028 (0.043)	−0.024 (0.042)	0.009 (0.089)	−0.246^a (0.058)
$(DEPR/L)$· Previous	−0.321^a (0.078)	−0.234^a (0.062)	−0.311^a (0.106)	−0.063 (0.124)
y^a. Bypass	0.163 (0.210)	0.502^a (0.165)	0.251 (0.323)	1.085^a (0.395)
$[(R-H-DEPR)/L]$· Bypass	−0.320^a (0.046)	−0.363^a (0.039)	−0.499^a (0.092)	−0.101 (0.064)
$(DEPR/L)$· Bypass	0.160 (0.126)	0.263^c (0.158)	0.203 (0.228)	0.248 (0.184)
External dummy	6.802 (19.482)	−4.614 (14.913)	5.968 (28.833)	–
Previous dummy	5.206 (21.201)	−3.542 (16.489)	−3.549 (31.302)	–
Bypass dummy	16.483 (20.606)	−1.044 (15.167)	28.324 (29.236)	–
Constant	−53.213^a (14.344)	−0.137 (23.656)	8.335 (17.496)	2.231 (2.00)
Regional dummies	Yes	Yes	Yes	No
Year dummies	Yes	Yes	Yes	Yes
Industry dummies	Yes	Yes	Yes	No
Adjusted R-squared	0.534	0.863	0.520	0.571
No. of observations	2290	1832	1832	1832

Notes:
1) Values in parentheses are standard errors.
2) a,b,c – statistically significant at 1 per cent, 5 per cent and 10 per cent on a two-tail test, respectively.
3) Firms serving as the base (constant) (a) did not have managers with bypass firms, (b) were not in part owned by external institutions and (c) were eventually privatized by the internal method.
4) The instrumental variables used are the same ones as those listed under Table 7.2.
5) In the level estimates, the constant term reflects the year 1991, firms in manufacturing industry, firms in Ljubljana region and firms that (a) had managers with bypass firms, (b) were not in part owned by an external institution and (c) were eventually privatized by the internal method.
6) In testing the hypothesis that $\gamma_2 = \gamma_3$ the values of relevant F statistics for OLS Lagged Levels, IV Levels, IV Lagged Levels and IV First Difference, models are 39.9, 71.8, 4.7 and 41.3 respectively. The hypothesis $\gamma_2 = \gamma_3$ is hence rejected in all four specifications.
7) In testing the hypothesis that $\gamma_1 = 1 - \gamma_2$ the values of relevant F statistics for OLS Lagged Levels, IV Levels, IV Lagged Levels and IV First Difference, models are 1.6, 0.54, 0.9 and 5.5 respectively. At the 5 per cent test level we cannot reject the hypothesis in all except IV First Difference Levels model.

given that workers in these firms know that in a few years they will be majority owners. They hence replace their firm's capital but also pay themselves wages at the expense of current surplus that they may otherwise have to remit in part to the government. Taking these results together, we find strong econometric evidence that workers in these firms appropriate part of the surplus (but not depreciation funds), and that they do so at the expense of investment ($\beta_2 < 0$ together with $\gamma_2 > 0$ and $\gamma_3 = 0$).

Firms that were eventually privatized to outsiders yield similar or somewhat higher coefficients γ_1 on the alternative wage, uniformly lower coefficients γ_2 on surplus and higher coefficients γ_3 on depreciation per worker than the insider privatized firms. In these firms, many of which have negative profit, one hence finds that wages are more related to the alternative wage and that workers boost their wages by appropriating depreciation funds and by not sharing in losses. The wage setting in these types of firms is hence driven by the available alternatives and the deficiency in corporate governance is manifested by the resistance of workers to share in losses and by their ability to appropriate depreciation funds. Combining these results with those in Table 7.2, we find that workers in these firms appropriate part of the depreciation funds but that this behavior is unrelated to firms' investment decisions ($\beta_2 = 0$ together with $\gamma_2 = 0$ and $\gamma_3 > 0$).

Previous ownership by an external institution has a relatively insignificant effect on the alternative wage and surplus coefficients. The exception is the IV first difference specification, in which the effect on the coefficient of the alternative wage is positive and on the coefficient of surplus negative. Combining these coefficients with those for the base set of firms, we find that firms with previous owners have coefficients on both the alternative wage and surplus per worker that are significant and in the [0, 1] interval in all specifications. Furthermore, relative to the base results, previous ownership diminishes the ability of workers to appropriate depreciation funds as wages. The estimated coefficient γ_3 is negative in all specifications and it is statistically significant in all specifications except for the IV first difference. The effect of previous ownership is hence relatively neutral with respect to β_2 and γ_2, but negative with respect to γ_3.

Finally, the effect of the CEO having a bypass company is to increase the tie of their own wage to the alternative wage (increasing γ_1) and reduce its link to the surplus generated by the firm (reducing γ_2). In only one of the four specifications (IV levels) is there also a marginally significant positive link between the presence of a bypass firm and the ability of workers to increase their wages at the expense of the depreciation funds ($\gamma_3 > 0$). The effect of a CEO with a bypass firm is hence to reduce the negative effect of β_2 (that is, to reduce the ability of workers to increase wages at the expense of investment), reduce γ_2 and exert virtually no significant effect on γ_3.

For the sake of completeness, we have also estimated the investment and labor cost equations jointly as a system of equations. The parameter estimates are similar to those obtained in the separate estimations of these equations in Tables 7.2 and 7.3 and we therefore do not present them here in order to economize on space. Our estimates are hence robust to single-equation versus joint-equation estimation.

7.5 Conclusions

The decline in investment, rise in wages, importance of strategic restructuring, and interest in the role of insiders in the transition economies have led us to analyze the determinants of (and tradeoff between) investment and wages in an unusual panel data set covering several important types of firms. In our analysis, which covers the 1991–95 period in Slovenia, we are able to exploit the fact that during this pre-privatization period the relevant decision-makers already knew how the firms would eventually be privatized in the mid-to-late 1990s. We are also able to divide the firms into those that ultimately would be privatized to insiders versus outsiders and we have taken into account whether during the pre-privatization period the firms were in part owned by an external institution and/or managed by CEOs who owned (their own) 'bypass' companies. With this stratification, we find that firms that were ultimately privatized to insiders (and had no previous ownership by an external institution or a CEO with a bypass firm) have a significant positive relationship between investment and value added, while firms that were ultimately privatized to outsiders do not. The effect of previous ownership strengthens, while the presence of a CEO with a bypass company weakens, this relationship. Firms that were ultimately privatized to outsiders as well as those with the CEO bypass firms hence appear to be less constrained in their investment behavior by the availability of internal funds than are firms ultimately privatized to insiders and those with previous ownership by an external institution. Anecdotal evidence indicates that firms privatized to outsiders, being predominantly large firms, have (a) stronger ties to suppliers that are willing to provide credit or tolerate arrears and (b) more assets (especially land) that can be used as collateral to obtain bank loans. Firms that were ultimately privatized to insiders are smaller and have a less powerful relationship with suppliers and banks. The elite CEOs with bypass firms appear to be able to overcome capital market imperfections on their firms, while previous external owners are (surprisingly) unable to do so.

Firms that were ultimately privatized to insiders register a very strong tradeoff between investment and wages, while those ultimately privatized to outsiders do not. The tradeoff is weakened by the presence of a CEO with a bypass company and unaffected by previous ownership of the firm by an external institution. Moreover, firms that were ultimately privatized to insiders and those with previous ownership by an external institution have wages that are relatively unrelated to the alternative wage, but strongly linked to the firm's surplus. In contrast, the firms that were eventually privatized to outsiders and firms with CEO bypass companies link wages to the alternative wage and display little surplus sharing. Workers hence have and exploit bargaining power in firms where they have obtained the government's permission to privatize the firm to themselves and their managers. Similarly, the lack of a link between wages and surplus in the firms that are to be privatized to outsiders is not a sign of lack of worker power since surplus in these firms is often negative. An interesting finding is that the CEOs with bypass firms are able to resist workers' demands for surplus sharing, while previous ownership by an external institution has the opposite effect. These findings suggest that theoretical modeling and policy formulation have underestimated the power of elite (and highly self-interested) managers to restrain wage demands of worker-insiders and overestimated such powers on the part of external owners.

Finally, while workers in firms with internal privatization, prior ownership and CEO bypass companies do not appropriate depreciation funds as wages, workers in the (frequently loss-making) firms with eventual external privatization do so. In the latter group of firms, workers hence do not share in losses but appropriate depreciation funds as wages. In contrast, workers who know that they will ultimately own the firm tend to replace their firm's capital but also pay themselves wages at the expense of current surplus that they may otherwise have to remit in part to the government.

Overall, our findings indicate that policy-makers in the transition and other emerging market economies should assign priority to establishing a proper legal and institutional framework as they relax or lose government control over firms. Insiders behave rationally and exploit legal and institutional opportunities, and appropriate part of rents (see also for example, Crombrugghe and Walque, 1997; and Estrin *et al.*, 1988).

Notes

1. Prašnikar's research on this paper was in part supported by the Ministry of Science and Technology grant no. 3411-97-25-7863 and by Phare ACE grant no. P96-6095-R. Svejnar's research was in part supported by NSF grant no. SBR95-12001 and Phare ACE grant no. P96-6095-R. The authors would like to thank Matjaz Koman and Lubomir Lizal for their useful comments. They would also like to acknowledge the excellent assistance in data gathering and processing by Matjaz Koman and Marko Grobelnik. Finally, the authors are indebted to the Slovenian Agency for Privatization, the Slovenian Statistical Office and numerous Slovenian enterprises for providing them with the data used in this paper. The usual caveat applies.
2. EBRD (1995, p. 67) for instance estimates that between 1985 and 1993 gross fixed investment declined from 29.5 per cent to 19 per cent in the former Soviet Union and from 24 per cent to 18 per cent in Eastern Europe. It should be noted that investment was an important subject of research already with respect to the communist economies. The principal focus at that time was on obsolescence of

capital over-investment, and the effects of foreign investment. See e.g., Thornton (1970), Desai (1976), Gomulka (1978), Green and Levine (1977), Weitzman (1979), Brada and Hoffman (1985), Terrell (1992, 1993), and Uvalic (1992).

3. See Aghion *et al.* (1994a), Aghion *et al.* (1994b), Blanchard and Aghion (1995), Grosfeld and Roland (1997), and Blanchard (1997).

4. The procedure for identifying the CEOs with bypass companies consisted of comparing the names and addresses of the chief executive officers of the 458 firms with the corresponding information in the registry of all private firms. The firms resented having CEOs with their own bypass firms and by 1994 they effectively banned the CEOs from establishing bypass firms.

5. We cannot distinguish whether these previous owners were domestic or foreign, although we know that the frequency of foreign owners was very limited.

6. See Prašnikar and Svejnar (1988).

7. On the demand side, much of the literature has focused on establishing the relative merits of the dynamic structural, Tobin's q, neoclassical, and accelerator models of investment, while studies on the supply side examined links between the firm's availability of internal finance and its investment (reflecting the effects of transaction costs and other market imperfections on the supply of capital). See for example, Fazzari *et al.* (1988, 2000), Kaplan and Zingales (1997, 2000) and Hubbard (1998).

8. As discussed in Lizal and Svejnar (2002), the basic capital accumulation constraint is given by $K_t = (1-\delta)K_{t-1} + I_t$, where $I_t = I_t^{Gross} = I_t^{Net} + I_t^{Replacement}$ and hence $I_t^{Net} = I_t - \delta K_{t-1}$. Denoting the optimal level of capital by K_t^*, the flexible accelerator (Koyck) model assumes that in each period a proportion λ of the gap $K_t - K_t^*$ between the actual and optimal level of capital is closed. The model further assumes that $K_t^* = \mu Y_t$ and net investment is hence given by $I_t^{Net} = \lambda(K_t^* - K_{t-1}) = \lambda\mu Y_t - \lambda K_{t-1}$, implying that the actual level of capital may be expressed as $K_t = \lambda\mu Y_t + (1\lambda)K_{t-1}$. Substituting this expression into the equations for $K_{t-1}, K_{t-2}, \ldots$, one obtains

$$K_t = \mu[\lambda Y_t + \lambda(1-\lambda)Y_{t-1} + \lambda(1-\lambda)^2 Y_{t-2} + \lambda(1-\lambda)^3 Y_{t-3} + \ldots],$$

which yields the corresponding net investment equation:

$$I_t^{Net} = K_t - K_{t-1} = \Delta K_t = \mu[\lambda\Delta Y_t + \lambda(1-\lambda)\Delta Y_{t-1}$$
$$+ \lambda(1-\lambda)^2\Delta Y_{t-2} + \lambda(1-\lambda)^3\Delta Y_{t-3} + \ldots].$$

Substituting back into the gross investment relationship one obtains Equation (7.1).

9. Note that the usual assumption on the form of heteroskedasticty of e_t leads to scaling with the reciprocal of capital. We therefore use ε_t to denote the transformed residuals.

10. Fazzari *et al.* (1988, 2000), Kaplan and Zingales (1997, 2000), and Hubbard (1998) provide overviews of this literature.

11. Value added is defined as profit plus labor cost plus depreciation. It is net of servicing loans and other costs.

12. Due to space limitations, we provide only a brief account of the principal features of the Slovenian transition. For a more detailed account, see for example, OECD (1997), Mrak *et al.* (ed.), (2004), Bole and Mramor (2006).

13. By the end of 1996 there were 33 banks operating in Slovenia, with the market share of 5 largest banks being about 60 per cent. Not all of the banks had equal operating licenses, with the limitations on bank operations varying with their capitalization and other factors.
14. See for example, Bole's (1997) analysis based on the theoretical framework of Stiglitz and Weiss (1981).
15. See for example, Cornelli *et al.* (1996) for the argument that in these types of circumstances demand for credit will be negatively related to profitability, as high profit firms are able and prefer to finance their investment internally rather than to borrow.
16. In comparison, in 1994 the ratio of bank credits to GDP attained 95 per cent in the Czech Republic, 63 per cent in Hungary, 33 per cent in Poland, and 13 per cent in Russia. By 1996, the corresponding percentages were 75, 27, 20, and 13. The range of values observed in developed market economies is 120–130 per cent (see Meyendorff and Snyder, 1997).
17. The Law did not apply to enterprises providing special public services, banks and insurance companies, enterprises engaged in the organization of gambling, enterprises that were transformed under the Law on Cooperatives, enterprises that were transformed under the forestry legislation, and firms in the process of bankruptcy.
18. The data are based on registered unemployed. The unemployment rate measured by labor force surveys also shows a major rise but it is about one-half of that measured by the unemployment registry data.
19. We use real assets as our measure of the capital stock.
20. One US\$ was approximately 10.5 Tolars (Dinars) in 1990. All Tolar values are in constant 1991 prices.
21. See Dreze (1989) for the theoretical underpinning of these arguments.
22. See for example, Hubbard (1998) for a survey.
23. This finding contrasts with that obtained by the studies of the Czech industrial firms (Anderson and Kegels, 1997; Lizal and Svejnar, 2002), where investment is positively related to sales. The reasons for this discrepancy include the fact that in the 1980s and early 1990s Slovenia was a more western-oriented market economy than the Czech Republic and that in the 1990s many Czech firms appear to have operated under softer budget constraints than their Slovenian counterparts.
24. The IV first difference coefficient is negative but statistically insignificant.

References

Aghion, P., O. Blanchard and R. Burgess (1994a) 'The Behavior of State Firms in Eastern Europe Pre-privatization', *European Economic Review*, 38 (6), 132–49.

Aghion, P., O. Blanchard and W. Carlin (1994b) 'The Economics of Enterprise Restructuring in Central and Eastern Europe', *Centre for Economic Policy Research Discussion Paper*, No. 1058.

Abel, A. B. and O. J. Blanchard (1986) 'The Present Value of Profits and Cyclical Movements in Investments', *Econometrica*, 54.

Anderson, R. and C. Kegels (1997) 'Finance and Investment in Transition: Czech Enterprises, 1993–94', *IRES Discussion Paper*, no. 9715, May.

Blanchard, O. J. (1991) 'Notes on the Speed of Transition, Unemployment and Growth in Poland', MIT, mimeo.

_____ (1997) *The Economics of Post-Communist Transition* (Oxford: Clarendon Press).

Blanchard, O. and P. Aghion (1995) 'On Insider Privatization', MIT, mimeo.

Bole, V. (1997) 'Stabilization in Slovenia: From High Inflation to Excessive Inflow of Foreign Capital', in M. Blejer, and M. Škreb (eds) *Macroeconomic Stabilization in Transition Economies* (Cambridge: Cambridge University Press).

Bole, V. and D. Mramor (2006) ' "Soft Landing" in the ERM2: Lessons from Slovenia,' in J. Prašnikar (ed.) *Competitiveness, Social Responsibility and Economic Growth* (New York: Nova Science Publisher).

Bond, S. and C. Meghir (1994) 'Dynamic Investment Models and the Firm's Financial Policy', *Review of Economic Studies*, 61.

Brada, J. and D. L. Hoffman (1985) 'The Productivity Differential Between Soviet and Western Capital and the Benefits of Technology Imports to the Soviet Economy', *Quarterly Review of Economics and Business*, 25, 7–18.

Burda, M. (1993) 'Unemployment, Labour Markets and Structural Change in Eastern Europe', *Economic Policy*, 16.

Commander, S. and F. Coricelli (eds) (1995) *Unemployment, Restructuring, and the Labour Market in Eastern Europe and Russia* (Washington, DC: The World Bank).

Cornelli, F., R. Portes and M. Schaffer (1996) 'The Capital Structure of Firms in Central and Eastern Europe', *CEPR Discussion Paper*, no. 1392.

Crombrugghe, A. and G. Walque (1997) 'Fiscal Norming of Wages to Promote Employment with Monopoly Power', *CEPR Discussion Paper*, no. 1766.

Desai, P. (1976) 'The Production Function and technical Change in Postwar Soviet Industry: A reexamination', *American Economic Review*, 66, 372–81.

Dreze, J. H. (1989) *Labor Management, Contracts and Capital Markets* (Oxford: Basil Blackwell).

European Bank for Reconstruction and Development (EBRD) (1995) *Transition Report 1995* (London: EBRD).

European Bank for Reconstruction and Development (EBRD) (1996) *Transition Report 1996* (London: EBRD).

Earle, J. S., S. Estrin, and L. L. Leshchenko (1995) 'Ownership Structures, Patterns of Control and Enterprise Behavior in Russia, Mimeo', *London Business School Discussion Paper*, no. 7.

Estrin, S., R. Moore and J. Svejnar (1988) 'Market Imperfection, Labor-Management and Earnings Differentials in a Developing Economy: Theory and Econometric Evidence from Yugoslavia', *Quarterly Journal of Economics*, 103 (3), 465–78.

—— (1988) 'Financing Constraints and Corporate Investment', *Brooking Papers on Economic Activity*, 1, 141–206.

Fazzari, S. M., G. R. Hubbard, and B. C. Petersen (2000) 'Investment-Cash Flow Sensitivities are Useful: A Comment on Kaplan and ZIngales' *Quarterly Journal of Economics*, 115 (3), 695–705.

Furubotn, E. and S. Pejovich (1970) 'Property Rights and the Behavior of the Firm in a Socialist State: The Example of Yugoslavia', *Zeitschrift fur Nationalokonomie* 30 (December), 431–454.

Gomulka, S. (1978) 'Import Technology and Growth: Poland 1971–1980', *Cambridge Journal of Economics*, 2, 1–16.

Green, D. W. and H. S. Levine (1977) 'Implications of Technology Transfers for the USSR', East-West Technological Co-operation.

Grosfeld, I. and G. Roland (1997) 'Defensive and Strategic Restructuring in Central European Enterprises', *Journal of Transforming Economies and Societies*, 3 (4), 21–46.

Hinds, M. (1990) 'Issues in the Introduction of Market Forces in Eastern European Socialist Economics', in S. Commander (ed.) *Managing Inflation in Socialist Economies in Transition* (The Economic Development Institute of the World Bank).

Hubbard, G. R. (1998) 'Capital-Market Imperfections and Investment', *Journal of Economic Literature*, 36 (1), 193–225.

Jorgenson, D. W. (1971) 'Econometric Studies of Investment Behavior: A Survey', *Journal of Economic Literature*, 9, 111–1147.

Kaplan, S. and L. Zingales (1997) 'Do Investment-Cash Flow Sensitivities Provide Useful Measures of Financing Constraints', *The Quarterly Journal of Economics*, 112 (1), 167–215.

Kaplan, S. and L. Zingales (2000) 'Investment-Cash Flow Sensitivities are not Valid Measures of Financing Constraints', *The Quarterly Journal of Economics*, 115 (2), 707–712.

Kopcke, R. W. (1985) 'The Determinants of Investment Spending', *New England Economic Review*, July, 19–35.

Koyck, L. W. (1954) *Distributed Lag and Investment Analysis* (Amsterdam North-Holland).

Lizal, L. (1977) 'Depreciation Rates in Transition Economy Evidence from Czech Panel Data',*CERGE-EI Working Paper*, October.

Lizal, L. and J. Svejnar (2002) 'Investment, Credit Rationing and the Soft Budget Constraint: Evidence from Czech Panel Data', *Review of Statistics*, 84 (2), 353–70.

—— (1997) 'Enterprise Investment during the Transition: Evidence from Czech Panel Data', *William Davidson Institute Working Paper*, No. 60a, Ann Arbor, MI.

Mencinger. J. (1991) 'Makroekonomske dileme republike Slovenije', *Gospodarska gibanja*, EPIF, 5.

Meyendorff, A. and E. Snyder (1997) 'Transactional Structures of Bank Privatizations in Central Europe and Russia', *Journal of Comparative Economics*, 25 (1).

Mrak, M., M. Rojec and C. Silva-Jauregui (eds) (2004) *Slovenia: From Yugoslavia to the European Union* (Washington DC: The World Bank).

Organisation for Economic Co-operation and Development (OECD) (1997) *Economic Survey of Slovenia*, (Paris: OECD) May.

Prašnikar, J. and J. Svejnar (1988) 'Economic Behavior of Yugoslav Enterprises, *Advances in the Economic Analysis of Participatory and Labor-Managed Firms*, 3, 237–312.

Prašnikar, J. and J. Svejnar (1991) 'Workers Participation in Management vs. Social Ownership and Government Policies: Lessons for Transforming Socialist Economies', *Comparative Economic Studies*, 4, 27–45.

Prašnikar, J., J. Svejnar, D. Mihajlek, and V. Prašnikar (1994) 'Behavior of Participatory Firms in Yugoslavia: Lessons for Transforming Economies,' *The Review of Economics and Statistics*, 76 (4), 728–41.

Stiglitz, J. and A. Weiss (1981) 'Credit Rationing in Markets with Imperfect Information,' *American Economic Review*, 71, 393–410

Svejnar, J. (1982), 'On the Theory of a Participatory Firm', *Journal of Economic Theory*, 27(2), 313–330.

Svejnar, J. (1986) 'Bargaining Power, Fear of Disagreement and Wage Settlements: Theory and Evidence from U.S. Industry', *Econometrica*, 54, 1055–78.

Terrell, K. (1992) 'Productivity of Western and Domestic Capital in Polish Industry', *Journal of Comparative Economics*, 16, 494–514.

Terrell, K. (1993) 'Technical Change and Factor Bias in Polish Industry', *The Review of Economics and Statistics*, 75, 741–47.

Thornton, J. (1970) 'Value Added and Factor Productivity in Soviet Industry', *American Economic Review*, 60, 863–71.

Uvalic, M. (1992) *Investment and Property Rights in Yugoslavia – The Long Transition to a Market Economy* (Cambridge: Cambridge University Press).

Vanek, J. (1970) *The General Theory of Labor-Managed Market Economies* (Ithaca: Cornell University Press).

Weitzman, M. L. (1979) 'Technology Transfer to the USSR: An Economic Analysis', *Journal of Comparative Economics*, 3, 167–77.

8
How Different Is Serbia?

Milica Uvalic[1]

8.1 Introduction

In 1991, the Socialist Federal Republic (SFR) of Yugoslavia was in a somewhat different position with respect to the other countries embarking on transition to market economy, as illustrated in my paper 'How different is Yugoslavia?' (Uvalic, 1991).[2] Despite having retained the most important systemic features of the socialist economy, including non-private property and state paternalism, SFR Yugoslavia at that time exhibited certain advantages: (a) a shorter reform agenda, due to a longer tradition in market-oriented economic reforms; (b) major economic decentralization, due to the dilution of powers from federal to lower-level political authorities and self-management mechanisms of policy coordination; and (c) greater openness towards the West, which brought many benefits including a higher degree of economic integration of the Yugoslav economy into world markets. The country also faced certain disadvantages which threatened transition-related reforms launched in 1989–90, including (a) a severe political crisis; (b) ambiguous property rights associated with 'social property' in combination with workers' self-management; and (c) resistance to change due to a higher degree of popular support for the existing regime. After the break-up of the Yugoslav federation, these systemic features inherited by its successor states have had very different implications in the different national contexts, thereafter leading to substantial divergence in the transition paths of the newly created states.

The present paper considers the case of Serbia, where until fairly recently the transition to market economy has been substantially delayed. Taking into account the specific features that Serbia had in 1991, it addresses the question of how different it is today with respect to other transition countries. In what follows, the most important political events of the 1990s will be recalled, and their impact on macroeconomic performance and economic reforms in Serbia during the first decade of transition (Section 2). The more recent economic reforms implemented by the post-Milosevic governments after October 2000 are then discussed (Section 3). Taking into account the overall results of transition, an assessment is made of the present systemic features of the Serbian economy (Section 4). A few concluding remarks are given at the end (Section 5). Although the focus is on Serbia, the analysis also refers to the Federal Republic (FR) of Yugoslavia, and after 2003 to Serbia and Montenegro, the country Serbia belonged to until June 2006.[3] Kosovo, although in January 2007 still officially part of Serbia, is explicitly excluded from the analysis.[4]

8.2 The slow pace of transition during the 1990s

The 1989 changes did not bypass Serbia. The transition to market economy and multiparty democracy in SFR Yugoslavia, and therefore Serbia, also started in 1989.[5] In December 1989 the federal Prime Minister Markovic implemented a bold macroeconomic stabilization program and launched the first privatization law, while the first multiparty elections were held in all republics soon after (in Serbia in December 1990). The transition was, however, interrupted by the severe political crisis and the break-up of the country in June 1991. Thereafter, a number of essentially political events have had very negative implications for most of its successor states, particularly Serbia. The disintegration of the Yugoslav federation was accompanied by the break-up of its economic and monetary union, loss of markets and of a common currency, four military conflicts in which Serbia/FR Yugoslavia has been directly or indirectly involved,[6] nationalistic policies which gave priority to political over economic objectives, high costs of maintaining almost one million refugees from Bosnia and Croatia, and substantial delays in political reforms which postponed effective democratization and the establishment of a functional state. On the international front, severe political and economic sanctions were imposed against FR Yugoslavia during most of the 1990s, culminating in the 11-weeks NATO bombardments in 1999. International sanctions interrupted not only normal trade flows and foreign direct investment (FDI), but also bank transfers, access to international financial markets, membership in international organizations, general inflow of information and free travel abroad, since airports were closed and visas introduced even by neighboring countries. Most of these events have had destabilizing effects for the whole Southeast European (SEE) region, but the implications for the Serbian economy have been particularly devastating. These events have also directly influenced the slow process of economic transition and integration of Serbia with the European Union (EU).

Following the disintegration of SFR Yugoslavia in June 1991, in just a few years the economy of the new FR Yugoslavia virtually collapsed (Uvalic, 2001a). By the end of 1993, GDP had fallen to just 43 per cent of its 1989 level. Expansionary monetary and fiscal policies necessary to finance the war in 1992–93 led to one of the highest and longest hyperinflations ever recorded in world history – by the end of December 1993, an average annual rate of 116.5 trillion per cent. The 1994 stabilization program of the

National Bank Governor Dragoslav Avramovic was very successful in halting hyperinflation (average inflation in 1994 was down to 3.3 per cent), introducing a convertible dinar, and reversing the trend of declining output, but these positive results were short-lived, essentially due to lack of systemic change. In the second half of the 1990s, despite economic recovery inflation again became double-digit, exports stagnated contributing to a rising current account deficit, and the black market exchange rate in 1997–98 remained six times the official rate. After the conflict in Kosovo in 1999, GDP declined by 18 per cent, industrial production by 21 per cent, and exports by as much as 50 per cent. Over the whole 1990–99 period, FDI amounted to just US $1 billion, almost entirely due to the only important privatization deal, the 1997 partial privatization of Serbian Telecom.

Very little progress has been achieved in reforming the economic system throughout the 1990s. Although there were attempts to re-launch some important reforms, such as privatization (see below), there were serious policy reversals in other areas and the return to practices long abandoned in SFR Yugoslavia. These included frequent price freezes, extreme protectionism in foreign trade (very high tariffs in combination with a complicated system of import quotas, licenses and various types of permits), foreign exchange rationing and the use of multiple exchange rates, applied on a discretionary, non-transparent and ad hoc basis, frequently in order to favor primarily the political and economic elite. During the years of sanctions, employment security was even strengthened through a law explicitly prohibiting lay-offs, thus postponing enterprise restructuring.

Regarding the enterprise sector, contrary to all other successor states of SFR Yugoslavia (including Montenegro within FR Yugoslavia), where 'social property' was first re-nationalized in an attempt to clarify property rights and thus facilitate privatization, in its new 1992 Constitution Serbia maintained 'social property' as one of the four property forms (alongside private, mixed, and cooperative property). Despite two new privatization laws and abundant related legislation (1991, 1994, 1996, 1997), since privatization was to be initiated voluntarily, by decision of the enterprise's General Assembly, the larger part of enterprises (and of the economy) remained under the ambiguous 'social property' regime.[7] There was no radical break with workers' self-management, since 'social property' also implied the partial maintenance of workers' management rights. Only a small number of firms in 'social property' (the most important ones) were re-nationalized and also excluded from privatization, in order to ensure government control over the strategically most important enterprises. These state-owned firms which under self-management were run relatively independently by workers and managers, came under the supervision and direct control of government ministries. Instead of demolishing state paternalism, there was a step backwards towards governance mechanisms abandoned more than half a century ago (Cerovic, 2000). Not surprisingly, by 2000 the contribution of the private sector to GDP was still less than 40 per cent. Only small-scale privatization had been partially implemented, mainly resulting in widespread ownership by insiders who frequently owned worthless shares (though there have been cases of successful insider-owned firms). Instead of breaking up large enterprises, economic power further concentrated in a handful of state-protected firms, for which soft budget constraints have been maintained through various direct and indirect privileges.

A decade of political and economic instability and very selective application of transition has had far-reaching social consequences. Along with falling incomes and living standards, there was notable social differentiation with adverse effects on the distribution of income and wealth. Absolute poverty roughly doubled during the 1990s. Social protection and health services rapidly deteriorated. The banking system was abused for political purposes, in 1992 through the freezing of citizens' foreign currency bank accounts,[8] and later through fraudulent financial pyramid schemes which deprived many Serbian citizens of their life-long savings (see Dinkic, 1995). Laws were arbitrarily implemented (if at all), with different criteria applied to the different segments of the economy, substantially weakening the rule of law. International sanctions created incentives for smuggling, illegal activities, organized crime and 'war profiteering' (Babic, 1999). New phenomena appeared in Serbia which could be characterized as elements of 'wild' capitalism (Uvalic, 2002). Parallel to the mass impoverishment of the larger part of the population, a new oligarchy was born recruited among directors of big factories and the closest political collaborators of President Milosevic. The political system was deeply corrupted and manipulated. The new oligarchs' strong influence over state institutions entailed significant benefits: they were in charge of the rules of the game throughout the 1990s, including foreign trade transactions which under sanctions secured enormous profits, and had used their position and various illegal and semi-legal channels to transfer capital to new private firms or personal bank accounts abroad. Many years of international isolation have contributed to the strength of the political elite, which has had a decade to entrench itself, forge new alliances (also with the underworld) and adapt to the post-1989 order (Kekic, 2000). Under sanctions, smuggling had also become the main source of earnings for many citizens, contributing to the flourishing of the informal economy. Various forms of criminality became common in everyday life, including robbery, kidnapping, murders and false suicides, for which those responsible have never been found. During the most difficult times when it was impossible to get a normal bank credit, the 'new rich' entrepreneurs were offering loans at weekly interest rates which were multiple the normal ones. A dramatic social differentiation of the Serbian society took place: a rapid decline in real incomes of the larger part of the population, parallel with the enrichment of a new and tiny social elite.

The severe economic and social problems that accumulated during the 1990s were frequently presented by the Serbian government as proof that the transition had prevalently negative effects, in this way also serving to justify the choice of a 'gradualist' strategy. In reality, vested interests of the political and economic elite prevented more radical economic and political reforms. The economic system for the most had changed little, or had regressed with respect to the model of market socialism that existed before 1989. The political system, though formally a multi-party democracy, was dominated by the Socialist Party of Serbia (SPS), or rather by its President Slobodan Milosevic and his closest collaborators.[9]

8.3   Post-2000 reforms: A radical change of regime

A radical change in the course of transition in Serbia came after the October 2000 political changes which marked the end of the Milosevic regime. Over the last 6 years, the new policies have produced impressive results in many areas, though more limited progress in others.[10]

One of the most urgent tasks of the Serbian/Yugoslav government in late 2000 was *macroeconomic stabilization*, given that price liberalization, necessary in order to eliminate major price distortions, initially also led to a high average *inflation* rate – of over 90 per cent in 2001. Substantial disinflation was achieved thereafter, by 2004 to a one-digit figure. Although average inflation in 2005 again jumped to 17 per cent (mainly due to higher oil and electricity prices and wage increases), in 2006 it is expected to decline to 12.7 per cent (see Table 8.1). Tight monetary policy has contributed to a strong real appreciation of the dinar (2001–03) followed by exchange rate stability,[11] introduction of current account convertibility and an impressive increase in foreign exchange reserves (US $11.7 billion by end-2006).

Table 8.1   Serbia: main macroeconomic indicators, 1999–2006

	1999	2000	2001	2002	2003	2004	2005	2006
Inflation (average, %)	37.1	60.4	91.1	21.2	11.3	9.5	17.2	12.7
Government balance (% of GDP)	Na	−1.0	−4.9	−8.3	−3.4	0.0	0.9	2.7
Real GDP growth (%)	−18.0	5.2	5.1	4.5	2.4	9.3	6.3	5.8
Unemployment rate (% of labor force)	14.5	13.3	13.3	14.5	16.0	19.5	21.8	Na
Current account balance (% of GDP)	−4.4	−5.1	−5.0	−17.5	−16.4	−14.8	−10.0	−10.4
FDI inflows (million US $)	112	25	165	475	1360	966	1550	4000

Source: EBRD (2006), except for: unemployment (Commission of the EC, 2006a); the 2006 inflation, GDP growth rate, and current account balance (Serbian Statistical Office, December 2006); and FDI (Economist Intelligence Unit, December 2006).

Serbia recorded relatively high *public deficits* in 2001–03, but thereafter achieved a balanced budget or even surpluses, in 2006 estimated at 2.7 per cent of GDP (Table 8.1). Radical fiscal reforms have included a major simplification of the tax system, the passage to gross wages for social contribution purposes, the introduction of value-added-tax, and measures to fight the informal economy (such as fines for the non-issuing of bills). Nevertheless, the structure and level of public expenditure has not changed much, in 2005 representing 43 per cent of GDP, but this is a problem common to other SEE countries (Croatia and Bosnia and Herzegovina have even higher public expenditure).

Growth performance has been impressive throughout most of the 2000–06 period (see Table 8.1). The real GDP growth rate was 4–5 per cent in 2000–02, it slowed down to 2.4 per cent in 2003, but was 9 per cent in 2004, 6 per cent in 2005–06, and is likely to stay around 6 per cent also in 2007. The strong economic recovery, however, has been largely insufficient to compensate for the very substantial fall in output during the 1990s. Although most other SEE countries are in a similar situation (by 2004, only Albania had attained its 1989 GDP level), Serbia is by far in the worst situation, having by mid-2005 reached at most around 60 per cent of its 1989 real GDP. In 2005, Serbia had a GDP per capita of US $3250 (at market exchange rates), therefore higher than Albania, Bosnia and Herzegovina, and Macedonia; or at Purchasing Power Parity (PPP) of US $6540, somewhat higher only of Albania (Economist Intelligence Unit (EIU), December 2006; see Figure 8.1). Serbia's present GDP per capita corresponds to about 30 per cent of the EU-25 average.

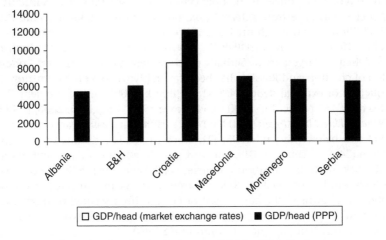

Figure 8.1   GDP per head in Southeast Europe, 2005 (in US dollars)
Source: Economist Intelligence Unit, December 2006, p. 4

Recent strong economic recovery has not yet brought employment growth, on the contrary. Over 2001–05, the *unemployment rate* (based on labor force survey) has continued increasing, from 13.3 per cent to 21.8 per cent, the long-term unemployment rate has also increased from 9.0 per cent to 17.3 per cent, parallel with a decline in the employment rate from 59.7 per cent to 51 per cent respectively (Commission, 2006a). Though these high unemployment rates overestimate the effective number of jobless workers since many are still active in the informal economy, unemployment is a key economic problem and is likely to worsen with further enterprise restructuring and privatization. Recent government measures have been largely unsuccessful in reversing these trends.

Serbia's *external sector* is also characterized by serious imbalances. The *trade deficit* has reached historical records, 25 per cent of GDP in 2004, though slightly declining thereafter (to 22 per cent in 2006). Serbia's exports have remained stagnant during the 1990s, but have roughly doubled in 2001–05, particularly to the EU facilitated by EU trade preferences granted in late 2000. However, the exports structure has not changed substantially, concentrated mainly in agricultural and low processed manufacturing products. The sluggish export performance is mainly due to the structural weaknesses of the economy, the limited restructuring and modernization of key industries which missed a whole decade of technological progress (though the strong real appreciation of the dinar has also hampered export growth). In 2002, exports were still dominated by state and socially owned enterprises, accounting for 45 per cent of total exports (World Bank, 2004, p. 55).

Serbia's *current account deficit* is also at critical levels and among the highest in the SEE region, despite recent improvements (from 17 per cent of GDP in 2003 it has been reduced to 10.4 per cent in 2006; see Table 8.1). Substantial financial assistance from international donors during 2000–06 (more than €2.5 billion only through the EU CARDS program) as well as workers remittances (10–12 per cent of GDP during 2001–03) have contributed to limiting the deficit. A large part of Serbia's external debt to the Paris and London Club of creditors and Russia[12] has been favorably written off, permitting the reduction of external debt to US $15 billion by 2005 and of the debt/GDP ratio from 167 per cent in 2000 to 64 per cent in 2005 (EBRD, 2006, p. 173).

Foreign Direct Investment (FDI) has been steadily increasing particularly after 2003 (see below). By end-2005, FDI stock in Serbia amounted to US $5.9 billion (24.4 per cent of GDP), but corresponding to just 1.5 per cent of total FDI stock in all 28 transition countries (EIU, September 2006). Record FDI inflows will be achieved in 2006, of around US $4 billion (EIU, December 2006). As elsewhere, the largest part of FDI has been secured through a few successful privatization deals in specific sectors (tobacco, base metals, and more recently banking and telecommunications).

In addition to improved macroeconomic performance, substantial progress has been achieved in transition-related *institutional reforms*. Looking

Table 8.2 EBRD transition indicators: Serbia (2000–06) and SEE (mid-2006)

	Enterprises				Markets and trade			Financial institutions	
	Private sector share of GDP (in %) mid-year	Large-scale privatization	Small-scale privatization	Governance and enterprize restructuring	Price liberalization	Trade and foreign exchange system	Competition policy	Banking reform and interest rate liberalization	Securities markets & non-bank financial institutions
Serbia									
2000	40	1	3	1	2+	1	1	1	1
2001	40	1	3	1	4	2+	1	1	1
2002	45	2	3	2	4	3	1	2+	2–
2003	45	2+	3	2	4	3	1	2+	2
2004	50	2+	3+	2	4	3	1	2+	2
2005	55	3–	3+	2+	4	3+	1	3–	2
2006	55	3–	4–	2+	4	3+	2–	3–	2
SEE 2006									
Albania	75	3	4	2+	4+	4+	2	3–	2–
B&H	55	3–	3	2	4	4–	2–	3–	2–
Croatia	60	3+	4+	3	4	4+	2+	4	3
Macedonia	65	3+	4	3–	4+	4+	2	3–	2+
Montenegro	65	3+	3	2	4	3+	1	3–	2–
Serbia	55	3–	4–	2+	4	3+	2–	3–	2

Source: EBRD, *Transition report 2006.*

at EBRD transition indicators in late 2000, the only areas where some economic reforms had been implemented in Serbia were small-scale privatization and price liberalization (see Table 8.2). Just a year later, the EBRD evaluated Serbia and Montenegro as 'the fastest reformer' among all 27 transition economies. Thereafter, many economic reforms have been carried forward successfully.

Privatization has progressed according to a new 2001 law, based on cash-based sales at tenders and auctions, which fundamentally changed the strategy away from the insiders' model used in the 1990s towards commercial sales. During the first 4 years of its application, some 1500 firms were privatized (out of 3000 envisaged for privatization) and small-scale privatization has been almost completed, though large-scale privatization has been delayed. The private sector share of GDP increased from less than 40 to 55 per cent during 2000–06, but fundamental problems remain in the enterprise sector. FDI has gone into a few best companies (by October 2004, only 39 firms were sold at tenders), whereas in many privatized firms the change of ownership has left many problems unresolved, including poor corporate governance and lack of restructuring. In the still non-privatized part of the economy, there are more than a thousand socially-owned firms that have not found potential buyers (end-2006); some of these are heavily indebted loss-making firms, that since 2001 have been waiting for a new bankruptcy law, adopted only in 2006. In addition, over 70 socially-owned enterprises have been selected for a special restructuring program, but its implementation has also been delayed without justification. The strategically most important firms nationalized in the early 1990s, representing 35 per cent of Serbia's capital, have started being privatized only in 2006–07 – such as the oil and gas company NIS or the Bor mining and smelting complex.[13] These are among the reasons why in 2006 Serbia still had a low 2+ EBRD score in *governance and enterprise restructuring*.

A lot of progress has been achieved in both *price* and *foreign trade liberalization*. By 2005 the average tariff rate has been reduced to around 7 per cent, the tariff structure has been greatly simplified, and trade liberalization has been implemented within the SEE region.[14] By contrast, very limited results have been achieved in *competition policy* (the EBRD score being the lowest of all, 2–). Only in September 2005 did a new competition law come into effect, while in May 2006 the Commission for protection of competition became operational. De-monopolization of the Serbian economy has been delayed, as many domestic state and socially-owned enterprises continue to be sheltered from competition from abroad through non-tariff barriers, or face soft-budget constraints and are often in a better position than private firms regarding access to bank credit or tax relief. Budget subsidies to large loss-making firms have remained among the highest in the SEE region, around 3.7 per cent of GDP; in 2003, according to a World Bank survey, some 12 per cent of Serbian firms perceived no competition on the local market (World Bank, 2004, p. 34).

As to *financial reforms*, a number of loss-making banks were closed at an early stage, including four of the largest banks representing 55 per cent of total assets of the banking sector. Though privatization of the banking sector was initially delayed, it speeded up after 2004 and by mid-2006, 18 foreign banks were operating in Serbia,[15] foreign ownership already accounted for 77 per cent of banking assets, while the remaining assets were in the hands of 19 domestic banks, 12 of which were state-owned (Commission, 2006a; Zdrale, 2006). Despite increasing competition, the net interest spread, though declining, has remained high: 11 per cent in 2005, substantially higher than the SEE average of 7 per cent or the Central East European (CEE) average of 4 per cent (Commission, 2006b). Currency substitution is also relatively high, as foreign currency deposits account for around 70 per cent of total deposits. Due to delays in privatization, the capital market remains underdeveloped, dominated by state bonds on frozen foreign currency deposits. Although in mid-2006, some 100 Serbian firms were quoted on the Belgrade stock exchange, traded stock amounted to only €500 million (Commission, 2006a). Regarding non-financial institutions, the National Bank of Serbia recently withdrew licenses of insurance companies not satisfying required standards.

The business environment has also substantially improved. According to the World Bank *Doing Business Survey*, Serbia and Montenegro was the top reformer in 2004, having been evaluated favorably in 8 of the 10 indicators (such as capital and time needed to start a new business, resolve commercial disputes, or labor legislation). In the 2006 *Doing Business Survey*, Serbia improved its relative position further in five of the ten indicators and ranked first among all six western Balkan countries, 13th among the 28 European and Central Asian countries (ahead of some of the EU new member states such as Poland), and 68th in the aggregate ranking of 175 countries, having been upgraded from the 95th position it occupied in 2005.

Overall, impressive results have been achieved but, as shown earlier, there is one important area where progress has been relatively modest. In mid-2006, with the private sector contributing just 55 per cent to GDP, Serbia was still lagging behind the large majority of transition economies (all except five).[16] The 'politically correct' model of privatization was chosen in 2001 based on commercial sales, as suggested also by World Bank experts, justified by arguments of economic efficiency, rather than social justice which has guided previous privatizations (see Uvalic, 2004). It would have been wiser to have adopted a multi-track privatization strategy; as anticipated in 2001 (Uvalic, 2001b), many socially-owned enterprises have not found potential buyers and are likely to survive well beyond the set deadlines. These enterprises should have been closed during the initial phase or, as a socially more acceptable solution, could have been given freely to workers, in line with the long tradition of self-management. Even if this would have led to a number of insider-owned firms, this could have been, also in Serbia, a highly pragmatic means of effecting initial privatization. As in many other transition economies, employee ownership would most probably have been a transitory form of organization, eventually leading to a shift in ownership from insiders to outsiders (Nuti, 1997, p. 179).

There are also other complementary areas of reform which could have facilitated faster progress in the real sector of the economy had they been implemented earlier, such as bankruptcy legislation, the general hardening of budget constraints, breaking up monopolistic structures, promoting competition, more substantial support of new private firms, radical reforms of the judiciary as to ensure the rule of law, better governance mechanisms and protection of property rights – in line with the 'New Washington Consensus' (Kolodko and Nuti, 1997; Kolodko, 2000). These conditions on their own could have delivered many of the advantages expected of privatization (Uvalic and Nuti, 2003, p. 13).

8.4   Is Serbia different? Systemic features of the Serbian economy

Given the overall results of market-oriented economic reforms implemented so far, how different is Serbia today with respect to other countries in transition?

Only 6 years ago, Serbia was lagging behind most transition countries and thus was compared with the other laggards in SEE or the Commonwealth of Independent States (CIS) (see Nuti, 2004, p. 184). In the meantime, from a laggard Serbia has become a frontrunner, and has caught up in many areas of reform, even surpassing some SEE (and many CIS) countries (see Table 8.2). Thus today there are no longer large differences between the results achieved in Serbia and other SEE (even some CEE) countries, particularly regarding price liberalization, the trade and foreign exchange system, small-scale privatization, or the business environment. In other fields progress has been much slower – enterprise governance and restructuring, development of securities markets and non-bank financial institutions, competition policy – but these are areas where fundamental changes have been much slower in other transition economies as well.

Despite major similarities to other transition countries, Serbia still retains certain specific features which explain why its post-2000 transition has been quite unique, much more complex than initially anticipated. This is due to essentially two groups of factors: its different socialist legacy, and the turbulent 1990s.

Socialist legacy: Has anything remained of Serbia's 1989 specific economic features?[17] The advantage of a shorter reform agenda has mainly been lost, due to many reversals in economic policies during the 1990s away from a market economy (as illustrated earlier). There is one advantage, however, latent during many years of isolation and sanctions, that has recently force-fully re-emerged: the rich experience accumulated during several decades of intense contacts with the West – of enterprises, commercial banks, government institutions, individuals – is today proving valuable for re-establishing relations worldwide at all levels.

As to the disadvantages, one of the elements of the old economic system that has robustly survived these 17 years of transition in Serbia is 'social property'. The same systemic feature that was a burden in 1991 – ill-defined property rights – has remained a burden today. Under socialism 'social property' could have been considered an advantage of Serbia/former Yugoslavia with respect to other socialist countries where enterprises were in state property, but after 1989 it has clearly become a disadvantage, since in many cases it has slowed down enterprise privatization and restructuring. The other disadvantage – resistance to change – today may still be more present in Serbia than in many other transition countries, but for different reasons than those in 1989 (see below).

Legacy of the 1990s: The transition in Serbia has proved to be rather complex not only because of the survival of pre-1989 economic features and the postponement of radical change for a whole decade, but because of the numerous problems which emerged after 1991. The 1990s was not simply a lost decade from the standpoint of transition (see Begovic and Mijatovic, 2005); it was a decade of particularly unfavorable overall conditions associated with wars, isolation, non-democratic regime, hyperinflation and reversals in economic reform, which have left profound traces on all segments of Serbia's society. The general conditions for re-launching transition in Serbia in late 2000 were consequently far worse than those in 1989 when the transition first started. More precisely, Serbia in late 2000 did not start its new phase of political and economic transformation from scratch, but with a heavy burden of the 1990s. The retrograde political and economic system set up in 1991 and a decade of political and economic mismanagement have left many negative consequences, some of which are felt still today – in the behavior of the still non-privatized enterprises, in the criminal and semi-criminal networks that made up much of the Serbian economy in the 1990s and have proved very difficult to fully dismantle, in the highly non-transparent and still non-reformed public administration, in the insufficiently modernized judiciary, in workers' mentality and their non-acceptance that the days of self-management are over, in the use of traditional communist methods and often highly non-democratic political culture, in citizens' mistrust of the government and of the transition.

Though features of continuity with the old regime are not an exclusivity of Serbia – also in other post-communist countries discontinuities with the old regime have frequently been more apparent than real (Kekic, 2000) – in Serbia the element of continuity has probably been even stronger. Because of substantial delays in radical economic and political reforms and the very negative heritage of the last 17 years, these elements of continuity are proving more difficult to eradicate.

This is closely related to the previously mentioned issue of resistance to change, which in Serbia today is present not simply because, as in many other countries, the losers from transition are still numerous. The reasons behind resistance to change in Serbia are much more complex. They include nostalgia – not only for the pre-1989 days, when the standard of living was apparently higher, employment more secure, pensions were paid regularly, travel abroad did not require burdensome visas and the country was respected worldwide; but also for some features of the 1990s system, such as the possibility of earning extra income in the still then tolerated informal economy, or subsidized prices of electricity, bread and milk – and the illusion that the clock can miraculously be turned backwards. Resistance to change also derives from the unfulfilled expectations associated with false promises of nationalism, continuous manipulations of facts by the pre-2000 government and the state-controlled television (if not all media), populist policies which for years have intentionally postponed the necessary adjustments, making today's costs of transition in Serbia particularly high.

Serbia's apparent ambivalence and slowness in embracing change is also a result of another key difference between Serbia and CEE countries with respect to the underlying drivers of transition and associated attitudes to the West. In the early 1990s, the geopolitical and national interests in CEE coincided with those of political and economic transition, since anti-Russian and pro-European sentiment strongly facilitated the post-1989 changes. By contrast, in Serbia the international geopolitical changes ran counter to its national interests (in particular, the negative impact of the break-up of the country for Serb minorities outside Serbia), and Western policy (which culminated in NATO's bombing in 1999) has been seen by many in Serbia as fundamentally hostile to Serb interests (Kekic, 2000).

Serbian citizens have lived a whole decade in international isolation, under sanctions and the veil of false promises of the Milosevic regime, in a world of unrealistic and irrational expectations. These are some of the factors which explain why a third of the voters in Serbia in January 2007 was still not ready to accept the new direction of change taken in late 2000, towards a capitalist market economy and full integration with the rest of Europe.

Taking into account the changing nature of the Serbian economy and its institutions, today we find the coexistence of ingredients of at least four different economic systems:

- Traditional socialism (soft-budget constraints, subsidies to loss-making firms, monopolistic practices);
- Self-managed market socialism ('social property' of enterprises, protection of workers rights);
- 'Wild' capitalism (inefficient judiciary, gaps in market regulation, insecure property rights, corruption); and

- Hyper-liberal capitalism (fast trade liberalization, substantial downsizing of the welfare state, balanced budget).

While these same elements were there in 2001 (Uvalic, 2002), what has changed in the meantime is their relative weight, as the capitalist components have gained importance. There is no doubt that today the dominant paradigm in Serbia is the liberal capitalist model. The remnants of the previous economic systems – the pre-1989 market socialist and the post-1989 socialist–capitalist system – are in the process of being emarginated, although perhaps not as quickly as desired or expected, for all the reasons discussed earlier.

8.5 Concluding remarks

Although transition to market economy and multiparty democracy in Serbia has proved to be rather complex and in many ways unique, Serbia is more and more resembling other transition countries. Today it is an open market economy with dominant private ownership, it has liberalized its trade with the EU and with its neighbors, it has reformed many of its institutions, its financial sector is dominated by foreign-owned banks and there is an emerging stock exchange. Serbia is also the fastest growing economy in the SEE region, it has reached substantial macroeconomic stabilization, it has a stable (or slightly appreciating) internally convertible domestic currency, it has accumulated substantial foreign exchange reserves greatly minimizing the risk of external insolvency, privatization opportunities are still abound and FDI has been on the upward trend.

Most importantly, the radical turn towards a fully-fledged market economy taken in late 2000 can now be considered irreversible. Economic transformation has reached a critical mass which precludes serious policy reversals, since eventual political changes could influence the speed of transition, but not its generally positive direction. There are still numerous challenges, the most important being further increasing competitiveness on world markets through further privatization and more substantial enterprise restructuring and modernization, but the economic prospects today have greatly improved with respect to only 5 years ago.

The more difficult challenges lie in the political domain. Although Serbia today has the status of a 'potential EU candidate', in May 2006 negotiations on a Stabilization and Association Agreement with the EU were interrupted due to the non-compliance with political criteria (essentially, the non-delivery of General Mladic). Considering that the very process of negotiations with the EU has recently been, also in Serbia, a very powerful engine of institutional change towards EU standards, Serbia should not be left without this important incentive for long. The other even more difficult issue is to find an acceptable solution for the status of Kosovo, which has been postponed for over 7 years and is unlikely to be definitely resolved without further complicating the history and geography of the Balkans.[18] It is to be hoped that the outcome of the January 2007 elections can be a new democratic government which will forcefully and coherently implement a pro-reform and pro-Europe agenda, so that the remaining political problems can also be resolved. This would allow Serbia to benefit from more permanent political stability, which would also clearly facilitate further progress in remaining economic reforms and economic integration with the EU.

Notes

1. I would like to thank Bozidar Cerovic, Renzo Daviddi, Saul Estrin and Laza Kekic for valuable comments on an earlier version of the paper.
2. The paper was published in the special issue of the *European Economy* on Transition in Central and Eastern Europe, prepared and coordinated by Mario Nuti and Richard Portes, both at that time advisors to the EU Commission in Brussels.
3. FR Yugoslavia, constituted in April 1992, consisted of Serbia with its two provinces, Voivodina and Kosovo, and Montenegro. The country changed its name into Serbia and Montenegro on 4 February 2003. Following the May 2006 referendum on independence in Montenegro, Serbia and Montenegro became two independent states in June 2006.
4. According to the UN Security Council Resolution 1244 adopted in mid-1999, Kosovo officially remained part of Serbia, but has since then effectively been governed by the United Nations Mission in Kosovo (UNMIK). All statistical data after 1999 on FR Yugoslavia/Serbia therefore do not include Kosovo.
5. It could be argued that transition to market economy in Serbia/SFR Yugoslavia started much earlier, but two fundamental changes marked a radical break with the previous economic and political system in 1989–90: privatization launched in December 1989, and the first free multiparty elections held soon after in all Yugoslav republics.
6. Chronologically in Slovenia (1991), Croatia (1991–92), Bosnia and Herzegovina (1992–95), and Kosovo/FR Yugoslavia (1999).
7. SFR Yugoslavia's 1974 Constitution defined social property explicitly as no-one's property, as property of the whole society. Enterprises were granted the right to use socially-owned resources, but not full property rights (Uvalic, 1992, pp. 60–1).
8. The problem of citizens' foreign exchange savings frozen in 1992 has been addressed only after the 2000 political changes: a part was paid back to citizens in cash, whereas another part was converted into government bonds.
9. As observed by the BBC correspondent, 'In almost all respects, the state in Serbia was synonymous with Milosevic's Socialist Party of Serbia, which in turn had offered the old bureaucracy and its dependants a new lease of life in rather ill-fitting democratic clothing' (Glenny, 1992, p. 40).
10. See Uvalic (2005). The initial achievements of the first post-2000 Serbian/Yugoslav government are described in Labus (2003). An extensive overview of economic reforms during 2001–05 is found in Begovic and Mijatovic (eds) (2005).
11. On exchange rate regimes in the western Balkan countries see Daviddi and Uvalic (2006).

12. Only in 2004, around US $2.5 billion of foreign debt was written off, as a result of deals with the London Club, the Paris Club and Russia.
13. A detailed account of privatization results in Serbia is found in Cerovic (ed.) (2006).
14. FR Yugoslavia has signed free trade agreements (FTA) with seven SEE countries, as envisaged by the Stability Pact's June 2001 Memorandum of Understanding on Trade Liberalization and Facilitation. These FTAs are in the process of being transformed into one agreement under the framework of the Central European Free Trade Agreement (CEFTA).
15. Société Générale, Raiffeisen Bank, HVB Bank, Hypo Alpe-Adria Bank, Banca Intesa, ProCredit Bank, Alpha Bank, National Bank of Greece, to mention just a few.
16. Among all 28 transition economies, in mid-2006 there were only five countries where the private sector share of GDP was lower or equal to that of Serbia: Belarus, Bosnia and Herzegovina, Tajikistan, Turkmenistan and Uzbekistan.
17. Some of the specific features recalled at the beginning of this paper, such as economic decentralization, or the political crisis, became irrelevant after the break-up of the country.
18. On 2 February 2007, an ambiguous 'blueprint for a deal' was laid out by the UN envoy for Kosovo Martti Ahtisaari without any mention of independence. The final status of Kosovo will have to be decided in a new UN Security Council resolution, announced for March.

References

Babic, S. (1999) 'Politica economica dell'adattamento alle sanzioni in Serbia', in M. Zucconi (ed.) *Gli effetti delle sanzioni economiche: Il caso della Serbia* (Rome: Centro Militare di Studi Strategici).
Begovic, B. and B. Mijatovic (eds) (2005) *Four Years of Transition in Serbia* (Belgrade: Center for Liberal-Democratic Studies).
Cerovic, B. (2000) 'Economy of FR Yugoslavia: transition or pre-transition economy?', Working Paper (Ljubljana: Faculty of Economics).
Cerovic, B. (ed) (2006) *Privatization in Serbia* (Belgrade: Faculty of Economics Publishing Center).
Commission of the European Communities (2006a), *Serbia 2006 Progress Report*, COM (2006) 649 final, Brussels, November.
Commission of the European Communities (2006b) 'The Western Balkans in transition', *European Economy Enlargement Papers*, no. 30, December.
Daviddi, R. and M. Uvalic (2006) 'Currencies in the Western Balkans on their way towards EMU', in F. Torres, A. Verdun, and H. Zimmermann (eds) (2006) *EMU Rules: The Political and Economic Consequences of European Monetary Integration* (Baden-Baden: Nomos), pp. 261–78.
Dinkic, M. (1995) *The Economics of Destruction: Can it Happen to You?* (Belgrade: VIN).
Economic Intelligence Unit (EIU) *Country Forecast – Economies in transition – Eastern Europe and the former Soviet Union – Regional Overview* (London: EIU), various issues.
European Bank for Reconstruction and Development (EBRD) *Transition report* (London: EBRD), various issues.
Glenny, M. (1992) *The Fall of Yugoslavia. The Third Balkan War* (London: Penguin Books).

Kekic, L. (2000) 'Yugoslavia: revolution or evolution?', *EIU Viewswire*, Economist Intelligence Unit, October.

Kolodko, G. W. (2000) *From Shock to Therapy* (Oxford: Oxford University Press for WIDER UNU).

Kolodko, G. W. and D. M. Nuti (1997) 'The Polish alternative – Old myths, hard facts and new strategies in the successful Polish economic transformation', *UNU/Wider Research for Action Series*, no. 33.

Labus, M. (2003) 'Transition in FR Yugoslavia a year after radical political changes', in D. M. Nuti and M. Uvalic (eds) (2003), pp. 285–92.

Nuti, D. M. (1997) 'Employee ownership in Polish privatizations' in M. Uvalic and D. Vaughan-Whitehead (eds) *Privatization Surprises in Transition Economies – Employee Ownership in Central and Eastern Europe* (Cheltenham: Edward Elgar), pp. 165–81.

Nuti, D. M. (2004) 'I sistemi economici post-comunisti, ovvero 2001 odissea nella transizione', in B. Jossa (ed) *Il futuro del capitalismo* (Bologna: Il Mulino), pp. 173–213.

Nuti, D. M. and M. Uvalic (eds) (2003) *Post-Communist Transition to a Market Economy. Lessons and Challenges* (Ravenna: Longo Editore).

Uvalic, M. (1991) 'How different is Yugoslavia?', *European Economy*, Special edition no. 2, *The path of reform in Central and Eastern Europe* (Brussels: Commission of the European Communities), pp. 199–213.

Uvalic, M. (1992) *Investment and Property Rights in Yugoslavia – The Long Transition to a Market Economy* (Cambridge: Cambridge University Press).

Uvalic, M. (2001a) 'Federal Republic of Yugoslavia', *Journal of Southeast Europe & Black Sea Studies*, 1 (1), Frank Cass, pp. 183–94; also in D. Daianu and T. Veremis (eds) (2001) *Balkan Reconstruction* (London: Frank Cass), pp. 174–85.

Uvalic, M. (2001b) 'Privatizacija u Srbiji deset godina kasnije' (in Serbian, 'Privatization in Serbia ten years later'), *Ekonomski anali/Economic Annales*, 45, May, Belgrade, pp. 121–24.

Uvalic, M. (2002) 'The Yugoslav way to capitalism: multiple ingredients, uncertain outcome', in Economics Faculty of Sarajevo *Economic Science before the Challenges of the XXI Century* (Sarajevo, Faculty of Economics), pp. 233–46; also in Italian 'La via jugoslava al capitalismo' in B. Jossa (ed.) (2004) *Il futuro del capitalismo* (Bologna: Il Mulino), pp. 231–46.

Uvalic, M. (2004) 'Privatization in Serbia: The difficult conversion of self-management into property rights', in V. Pérotin and A. Robinson (eds) (2004) *Advances in the Economic Analysis of Participatory and Labor-Managed Firms*, 8, Chapter 9, pp. 211–37.

Uvalic, M. (2005) 'Tranzicija v Srbiji in Crni Gori: Od ponavljajocih se kriz do prizadevanj za vstop v EU' (in Slovene, 'Transition in Serbia and Montenegro: From recurrent crises towards EU integration'), in J. Prašnikar and A. Cirman (eds) (2005) *Globalno gospodarstvo in kulturna razlicnost* (Ljubljana: Casnik Finance), pp.291–305.

Uvalic, M. and D. M. Nuti (2003) 'Twelve years of transition to a market economy', in D. M. Nuti and M. Uvalic (eds) (2003), pp. 9–19.

World Bank (2004) *Serbia and Montenegro – Republic of Serbia: An Agenda for Economic Growth and Employment*, Report no. 29258-YU, December, Washington DC.

World Bank, *Doing Business Indicators*, www.doingbusiness.org, Washington DC, The World Bank Group, various issues.

Zdrale, J. (2006), 'Transformation of Serbia's banking sector: Ownership structure and growth of balance categories, December 2003–March 2006', *Quarterly Monitor of Economic Trends and Policies in Serbia*, no. 4, pp. 92–100.

9
The Search for Identity: Where Is Russia Heading?[1]

Padma Desai

9.1 Introduction

Individuals belonging to a country define their identity in terms of a cultural heritage and a shared history. Culture is an amalgam of influences originating in religion, language, art forms, and food. History for most consists of shifting political arrangements over time in which they may have been passive observers or active participants. Finally, people define their cultural and historical identity over a geographical area they call their country or their nation. Without this space, they would be homeless.[2]

Shared culture, history and a common home provide individuals with a nurturing collective identity. But how is this collective identity formed? How do personal preferences result in a collective outcome for people who consider themselves citizens of an established nation? Even when the environment is stable, the presence of a minority of individuals belonging to a distinct ethnic or linguistic group complicates collective identity formation. In that case, two scenarios are possible. A collective identity may be imposed from the top forcing some individuals to submerge or even forego their cultural identity. They must construct their identity to conform to the majority norm in terms of, say, a given language. On the other hand, the transformation of individual identities into a collective identity in the presence of cultural differences can transpire in a participatory fashion. For example, constitutional guarantees may require that an elected majority safeguards minority rights with regard to the choice of the minority member's occupation or location. Thus, the process of collective identity formation in a settled geographical environment may operate in a participatory, somewhat chaotic, fashion as in India, or take place in an involuntary mode from the top down as in China.

By contrast, identity formation and its outcome become unpredictable under unstable political and social circumstances. Convulsive regime changes occasionally associated with a nation's breakup imply that all individuals, including those belonging to a majority, must begin the search by collecting a few identifiable pieces, discard the rest, and create a fresh identity in a new geographical space. The historical continuity is damaged as well. In the second half of the twentieth century, several countries of Africa faced these daunting challenges when colonial rule was overthrown. So have Russia and the new independent states in its neighborhood as a result of the breakup of the Soviet Union. 'When the Soviet Union disappeared as a state at the beginning of the 1990s, "Soviet" suddenly ceased to be a viable identity' (Fitzpatrick, 2005, p.10). 'For many Russians, it was hard to recover the sense of being Russian rather than Soviet and even harder to accept the loss of empire that required this. As one teenager put it, "The hardest thing I had to get used to was saying 'Russia"'. One of the very first things we learned was where we lived – in the Union of Soviet Socialist Republics, the USSR, the *soyuz*. And then it was Russia, Russia, Russia' (Fitzpatrick, 2005, p. 314). These challenges not only involve the choice of the mechanism, voluntary or top-down, for the conversion of individual identities into a collective whole, but also for the creation of a new space. The fresh choices range from the selective rejection of past history to the possible adoption of foreign ingredients in the mix and the speed with which both can be managed.

Identity formation in Russia from Yeltsin to Putin falls in the 'shattered space' category, raising a number of questions. What specific features of the past have been discarded by each leader? In what way has their choice of political and economic arrangements advanced Russians' search for identity? What has been the contributory role of a foreign model in the progression? Have Russians succeeded in discovering identifiable cultural norms?

Before turning to issues of the two leaders' selective rejection of history, their choice of political and economic arrangements, and the impact of foreign features in the process, I briefly outline the American model that can serve as a template for judging its applicability, howsoever faint, in Russian identity formation. It will also help me differentiate the emerging aspirations of an average Russian from the well-established goals of an American, and judge the Russian progression from individual goals to their collective fulfillment. Such a comparative approach is not altogether misplaced considering that throughout history, Russia has turned to external sources for resolving a variety of dilemmas. Thus, according to Billington,

> In the economic sphere, the new Russian state [under Yeltsin] looked primarily to the West, and moved rapidly to institute private property and a market economy. In so doing the Yeltsin government was following an old Russian tradition of suddenly instituting sweeping changes by adopting wholesale the model of their principal foreign adversary. Russians had taken their religion and art from a Byzantium they had previously raided, their first modern governmental structures (under Peter the Great) from a Sweden they had long been fighting, and their

models for industrial organization from the Germans that they were about to fight in two world wars. In the 1990s, they basically adopted the model of the United States, their longtime Cold War adversary. (2004, p. 48)

9.2 The US model of identity formation

The founding fathers proclaimed Life, Liberty, and the Pursuit of Happiness to be the goals with which Americans should identify. The preamble to the US Constitution also declares that All Men are Created Equal, although the recognition of equal rights for women and for African–Americans, the latter with the passing of the Civil Rights Act of 1964, stretched over more than 200 years. Over time, the unfolding amendments to the Constitution have been designed to provide all citizens equal protection before the law and endow them with the freedoms to pursue their choices. While the election procedures and their outcomes conform to majority views and votes, majoritarianism cannot endanger the rights of minorities because these are protected by laws and institutions that treat all citizens equally. Often minorities, women among them, must struggle to have their rights confirmed in law, such as Roe vs. Wade, and make sure that they are not overturned.

Overall, the ideals and arrangements encourage individuals to fulfill their personal aspirations as part of a collective enterprise. Even so, minorities with a different religious and linguistic heritage may feel compelled to identify with the English language although not with the Judeo-Christian practices of the majority. So far as occupational and economic fulfillment is concerned, the American arrangements go a long way in allowing individuals to formulate their choices. Indeed, the free market environment, in which all must compete and fulfill their individual quests, produces unequal outcomes calling for government remedial intervention. With this caveat, the liberal model combining political and economic freedoms with legal guarantees is acknowledged as an ideal underpinning for defining personal identities and realizing them.

These features, which have matured over time in the US, cannot be reproduced in other environments expeditiously, but require careful adaptation as the existing arrangements, political and economic, are changed. At the very outset, Russia's search for identity required that the authoritarian arrangements of the past be overturned, a process initiated by Boris Yeltsin in early 1992, a topic to which I turn immediately below.

9.3 The political and economic changes interacting with external features: from Yeltsin to Putin

9.3.1 The Yeltsin legacy and the demolition project

In an October 2003 interview, Yeltsin, looking back, described the risky choice of 1991 in the following words:

I had a perfectly clear idea of the task to be solved. The political system had to be overturned, not just changed. In place of the Soviet political system, a democratic one had to emerge. The administrative command economy had to be replaced by a market economy, and freedom of speech had to replace censorship. . . . What was needed was a kamikaze crew that would step into the line of fire and forge ahead, however strong the general discontent might be. . . . I had to pick a team that would go up in flames but remain in history. (Desai, 2006, pp. 79–80)

It is incontestable that Yeltsin's reformers firmly and irretrievably planted the liberal idea in the land of Lenin and Stalin. They dismantled the Communist planned economy and the authoritarian political arrangements that had prevailed over nearly seven decades. However, controversy over Yeltsin's economic reforms and political changes has raged ever since. Dissenting voices have multiplied over the provisions of the 1993 Constitution, the election procedures, and the freedom of the media throwing doubt over the emergence of an American-type liberal environment in Russia under Yeltsin.

9.3.1.1   The Constitution of 1993, the election procedures, and media freedom

The Russian Constitution adopted in October 1993 on the basis of a public referendum represented a significant political triumph for Yeltsin over the Communist-dominated Supreme Soviet (parliament) that had opposed the constitution. However, according to Sergei Rogov, Director of the US–Canada Institute:

We adopted a constitution toward the end of 1993 that gave enormous authority to the executive without appropriate checks and balances. The legislative branch is weak and is dominated by the executive authority. The judiciary is not independent. The executive branch is divided into the presidential administration, the federal government, and the federal authorities in the region. Russia today [mid-2003] has more bureaucrats than in the pre-Yeltsin days. Yeltsin the boyar, established democracy via the bureaucrats, who had no control from the legislative branch. (Desai, 2006, p. 208)

The original draft of the constitution recommended the adoption of an American-style presidency with checks and balances (Billington, 2004, p. 52). The final version, however, resembled the French presidency, conferring enormous powers on the president who could, in effect, rule via presidential decrees bypassing the legislators, a procedure Yeltsin frequently adopted (until his resignation in December 1999) whenever the Communist legislators in the majority opposed his decisions. Boris Jordan, one of Russia's leading financiers, judged the situation from early 1992 to December 1999 in the following words:

The Yeltsin-era freedoms did not bring forth a democratic political system in Russia. I think the West saw several likable faces, heard familiar pronouncements, witnessed seemingly positive events, and took them as signs of a more developed democracy than actually existed – features such as elections, political parties, democratic rhetoric from businessmen and officials, massive privatization, a vocal private interest, and an outrageously open and bold press. A closer examination suggests that these were marks of a Potemkin democracy. They did not represent genuine public involvement and resulted in policies that most of the people strongly opposed. The most telling misperception centered around Yeltsin's 1996 election. It was hailed in the West as a major coup for democracy, although he and his policies had become unpopular by the time of the election, and the balloting process was acknowledged as flawed. (Desai, 2006, p. 307)

The Yeltsin-era record in the field of media freedom needs to be examined objectively as well. During his presidency, Russian TV networks and the press, strapped for money and lacking in advertisement revenues, turned to government bureaucrats and the cash-wielding oligarchs. The result? They became propaganda outlets for their sponsors, rather than independent information sources or competitive, rule-based businesses. According to the Russian Media Fund, a private US media project, draconian Yeltsin-era laws constrained them from exploring avenues of financial sources and moving into the world of US style media culture. In particular, non-media oligarchs moved into the media business in order to take advantage of the tax exemption for profits enjoyed by media companies.

While Yeltsin's political record on presidential governance, election procedures and media practices was far from ideal, the economic measures and outcomes maneuvered by his 'kamikaze crew' were shot through with problems as well. They ended up paying insufficient attention to the politics of the reform process they had launched. Their technocratic stance under-emphasized both the need to work at getting public acceptance of their programs and at countervailing the adverse distributional implications of some of the key reforms. According to Rogov,

> The so-called Yeltsin liberals went for the right-wing conservative ideology of the United States as an alternative to the Communist planned economy. They exchanged Marxism–Leninism for Friedmanism. For most of the post-Gorbachev period, the [reformist] Russian government was dominated by policy makers who would make the Cato-Institute gang look like a Democratic outpost in Washington, DC. (Desai, 2006, p. 209)

As a result, public discontent materialized from three directions.

9.3.1.2   Public discontent and fragmented collective identity

The freeing of prices caused the costs of essential goods to rise dramatically, in a way that essentially wiped out the savings people had accumulated during the Soviet days. Bread lines disappeared but bread prices climbed higher than wages. Moreover, price decontrol also destabilized enterprise balance sheets, forcing them to withhold wage payments to workers and tax payments to the government, and shortfalls in budget revenues created government defaults of wage payments to state sector employees and pensions to retirees. The pervasive withholding of wages from workers and nonpayment of pensions to retirees from 1994 to 1998 intensified public discontent. Finally, the voucher scheme, designed to ensure public participation in asset privatization, did not buy enough stock to be of significant value to an average Russian, and voucher privatization led to uneven and unregulated ownership. At the same time, the second phase of privatization, that began from mid-1995, involved loans by Russian oligarchs to the government in exchange for their eventual capture of state shares in Russian companies. The Russian voters judged this loans-for-shares scheme as a corrupt maneuver to enrich the few while depriving them of their legitimate share in assets created collectively during the Soviet Communist period.

9.3.1.3   The positive features

However, in demolishing the political and economic kit and caboodle of Soviet Communism, Yeltsin and his reformers chalked up a few accomplishments. Politically, by the end of 1999, several formal procedures marking a departure from the past were introduced. Among these were a federal constitution, an elected president as the head of state, parliamentary elections, an active electronic media, and a lively press. In actual practice, however, the benefits flowing from these new arrangements were tilted in favor of a few rather than the wider public. The constitution gave extraordinary powers to the president who could also manipulate the presidential election, assisted by the oligarchs who came to possess the most lucrative assets of the economy. On the other hand, the parliamentary elections endowed majority representation to the Communist Party, which, until the end of 1999, remained the most organized political force. Russia's collective identity at the apex of the political decision making was thus bifurcated.

At the same time, several policy instruments were launched marking a sharp departure from the Communist-era administered prices, physical quotas of factory outputs and foreign trade quantities, and an artificially fixed ruble that really did not regulate foreign trade flows. By contrast, market prices began to operate except in the monopoly sectors; the federal government relied on taxes for collecting revenue; the ruble began to be traded on foreign-exchange markets; stock exchanges, brokers, and commercial banks appeared too; the Russian Central Bank began to assume a role in formulating monetary policy.

However, these departures from the past lacked a firm legal and institutional underpinning and, thus, failed to contribute to a collective identity formation.

9.3.1.4   *The failure to forge a collective identity*

Most of all, the mounting public discontent pitted the president, his reformist team and a few among the young and the elite against the many who rejected the reforms. According to Rogov,

> On the one hand, we have the young people who are more aware of their needs and interests. This is the 'me' generation, which comes into conflict with the authoritarian collectivist traditions of Russian and later, Soviet history. Such tension between individualism and collectivism exists everywhere, but in Russia the story is complex. Contrary to common impression in the West, the experience of the 1990s produced a reverse input and popular disengagement that discourage voluntary participation for the common good. Let me explain. Ten or fifteen years ago, in the early days of Boris Yeltsin, there were enormous expectations. People came out by the thousands in the streets of Moscow, demanding immediate and fundamental changes. Later, people felt they had been betrayed and manipulated by the government. There was frustration followed by fragmentation. Since the expectations were so high, the letdown was massive too. Most Russians today [mid-2003] do not think they can do anything to bring about a positive turnaround. They have plainly retreated into a do-nothing pessimism. They do not believe the government wants to help them. (Desai, 2006, p. 205)

Toward the end of 1999, the breakdown of a consensual contract indispensable in the forming of a collective identity was ultimately reflected in Yeltsin's approval rating that had collapsed to below 5 per cent, and his surprise resignation as president of Russia on 25 December 1999. His decision to appoint Vladimir Putin as his successor in late 1999 demonstrated his acute unease over the breakdown of political cohesion and economic dissatisfaction and the urgency of restoring stability in Russia. 'He [Putin] is not a maximalist, and this is what set him apart from the others,' Yeltsin responded in the October 2003 interview when questioned about the choice. Predictably, Putin set about the task of consolidating state authority and restoring order following his election as president in April 2000, which in turn prompted concern as to whether Putin was undermining Russia's nascent democracy and imposing a collective identity from the top.

9.3.2   The Putin project: reconstructing the shattered space

In Putin's view, the need to enhance presidential powers arose from the danger posed to national integrity by the virtually nonfunctioning federal system he had inherited. The 1993 constitution formally designated Russia as a federal state. However, state authority across the hierarchy from the center to the periphery could not be exercised because the requisite institutions were missing. At the same time, while the Russian federation's political makeup was disorderly, its economic management also lacked a uniform, legal infrastructure. A 2001 report by the Organization for Economic Cooperation and Development (OECD) characterized the situation thus: 'There is no unified economic space, no "level playing field" for businesses in Russia, because of the multitude of administrative barriers and obstacles encountered by investors, particularly at the regional level, often in contravention of federal legislation and regulation' (Desai, 2006, p. 45).

The consolidation of federal authority which began in 2000 progressed in several directions after a group of terrorists attacked a school in Beslan, a small town in the Caucasus region of Russia, and more than 330 hostages, including scores of children, were killed.

9.3.2.1   *Consolidation measures: gubernatorial elections and political party formation*

In Putin's view, the twin objectives of restoring a functioning Russian federation and controlling terrorism called for enhanced federal authority. Unlike the Yeltsin presidency during which the Duma, the lower house of the parliament, was controlled by the Communist majority, the pro-Putin United Russia party dominated the Duma after the December 1999 elections, continuing right up to the December 2006 elections, facilitating the adoption of measures proposed by the government. According to the laws passed by the Parliament in 2000, regional governors were to be nominated by the president for subsequent approval by the regional legislatures rather than be elected by voters. The new laws also eliminated the election of independent, single-mandate contenders to the Duma, the lower house of the Parliament. Members would be elected solely on the basis of proportional votes garnered by party-list contestants to the exclusion of single mandate-constituencies. Moreover, a party must get 7 per cent of the vote instead of the previous 5 per cent in order for the winning candidates to gain eligibility as Duma members. Parties must have organizations in at least half of the 89 regions of Russia in order to qualify for electoral contests. These tougher requirements were calculated to eliminate splinter groups and promote political party formation.

Not surprisingly, reformers and analysts, Russian and foreign, reacted to the political tightening with alarm. Gaidar, former acting prime minister in the Yeltsin government in 1992, provided a historical perspective on the presidential selection of regional governors: 'Russia was ruled like that from Moscow for centuries. . . . It did not prevent two revolutions, namely the end of the tsarist regime in 1917 and the breakup of the Soviet Union in 1991' (Desai, 2006, p. 111). According to Strobe Talbott, former Deputy Secretary of State in the Clinton Administration, 'The tsars and the commissars tried to impose unity and order by a more brutal version of the methods Putin is now applying. They failed and so may he' (Desai, 2006, p. 184). As for the streamlined electoral procedures and the abolition of single mandate constituencies, evidently calculated to promote a party system, Gaidar reacted with concern: '[The] independent deputies, who obtain entry via individual contests, will be absent from the Duma. The party loyalists will then take over. That I think is an alarming prospect' (Desai, 2006, p. 110). Richard Pipes, the distinguished historian, sized up the prospects of party formation in Russia: 'The notion that political parties can express the interests of society is alien to Russian political culture' (Desai, 2006, p. 368).

On this issue – which encompasses Putin's political authority relating to gubernatorial elections and political party formation – the majority of Russians express opinions that are decidedly middle-of-the-road and mature. Thus, in a late September 2004 poll, 55 per cent opposed appointments of mayors and governors by higher authorities, warning their president against 'tugging the administrative blanket' in his direction.[3] According to an early November 2004 poll, more than 50 per cent believed that Russia needed a robust opposition party; 30 per cent were ready to vote for a united liberal party in the December 2007 Duma election – a signal to Russia's squabbling liberal groups to set aside their personal differences and unite as a single party. These opinions, combined with Putin's favorable rating, suggest that, while Russians want their leader to exercise his power (*vlast'*) as an absolute figure, they desire that he remain fair and flexible. The dialogue between the president and the people expressed in these polls is qualitatively different from the non-paternalistic connection between elected leaders and the electors in Anglo-Saxon democracies.

The systematic consolidation of political authority at the federal level was accompanied by a similar reshaping of Russian big business including the energy sector, and a slowing of economic reforms which the reformist groups called a reversal. The economic reconfiguration raised doubts about Putin's support of a continuing evolution of competitive markets in Russia. The question arises: Does he believe in a market system that contributes to the fulfillment of individual choices?

9.3.2.2 Does Putin believe in markets?

While Yeltsin categorically supported market-based changes, Putin's credentials as a market reformer and a supporter of private property have been frequently put under the microscope. Boris Nemtsov, the young reformist governor of the Nizhni Novgorod province and later first deputy prime minister in the Yeltsin government, brought out the contrast between Yeltsin and Putin saying that Putin believes that Russia needs a healthy market economy but,

> unfortunately he doesn't believe that Russia also needs a democracy. It is difficult to explain to someone with a KGB background that a connection exists between democracy and competitive markets. That is the real difference between Putin and Yeltsin. Yeltsin believed in this connection in his very soul, especially after he visited the United States and went to a supermarket. 'I am for democracy, and I am for private business,' he said. He kept that pledge to the end of his career. (Desai, 2006, p. 127)

By contrast, Martin Malia, the eminent historian, suggested a nuanced pro-market hypothesis in Putin's favor in his pre-Beslan interview:

> To speculate a bit on the basis of very little evidence, I would say that one of the traumatic experiences of Putin's life must have been his experience in East Germany, for while there he witnessed the complete collapse of the Soviet system, a system in which he believed when he joined the KGB in 1975. This could only have impressed on him the extraordinary vulnerability of the system and the contrasting dynamism of its rival, which he had always been taught to hate as 'capitalism' . . . Putin could only have concluded that what he had been brought up to believe as progress for Russia – that is, socialism – was in fact a burden. The corollary of this was that Russia had to chuck the old Muscovite ways of Stalin and adopt the new modern ways of the so called capitalist world. So when he returned to St. Petersburg after having lost his job in East Germany, he joined the reformers. (Desai, 2006, p. 342)

In actual practice, however, the market idea, in Putin's design, was modified in three ways.

9.3.2.3 *The modified model for the economy*

The policy framework of the market system, including free prices, monetary and fiscal policy instruments (the former under the management of the Russian Central Bank and the latter of the Ministry of Finance), an increasingly convertible ruble, and a reasonably open trading system, was to continue functioning. But reform of the Russian monopoly sector and the Soviet-era social contract with guaranteed entitlements to the citizenry would proceed at a speed that did not damage public welfare. Finally, the privatization of Russian industry accomplished under Yeltsin was not to be overturned. But Russian big business, the energy sector in particular, would be consolidated via mergers and be monitored by Kremlin watchdogs so as to safeguard Russian national interests.

During Putin's first term as president (2000–04), the government of the reformist Prime Minister Mikhail Kasyanov successfully steered a series of pro-market laws through the Duma, including the adoption of a tax code (which had a uniform personal tax rate of 13 per cent, and lowered the corporate tax rate from 35 to 24 per cent), a land transactions bill, a criminal code, and a joint stock company law. However, the challenges of economic reform facing Putin and his government during the second term remained complex. For example, converting the Soviet-era real entitlements into monetary payments would affect as many as 40 million recipients, including pensioners, veterans, and people with disabilities. In January 2005, the government measures to monetize free travel allowances and medical benefits, which were to be followed by reduction of subsidized utilities and housing, brought protests throughout Russian cities. At the same time, higher cash allowances for the purpose could push up the inflation rate. Finance Minister Alexei Kudrin, a pro-market policy-maker, consistently pointed to the inflationary consequences of hurrying with the conversion of real entitlements into cash payments. The reform, similar in its complexity to the US social security overhaul, was postponed in view of the December 2007 Duma elections.

Reforming the monopolies, among them Gazprom, the natural gas monopoly, United Energy Systems (the electric power company), and the railroads, involved complex decisions about their breakup into separate units before the prices of the services they provided to households and industry are decontrolled. The prices of passenger and railway freight, and of natural gas and power for industry have gradually been raised, each time creating a blip in the price level, yet Gazprom charged its Russian customers 10 per cent of world prices. According to the cabinet decision in December 2006, natural gas and electricity charges for domestic consumers would be brought up to market levels by 2011. Till then, the profitability of these companies will continue to be low because of the below-market pricing of their products. Finally, the restructuring of the three companies was predicated on their division into natural monopolies such as the electric power transmission lines and the railroad tracks from the rest of the units. In short, Russian monopoly reform involved complicated decisions because of the excessive physical integration of the companies under Stalinist planning, as well as the internecine turf wars among the decision makers in the Kremlin, the relevant ministries, and the companies.

In any case, the companies privatized during the Yeltsin years were ensured ownership of their assets. The Audit Chamber of the Duma, which investigated 1500 companies, announced in late 2004 that their deprivatization was out of the question. Throughout the long winded Yukos prosecution, Putin had emphasized that Russian companies would remain privately owned. As early as April 2000, Gaidar had singled out Putin's adherence to private ownership while raising doubts about his commitment to a democratic order:

'He does not have a good record in the field of democratic freedoms. . . . There are very few subjects in economic policy on which he is clear, but he has been clearest in his commitment to the protection of private property and his strong opposition to renationalization' (Desai, 2006, p. 100).

There was, however, a sting in the tail, a selective and ferocious one, that appeared in late 2003 with the prosecution of Yukos chairman Mikhail Khodorkovsky on charges of tax evasion and fraud ultimately ending in June 2005 with his jailing for a nine-year prison term and a well-orchestrated destruction of the oil company.

9.3.2.4   Yukos: The oil oligarch versus the Russian state

Having bought Yukos at a cost of a little over US $300 million in 1995, Khodorkovsky transformed it to Russia's leading oil company, raising its market capitalization to US $15 billion by 2003. With vast resources at his command, he was bent on influencing the composition of the Duma resulting from the December 2003 elections. His financial support extended to political parties and groups across the ideological spectrum, from the reformist groups to the Communist Party of the Russian Federation. At the same time, Khodorkovsky reportedly supported as many as seventy single member constituencies. Capturing a significant number of Duma seats would have given him a strong institutional voice in the Duma and in the government. In short, his tactics resembled the pre-1832 English-type 'pocket-boroughs' in which parliamentary representation was owed to a family or an individual.

The singularly uneven combat between the chair of Yukos and the president of Russia involved complex economic, political, and legislative issues, which went far beyond the company's non-payment of its tax liabilities. It prompted a reaction from several directions, including from German Gref, Minister for Trade and Economic Development, a staunch pro-market, anti-monopoly policy-maker. While describing the federal prosecutor's Yukos investigation on charges of fraud and tax evasion as 'cheap populism,' Gref also highlighted Khodorkovsky's heavy-handed tactics for amending federal laws in favor of his business: 'I don't think much of Khodorkovsky. He once said to my face: "Sorry, but either you repeal this law, or we'll replace you. It's your choice"' (*Nezavisimaya Gazeta,* 15 October 2004). Yukos was dismantled to signal to the privatized companies that the state was not ready to let a single corporation in one sector influence legislation in favor of its business or to allow Russia's natural resources (for example, oil and gas) to be controlled solely for private gain.

The strategy in pursuit of this goal involved majority state ownership in the natural gas sector, consolidation of several basic industries, and their monitoring by Kremlin appointees.

9.3.2.5   *Energy sector and big business consolidation*

In March 2005, the energy ministry announced that only companies with 51 per cent Russian ownership would in the future qualify to bid in auctions of oil and gas fields. Soon thereafter, Gazprom, 51 per cent state-owned, acquired Sibneft, a Siberian oil producer, thereby converting itself into a global energy player in natural gas as well as oil. At the same time, Rosneft, already fully state-owned, acquired Yugansneftegaz, the Yukos oil field, in a questionable transaction. These acquisitions pushed state share of oil production from 18 per cent in 2000 to almost 40 per cent in 2006. Mergers proceeded in other sectors as well. Aluminum and aircraft manufacturing was consolidated in 2006. The combined Rusal and Sual in the aluminum industry are larger than US Alcoa. The merged aircraft manufacturer was calculated to ultimately rival Boeing and Airbus. Steel and auto industry restructuring was proceeding apace. These consolidation forays raised doubts about whether the units placed under scrutiny by Kremlin gatekeepers would act as dependable players in the global economy spurred by rules of the market.

At the same time, existing or potential contracts with foreign collaborators were sought to be revised. Royal Dutch Shell and its Japanese partners were charged with environmental law violations in their operation of generating liquefied natural gas and oil via gas pipelines and oil terminals under a production sharing agreement in Sakhalin-2. The signals and countersignals, often clumsy and confusing, emanating from several Moscow ministries were actually calculated to enable Gazprom eventually get 50 per cent plus one share majority stake in Sakhalin-2, reducing the foreign partners as minority shareholders in the project. The doubling of the cost of the project to US $20 billion by Shell in late 2006 intensified the battle for control, because it postponed far into the future the date by which the Russian government could receive oil or gas from the production sharing agreement from which a foreign company must first recoup all its costs before Russia, the host country, started acquiring pecuniary benefits.

What was Putin's game plan in consolidating domestic units in the economy and playing hard ball with a foreign company?

9.3.2.6   *The revised contract between the state and big business*

Putin had in fact reformulated the contract between the Russian state and big business, Russian and foreign, by introducing two elements. First, Russia's national interest combined with profit-making would play a decisive role in these units. Second, the state would not outright nationalize these units but instead monitor them because their departure from the assigned mission of fulfilling national interest could not be penalized by the nascent legal system still evolving in Russia. Under his predecessor Boris Yeltsin, by contrast, the Russian oligarchs who captured industrial assets in the oil, mineral, and steel sectors, could flout Russian laws and act against Russia's interest. Winston

Churchill, years ago, had described the Soviet Union as a riddle wrapped inside a mystery in an enigma, adding that the key to solving it was national interest. In the long stretch of Russian history, Putin was the latest leader seeking to carry out that agenda via a strong state.

But was Putin reenacting history by enforcing his mandate on Russia's big business in order to fulfill national interest? In his interview, Malia drew a parallel with Peter the Great, but noted the difference that Putin was a modern leader with a mission for the twenty-first century:

> Putin cannot be Peter the Great because the twenty-first century is not the eighteenth.... All he [Peter] had to do was to call himself emperor and create a European, Versailles-like court, and he was modern. In the twentieth century, modernization or Westernization means much more than an army or navy. If Putin wants to make Russia strong, he must make it advanced technologically, and that means fostering education. Advanced technology and education mean an independent-minded, diverse, civil society. You cannot run a modern, technological, and educated society the way you run an eighteenth-century military monarchy. I think that Putin understands this, for he considers himself in the Petrine tradition. He's from St. Petersburg.... it [Petrine] is a historian's word. And it connotes building a strong Russia internationally by creating a strong state internally so as to foster Westernization and modernization from above. But... Westernization in the twenty-first century does not mean the crude and simple thing it meant at the beginning of the eighteenth. It means creating a sophisticated, modern, technological society and market economy, and Putin understands that. (Desai, 2006, pp. 341–42)

In his pre-Beslan interview, Talbott also referred to Putin's 'Western vocation' by invoking the term *zapadnichestvo*.

> *Zapadnichestvo* is actually a nineteenth-century word that was used by the [Russian] Westernizers, to be sure, and the way I would translate it is 'Russia's Western vocation.' I was quite interested to discover, in the first several meetings that I had with Putin, that he uses it as part of his vocabulary, whereas both Gorbachev and Yeltsin didn't like to talk about the West because they thought the very word 'West' discriminated against Russia. Russia could never be part of the West. I don't think that is Putin's view. (Desai, 2006, p. 182)

Along with the political tightening and big business consolidation, Putin has continued his modernizing and Westernizing vocation for Russia in the midst of sustained economic performance led by high oil prices. Toward the end of 2006, Russian business, especially in the energy sector, was poised to attract capital, technology and management expertise from abroad.

United Energy Systems was set to raise US $10 billion from markets, and invite Western participation in energy generating units. Gazprom, its stock registered as American Depository Receipts on the New York Stock Exchange, hoped to raise US $75 billion in the next decade for new natural gas explorations. Foreign investment flows had soared to US $35.3 billion in the first 9 months of 2006 as the economy, driven by high energy prices and oil export revenues, chalked up a series of robust indicators starting from 2000. The annual growth rate of the real GDP averaged 6.5–7 per cent; the budget surplus averaged 6 per cent of GDP; the annual inflation rate remained between 8 and 10 per cent; the foreign exchange reserves of the Central Bank of Russia had risen to US $260 billion by the end of 2006, third highest after those of China and of Japan; and the foreign debt liability as a share of GDP had declined to 25 per cent.

Most of all, the relative share of the poor had declined sharply from 30 per cent in 1990 to 10 per cent by 2006. In public opinion polls, an increasing number of Russians expressed satisfaction with their life. Despite the consolidating measures, political and economic, Russians could choose jobs, select their place of residence, own property, travel, and protest. The television reporting was controlled and Chechnya was largely absent from news coverage, but the entertainment and educational programming was varied and engaging. The majority of Russians felt that they could begin to define their personal goals in a stable political environment.

This feature marked a solid step forward for Russians in the realm of personal identity formation at the end of Putin's 6 years in power in contrast to their rudderless drift with increasing impoverishment under the Yeltsin presidency.

9.3.2.7 Personal identity formation in terms of a profession

During the long march from the post-Stalin to post-Soviet years, the economic contours of personal identity formation by Russians were beginning to be defined somewhat superficially in terms of a profession. According to Fitzpatrick,

> In the realm of identity, the most important postwar development was that class, the great focus of identity concerns in the 1920s and 1930s, became less central. Local authorities in the Russian provinces in the late 1940s were still entering class data in personal dossiers including parents' class . . . In Moscow, however . . . the party had become markedly less responsive to class denunciations (kulak uncles, capitalist grandfathers, and so on) than it had been before the war. (Fitzpatrick, 2005, pp. 23–24)

However, the actual progression to professional identity formation was slow. Under Leonid Brezhnev (1964–82), personal choices of occupation and location were still ruled out because the plan and planners assigned both.

The collapse of 1991 initiated a process of 'behavioral and psychological responses' to the new economic opportunities that the unraveling of the planned economy opened up. 'Former Soviet citizens might now reinvent themselves as *menedzhery*, *brokery*, and *biznesmeny* (feminine: *biznesledi*, *biznesmenki*, *biznesmenshi*); practitioners of *konsalting* or *pablik-rileishnz*; *rieltory* and *reketiry*; *programmisty* and *khakery*; *seks-bomby* and *iappi*; *gei* and *biseksualy* – identities whose novelty is conveyed by the exoticness of the newly borrowed terms' (Fitzpatrick, 2005, p. 304). However, the solid economic recovery that began in 2000 converted these 'impersonations' into concrete occupational and economic realities with corresponding functional retooling. The steady climb in higher education and improved training contributed to greater occupational mobility, higher earnings, and improved standard of living reflected in more housing, cars and telephones.[4] Russians were beginning to live better although, 'No Russian version has emerged of the American dream that whatever the problems of today, tomorrow will always somehow be better than yesterday' (Billington, 2004, p. 153).

While the improving economy has afforded more Russians identity choices in terms of diversified occupational possibilities, Putin's pragmatic foreign policy has provided them with the psychological lift they needed after the breakup of the Soviet Union and the loss of a homeland. Along with reorienting Russia's energy sector and big business toward fulfilling Russia's economic interests, Putin has reformulated foreign policy in an independent, pragmatic mode in his interaction with the US and Europe. It marked a sharp departure from the foreign policy implementation under Gorbachev and Yeltsin during whose leadership Western and Russian interests and values coincided. That was no longer true.

9.4   The new foreign policy to serve the Russian national interest

Putin's consolidation of federal authority departed not only from the political liberalization under Yeltsin but also under Mikhail Gorbachev who launched the process in the 1980s. The Reagan–Gorbachev years from 1985 to 1988 saw the end of the Cold War followed by the dissolution of the Soviet Union, both outcomes meeting US strategic goals. At the same time, the liberalizing initiatives under Gorbachev fulfilled the US desire for the initiation of liberal values in the Soviet Union. The complete identification was caught in this conversational banter as the two presidents strolled the Kremlin grounds in May 1988, followed by a group of journalists.

The US president was asked: 'Is this still the Evil Empire?' He said, 'No, that was another era, another time.' Then someone asked, 'Well, who is responsible?' And he said, 'Mr. Gorbachev, of course. He is the leader of this country.' One more question [to Reagan]: 'Who won?' 'Well, certainly, the Cold War ended on terms that had been set by the West, and specifically by the United States, and yes I think both sides won. (Desai, 2006, pp. 330–31)

Similarly, the energetic enterprise jointly undertaken by Clinton and Yeltsin to end the Communist system fully promoted US interests and principles. According to Talbott, 'Bill Clinton bonded with Boris Yeltsin. Big time. And he used that bond to get Yeltsin to do things that were hard for Yeltsin but important to us. That is the story of the last eight years more than any other single thing' (Desai, 2006, p. 180). At one point, Clinton had reportedly summed up the interaction imperative in a memorable one-liner: 'We can't ever forget that Yeltsin drunk is better than most of the alternatives sober' (Talbott, 2003, p. 185).

By contrast, under the Bush–Putin joint leadership starting in 2000, the United States and Russia began cooperating on a number of issues of common concern, among them terrorism control, nuclear non-proliferation, and bilateral nuclear parity management. But Putin has chosen to resist blandishments and bonding and instead toe an independent line by separating the resolution of these areas of mutual US–Russian concerns from the strengthening of political democracy in Russia. Thus, the policy stance with the Western leaders has been crafted to advance Russian interests in a constructive mode via negotiations with top leaders and partnership agreements with private business. By contrast, the approach with leaders of the independent states, of Ukraine and Georgia, in particular, was marked by tough posturing and occasional muscle-flexing. In early 2006, gas supplies to Ukraine were interrupted, and sanctions were imposed against Georgia later in the year as retribution for the capture and subsequent release by Georgian authorities of four Russian military personnel. On a less punitive level, Gazprom announced that it would lift subsidized prices and begin charging market prices to customers in the neighborhood, knowing fully well that the West would not help them meet the pricing differential.

Supported by economic resurgence and political stability, the dual foreign policy approach fulfilled two objectives. First, it signaled to the Western powers to stop treating Russia as a victim of their aggressive designs. It also conveyed to the independent states in the neighborhood that they must adjust to the new reality of a strong Russia, and her readiness to act as their partner rather than as an aggressor. Second, the predominantly negotiating, give-and-take mode marked by occasional muscle-flexing contributed to reining in the emergence of extremist nationalist forces in Russia.[5]

9.4.1 The new Russia: aggressor or victim?

With the breakup of the Soviet Union in 1991, Russia ceased to be an empire and became for the first time in its history a nation. Russians started describing their country as a nation (*natsiia*), although the word for the state (*gosudarstvo*) originates from *gosudar'* an autocratic ruler (Billington, 2004, p. 2). The new reality of a nation-state, however, has been burdened with the old dichotomy of whether Russia was a victim or an aggressor. Whereas Russians consider themselves victims of foreign invasions by predatory empires from the Mongols and Teutonic knights to Napoleon and Hitler, Russia's neighbors continue to see themselves as victims of relentless expansion by a much larger country (Billington, 2004, p. 3). Despite the end of the Cold War, these contradictory perceptions have persisted.

Putin has sought to resolve the victim–aggressor dichotomy by pursuing a selective, pragmatic foreign policy that has been marked by tough negotiations and avoidance of military adventurism in the new independent states. While foreign reaction to this mode has been that of a resurgent Russian aggression, most Russians view it as an effective tit for tat against NATO's eastward expansion and Western meddling in Russia's neighborhood via support of the 'color revolutions' in Ukraine and Georgia. According to a June 2006 poll, 50 per cent of Russian citizens believed that NATO presented a threat to Russia's security. With regard to Georgia, the majority of Russians, at 51 per cent in an October 2006 poll, blamed Georgian authorities for the conflict, while only 5 per cent thought that the Russian authorities were at fault. The same poll suggested that 44 per cent believed Georgia was acting under the direction of the United States rather than in the interest of its people. The majority of Russians also supported the imposition of sanctions and the closure of rail and postal links to Georgia, reflecting a determined willingness on their part to punish Georgians, who are ethnically different. This foreign policy packaging has kept the ultra-nationalist forces within Russia at bay but lifted Russians' collective psyche after the breakup of the Soviet Union, and contributed to the emergence of a middle-of-the road Russian identity.

More to the point, support for an activist pro-Russian foreign policy in the 'near abroad' has extended beyond the Russian rank and file and is often articulated by liberal voices.

9.4.2   Hard-line approach with states in the neighborhood

The interruption of natural gas supplies to Ukraine and the imposition of sanctions against Georgia followed by the expulsion of several Georgians from Russia in 2006 were troubling maneuvers. The former was imposed to warn Ukraine from stealing gas from the pipeline en route to Western Europe and the latter were calculated to prevent the Georgian leadership from reclaiming the two breakaway units of Southern Ossetia and Abkhazia back in Georgian territory via military action. However, such altercations, light or heavy, will continue into the future because Russian public opinion, including that of Russia's leading reformers, regards the surrounding independent states, all former republics of the Soviet Union, as Russia's sphere of influence.

Thus, former Prime Minister Mikhail Kasyanov, who successfully carried out a series of reformist laws during his tenure as head of the government from 2000 to 2004, acknowledged that Russia had 'special interests and responsibilities' in its immediate neighborhood. 'We have a long history of shared problems and common traditions, although the former Soviet republics are now independent states.... Russia will continue to be a global player, especially in the regions where, because of its history and geography, it has continuing interests and responsibilities' (Desai, 2006, p. 167). Anatoly Chubais, the legendary privatizer of Russian industry, was more explicit in suggesting that Russia should become a 'liberal empire' and assume a 'mission of leadership.' Of course, the reformers' weapons of choice would consist of negotiations and aggressive bargaining rather than Putin-style intimidation which has, nevertheless, excluded military intervention except in Chechnya.

Indeed, not only has Chechnya eluded an effective resolution, political or military, but the Russian public's concern for the plight of the Chechens has been marked by collective indifference, which is reflected in the measures Russians are willing to put up with in order to control terrorism.

9.4.3 Approval of terrorism control measures and discriminatory treatment of ethnic minorities as instruments of collective identity formation

When questioned by pollsters about their readiness to part with their freedoms in order to rein in terrorism, Russians reacted overwhelmingly in support of the necessary restrictions. Toward the end of 2004, opinion polls dealing with terrorism reflected respondents' all-out willingness to surrender many freedoms in order to stamp out terrorism. As many as 57 per cent were willing to let the secret police freely eavesdrop on telephone conversations and intercept mail, and a staggering 82 per cent were willing to allow the police to check their documents on the street. Russians, however, expressed their desire to preserve their basic political freedoms to protest, strike, and vote in elections.

At the same time, the Russian public's viewing of the Chechen wars had taken a 180-degree turn over a decade. According to Gaidar, the Russian public supported the first Chechen War under Yeltsin (1994–96), as a struggle for self-determination on the part of the Chechens. However, 'after the war, Chechnya became an increasingly serious problem for Russia with kidnapping, imprisonment, and trafficking in people.... the situation changed dramatically when ... [in August 1999] a few thousand well-armed and trained people [entered] Dagestan from Chechnya, [and the Dagestani people] asked for Russian military support' (Desai, 2006, pp. 97–98). Later, following the terrorist attack in a Moscow theatre in October 2002 in which 129 hostages were killed, and the death of 330 hostages, including scores of schoolchildren, in Beslan, Russian public opinion hardened to total indifference even with regard to the violations of Chechens' rights by the Russian military. According to Rogov, 'Right now [mid-2003] the public is in a leave us alone mood with the Chechen war. "If my family is not serving in Chechnya, then I wake up in the morning, drink my coffee, watch TV, and survive." And you know the TV does not carry any news about Chechnya' (Desai, 2006, p. 211). At the same time, according to Jack Matlock Jr., US ambassador to the Soviet Union from 1987 to 1991 under Gorbachev, the result of simply granting Chechnya independence would be more like Afghanistan under the Taliban than Algeria after the French left. Russian leaders can win the struggle if most Chechens oppose the terrorists.

In the midst of the tangible public indifference and the deadlocked situation defying a political resolution of the continuing military engagement, the Moscow journalist, Anna Politkovskaya, who reported on human rights violations in Chechnya, was murdered in early October 2006. In commenting on Politkovskaya's murder, Putin acknowledged, according to a *New York Times* report of October 11, that the killing was 'a crime of loathsome brutality,' and then added, 'she was known in journalist and human rights circles, but her influence in political life in Russia was minimal.' Rather than downplaying her courage in reporting human rights violation in Chechnya, he was implying that the Russian public was indifferent to these abuses and to her work. According to an October 2006 poll, 53 per cent of Russians admitted that they had not heard of Anna Politkovskaya prior to her murder.

These discriminatory attitudes bordering on callous indifference toward minority groups have persisted, although Russia has been opened up and Russians have been subjected to a blitzkrieg of external influences. At the same time, the population of the new Russian Federation, now four-fifths Great Russian compared to only one-half Great Russian in the Union, has contributed to Russians thinking in terms of a common identity that is ethnically Russian (*russkii*) rather than a pluralistic mix of 'all those within Russia' (*rossiiskii*) (Billington, 2004, p. 68). In early December 2006 remarks, Putin called upon civic groups and political parties to preach and practice religious and ethnic tolerance while acknowledging that countering extremism was a state responsibility. Despite the enactment of laws to safeguard minority rights and Putin's frequent pronouncement to prevent extremism in Russia, a mid-November 2006 public opinion poll suggested higher intolerance among Russians toward ethnic groups. While 55 per cent declared lack of 'irritation' toward such groups, 62 per cent desired restricted access by them in their neighborhood and 52 per cent wanted such groups to be settled elsewhere. It would seem that the cultural and religious norms of Russians tend to be exclusive, even intolerant of outsiders.

At the same time, Russians are beginning to rediscover their own roots giving them a strong cultural and religious self awareness.

9.5 Cultural identity formation: the reappearance of old values

To what extent have Russians succeeded in constructing a cultural identity in the new home in which they clearly dominate politically and numerically?

Culturally, the Russian empire lacked secular cultural criteria such as ethnicity and language. Peasants as well as the nobility defined their identity in terms of service to the tsar, adherence to the Orthodox Church and residence on the land. Tsar Nicholas I (1825–55) added 'nationalism' (*narodnost'*) to the two traditional components 'autocracy' and 'orthodoxy,' as debates about national identity began swirling between the Slavophiles and Westernizers, the former emphasizing the role of the Orthodox faith, Slavic ethnicity and communal organizations and decision making in Russian identity, the Westernizers stressing the role of individual freedom, legal accountability in government and international commerce (Billington, 2004, pp. 9, 14).

The convulsive changes that commenced in 1991 irretrievably affected the trinity of 'autocracy,' 'nationalism,' and 'orthodoxy.' Under Yeltsin, the old-vintage autocracy, both tsarist and Communist, was gotten rid of. Russians also found a *natsiia* with an overwhelming representation of close to 80 per cent. Finally, they began to rediscover religion by embracing Orthodoxy and attending church services.[6] At the same time, the recovery of Russianness, a major preoccupation, has existed 'uneasily with the assumption of modern Western identities' (Fitzpatrick, 2004, pp. 313–17). Overall, the economic recovery, political stability, and an open society are set to promote a fusion between the opposing identities over which the Slavophiles and the Westernizers battled.

9.6 Conclusions: the Putin-style paternalistic majoritarian model

In conclusion, Putin's 6-year policy record has been marked by five dominant features that have contributed to the formation of a collective identity and are reinforced by the faint beginnings of professional and cultural aspirations for the majority of Russians.

- Yeltsin's kamikaze crew demolished the Communist planned economy and the authoritarian political arrangements of 70 years and irretrievably planted the liberal idea in Russia. However, the reformers' technocratic approach was devoid of concern for the impoverishment of the majority of Russians. The declining economy and the accompanying political disorder in the vast country had a negative impact on the formation of individual as well as collective identities in Russia. The dissolution of the Soviet Union in December 1991 accentuated this tendency from 1992 to 1999.

- The emergence of the pro-Putin United Russia party in the Duma, the lower house of the Russian parliament, in the December 1999 elections set the stage for the adoption of reformist legislation and for the consolidation of federal authority by the lawmakers. This marked a sharp contrast from the Yeltsin years during which reform progression relating especially to asset privatization was carried through via presidential decrees and government resolutions bypassing the Communist- dominated legislature until December 1999. The collective political identity at the top was bifurcated from 1992 to 1999.

- With regard to the consolidation of presidential authority, the majority of Russians caution the president against excessive political tightening while at the same time accepting his leadership reflected in his consistently high approval rating at 70 per cent. Most Russians, excluding the reformers and the vocal intelligentsia, evidently accept the political consolidation as a tradeoff in favor of stability, and big business consolidation as contributing to Russian national interest. While running counter to full-blown political and economic liberalism, the nod of approval by the majority with regard to these measures suggests the emergence of paternalistic majoritarianism in Russia under Putin which eluded the Yeltsin presidency.

- The sustained economic recovery, fuelled by high energy prices, has resulted in better living standards, increasing professional choices, and an optimistic view of the future by an increasing number of Russians. At the same time, as a distinct majority with 80 per cent representation, Russians have begun reviving old traditions, among them church-going, while adopting Western practices. The fusion of the old Russian and the new Western elements will proceed in a manner and at a pace preferred by individual choices.

- The most troubling feature of this majoritarian phenomenon among Russians consists in their indifference with regard to the rights of ethnic minorities including the Chechens although it falls short of xenophobic nationalism. Despite laws that punish extremist political activity and ban such parties from elections, the collective identity based on intolerant predisposition among Russians runs counter to the American style liberal arrangements under which minority rights are effectively protected by laws and corresponding institutions. Despite Putin's exhortations for tolerance, and legal safeguards in favor of minority groups, his selective muscle-flexing against minorities promotes the emergence of a top heavy, Russian-centered majoritarian collective identity.

Notes

1. Mariya Konovalova's research assistance is gratefully acknowledged.
2. In this essay, 'individual or personal choice or identity' includes 'real life phenomena' among them, native language, occupation, religion, and marital status while excluding the ontological category of 'who am I really?' My usage also refers to identities as ' "constructed", that is, learned from the surrounding culture rather than innate' (Fitzpatrick, 2005, p. 11). In her Introduction, Fitzpatrick has an illuminating discussion of these issues from the perspectives of social and cultural historians, sociologists and philosophers.
3. Russia has three major polling agencies. They are: VTSIOM (the All-Russian Public Opinion Research Center), FOM (the 'Public Opinion' Foundation), and the Levada-Center. References to the polling data in this paper are collected from polls conducted by these agencies which use a representative sample of Russians. The poll citations are available on the agency websites at www.wciom.ru, www.fom.ru, and www.levada.ru.
4. According to Hellevig (2006), additions to existing housing stock has been proceeding apace at the rate of 10 per cent; automobile ownership has increased from 59 per 1000 people in 1993 to 250 per 1000 in 2005; fixed line telephones have gone up from 16.7 per 100 people in 1992 to 29.8 per 100 in 2005. Above all, 70–80 per cent of college age youngsters attend higher education institutions, in turn creating improved occupational choices for themselves as the economy continues improving.
5. Commenting on the popular appeal and possible emergence of 'xenophobic nationalism' or 'authoritarian Eurasianism,' Billington writes: '[If] Russia were to succumb to negative nationalism and take a sharp autocratic turn, it would probably not last for long. Repression would be difficult to sustain in a vast country that has been so dramatically opened up to political freedoms and to the outside world in the information age. Nor does Russia have a large enough population or the military resources to sustain the kind of foreign policy that hypernationalistic states generally need to maintain their legitimacy' (Billington, 2004, p. 88).
6. For a detailed discussion of Russians' ongoing search for a new cultural identity, see Fitzpatrick, 'Becoming Post-Soviet' (2005, pp. 303–17).

References

Billington, J. H. (2004) *Russia in Search of Itself* (Baltimore: The Johns Hopkins University Press).

Desai, P. (2006) *Conversations on Russia: Reform from Yeltsin to Putin* (New York: Oxford University Press).

Fitzpatrick, S. (2005) *Tear off the Masks!: Identity and Imposture in Twentieth-Century Russia* (Princeton: Princeton University Press).

Hellevig, J. (2006) 'The Russian Middle Class', http://hellevig@hku.ru.

Talbott, S. (2003) *The Russia Hand: A Memoir of Presidential Diplomacy* (New York: Random House).

10
The Effects of Privatization on Company Performance in Belarus[1]

Saul Estrin, Marina Bakanova, Igor Pelipas, and Sergei Pukovich

10.1 Introduction

Privatization is usually argued to improve corporate performance in all situations (see Megginson and Netter, 2001; Megginson, 2005), though the situation has been less clear-cut in transition economies (see Djankov and Murrell, 2002), perhaps because the institutional framework was insufficiently developed. One way to explore the relationship between privatization and institutional development more deeply is to focus on the impact of private sector development on corporate performance in an economy where institutional development has been limited. In this paper, we focus on Belarus, a country which has been lagging from the outset in the reform process (see EBRD Transition Report, 2005). Indeed, Nuti (2004) argues that Belarus is not in transition at all; rather he describes it as a 'command economy'.[2] We use a new dataset on Belarusian firms to investigate how privatization and new firm entry has acted on a variety of measures of enterprise performance. Our findings are compared with those in the literature for transition economies which are more advanced in the reform process.

The literature on the relationship between ownership and company performance (for example Megginson and Netter, 2001) suggests two hypotheses to guide empirical work in transition economies. The first is that privately owned (and privatized) firms will perform better that state-owned ones. This is because private ownership is expected to guarantee superior corporate governance via the role of external owners in monitoring managerial performance and in ensuring a single-minded concentration on profitability as the objective of the firm (see Estrin, 2002). Moreover, because of the legacy effects of the planning system and state ownership (whether current or former), *de novo* firms will perform better than privatized or state-owned companies (McMillan and Woodruff, 2002). The measures of company performance used include growth in sales, employment and exports as well as productivity.

In this paper we use an important new dataset of Belarusian firms to explore these hypotheses empirically. The dataset is based on a survey in 2004 of 402 enterprises in the Belarusian industrial sector (out of 2200 firms in total). It contains new firms (DNs) as well as state-owned (SOEs) and privatized former state-owned firms (PFs). We also draw on surveys undertaken by the Institute of Privatization and Management (IPM) in 2000 and 2003.

As Nuti (2004) noted, Belarus lags behind all transition economies in reform indicators except Turkmenistan and Uzbekistan (see EBRD, 2005). However, since the post-reform recession, which lasted to 1995, growth performance has been good by post-Soviet standards and macroeconomic policies have included unification of the exchange rate, and a gradual reduction in quasi-fiscal activities and barter operations (see World Bank, 2005; Bakanova and Freinkman, 2006). But, the private sector share has remained very low (only 25 per cent in 2004), 'bottom up' privatization had run its course by 1994 and there have been few privatizations (except of firms performing badly) since 2000. Nuti (2004) summarized the situation as follows, 'Economically, under a thin layer of markets, Belarus is a command economy without central planning, similar to pre-transition Poland in the second half of the 1980s' (p. 111).

The paper has three further sections. In the following section we summarize the findings of the dataset with respect to enterprise performance, in comparison with experience elsewhere. We report our econometric results in the third section and draw conclusions in the fourth.

10.2 Enterprise performance and restructuring in Belarus

Our work draws on three surveys of Belarusian industrial firms. The first two were undertaken in 2000 and 2003 and cover 222 firms, 119 of them SOEs and 103 PFs. The most recent one was in 2004 and covers 402 industrial enterprises, 23.1 per cent SOEs, 48 per cent PFs and 28.9 per cent DNs. The sample is a structured random one so as to ensure adequate representation of large firms.

Table 10.1 provides a snapshot of Belarusian firms in 2004. On average the three ownership categories are all relatively large in terms of employment, especially the SOEs, but even DNs. This it true even by the standards of other transition economies. Belka *et al.* (1995) report that in early-transition Poland, SOEs on average employed 703 workers, PFs employed 1007 if they were majority state-owned (594 if privately held), and DNs employed 111. The figures for Russia are also similar; Linz and Krueger (1998) report that their Russian sample varied in size between less than 200 and more than 10,000 workers, though 80 per cent employed between 2000 and 5000.

Table 10.1   Characteristics of Belarus enterprises

	Sample average	SOE	PF	DN
Employment	594	1237	565	146
% firms exporting to:				
developed economies	25.1			
former socialist economies	35.1			
Russia	70.6			
Share of exports in revenue (%)	25.8	28.7	28.0	19.1
Years of service of general manager (LOS)	12.1	17.6	12.4	7.4
% firms with or in a joint venture (JV)	5.5	7.5	6.2	2.6

Source: Institute of Privatization and Management (IPM), 2004.

Exports are a surprisingly low share of sales for what one might expect *a priori* to be a small open economy: less than 30 per cent. DNs export the least and SOEs the most. There had been little progress by 2004 towards Belarusian integration into the world economy; exports to Russia and the former communist bloc still predominate. As also noted by Nuti (2004), foreign direct investment (FDI) is negligible and only around 5 per cent of firms are in a joint venture. The comparable figure for Poland in 1994 was 14 per cent (Belka *et al.*, 1995). Another sign that reforms have not yet taken root come from managerial turnover. On average, managers have worked with their firms for more than 12 years, more than half of them in the top post. Thus most managers have stayed in post throughout the transition from planning. Managerial turnover is particularly low in SOEs, where the average tenure is nearly 18 years, but even in PFs, managers have worked for the firm on average for more than 12 years.[3]

There are interesting differences in the sources of financing by ownership type. *De novo* firms rely largely on retained earnings while former and especially current state ownership is associated with superior access to bank loans, selling or leasing unused assets and an enhanced ability to obtain subsidy, government exemptions and preferences. Overall, some 39 per cent of all firms in Belarus still continued to benefit from some form of government concession in 2004, down from 49.1 per cent in 2000.

Finally, there has been little progress in separating the functions of enterprise and welfare systems. Table 10.2 reveals that the levels of social provisions were still higher in Belarus in 2004 than they were in Poland in 1993, and that there has been almost no restructuring at all of social assets since the fall of communism in either state-owned or privatized firms.[4] This seems consistent with Nuti's evaluation of Belarus as being in a comparable situation to pre-reform Poland. There are some differences between SOEs and PFs in the structure of the provision of social assets; for example SOEs provide on

Table 10.2   Share of enterprises having social assets, %

Social asset	Form of ownership			
	SOE		PF	
	1991	At present	1991	At present
Canteen, café	64.5	63.4	46.1	45.1
Holiday center, recuperation center	22.6	20.4	12.4	11.4
Cultural center, club	26.9	22.6	18.1	17.1
Information and education centers	5.4	3.2	4.7	3.6
Residential houses	47.3	44.1	30.6	32.1
Sport facilities	20.4	21.5	13.5	14.5
Health facilities	43.0	45.2	23.8	23.8
Day care centers, nurseries	47.3	18.3	28.5	11.4

Source: Institute of Privatization and Management (IPM), 2004.

average more canteens and day care centres, but the differences that existed in 1991 between the firm types remain in 2004.

10.3   The impact of ownership on company performance in Belarus

In this section, we outline our empirical strategy and the specification of equations. We go on to report the result of our econometric analysis and discuss the implications of the findings for our hypotheses.

We summarize our hypotheses in a simple equation,

$$X = f(O, Z) \qquad (10.1)$$

where X is a vector of performance variables; O is ownership (three categories; SOE, PF and DN); and Z is a vector of control variables. A number of variables have been employed extensively in the literature to control for the factors in addition to ownership that might influence company performance. Large firms, which can exploit scale economies, may be more productive than smaller ones, especially in the industrial sector and size can also bring pecuniary benefits, for example lower input costs or higher prices because of monopoly power. We use the number of employees (EMP) in the firm to proxy for size. We also control for the institutional environment with the share of barter in revenue (SBC and SBC1).[5] Different sectors have different technologies, capital intensities and factor productivities, and may also have different market structures and price–cost margins. We control for industry-specific effects with sectoral dummy variables and a variable for the intensity of competition (COMP). Since transition economies often have regionally fragmented markets, we also use a dummy for Minsk (GEO). The literature stresses the importance of dominant ownership (insider versus outsider) for company performance (Djankov and Murrell, 2002) and we control for this using a dummy variable for insider (managerial) ownership (MAN). Finally, because foreign-owned firms are argued to perform better (Sabirianova *et al.*, 2005) we include a dummy variable for whether the firm is engaged in a joint venture (JV) and we control for managerial quality with a variable for the duration of manager's tenure in the company (LOS).

We follow the literature (Claessens and Djankov, 1999; Frydman *et al.*, 1999) in using a variety of measures of enterprise performance:

1. *Enterprise productivity and profitability*: sales per worker (SL), and profitability (ratio of profits to sales) (PS). Since these are continuous variables and the data is cross-sectional, we use OLS estimation methods in these regressions.
2. *Export performance*: we use the export to sales ratio (EXP) and the expected change in future exports (DEX) and in exports to the West (DEX1). The latter are limited dependent variables (taking the value of unity if exports (exports to the west) increased and otherwise zero) so we estimate using probit methods, and use OLS for the former.
3. *Changes in company performance*: productivity change (DSL) and change in employment (DEMP).[6] The former is a limited dependent variable (taking the value of unity if sales per worker increased) so the estimation method is probit, but OLS is used for the employment change equation.[7]

Our hypotheses concern the sign and significance of the firm type dummies, DN and PFs, relative to SOEs, in these seven performance equations. We also further sub-divide the category of privatized enterprises to take account of the fact that some firms, which have formally been privatized, continue to have majority state ownership. Thus while all former state-owned firms, including those with majority state ownership, are denoted PF, privatized firms with majority private ownership are denoted PF1. The SOEs are the omitted ownership category in the regressions.

Because SOEs are typically larger, and DNs smaller than PFs, we provide estimates that both exclude and include the employment variable, columns (1) and (2) of each regression respectively.[8] We report the productivity equations in Table 10.3, exports in Table 10.4 and performance change equations in Table 10.5.

The sales per worker equation in Table 10.3 suggests that industry effects are significant in understanding productivity differences between firms, with enterprises in the timber, woodworking, and pulp and paper industry being significantly more productive. Moreover, though Belarus operated a system of largely administered prices (see Nuti, 2004), monopoly power is found to yield higher prices, and therefore revenues and sales per worker, since COMP

Table 10.3 Performance equations: productivity and profitability

	Productivity (SL)		Profitability (PS)	
	(1)	(2)	(1)	(2)
DN	0.022	0.017	−0.107	−0.061
	0.203	0.154	−0.986	−0.519
PF	0.106	0.104	−0.113	−0.143
	0.811	0.786	−0.876	−1.068
PF1	−0.205*	−0.207*	0.182	0.261**
	−1.828	−1.83	1.598	2.202
MAN	0.194**	0.195**	0.029	0.033
	2.154	2.152	0.347	0.381
GEO	−0.045	−0.046	−0.013	−0.04
	−0.565	−0.568	−0.161	−0.489
LOS	0.045	0.043	−0.077	−0.078
	0.591	0.548	−1.037	−1.013
JV	−0.012	−0.012	0.065	0.042
	−0.174	−0.162	0.933	0.588
SBC	−0.052	−0.05	0.003	0.023
	−0.663	−0.637	0.033	0.291
SBC1	−0.095	−0.093	0.052	0.035
	−1.187	−1.152	0.655	0.438
COMP	−0.158**	−0.158**	−0.038	−0.058
	−2.28	−2.26	−0.567	−0.84
EMP		−0.013		0.108
		−0.159		1.329
Industry dummies	Yes***	Yes***	Yes***	Yes***
R^2	0.102	0.102	0.071	0.099

Figures below estimated coefficient are t statistics, * denotes significance of 10 % level, ** at 5 % level and ***at 1 % level.

is negatively associated with productivity and we find a positive effect from managerial ownership.[9] However, privately owned firms – both privatized and created *de novo* – are not found to perform better than state-owned ones. Indeed private ownership, when it takes the form of majority control being placed in private hands, is actually found to be associated with lower productivity than state ownership. We also find no significant difference between the profitability of former state-owned firms, new firms or state-owned firms. We find that firms that have been privatized fully (PF1) are more profitable but the equation is so poor that the result is not robust. Thus

Table 10.4   Performance equations: exports and export growth

	Exports (EXP)		Change in exports (DEX)	Change in exports to the West (DEX1)
	(1)	(2)	(1)	(1)
DN	0.162*	0.26***	0.284	0.707
	1.806	2.683	0.927	1.429
PF	0.081	0.106	−0.019	0.041
	0.747	0.946	−0.051	0.08
PF1	0.019	0.071	0.471	−0.674
	0.203	0.712	1.285	−0.88
MAN	0.067	0.07	−0.127	−0.018
	0.96	0.993	−0.52	−0.043
GEO	−0.275***	−0.251***	−0.761***	−0.694*
	−4.154	−3.654	−3.65	−1.878
LOS	−0.204***	−0.163**	−0.232	−0.253
	−3.25	−2.531	−1.145	−0.765
JV	0.014	−0.013	−0.449	−0.052
	0.233	−0.224	−1.586	−0.122
SBC	0.144*	0.129*	0.297	0.344
	1.769	1.953	0.831	0.85
SBC1	0.17**	0.114*	0.246	0.622*
	2.555	1.678	1.117	1.695
COMP	0.082	0.111*	0.121	0.133
	1.445	1.93	0.618	0.402
EMP		0.257***	0.000***	0.000**
Industry Dummies	Yes***	Yes***	Yes***	Yes***
R^2		3.785	2.736	2.455

Figures below estimated coefficient are t statistics, *denotes significance of 10% level, **at 5% level and ***at 1% level.

our equations on productivity provide no convincing evidence that capital market discipline has led to improved company performance in Belarus.

The regressions in Table 10.4 concerning export performance have a better fit. Commencing with export shares, we find that larger firms export more, have faster growth of exports and increase their exports to the West more. Length of service seems to be a (negative) indicator of managerial quality, in that export shares are significantly lower in firms in which managers were appointed before 1996. There are also strong sectoral and regional effects, with a base in Minsk being a significant disadvantage for all three measures of export performance. Export shares are also positively related to both measures of softness of budget constraint, perhaps indicating that firms may need to be subsidized to maintain high levels of exports. This result holds when we control for size of firms. There is also some weak evidence that firms in receipt of soft budget constraints may be increasing exports to the West faster. However, once again there is no evidence that privatized or new firms significantly increase exports or exports to the West faster than state-owned firms, though new firms are found to have higher export shares.

We consider changes in enterprise performance in Table 10.5. The change in the employment equation contains rather few significant determinants, with firm size, soft budget constraints and product market competition all insignificant and there are also no significant effects from managerial quality

Table 10.5 Performance equations: productivity and employment growth

	Productivity growth (DSL)	Employment growth (DEMP)	
	(1)	(1)	(2)
DN	−0.66**	0.074	0.092
	−2.256	0.73	0.873
PF	−0.116	0.053	0.062
	−0.317	0.437	0.5
PF1	−0.252	0.27**	0.277**
	−0.718	2.533	2.579
MAN	−0.213	−0.141*	−0.142*
	−0.921	−1.754	−1.764
GEO	−0.115	0.031	0.032
	−0.562	0.415	0.427
LOS	−.340*	0.065	0.073
	−1.732	0.939	1.041
JV	−0.107	−0.01	−0.013
	−0.392	−0.161	−0.198
SBC	0.357	−0.041	−0.047
	1.058	−0.578	−0.653
SBC1	0.576***	−0.066	−0.072
	2.716	−0.898	−0.977
COMP	0.236	−0.018	−0.02
	1.285	−0.287	−0.321
EMP	0		0.047
	0.831		0.635
Industry Dummies	Yes***	Yes***	Yes***
R2		0.129	0.13

Figures below estimated coefficient are t statistics, *denotes significance of 10% level, **at 5% level and ***at 1% level.

or the presence of JVs. Indeed the only significant control effects are sectoral and via insider ownership.[10] Employment change does not vary according to whether a firm is state-owned, privatized or *de novo*, though former state-owned firms in which private owners hold a majority stake do adjust employment significantly more than the other types of firms. The productivity growth equation is interesting in that soft budget constraints are again found to have a positive effect, and length of managerial service a negative one. However, once again there are no significant differences between any PF and SOEs though DNs display significantly slower productivity growth.

These equations taken together suggest that the determinants of company performance in Belarus, using a wide variety of indicators, are not for the most part those that are relevant in most other transition economies; the fits are poor and few 'economic' variables are significant. However, we are still able to explore the relationship between company performance and ownership. We find the hypothesis that privatized firms will perform better than state-owned ones to be rejected in every equation: the coefficient on PF is never significant. This may be because the state retains significant stakes in privatized enterprises, but when we separate out the group of privatized firms that have non-state majority owners, there are still only a few significant effects and these are mixed in sign. Majority private ownership of former state-owned firms is associated with greater profitability and productivity growth, but also lower productivity levels and less property restructuring.

The results with respect to new firms are even more emphatically negative. For the most part, new firms in Belarus are not found to perform any differently to state-owned or privatized firms. However there are two contradictory exceptions; exports, which are greater in DNs, and productivity growth, which is found to be slower.

10.4   Conclusions

Mario Nuti (2004) has argued that Belarus is not a transition economy in the sense that it is not on a reform path from communism to capitalism. Rather it is only slightly reformed in institutional structures and is not at the moment seeking further movement. This is consistent with our findings that despite an apparently good macroeconomic performance since the late 1990s, Belarusian firms have made very limited progress in enterprise restructuring. We will focus on three aspects of these difficulties: the failure to integrate sufficiently into the world economy, the effects of soft budget constraints and the institutional environment for privatized and new firms.

Studies of other transition economies suggest that foreign firms could have a very important role to play in enterprise restructuring. They can provide new technologies and mechanisms to benefit from the global division of labor including export growth, capital investments and managerial skills. In Belarus, we find the levels of FDI and joint ventures to be low, and in our equations, we do not find that membership of a JV yields any benefit in terms of improved performance. This may be an important reason for the limited progress in enterprise restructuring in Belarus.

We also find that firms in receipt of direct or indirect subsidy never perform significantly worse and sometimes perform better. One might interpret this result as indicating that soft budget constraints are effective in improving company performance. However, this conclusion is probably misleading. As we have seen, the Belarus economy has only partially moved in a direction of the market. Firms are financially constrained and financial instruments other than retained profits or sale of socialist assets are virtually non-existent. In such a situation, resources from any source may allow firms in receipt of them to improve their own performance somewhat. However, soft budget constraints also dull the incentives generated by the market economy, and their continued relevance in the Belarus environment may indicate why other variables proxying for market incentives in our equations are rarely found to be significant.

For the most part, in our study privatization is found to have no significant effect on a variety of aspects of company performance in Belarus. This could be because the new owners were inappropriate, but the study does not indicate that insider ownership is the key issue. It seems more plausible that privatization is having no impact because the new owners are not able to exercise effective corporate governance because of weaknesses in the enforcement of property rights, restrictions on the operations of product markets and softness of budget constraints. The extended length of service of managers in privatized firms also suggests that the new private Belarusian owners have not changed management post-privatization and this is indicative that ownership changes alone have not been enough to engender behavioral shifts.

Evidence is emerging that the path of institutional development between the former Soviet Union countries and Central and Eastern Europe is diverging (Djankov and Murrell, 2002), particularly in the area of property rights and institutions conducive to the emergence and growth of a dynamic *de novo* sector (see Estrin *et al.*, 2006). Such institutions include a flexible capital market, a sound commercial code, enforcement of property rights, a limitation on rules and bureaucracy, especially for small and medium-sized enterprises, and relatively low levels of corruption (see Kornai, 1990). The institutional differences with respect to the business and legal environment for new firms seem to be strongly associated with the rate of creation of new enterprises, and therefore productivity and economic growth. Our findings that new firms in Belarus are rarely different from current and former state-owned firms with respect to performance are contrary to the transition literature that identifies new firms as an important potential source of restructuring and growth. The results seem once again likely to be explained by the particular legal, institutional and business environment in which *de novo* firms operate in Belarus.

Notes

1. The authors acknowledge comments from Lev Freinkman, Mario Nuti, and participants in a World Bank seminar in Minsk in June 2005. Research assistance from Rhana Neidenbach and Yevheniya Bazhenova is also gratefully acknowledged. Any remaining errors are our own.
2. Thus Nuti's paper is entitled 'The Belarus Economy: Suspended Animation between State and Markets'. However one interprets the reform process in Belarus, the institutional weakness make it an interesting economy to explore the interdependency between privatization and other institutional reforms.
3. Interestingly, joint ventures are slightly more common with SOEs and PFs, than with DNs, perhaps indicating foreign firms' preference for arrangements with larger or better connected enterprises or an institutional bias against DNs in the granting of licenses.
4. Estrin, Schaffer and Singh (1997) undertook a study of such restructuring for Poland, and found that while SOEs had only restructured slightly, there was somewhat more change in the ownership and provision of social assets among privatized firms. *De novo* firms, since they did not inherit such structures from the socialist period, owned very few social assets.
5. In a partially reformed environment like Belarus, where resources are scarce and capital markets underdeveloped, soft budget constraints may represent access to resources and enhance firm performance. SBC equals unity if the firm reports that subsidies or exemptions and preferences granted by the state are an important source of enterprise funding and SBC1 equals unity if the state has granted the firm any soft loans, targeted budgetary financing and subsidies, customs or tax exemptions, sale of foreign proceeds on privileged terms, soft settlement regime for energy payments or writing off unpaid dues to the budget.
6. The equation for employment growth must be interpreted differently. Faster output or productivity growth in a given sector in DN firms than privatized ones would be a consequence of better management but current and former state-owned firms would almost certainly be over manned so employment might fall whatever was happening to output and sales.
7. Productivity and profitability are positively correlated, and firms with higher labor productivity also have greater exports to the West. Productivity growth is strongly correlated with other measures of good performance, including high export shares and growth, including to the West. The improvement of exports to the West is correlated with SL, DSL, EXP, DEX, but not correlated with profitability or employment growth. Indeed employment growth is not correlated with any other performance measures. Profitability is not associated with productivity, employment growth, or exports.
8. New firms are also concentrated in Minsk, and are more likely to have joint ventures, but this does not influence any of our results so we do not report regressions with these variables omitted.
9. The causality here is not unambiguous – managers may have taken ownership stakes in more productive firms. We are not able to explore this issue further in this paper.
10. Firms with managerial ownership reduce employment more slowly. This is consistent with the view that insiders will act to slow the pace of restructuring.

References

Bakanova, M. and L. Freinkman (2006) 'Economic Growth in Belarus (1996–2004): Main Drivers and Risks of the Current Strategy', in V. De Souza and L. O. Havrylyshyn (eds) *Growth resumption in the CIS* (Elsevier).

Belka, M., S. Estrin, M. Schaffer and I. Singh (1995) 'Enterprise Adjustment in Poland: Evidence from a Survey of 200 Private, Privatized and State-Owned Firms', *LSE Centre for Economics Performance Discussion Paper*, 223.

Claessens, S. and S. Djankov (1999) 'Enterprise Performance and Management Turnover in the Czech Republic', *European Economic Review*, 43 (4–6), 1115–24.

Djankov, S. and P. Murrell (2002) 'Enterprise Restructuring in Transition: a Quantitative Survey', *Journal of Economic Literature*, 40 (3), 739–92.

European Bank for Reconstruction and Development (EBRD), *Transition Report* (London: EBRD), Various years.

Estrin, S. (2002) 'Competition and Corporate Governance in Transition', *Journal of Economic Perspectives*, 16 (1), 101–24.

Estrin, S., K. Meyer and M. Bytchkova (2006) 'Entrepreneurship in Transition', in M. Casson, B. Yeung, A. Basu and N. Wadesdon, (eds) *The Oxford Handbook of Entrepreneurship* (Oxford University Press).

Estrin, S., M. E. Schaffer and I. J. Singh (1997) 'The Provision of Social Benefits in State Owned, Privatized and Private Firms in Poland', in M. Rein, B. Friedman and A. Wörgötter (eds) *Enterprise and Social Benefits after Communism* (Cambridge: Cambridge University Press).

Frydman, R., C. Gray, M. Hessel and A. Rapaczynski (1999) 'When Does Privatization Work? The Impact of Private Ownership on Corporate Performance in the Transition Economies', *Quarterly Journal of Economics*, 114 (4), 1153–92.

Kornai, J. (1990) *Road to a Free Economy* (New York: Norton).

Linz, S. and G. Krueger (1998) 'Enterprise Restructuring in Russia's Transition Economy: Formal and Informal Mechanisms', *Comparative Economic Studies*, 40 (2), 5–53.

McMillan, J. and C. Woodruff (2002) 'The Central Role of Entrepreneurs in Transition Economies', *Journal of Economic Perspectives*, 16 (3), 153–70.

Megginson, W. (2005) *The Financial Economics of Privatization* (Oxford: Oxford University Press).

Megginson, W. and J. Netter (2001) 'From State to Market: A Survey of Empirical Studies of Privatisation', *Journal of Economic Literature*, 39 (2), 321–89.

Nuti, D. M. (2004) 'The Belarus Economy: Suspended Animation between State and Markets', in S. White, E. Korosteleva and J. Lowenhardt (eds) *Postcommunist Belarus* (Lanham MD: Rowman & Littlefield).

Sabirianova Peter, K., J. Svejnar and K. Terrell (2005) 'Foreign Investment, Corporate Ownership, and Development: Are Firms in Emerging Markets Catching up to the World Standard?', *IZA Discussion Papers*, 1457.

World Bank (2005) 'Belarus: Window of Opportunity to Enhance Competitiveness and Sustain Economic Growth', *Report No. 32346-BY*.

Part III
Beyond Transition

11
Complexity and Systemic Failure

Vito Tanzi

11.1 Introduction

Among his many achievements, in his long career as a successful and influential economist, Mario Nuti has been one of the leading students of centrally-planned and transition economies. Better than most, he has fully understood the inner workings of these economies. I am sure he would agree that the three factors leading to the collapse of the centrally-planned (or socialist) economies were: (a) the limited economic incentives that they provided for the efforts of individuals; (b) the growing corruption that affected them, and especially the Soviet Union, over the years; and (c) the growing complexity of these economies, that made economic planning more and more difficult.

The question of incentives in socialist economies is an old question that has been debated often over the decades. For economists schooled in market economies, where the compensation that a person receives is expected to be based on what the person contributes to the economy, it has always been difficult to understand how a socialist economy could operate efficiently and grow, without strong personal incentives, once the initial revolutionary or ideological enthusiasm began to wear out. Economists in market economy justify huge differentials in the incomes of individuals, as long as these differences are market determined. For these economists it is difficult to understand how an economy can be efficient without clear links between the performance and the income of individuals.

The question of corruption is perhaps a bit more controversial because to some extent corruption exists in all countries. It is not obvious that it was more significant in centrally-planned economies than in some market economies. Here the key hypothesis, and one that cannot be validated empirically, is that time made centrally-planned economies progressively more corrupt because the original idealistic belief, that it was possible to create economies without class distinctions and with substantial income equality, started giving place to doubts and to a growing cynicism that led to the extremes of corruption in the Breshnev's era in which it became necessary to bribe someone even to get a dead body into a morgue (see Simis, 1982; David Remnick, 1994). The levels of corruption described by Remnick, Simis and some other writers, such as Shleifer and Vishny (1999), are unlikely to have been reached in industrial countries.

The third factor, the role of complexity, has attracted far less attention. It is evident that in a command economy, the bureaucrats who must make the economic decisions on what to produce and on how to allocate what is produced to the citizens, who are not a homogeneous group ('workers'), find their task easier when the economy is poor and simple, produces few essential products, and produces them at a low level of quality, standard design, and, where relevant, in few sizes. It is far easier to plan and distribute potatoes, standard bread, rice, and 'one size fits all' Mao tunics than Armani suits, tailor-made to fit every person, and a growing number of heterogeneous services which reflect the needs or desires of individuals with higher incomes. Once the centrally-planned economies passed the primitive state, in which production consisted mainly of a few basic, standard products, allocated mostly through rationing, or long waits in lines, rather than through prices, and started producing less standard and more sophisticated products and services, they faced the problem of complexity.

Command economies did not have the tools – mainly the automatic work of the price system in a market economy – to deal with this increasing complexity. They attempted to deal with it by developing progressively more elaborated input–output tables and by developing advanced mathematical tools. But this was still an *Economics of Shortage*, in Janos Kornai's appropriate description. In the end, it became evident that centrally-planned systems could operate much better in simple economies than in complex, modern economies (see also Kornai, 1980). Some of these countries, in later years, had literally thousands of 'excise taxes', taxes that were not legislated but were created and changed administratively. By mimicking the price mechanism for consumers, these taxes helped the bureaucrats to bring the demand and supply for specific products closer in line. The planners could change the tax rates for items for which too much or too little had been produced in order to induce a desired demand response.

In the rest of this paper I shall not pursue this question of complexity in centrally-planned, or command economies. Rather, I shall argue that complexity is a phenomenon or problem not limited to centrally-planned economies. It is a problem that is becoming more common in today's world raising the probability of failure in various systems. I shall argue that market economies are not immune to it. Sooner or later they also suffer the consequences of excessive complexity. Section 2 discusses the phenomenon of complexity in a selected number of manifestations. Section 3 focuses specifically on how advanced economies can be affected by it. Section 4 draws some general conclusions.

11.2   Complexity in the modern world

Perhaps the issue is so obvious that most of us have not given much thought to the fact that life is becoming progressively more complex and that complexity can lead to systemic failure. Complexity seems to have crept into many actions, from making doctors' appointments, to buying plane tickets, to deciding what to do with the money we have saved, and so on. As choices have increased, so has complexity. In many instances, complexity is just an annoyance. In some it can become a big problem. I will skip the annoyance part and focus on the problem.

Complexity can have damaging consequences for technological, financial, economic, and even political systems, by creating situations for which the outcomes are hard to predict and to cope with. The problem can be described best through a few examples, chosen from the four areas mentioned above.

11.2.1   Technological failures

On 28 March 1979, at 6:00 AM an atomic reactor located at Three Miles Island in Pennsylvania, a location 90 miles from Washington, DC, came close to a 'critical meltdown'. 'The unexpected lineup of a feed water cutoff, a valve failure, and a control room miscalculation quickly escalated into the nearest think to a nuclear disaster . . . ' (see Preface to the New Edition of *The Warning*, a very informative book by Gray and Rosen, 1982). This could have been a disastrous event that, under certain atmospheric conditions, could have contaminated the nation's capital with lethal radiation. At that time I knew one of the commissioners of the Nuclear Regulatory Commission, the agency that supervises atomic plants. He was a brilliant scientist with very strong academic credentials. A few weeks after the accident, he commented that what had scared him the most about the crisis was the realization, for the first time, that none of the leading scientists that the Commission had consulted for advice understood the whole atomic plant. They were all specialists and the world's leading experts on *parts* of the atomic plant. The plant had become too complex for any one person to understand in its entirety and to anticipate all the possible interactions of its parts that could lead to failure. The lineup reported above had not been anticipated by any simulation scenario and it was just one of many possible disaster scenarios.

On 28 January 1986, at 11:39 AM, the Space Shuttle *Challenger* was destroyed 73 seconds into its flight killing its crew of seven astronauts. The lengthy investigation by a Presidential Commission (the Rogers Commission), which included among its members Richard Feynman, the famous physicist, attempted to identify the cause of the accident. At first it had great difficulty until, in a famous televised experiment, Feynman showed that when rubber O-rings, used as seals on the solid rocket booster, were immerged in icy water they became brittle and were no longer capable of performing their sealing function. Florida temperatures are normally well above freezing, therefore the design of the shuttle had not contemplated the consequences of very cold temperatures during takeoff. A series of unexpected circumstances, that had included delays in the launch, combined with abnormally low temperatures in Florida, had generated the conditions for a disaster that was not supposed to occur.

On 1 February 2003 another space shuttle, *Columbia*, exploded on its return to Earth killing again its crew of seven astronauts. This time, after a 7-month investigation, the Investigation Board concluded that 'the physical cause of the loss of Colombia and its crew was a breach in the Thermal Protection System . . . .' '. . . this breach allowed superheated air to penetrate through the leading edge insulation and progressively melt the aluminum structure of the left wing . . . .' (see *Columbia*, p. 9). The Investigation Board stated that 'the Space shuttle is one of the most complex machines ever devised. Its elements . . . are assembled from more than 2.5 million parts, 230 miles of wire, 1060 valves, and 1440 circuit breakers' (op. cit., p. 14). It is obvious that (a) nobody understands the whole system, and (b) that, given the number of parts, it would be impossible to anticipate and protect against all the combinations of circumstances that could lead to failures of some of the parts.

There have been other scientific or technological breakdowns in very complex systems for which it has been difficult to identify the reasons in order to anticipate the problems. These have included plane accidents – TWA flight explosion outside New York; El Al crash in Holland, and so on, blackouts, and other such failures. In all cases, the systems had become too complex to fully understand and complexity had created the possibility of combinations of circumstances and outcomes that could not have been anticipated and that could lead to failure. The systems are often made up of independently designed and built components. It is impossible to anticipate how all these separate components will interact in particular, unanticipated circumstances.

11.2.2 Financial failures

There have been financial crises that, like the technological ones, have had their genesis in the complexity of financial systems. For financial systems there is the aggravating circumstance that complexity makes it easier for some individuals to engage in acts of corruption that increase the probability of failure. Corruption is not an essential element but it is often an accompanying one. Many examples could be mentioned but perhaps the most egregious ones in recent years are provided by failures involving Enron, Parmalat, Fannie Mae, and Long Term Capital management (LTCM).

In the year 2000, Enron had reported revenues of US $101 billion and in 2001 had ranked seventh on the Fortune 500 list. For 6 consecutive years, it had been named by *Fortune* magazine 'America's Most Innovative Company'. It was a much-admired company. In August 2000, the value of its shares had reached US $90 making Enron one of the most valuable companies in the United States. By the end of 2001, the value of Enron's shares had dropped to US $0.30 and the company had been declared bankrupt. How could this happen and in such a short time? Complexity had covered this company with a deep fog that had misled outsiders and had allowed some insiders to fool shareholders, regulators, tax authorities, brokers, presumably accounting companies, and possibly themselves. Thus, in this case complexity had combined with, and made easier, some acts of corruption. It was never clear what this 'most innovative company' produced. Much of its 'output' was in 'trading'. It traded more than 800 different products and information on the trades was not available to outsiders and probably to many inside the company. Complexity facilitated insider trading and allowed managers to cash billions in options while hiding losses in off-budget accounts (see Smith and Emshwiller, 2003). Its collapse had various consequences: it led to large losses to shareholders; loss of jobs and pensions to employees; the dissolution of Arthur Andersen, one of the big four accounting firms; and the passage of the Sarbanes–Oxley Act in the US that required companies to better report on their activities. This Act would lead to complaints by corporations about the increasing reporting costs.

Parmalat was an Italian 'national champion'. It was an apparently very successful company, and a much admired one, with significant activities in at least 30 countries. It was one of Europe's largest and most global companies with some 36,000 employees on its payroll and its products were globally known. Then all at once a huge hole of some US $14 billion losses appeared in its accounts. How could the company have lost so much money without anyone noticing? And once again, how could it have fooled on such a grand scale all the 'keepers of the gate', all those who are supposed to closely follow these large companies? It turned out that fraud by insiders *vis-à-vis the company* may have been less of a factor in Parmalat than it had been at Enron. The company, largely family-owned and managed, had started losing money, years back, in some of its foreign operations, and had started to 'cook the book' to hide the losses in order to continue its operation by attracting credit from banks. In the process it had been able to fool the accountants, the banks, other creditors, the regulators, the tax authorities, the brokerage firms, and others to the tune of US $14 billion, or about one per cent of Italy's GDP. Once again complexity had made this possible. The illusion that such large and global companies can be controlled and correctly audited is just that, an illusion.

Complexity must have also contributed to the US $11 billion 'accounting error' made by Fannie Mae, the huge American enterprise that buys the mortgages that banks provide to house buyers by issuing bonds. The 'error' allowed some of its managers to get huge bonuses that had been tied in their salary contracts to the reported short-run profits of the company. In the process Fannie Mae had broken various accounting rules. It turned out that the concept of 'profits', so often used by economists and assumed by many to be a well-defined and clearly measured parameter, is, after all, not as objective a concept as believed. As a newspaper report put it, it was '... largely a function of complex estimates that could be squeezed or stretched' to get the desired results. These results determined the compensation packages of the managers. Therefore, accounting is not as precise a field as one had been led to believe (see *Washington Post*, 28 February 2006, p. D-4). Fannie Mae settled with the government by paying a fine of US $400 million but the former managers have so far kept their bonuses. An investigation of Fannie Mae's accounts required a review of more than two million letters, e-mails and other documents over many months by 1500 investigators.

Another example worth reporting from the financial area is that of *Long Term Financial Management* (LTFM), the hedge fund that in 1998 suddenly imploded almost taking with it the entire financial system after Russia defaulted in August 1998. The Russian default had changed dramatically and in the wrong direction with respect to the risk premia against which LTFM had taken bets. The New York Federal Reserve Bank had to intervene to prevent a financial catastrophe. LTFM had lost US $4 billion but behind this money there was about a trillion dollars in derivative contracts related to currency and treasury markets. The managers of LTFM, that included two high-flying recent Nobel Prize in economics winners, Robert Merton and Myron Scholes, had created a system that had become too complex perhaps even for them to understand and control (see Lowenstein, 2000).

Other examples could be easily provided from the financial area. They would all point towards the same conclusion. Complexity creates a thick fog around reality and contributes to the creation of potential combinations of damaging events that cannot be anticipated or controlled. It, thus, creates a fertile ground for 'perfect storms' or for unexpected events while, at the same time, making it easier for unscrupulous individuals to manipulate accounts in order to present a reality different from the real one and occasionally to take advantage of the situation for personal gains.

Similar problems have arisen in economic crises that from time to time hit particular countries. Some of these crises are anticipated and generate no surprises to experts, others much less so. In these latter cases complexity is often found to have played a key role. Take for example, the financial crises that hit Korea and Indonesia in 1997. Both of these countries had been considered, by many economists, including those working in international organizations, to be very successful economies and both crises were unannounced. The economists of the International Monetary Fund, who had been closely following these countries, were caught by surprise. The OECD had just admitted Korea among its members because of its good economic policies and institutions. In both cases, complex financial arrangements, involving loans and the contingent use of foreign reserves had created non transparent situations that at some point led to major difficulties. Interestingly these arrangements were similar to those in which the management of Enron had engaged.

Complexity can, of course, also contribute to political difficulties. Although the connection is less direct and less obvious, it could be asserted that the situations that have developed in particular geographical areas, such as Iraq and Afghanistan, have been the result of the nonanticipation of the role of complexity. The ignorance of complexity by policymakers led to policies that *ex post* appeared naïve and unimaginative. Also complexity has affected elections, the results of which have often been questioned.

11.3   Complexity and the future of market economies

In the first section of this paper it was argued that an important cause of the collapse of centrally-planned economies was the growing complexity of these economies that made dirigisme increasingly difficult. Market economies do not have economic planning. The free working of the market and the 'invisible hand' are supposed to do much of the basic work of allocating resources to productive uses and distributing the output to consumers. The role of the state is supposed to be limited although it has been growing over the years especially in income distribution and stabilization (see Tanzi, 2005).

While market economies do not have economic planners, they have policymakers and managers of policies that are supposed to ensure that the invisible hand operates in an environment that is transparent, efficient, and fair. Thus, a relevant question is the extent to which complexity is making this environment more opaque and the policy tools less effective, raising questions about the legitimacy of the outcome. This is a difficult question that would require far more space to answer satisfactorily than is provided by a short article. The discussion here will be limited to a few examples.

While largely self-regulating, modern market economies need efficient governments to play the role of referee and regulator in a game of allocation and distribution of resources and to supply public goods and subsidize (tax) goods that produce positive (negative) externalities. Governments play this important role through fiscal, monetary, and regulatory policies. The more able and honest the policymakers are, and the more efficient the policies that they enact, the better the outcome and the more sustainable and legitimate the game. There is growing evidence that some policies have become less effective than in the past and that complexity may be playing a role in this process. We shall highlight a few important trends, using mostly information from the United States, the mother of all market economies.

11.3.1   Complexity and the use of fiscal tools

Let us start with the tools available to pursue fiscal policy. Most observers assume that the government knows exactly what it is doing when it legislates new tax laws, and that it has a clear view of the incidence of the tax system and the impact that the taxes have on taxpayers. However, this may be far from the truth. In 1913, when the Federal income tax was first introduced in the United States, a policy that required an amendment to the US Constitution, 400 pages of federal tax rules (including the Code, regulations and IRS rulings) were required to inform and guide the taxpayers. By 1939, or 26 years later, the pages had increased a little, to 504. Thirty years later, in 1969, they had increased to 16,500. By 2006, or 37 years later, the number of pages had increased to an extraordinary 66,498 (see Edwards, 2006). Twenty thousand pages were added in the past 6 years alone! If this trend should continue, and there is no reason to believe that it will not, the system will become truly unmanageable for tax administrators, and incomprehensible to most taxpayers, if this has not already happened.

The gap between federal taxes owed and actually paid has been estimated to have risen to US $345 billion annually (see General Accountability Office, 2006). The number of IRS tax forms that may be required by different taxpayers to pay taxes has risen to an incredible 582. Federal income tax compliance costs have been estimated at US $265 billion in 2005. The growing complexity of the tax system is inevitably and frequently raising questions about its fairness at a time when Gini coefficients indicate that the income distribution in the United States is becoming progressively more uneven (see below). It has also raised questions about the impact of the tax system on economic activities. A recent survey of taxpayers has reported on their confusion *vis-à-vis* the complexity of the tax code (see CCH, 2005). This problem is not limited to the United States but it is a growing one in many countries (see Tanzi, 2006b).

Complexity is not limited to the revenue side of the budget but extends to the expenditure side. Here 'contingent liabilities', off-budget accounts, unfunded commitments about future payments related to pensions and medical expenses, that do not appear in the budget data, and other potential or actual expenses have made the annual budget a progressively less useful or informative indicator of fiscal policy and a less useful instrument for pursuing the correct policy (see Tanzi, 2006a). Uncertainty about future developments and what measures to take have increased significantly (see Heller, 2003). For example, in 2001 the Congressional Budget Office had forecast huge fiscal *surpluses* over future years that would wipe out the public debt within a few years. At that time there was a lot of discussion about what to do with the surpluses. The forecast proved to be totally wrong so that a few years later the budget was again in deficit in the hundreds of billions of dollars and the public debt was once again increasing at a fast rate.

Public expenditure for health has been growing at a very fast pace promoted in part by the complexity of the health system that has made it easy for hospitals and other health providers to overcharge and to engage in acts of corruption. These acts include overbilling, billing for services not provided, providing services not needed, using the most expensive options when cheaper ones are available, and so on. Attempts to reduce these acts through more detailed reporting requirements have also added hundreds of billions of dollars in administrative costs (see Woolhandler and Himmelstein 1997). Attempts by doctors and hospitals to protect themselves against lawsuits, for presumably bad practices, have added additional billions and contributed to future uncertainty. Some major economists, such as Nobel Prize winner, Robert Fogel, have estimated that by 2030, the health care industry in the United States will account for 25 per cent of the US GDP. Unfortunately this expenditure is not leading to better results in terms of life expectancy compared to countries that spend much less.

Contingent liabilities by the government, *vis-à-vis* particular events such as hurricanes or default in public pensions, are also contributing to the complexity of the budget and reducing the informational value of the fiscal data. Some of these liabilities may be implicit as those *vis-à-vis* a failure by, say, Fannie Mae. It is becoming progressively more difficult to know what the fiscal policy is and what the optimal fiscal policy should be. A 'balance sheet' or 'net worth' approach to fiscal policy has been recommended by some economists. Such an approach would presumably provide a more complete assessment of the fiscal situation of a country. However, difficulties connected with the needed assumptions for variables over many decades, combined with legal obstacles on the transformation of assets owned by the government (stocks) into revenue flows renders this approach of limited practical value. The bottom line is that fiscal policy is becoming progressively more difficult to assess and implement thus reducing the usefulness of one of the government's key policy instruments to pursue socially significant objectives (see also Schuknecht, 2005, pp. 77–78).

11.3.2   Complexity and monetary policy

Let us consider next how complexity may be affecting monetary and financial tools. In market economies central banks are expected to control monetary and financial developments to ensure price stability and to maintain growth. They do this mainly through the discount rate and their regulatory powers. Given the regulatory rules, economic and, especially, inflationary developments are influenced through the raising and lowering of the discount rate. In the past, the decisions of the central banks were transmitted to the commercial banks which were the main intermediaries between the central bank and those who borrowed money for most purposes. The banks reflected the actions of the central banks in their lending policies. The system was relatively simple. When financial crises occurred, they were the consequence of bad policies, inefficient regulations, or occasionally acts of corruption.

In recent years, and especially over the past couple of decades, the situation has changed dramatically and has become far more complex. First, there has been an explosion of new financial *instruments* that have created new markets and have allowed borrowing for all kinds of risks. Second, there has been the emergence of many new *intermediaries* that have come to compete with the commercial banks. These include investment banks, insurance companies, public pension funds for state and municipal employees, hedge funds, or even corporations that over the years have dramatically increased their financial activities. Many of these institutions do not face checks and balances on their financial activities in spite of their size and complexity. Third, the financial market has become truly globalized thus reducing the influence of *national* central banks and increasing the financial links across countries. This has created a new world that is much more difficult to fully comprehend and manage than the one that existed before.

The financial instruments, including those related to *securitization* and *derivatives*, have become very different from, and more complex than, the saving accounts and bonds of past years. At times they have become so complex that they have literally required 'rocket scientists' to develop them and a mathematical background to fully understand them. There is a lot of anecdotal evidence that indicates that those who invest in these instruments often have little knowledge of their nature and of the risks associated with them. This has been the case with managers of private pension funds and private investors in hedge funds who, at times, have watched the value of their assets vanish over short periods of time. This implies that problems of asymmetrical information between those who invest their savings in some financial institutions and the managers of these institutions have become more significant.

Among the intermediaries that have expanded beyond commercial banks, that include investment banks and specialized government-sponsored institutions such as Fannie Mae, a growing role has been assumed by 'hedge funds'. Hedge funds were almost unknown only a couple decades ago but have become major and growing players in the financial market. There are now about 10,000 such funds. They manage assets that may be approaching 1.5 trillion dollars, up from only US $38.9 billion in 1990. These hedge funds are largely unregulated and many are not even registered which makes the counting of them difficult. Because many new ones enter the field all the time, while some exit it, after large losses, statistics on them are not as good as they should be. These hedge funds deal in derivatives, that is in contracts whose value 'derives' from the prices of bonds, stocks, currencies, commodities, and so on. They use proprietary mathematical models that are supposed to identify imperfections in the pricing of financial instruments allowing them to exploit these imperfections for gains. These imperfections are identified on the basis of *past* performances.

The hedge fund industry has made it possible for some managers to get enormous incomes. *Forbes' 2006 Report* on the 400 richest Americans includes 12 hedge fund managers among them. In 2005, James Simons, of Renaissance Technologies, and T. Boone Pickens Jr, of BP Capital Management, reported incomes of US $1.5 billion and US $1.4 billion respectively from their hedge fund activities. Each of the top ten hedge fund managers had salaries that exceeded US $300 million in 2005. These are incredibly large incomes that raise legitimate questions about what these individuals were contributing to society that deserved such enormous compensation, especially when many economists continue to believe that capital markets are efficient. There are also questions as to whether these funds have not in fact increased the volatility of some markets. Apart from these important questions, there is the problem that the form of contracts used to make investments in hedge funds tends to encourage hedge funds' managers to take excessive risks. Much of their compensation comes from being able to beat some market indexes. A single good year can make these managers rich for the rest of their life. Thus, the managers have incentives to take large risks. When they lose in these bets, they may close the hedge funds they had been guiding and may open new ones. At times, within days, they go from reporting large gains for a year to reporting enormous losses, as happened to 'Amaranth Advisers' between August and September 2006. There are no firm data to indicate that *as a group, including those that fail*, hedge funds' earnings systematically beat the market.

The risks associated with the growth of the hedge fund industry are several. Some are mentioned here without much elaboration.

First, as the number of hedge funds rises, it is not likely that there will be enough 'market imperfections' in the pricing of financial instruments that can be exploited by them to support their activities. The mathematical models developed are based on the historical behavior of financial variables. This behavior may change suddenly. The models also do not reflect systemic risk. But, as LTFM discovered in 1998, historical relationships for specific variables become irrelevant when whole systems fail.

Second, as mentioned above, the contracts that investors have with the managers of the hedge funds invite the taking of excessive risk: the managers gain when they beat the market while the investors in the hedge funds are the main losers when the funds do badly. The investors who lose money often complain that they had not received precise information on the operations of these hedge funds.

Third, as the number of hedge funds increases, and there is mobility of personnel among them, the mathematical models that they use inevitably tend to become more similar thus increasing the probability that herd instinct will guide behavior.

Fourth, the money that investors invest in the hedge funds supports contracts or positions that are a large multiple of that money. For example, by the spring of 1996, Long Term Capital Management had US $140 billion in assets, or 30 times the capital that investors had placed in it (Lowenstein, 2000, p. 80). This leveraged position forces them to borrow enormous amounts of money from banks which later may claim that they were not fully informed about the fund's activities. Some reports have indicated that the total value of the derivative contracts entered by hedge funds is now (September 2006) more than 22 times the gross domestic product of the United States. This gives a clear idea of the role of hedge funds in the financial market and the danger that a systemic crisis involving them could create for the financial system. It should be recalled that the Federal Reserve Bank of New York had to intervene in 1998 to prevent a financial meltdown, after Long Term Capital Management failed as a consequence of the Russian default. Since that time the number of hedge funds and their activities has increased sharply.

Finally, and a growing concern for the monetary authorities, many of the derivative contracts (or trades) entered by the traders on behalf of the hedge funds that they represent *remain unconfirmed* for significant periods of time. During this time these contracts are essentially informal and unregistered promises. This means that a major failure on the part of a large enterprise or a country could create major difficulties in determining *quickly and precisely* who owes and who is owed money. Should such an event occur in connection with a technical failure on the part of a large-value payment system, as happened to a computer at the Bank of New York in 1985, the consequences could be very serious.

The payment systems have been called 'the transportation systems of a monetary economy' – because they are the vehicles that carry the enormous and increasing flows of daily payments. Quoting a report of the European Central Bank (ECB):

> credit risks in a net settlement system are extinguished only with the settlement of all net positions in the system . . . As a result, the failure of one participant to meet its obligations at the time of settlement could lead to the unwinding of payments that other participants had already treated as final.

This could lead to a 'domino effect' and to systemic risk (see ECB, 2006, p. 73; see also De Bandt and Hartmann, 2002, especially pp. 273–76).

There have been frequent statements on the part of concerned central banks on the need to impose more stringent rules on the hedge funds, including the need for them to register and to better report on their activities. So far the hedge funds have resisted these initiatives on the grounds that these steps would increase costs and slow down technical advances. This potential conflict between safety on one hand, and technical progress (and presumably efficiency) on the other is becoming more frequent in market economies and is often used as an argument for resisting controls and regulations.

Complexity makes it more difficult to anticipate crises, to predict how crises will evolve, what will be their consequences, and what policy tools the policymakers could use in such events. The fact that markets and countries have not only become more complex but also more interrelated, which is itself another dimension of complexity, can present scenarios never faced before. Assume for example, that the United States and China get into a political spat. China could transfer into euro a few hundred billions of dollars held in dollar reserves. The value of the dollar would fall. The Federal Reserve would be forced to increase interest rates to attract capital inflows and to limit the inflationary impact of the devaluation. Those who had bought houses, in the United States, with little or no equity and flexible rates, especially when the prices of houses were high, would face higher interest rates with reduced property values. Many would default on the payments creating problems for the banks and for the institutions, such as Fannie Mae, that ultimately hold the mortgages. Derivative contracts would face systemic turbulence. Many would fail. This and other possible crises scenarios would have similar ingredients: (a) the complexity of the systems; (b) limited flow of information among various actors; (c) the inability to anticipate possible failures; (d) interactions among parts of the whole system; and (e) fragment-ation of responsibilities because of specialization. While the probability of such scenarios is probably low, it is not zero.

There is surprisingly little attention paid by economists to the connection between increasing complexity and increasing risk of failure in financial markets. A few papers, however, have started to recognize the potential danger. For example, Rajan (2005) has called attention to the increased risk to economies created by the emergence of a whole range of new intermediaries. He has concluded that 'under some conditions, economies may be more exposed to financial-sector-induced turmoil than in the past' (p. 1). Hart-mann *et al.* (2005) have concluded that 'structural stability tests . . . suggest a general increase in systemic risk taking place over the second half of the 1990s . . . ' and that 'for the U.S. . . . . some of the strongest increase in extreme systematic risk seems to be concentrated among the largest players and the main credit banks' (p. 38). De Nicolo and Kwast (2002) have concluded that 'the creation of . . . increasingly complex financial institutions . . . ' have increased . . . 'the systemic risk potential in the financial sector . . . over the last decade'. (p. 1).

11.3.3   Complexity and the income distribution

In democratic countries, to retain legitimacy and political support for its outcome, the private market must (a) allocate resources efficiently, to promote economic growth, and (b) distribute income in a manner that is considered legitimate and fair by the majority of the country's citizens.

When the distribution of income becomes *very* uneven, and a majority of the citizens comes to consider that distribution as unfair, sooner or later populist politicians will appear proposing economic policies that would damage the market economy. The more the distribution of income comes to be considered unfair, the more votes the populist politicians will get from the electorate. Thus, high income inequality can, over the long run, lead to adverse social and economic consequences (see Alesina and Rodrik, 1994; Persson and Tabellini, 1994, for empirical support of this plausible thesis).

In the past couple decades the income distribution has become much less even in industrial countries, and especially in the United States. Between 1967 and 1980 there was little change in the US income distribution, as measured by the Gini coefficient. That coefficient remained around 0.40, not a particularly good value by industrial countries' standards, but a stable one. After 1980, it started rising rapidly and reached 0.47 by 2005. At this level it enjoyed the company of mostly Latin American and African countries. By comparison, the most recent data available give a Gini coefficient that is 0.40 for Russia and 0.44 for China. Other industrial countries have Gini coefficients far below that of the United States.

Another indication of the increasing inequality in the United States can be seen from the comparison between the *mean* and the *median* income. In 1967 the median income was 89.4 per cent of the mean income. By 2005 the percentage had fallen to 73.1 per cent, reflecting the increasing concentration of income at the top. Between 1967 and 2005, while the median income, that reflects mainly the income of workers, had grown by 30.7 per cent in nominal terms, the mean income had grown by a remarkable 59.8 per cent. Workers have hardly experienced any increase in their real wages over this period. Much of the income growth had gone to those at the top. This deterioration has had an impact on the results of surveys that indicate considerable unhappiness, on the part of a majority of those interviewed, about the economy. This has happened in a period of remarkable economic growth that should have made everyone happy. In its annual 'Special Report on the 400 Richest Americans', *Forbes Magazine* has concluded that these were billionaires in dollars, with a total combined wealth of US $1.25 trillion, that is close to the GDP of Italy. In 1982 there had been only 13 billionaires on the list.

The deterioration in the income distribution has been attributed to various factors and especially to the effects of globalization and technological developments. The question to be raised here is whether complexity, interpreted in a broad sense, might not have been one of these factors. It may not be a coincidence that the very high incomes were received by individuals that were either in sectors characterized by complexity (such as those working in the financial market) or that could themselves create complexity to get larger compensations (such as the CEOs of large corporations) (see also Forbes' list).

We have already reported the earnings of some of the managers of hedge funds. Those working in investment banks did not do so badly either. For example the 25,647 employees working for Goldman Sachs received an *average* compensation of US $521,000 in 2005. The five top executives in that enterprise received a combined US $143 million. Compensation in 2006 is expected to be even higher. The CEOs of corporations benefited from a different kind of complexity. They could often select the members of the boards of their corporations, that is the individuals who must approve their compensation package. In large corporations the shareholders hardly play a role. Much of the real power rests with the CEOs who are hired to run the corporations. Their compensation contracts are often complex, and their details are generally kept confidential. The use of stock options and bonuses and the ability of managers to date the options at a time that maximizes earnings can lead to enormous compensation packages. These maneuvers have recently attracted the attention of the Federal Bureau of Investigation (FBI).

Huge salaries have been reported even for heads of corporations that do not do particularly well or lose money. A recent article in the *New York Times* called attention to this problem. As the article put it, 'watching mountains of money go to managers *who destroyed value* in recent years, stockholders have learned that while their shares may sink, executive pay rarely does' (italics added). Citing a report by Glass Lewis and Company, the article states that: 'At ... 25 companies ... chief executive pay averaged US $16.7 million in 2005. The stock of these companies ... fell an average 14 per cent while [the companies'] overall net income dropped 25 per cent, on average.' Furthermore, ' ... the average chief executives' pay totaled 6.4 per cent of these entities' total net income'. This is not an example of an economy in which incomes reflect a person's contribution to total output.

What could be the consequences of increasing inequality for market economies? An interesting paper by Glaeser *et al.* (2002) provides a formal answer to this question. The paper argues that (high) income inequality can be damaging, over the long run, to institutions that are necessary for the good functioning, and especially to institutions that secure property rights, institutions that have been shown to be of great significance for growth. Inequality allows the rich to capture and distort these institutions to their advantage. As they put it, inequality 'enables the rich to subvert the political, regulatory, and legal institutions of society for their benefit'. 'If political and regulatory institutions can be moved by wealth or influence, they will favor the established, not the efficient'. The rich will be able to do so ' ... through political contributions, bribes, or just deployment of legal and political resources to get their way' (p. 2). Lobbying will be an integral and important part of this process.

It is easy to see how, in addition to its initial role in increasing income inequality, complexity could greatly facilitate this subversion process. The subversion of institutions will be made easier by the increasing complexity of laws and regulations. This has clearly happened with the tax system and is happening increasingly in the regulatory system. Inequality, assisted by complexity, creates an asymmetry between the power of the rich and that of the masses, an asymmetry that can be exploited to the advantage of the rich but that can also damage the market economy over the long run. To some extent the tax system and the legal system are becoming tools of the super rich in the United States.

11.4 Concluding remarks

This paper has dealt with an ambitious and broad theme. It has called attention to the increasing complexity that has come to characterize some aspects and institutions of market economies. The paper has also attempted to outline some consequences of this phenomenon.

Complexity may be a natural by-product of technological developments. Some, however, is largely man-made. We may have little power to stop the first, without stopping technological progress. But it may be possible to reduce the second. Building a space shuttle, or an atomic power plant, are examples of complexity that cannot be avoided, although the consequences must be taken into account. It may simply not be possible to go to the moon or to produce atomic energy without complex machines. Thus, the choice is between having this kind of progress or not having it taking into account the cost of occasional failures. On the other hand the creation of a tax system that requires 65,000 pages of laws and regulations is clearly an example of complexity that is man-made and avoidable. Several aspects of the financial market also reflect this avoidable complexity. One suspects that there are intrinsic forces, or vested interests, that benefit from this complexity.

More complexity is likely to contribute to systemic failure. It also (a) facilitates corruption and especially what could be called 'legal corruption', that is redesigning rules to reach particular outcomes; (b) increases the power of lobbies and their ability to promote the interests of some groups at the disadvantage of others; (c) contributes to the increasing inequality of the distribution of income and wealth; (d) creates asymmetry in the ability of the rich and the poor to use the legal, tax, regulatory and other systems to their advantage. The more complex the systems become, the greater will be the advantages for those with greater means. When a system becomes very complex the cost for the average citizen of staying informed becomes very high. Thus many areas are left to 'experts' who can be hired by those who have the means.

It is not too farfetched to maintain that, as complexity comes to characterize the institutions of market economies more and more, and as it contributes to income, legal, and political inequality, this process will in time affect the legitimacy of the market system and increase calls for populist alternatives. These alternatives could damage or even destroy the free market system and create economic problems that over the long run can lead to economic decline. Thus, complexity might play a role in market economies similar to the one it played in command economies.

Transparency and simplicity should become driving principles for policy-makers in market economies. In their regulatory roles and in their legislations, governments must give much more weight to these principles and less to the usual arguments that almost any controls or regulations will damage economic efficiency and slow down economic and technical progress.

References

Alesina, A. and D. Rodrik (1994) 'Distributive Politics and Economic Growth', *Quarterly Journal of Economics*, 109, 465–90.

CCH (2005) *Complete Tax Survey Suggests Taxpayers Confused by Tax Code Complexity* (Washington: CCH Wolters Kluwer), March 16.

Colombia Accident Investigation Board (2003) *Accident Investigation Report*, vol. 1, August.

De Bandt, Olivier and Philipp Hartmann (2002) 'Systemic Risk in Banking: A Survey', in C. Goodhart and G. Illins (eds) *Financial Crises, Contagion, and the Lender of Last Resort: A Reader* (New York: Oxford University Press) pp. 249–97.

De Nicolo, G. and M. L. Kwast (2002) 'Systemic Risk and Financial Consolidation: Are They Related?', *Journal of Banking and Finance*, 16, 861–80.

Edwards, C. (2006) 'Income Tax Rife with Complexity and Inefficiency', *Tax and Budget Bulletin*, 33, April.

European Central Bank (2006) 'The Evolution of Large-Value Payment Systems in the Euro Area', *Monthly Bulletin*, August.

European Central Bank (2005) *Financial Stability Review*, December.

Forbes (2006) 'The 400 Richest Americans: Special Report', *Forbes Magazine*.

General Accountability Office (2006) 'Tax Gap', *GAO-06-453T*, February 15.

Glaeser, E., J. Scheinkman, and A. Shleifer (2002) 'The Injustice of Inequality', July 29, mimeo.

Gray, M. and I. Rosen (1982) *The Warning* (New York and London: W.W. Norton & Company).

Hartmann, P., S. Straetmans and C. de Vries (2005) 'Banking System Stability: A Cross-Atlantic Perspective', *National Bureau of Economic Research, Working Paper*, 11698.

Heller, P. (2003) *Who Will Pay? Coping with Aging Societies, Climate Change, and Other Long Term Fiscal Challenges* (Washington: IMF).

Hilzenrath, D. (2006) 'Fannie Report Details a Calculated "Catch Up" ', *Washington Post Business Section*, D1.

Johson, S. N., R. Herring, and R. Lilan (2005) *The Top Ten Financial Risks to the Global Economy: A Dialogue of Critical Perspectives*, Conference Proceedings, Fall.

Kornai, J. (1980), *Economics of Shortage* (Amsterdam: North Holland).

Lowenstein, R. (2000) *When Genius Failed: The Rise and Fall of Long-Term Capital Management* (New York: Random House).

Persson, T. and G. Tabellini (1994) 'Is Inequality Harmful to Growth?', *The American Economic Review*, 84, 600–21.

Presidential Commission on the Space Shuttle Challenger Accident, (Rogers Commission Report) (1986) *Report of the Presidential Commission on the Space Shuttle Challenger Accident*, vol. 1.

Rajan, R. G. (2005) 'Has Financial Development Made the World Riskier?', *NBER Working Paper,* no. 11728.

Remnick, D. (1994) *Lenin's Tomb: The Last Days of the Soviet Empire* (New York: Vintage Books).

Schuknecht, L. (2005) 'Stability and Growth: Issues and Lessons from Political Economy', *International Economics and Economic Policy,* 2, 65–89.

Shleifer, A. and R. W. Vishny (1999) *The Grabbing Hand: Government Pathologies and their Cures* (Cambridge and London: Harvard University Press).

Simis, C. M. (1982) *USSR: The Corrupt Society. The Secret world of Soviet Communism* (New York: Simon and Schuster).

Smith, R. and Emshwiller (2003), 24 Days (Harper Business).

Tanzi, V. (2005) 'The Economic Role of the State in the 21st Century', *The Cato Journal,* 25 (3).

_____ (2006a) 'Fiscal Policy: When Theory Collides with Reality'. *Center for European Policy Studies Working Document,* no. 246.

_____ (2006b) *Past and Future of Taxation,* paper presented at Politeia Lecture Series 2006, London.

Woolhandler, S. and D. Himmelstein (1997), 'Costs of Care and Administration at For-profit and other Hospitals in the United States', *The New England Journal of Medicine,* March, no. 11.

12
Risk Management and Systemic Risk

John Eatwell

The objectives of regulation and regulatory components could be more expressly linked to the goal of system-wide financial stability. The standards are useful to regulators charged with assessing the strength of regulated entities within each sector. However, their use in addressing system-wide stability issues is limited, partly because they were not written for this purpose. The standards take little account of structural issues, or of inter-linkages among different types of financial firms and markets.
(*Financial Sector Regulation: Issues and Gaps*, IMF, 2004a, p. 30).

12.1 Introduction

Financial policy is today a central concern of economic policy. This has not always been the case. Prior to the financial liberalization initiated in the early 1970s, financial issues did not play a major role in post-War policy-making. Liberalization, combined with remarkable developments in financial analysis, has dramatically changed the policy terrain. Today, whether in developed, transition, or developing economies, financial issues, domestic and international, are a major component of any policy debate.

In contrast to many of the international regulatory developments in finance since 1975 (the Basel Accord of 1975, Basel I in 1988, and so on) a lack of focus on the changing *systemic* characteristics of the international financial system has become a characteristic of international regulatory developments in the past few years. It is certainly a characteristic of Basel II, surely the most important practical expression of the contemporary theory of international regulation. And via Basel II, it will be a characteristic of the European Union's regulatory directives, and, indeed of the regulatory initiatives now being taken by the IMF and the World Bank, and the Financial Stability Forum.

What are these 'changing systemic characteristics'? The *Background Paper* that accompanies the IMF's *Issues and Gaps* paper lists them as (IMF 2004b, pp. 4–17):[1]

- Increased conglomeration and risk transfer;
- Significant and growing internationalization;
- Growing dollarization.

Paradoxically, in the face of these significant *macroeconomic* trends, regulatory standards have retreated from macro concerns, concentrating on essentially *microeconomic* issues – as is the case with the Regulatory Standards. Pillar 1 of Basel II in which regulatory capital requirements are based on the risk models *of firms* is another major example. And at the same time, the impact of the externalities created by risk-taking institutions has been lost in the emphasis on market-compatible regulation – consider Pillar 3 of Basel II that seeks to enhance disclosure, transparency and market discipline.

Efficient risk-management by firms is a fundamental component of competitive success in today's financial markets. It also makes an important contribution to general market stability – in normal times. However, in the face of extreme events (even 'moderately' extreme events) rational risk-management by individual firms may precipitate a macroeconomic reaction that is destabilizing, can place those firms in jeopardy, and result in a general welfare loss.

The objective of this paper is to explore some of the linkages between risk management at the microeconomic level and systemic risk. Some important arguments recently advanced by Caballero and Krishnamurthy (2006) will be used to illustrate these linkages. A key element in the argument will be played by the concept of 'Knightian uncertainty' (see Gilboa and Schmeidler, 1989). The essence of Knightian uncertainty is that an agent has too little information to form a prior, and hence considers a set of priors as possible. Being uncertainty averse, the agent acts on the basis of the minimal expected utility when evaluating any particular trade or contract. It will be argued that this concept captures a key element of the relationship between risk management and systemic risk. It also throws important light on the role of the lender of last resort.[2]

12.2　Externalities and the macroeconomics of systemic risk

Financial risk-taking is a concern of public policy because associated with the risk-taking actions of individuals there are externalities; that is costs and benefits accruing to the society that are *external* to the calculations of the individual investor, and not accounted for in the market place.[3] A major financial failure imposes costs on society going far beyond the losses suffered by the investors. In an economy where there are important externalities, competitive markets will be socially inefficient. The task of public policy, in this case of financial regulation, is to attempt to mitigate these inefficiencies.

Financial externalities are particularly potent because they are transmitted *macroeconomically*, via interest rates, or the exchange rate, or the general level of stock prices. Financial markets are markets for stocks of current and future assets, the value of which today is dependent on the expectation of their future value. To the extent that expectations are shared, any factor that leads to a general shift in expected future values will have an immediate impact on financial markets, and on the major macrofinancial variables, such as the interest rate and the exchange rate.

So the failure of a single firm can, by influencing expectations, have an influence not only on its immediate counterparties, or even just on firms dealing in similar products, but also, through its impact on expectations, on financial markets as a whole, and then via the interest rate or the exchange rate the contagion may spread to the real economy at home and abroad.

Yet despite the presence of externalities and potential contagion, a peculiarity of market expectations is that they can be remarkably stable (or tranquil) for substantial periods of time, even when underlying real circumstances might be decidedly unpropitious. In consequence, the financial markets can resemble the cartoon character who, having run off the edge of the cliff remains suspended for some time in mid-air, with no visible (or rational) means of support, before suddenly plunging into the abyss.

Periods of tranquility defined by stable expectations and stable market confidence may sustain the illusion that financial markets are truly reflecting a strong real economy. The shattering of that illusion can be catastrophic. One of the tasks of a lender of last resort and of financial regulation is to keep markets away from the cliff edge, and when they rush over, to ensure that the damage to the economy as a whole is minimized. In this respect regulation and the lender of last resort function are mutually reinforcing, the task of regulation being both to manage the systemic components of risk-taking by firms and to limit the moral hazard inherent in the actions of a lender of last resort always willing to provide liquidity to a stressed market.

12.3   The analytical framework

The origins of the externality of systemic risk are in large part manifest through what the economist John Maynard Keynes called a 'beauty contest'. In Keynes's contest beauty is not in the eye of the beholder. Instead, the game is won by those who can accurately assess what others think is beautiful. In financial markets, it is knowing what others believe to be true that is the key to knowing how markets will behave. The market is driven by participants' belief about what average opinion believes average opinion believes . . . and so on (Keynes, 1936, Chapter 12; Eatwell and Taylor, 2000, Chapters 1 and 3).

If such markets are to be liquid and reasonably stable then, as Avinash Persaud has emphasized (Persaud, 2000, 2001) it is not enough that markets should be large, it is also a fundamental requirement that they should be characterized by a wide range of participants with heterogeneous objectives *and* with confident expectations that markets will be stable.

A market is liquid when buyers are broadly balanced by sellers.

Markets become illiquid when objectives become homogeneous. When everyone believes that everyone will sell, liquidity vanishes (as it also does when all wish to buy). Markets fall over the cliff when average opinion believes that average opinion has lost confidence in financial assets.

So what contributes to heterogeneity?

First, individual investors and traders must be highly heterogeneous, with different financial objectives, different methodologies, different institutional structures and infrastructures. In traditional economics this was described as the difference between those seeking income certainty and those seeking wealth certainty, with different patterns of risk aversion, different investment time horizons and so on (Robinson, 1951).

Second, investors may have differing access to information, so even if their goals might be the same they will behave differently.

Third, when average opinion believes average opinion believes that markets are stable, then stability becomes a convention. Convention (meaning belief in stability) is vital in financial markets, because convention *creates* and *sustains* heterogeneity. This power of stable expectations should not be underestimated – by defining the *expected* range of movements in asset prices it fixes the *actual* range of fluctuations in current asset prices. But of course once convention is breached, then the flood will follow.[4]

Fourth, investors may be forced, by government regulation, into segmented markets – heterogeneity is effectively imposed by the authorities. For example, the UK mortgage market used to be legally separated from other investment markets, and allocation of mortgages was not entirely by price – queuing was also important. Similarly the Glass–Stegall Act segmented US financial markets, and exchange controls segmented national financial markets.

The classic example of a systemic risk is a bank run. A depositor at a particular bank would be willing to leave funds on deposit, but believes that other depositors are likely to withdraw their funds, forcing the bank to call in loans or sell securities and suffer losses, perhaps even suspending payments. Consequently, a rational investor will seek to be the first to withdraw funds. Hence all withdraw their funds as rapidly as possible resulting in a 'run'. A run on one particular bank necessarily effects the perception of the liquidity of other banks and the run spreads to other, nominally solvent, banks. More formally, whilst a depositor may be certain about the probability of suffering a liquidity shock, the depositor cannot be certain about the probability that his or her shock will occur early or late relative to others. In other words, the depositor cannot be sure where they will be in the queue to withdraw funds. And the position is made yet more uncertain the more homogeneous are the depositors. Depositors therefore treat their uncertainty as 'Knightian', pursuing a maximin strategy over the set of presumed probabilities (Caballero and Krishnamurthy, 2006, p. 8). The result is the rush to withdraw funds.

However, not only has the bank run become a very rare event – whether due to the profitability of banks, the insistence of the regulators on strong balance sheets, the growth of credit risk transfer, or the perceived willingness of the public authorities to provide liquidity when necessary (of which more details given below) – but also the structure of financial markets has changed, shifting from a bank-based to a market-based financial system (Hendricks *et al.*, 2006). Financial intermediation has moved from institutions into markets, and financial crises are now manifest in markets rather than institutions. Accordingly the analytical interest has moved from bank runs to 'market gridlock' as a source of systemic risk. The market oriented systemic crisis is a breakdown in the functioning of markets for traded assets. It may be triggered, for example, by a sharp decline in the price of one asset that sparks a widespread sell-off in the general rush for liquidity.

In Knightian terms, the individual agent knows the probability of a shock, but does not know the probability of being able to trade with the market counterparties on whom his or her liquidity depends. Not knowing, and being averse to uncertainty, the agent (and all other agents) pursues a maximin strategy over the set of possible priors, resulting in a collective bias toward liquidity (Caballero and Krishnamurthy, 2006, p. 15). The collective rush for liquidity produces the market gridlock characteristic of market-based systemic crises. Liquidity dries up as increasingly homogeneous traders all attempt to move in the same direction. It is important to note that a relatively small event can produce this gridlock in very large markets if agents' behavior is sufficiently homogeneous.

12.4 Recent developments in financial markets

The systemic changes identified in the IMF paper, *Issues and Gaps*, have tended to increase the homogeneity of markets – and in many cases this tendency has been reinforced by the regulatory response.

The liberalization and hence internationalization of financial markets that has taken place over the past three decades has inevitably reduced heterogeneity in financial markets. By definition liberalization and internationalization have broken down market segmentation – cross-market correlations have risen sharply.

And with liberalization has come a growing professionalization of financial management (BIS, 1998, Chapter V), and extensive conglomeration of financial institutions (Group of Ten, 2001; IMF 2004a, 2004b; Hendricks *et al.*, 2006, p. 8). Most investments are now managed by mutual funds, pension funds, insurance companies and so on; and these funds are themselves locked into sophisticated wholesale money markets, securitizing and re-packaging and hence homogenizing funds from previously segmented markets. Professionalization has reduced the heterogeneity of investor preferences as expressed in the marketplace. The professional investor is subject to a continual competitive pressure to maximize (short-term)[5] returns, and is constrained by the well-known institutional dilemma that 'it is better for reputation to fail conventionally than to succeed unconventionally' (Keynes, 1936, p. 158). So whatever the preferences of the private investor might be, convergence on 'professional' or 'conventional' strategies by institutional investors are homogenizing the market. And with professional investment go professional information services – both in sources and processing – again making for a more homogeneous environment.

Conglomeration is clearly a major homogenizing force too. As conglomeration proceeds risk management procedures acquire common characteristics throughout the financial sector, whether in banking, securities or insurance. Where once management techniques were sector specific, they are now becoming firm specific, applied across sectors.

Dollarization has also reduced the heterogeneity of policy response. National institutions that might have pursued distinctive policies related to national needs find their powers significantly diminished. In addition to the familiar problem of balance sheet currency mismatch, the central bank has little scope to pursue an independent policy on dollar deposits (IMF 2004b, p. 11).

Finally, what of the impact of increased risk transfer? In principle risk transfer should enhance the heterogeneity of risk bearing, transferring risks toward those with a previously unrequited appetite for risk. A number of questions arise: Has risk indeed been transferred or has it been concentrated (there is clearly a significant concentration in credit risk transfer (CRT) intermediaries, most notably JP Morgan Chase)? Has risk been transferred to those institutions with not just a greater appetite for risk, but also a greater capability for managing risk? When there is a lack of liquidity is the central bank still able to effectively target the provision of liquidity to the market? How will CRT change the risk-taking behavior of both buyers and sellers of risk? All these questions are at present unresolved, with only tentative answers on offer (see Bank of England, 2001; FSA, 2002; BIS, 2005; BCBS, 2004; IAIS, 2004; Wagner and Marsh, 2004). However, what does seem clear is that risk transfer will become a powerful homogenizing force across financial institutions.[6] The efficient management of banking risk by non-banking risk purchasers will tend to converge with efficient management of banking risk by banks.

It would therefore appear that underlying the concern expressed in the IMF paper over the impact of changing systemic characteristics of the international financial system is the tendency of these changes to reduce heterogeneity in financial markets.

12.5   Regulatory principles

As has already been noted, financial sector regulators are tending to reinforce this homogenizing process. The most important reaction to the recurring crises that have followed the process of liberalization since the 1970s has been the development of international regulatory standards and procedures. In this context the IMF-World Bank Financial Sector Adjustment Program (FSAP) is of particular note since it locates regulation within a treaty framework under Article IV of its Articles of Association. FSAP surveillance concentrates on the adherence of national regulation and practices to core principles developed by the Basel Committee, together with the International Organization of Securities Commissions (IOSCO) and the International Association of Insurance Supervisors (see IMF, 2004a, 2004b). But it is the principles underlying Basel II that embody the most important intellectual foundations of the new international financial architecture.

These principles are expressed through the three pillars of Basel II: Pillar 1 – the determination of regulatory capital now heavily weighted toward use of banks' internal risk weighting models, as well as the views of ratings agencies; Pillar 2 – supervision; and Pillar 3 – market discipline enforced by greater disclosure of banks' financial status as well as their internal risk management procedures.

What is particularly noticeable is the emphasis on the role of firms' own risk management procedures and on market discipline. A rather odd way to confront systemic risk, which is by definition an externality that internal procedures do not encompass and is not accounted for in the market place.

But perhaps of even greater importance is that the powerful tendency of Pillar 1 and Pillar 3 will tend to increase the homogeneity of financial markets.

First, there is the emphasis on the use of firms' internal risk management systems, systems that are by definition, market sensitive. Whilst firms' models may differ in detail, they are constructed on similar analytical principles, estimated on similar historical data, and sensitive to the same market information.

Good risk management will result in firms holding a portfolio of assets that are not volatile and the prices of which are not highly correlated – not correlated in normal times that is. Suppose however that the volatility of a given asset rises sharply, the models will tell all the firms to sell. As all try to sell, liquidity dries up. As liquidity dries up, volatility spreads from one asset to another. Previously uncorrelated assets are now correlated in the general sell-off, enhanced by the model driven behavior of other institutions caught up in the contagion.[7] Whilst in normal times such models may encompass a wide range of behavior, in extreme circumstances the models will encourage firms to act as a herd, charging toward the cliff edge together (Persaud, 2000).[8]

Second, the emphasis on disclosure reduces the diversity of information that has in the past created diversity of views. Today information is ever more readily available, and disclosure of price sensitive information is legally required. Insider dealing on private information is, rightly, characterized as market abuse. But the attainment of equal information is bought at a cost – increased homogeneity and hence potentially reduced liquidity.

In the light of the enforcement of greater homogeneity by Pillars 1 and 3, considerable weight is placed on Pillar 2 (enhanced supervision) to inhibit the behavior that generates systemic risk. Unfortunately it is not at all clear that an essentially subjective, personal interaction between bureaucrat and risk taker can be either consistent or effective, particularly on an international scale (Ward, 2002; IMF 2004a).

The drive toward homogeneity is not confined to the Basel II banking proposals. Regulators are responding to the creation of seamless financial markets, spanning banks, securities firms, insurance companies, pension funds, and so on, by requiring that they all follow the same regulatory regime. For example, in considering the relationship between banking and insurance, Sir Howard Davies of the UK Financial Services Authority argued 'Our general view is that the capital treatment should in principle be the same, where the risks are the same' (Davies, 2002). The homogenizing pressure exerted by the regulators was evident in the Financial Services Authority's (FSA) Consultation Paper 142 on *Operational risk systems and controls* (which enunciates policies that apply to all regulated firms) and is a defining theme of the EU directives, the *Capital Requirements Directive* and the *Market in Financial Instruments Directive*.

The competitive pressures for homogenization throughout financial markets are being reinforced by the regulators.

12.6 Macroeconomic policy

The IMF has justified its move into financial regulation by reference to the powers of macroeconomic surveillance embodied in Article IV. It might therefore be hoped that the macroeconomic dimension of systemic risk would be to the fore both in its analysis and in its regulatory proposals.

And indeed, the IMF has proposed the construction of 'macroprudential indicators' (MPIs) to assess the 'health and stability of the financial system'. MPIs 'comprise both aggregated microprudential indicators of the health of individual financial institutions and macroeconomic variables associated with financial system soundness' (Hilbers *et al.*, 2000; see also Evans *et al.*, 2000).

This attempt to link micro risk to the performance of the macro economy is laudable, and is exactly where the debate on effective international regulation should be going. However, there is a flaw in MPIs as currently conceived: there has been no attempt to link the microeconomic risk-taking to the risk created by the inter-actions of firms.[9] Just adding up micro data would not do (White, 2006). The whole is not just greater, but behaves very differently, from the sum of the parts. It is not that the key issue of homogenization is not addressed, by concentrating on microstructures it is regarded as a virtue.

A complementary manifestation of the relationship between microeconomic risk and macroeconomic performance derives from the links between risk management, financial contagion and the trade cycle. Strict regulatory requirements on risk exposures will result in firms reducing lending as a result of a downturn in the economy, thus exacerbating the downturn. In an up-turn, the perceived diminution of risk and the availability of regulatory capital will tend to increase the ability to lend, stoking up the boom (see Jackson, 1999; BIS, 2001).

This procyclicality of regulation is further amplified by the contagion-inducing techniques of the micro risk management encouraged by the regulators. During the Asian crisis, for example, financial institutions followed the instructions of their risk models by reducing their exposure to emerging markets throughout the world. These cutbacks helped spread the crisis, as reduced lending and reduced confidence fed the financial downturn. The key to the problem is, once again, the link between microeconomic actions and macroeconomic consequences. Rational risk-management by individual firms precipitates a macroeconomic reaction that, in a downturn, can place those firms and other firms in jeopardy, indeed could overwhelm the firms' defenses entirely.

Yet there is no coherent policy response to this perverse consequence. Under pressure, regulators have adopted the pragmatic solution of 'regulatory forbearance'. At the onset of the Latin American debt crisis in the early 1980s many major US banks were technically bankrupt, since Latin American assets held on their books had lost their entire market value. Nonetheless, US regulators allowed those worthless assets to be evaluated in the banks' balance sheets at their value at maturity, hence boosting the banks' notional capital and preventing a sudden collapse in lending and liquidity.[10] In the autumn of 1998, many assets held on the balance sheets of financial institutions in London and New York were, if marked to market, worth nothing. Again, the regulators did not insist on an immediate (potentially catastrophic) write down.

For all countries, there is the further difficulty that even if some sort of macroeconomic response were available to offset the procyclicality of regulation, macroeconomic policy is essentially national, whilst the problem may well be international in origin and scope.

12.7 An international approach

And it is the international dimension that is notable, and oddly, missing in the IMF's new approach. The FSAPs are appraisals of *national* financial systems. Yet many of the risks faced by a given national economy may well, in a seamless international financial system, emanate from outside the juridical boundaries of the nation state. It is precisely the national focus of regulators that has been persistently exposed as inadequate in recurrent crises in the past 20 years. It seems quite unsatisfactory to conduct an appraisal of the financial health of Colombia, for example, when many of the risks to which that country is exposed are external. And it seems equally unsatisfactory to conduct an FSAP of UK confined to UK institutions and markets alone, when Britain is so obviously an integral part of a worldwide financial system. At very least IMF should be conducting FSAPs on major collectivities of states, say the G7, or the East Asian economies taken together.

The current approach to reform the international financial architecture is increasing the homogeneity in behavior, is struggling to construct its policy proposals to take account of the inter-relationship between microeconomic risk-taking and macroeconomic performance, and is still trapped within the historical perspective of the nation state. In these circumstances the likely consequences cannot be regarded with equanimity.

12.8 The lender of last resort

> ... Policy practitioners operating under a risk-management paradigm may, at times, be led to undertake actions intended to provide insurance against especially adverse outcomes... When confronted with uncertainty, especially Knightian uncertainty, human beings invariably attempt to disengage from medium to long-term commitments in favor of safety and liquidity.... The immediate response on the part of the central bank to such financial implosions must be to inject large quantities of liquidity... Alan Greenspan (2004)

It is the task of the public authorities to minimize welfare losses that derive from the volatility and/or procyclicality of financial markets. It is essentially a post-hoc task. Despite huge research efforts it has not proved possible to predict shocks in a useful way. So important aspects of policy are responsive rather than preventative.[11] The main response is the provision of liquidity by the lender of last resort. Given that market developments are likely to enhance homogeneity over the foreseeable future, this provision is likely to become yet more important, and to acquire an international dimension.

The link made by Greenspan between Knightian uncertainty and the lender of last resort is an important one. As discussed above, Knightian uncertainty arises because the individual agent simply cannot know whether a bank-run or market gridlock will leave him or her bereft of liquidity. However, the central bank, whilst concerned about the economic health of the economy as a whole, is presumably indifferent to the fate of particular individuals. The bank should be able to take a macroeconomic view of the impact of shocks, and hence have the option of 'leaning against the wind' by providing liquidity to the markets. The central bank's provision of liquidity has a multiplier effect, the direct effect being supplemented by the private sector liquidity that is 'unlocked'. The provision of liquidity leads market agents to reassess the probability of them having access to liquidity. This re-assessment will tend to lead to the release of liquidity, by raising the confidence of market counterparties that the sequence of trades will not break down (Caballero and Krishnamurthy, 2006). An important outcome is that the scale of the injection of liquidity may well be very small relative to the size of market liquidity that is unlocked. It might even be zero! The declared willingness of the Federal Reserve to provide 'as much as is needed' has meant that it has had to provide relatively little.

It is the international dimension of the lender of last resort's function that is problematic. This dimension is probably not very important when the dollar is effectively 'international money', when market linkages and contagion tend to translate any significant financial crisis into a dollar denominated crisis, and when the Federal Reserve is committed to maintaining liquid dollar denominated markets. Of course, the relative stability achieved in dollar denominated markets may well not be reflected in other markets. But at least the center of the international financial system is reasonably stable.

This should provide the platform for the extension of the lender of last resort's function to markets outside the US, presumably by the IMF. Unfortunately, no satisfactory institutional framework has been developed internationally to provide liquidity on the (potential) scale and on the terms required by an effective lender of last resort. The FSAPs are intended as the regulatory counterpart of a lender of last resort. But the IMF lacks the treasury department that is the necessary foundation of the lender of last resort. Its lack of credibility undermines its ability to unlock liquidity gridlock.

A complementary approach to reducing the economic losses imposed by the increasing volatility of financial markets would be to seek to increase liquidity by enhancing heterogeneity, by strengthening the forces of underpinning stabilizing convention, and by considering the possibilities of macroeconomic measures to reduce systemic risk.

12.9 Policy response

In normal times, when risk is predominantly confined to the individual institution, modern risk management is likely to reduce the probability of failure, and so be substantially stability enhancing. But it is when the interlinkages between firms and markets come to dominate behavior, that is at times of extreme events, that the homogenizing impact of common risk management techniques is likely to predominate, increasing instability and market volatility. Effective regulation in normal times creates destructive behavior at times of crisis.

Faced with a collapse in liquidity in the 1930s the policy response was to severely segment financial markets, a market structure that was further reinforced by the Bretton Woods agreement. Controlled financial markets served the immediate post-war era rather well.

But alternatively the benefits of an open international financial system can be secured if there is a far greater recognition of the risks imposed on society by individual risk-taking investors, and that investors are made to bear a fairer proportion of the social costs of those risks. This would mean paying far greater attention to the accumulation of macroeconomic risks that tend to signal the transition from normal times to extreme events, and developing a far more powerful structure of international rules and charges associated with risk-taking investment. For example, the increasing size of bank mergers represents a threat to systemic stability. Yet the banks are not paying the costs of the potential risk they create – they reap the benefits, but shift the costs onto society at large. Of course, the externality varies between banks and financial institutions according to their size, ability to manage risk, and so on. But the externality should attract a charge. Similarly, proposals to impose bailout requirements on lenders and to permit repayment standstills in the face of financial crises are steps in this direction. These measures will tend to increase the cost of funds. But this is what should happen, since too often funds are available today, and risks are taken, at well below their true social cost.

Effective international action will require a new financial architecture that encompasses macroeconomic risk management concerns. The Financial Stability Forum was founded in response to these concerns, linking regulators with treasury departments as well as central banks. This approach should be extended, particularly with respect to developing countries. They should be permitted to substitute macroeconomic controls for the resource intensive firm-level regulation that is espoused in the current FSAP approach.

Efficiency requires that the domain of the regulator should be the same as the domain of the market. None of the standard tasks of a financial regulator – authorization, the provision of information, surveillance, enforcement, and the development of policy – are currently performed in a coherent manner in international markets.

The establishment of a World Financial Authority (WFA) was recommended in 1998 (Eatwell and Taylor, 1998). The role of the WFA was to create a framework of truly *international* regulation. The probability of a WFA being actually established is not far from zero. But the proposition is valuable as a test of the regulatory needs of today's liberal financial markets. Whether a WFA is created or not, the tasks that the model WFA should perform must be performed by someone if international financial markets are to operate efficiently.

Today an institutional structure of international financial regulation is emerging which embodies, albeit imperfectly, a few of the features of an idealized WFA:

- The authorization function is the responsibility of national regulators, with access to markets being determined by agreements specifying the terms of mutual recognition.
- The information function is performed by national regulators supplemented by the international financial institutions, particularly the BIS and by the International Financial Reporting Standards of the International Accounting Standards Board.
- The surveillance function is performed by national regulators, supplemented now by the World Bank-IMF financial sector program.[12]
- The enforcement function is the responsibility of national regulators, but is being developed internationally as an implicit outcome of the World Bank-IMF financial sector program.
- The policy function is in the hands of the BIS committees, IOSCO and the IAIS, the Financial Stability Forum, the IMF, and national authorities.

This list of international regulatory activities has three major features:

1. If the same list were compiled 10 years ago most of the regulatory functions would lack any international dimension. Today in all areas other than authorization, international bodies are taking up some of the regulatory tasks.
2. The list deals only with major international regulatory developments, and omits the growth of *regional* regulation, notably in the European Union.
3. Measured against the template of a WFA, the international regulatory structure is limited, patchy, and even incoherent. It portrays a response to crises rather than a coherent reaction to the international propagation of systemic risk.

12.10 Conclusions

A number of principles should guide the development of the international financial institutions and policy:

- full cognizance should be taken of the social costs of the externality of systemic risk, particularly its macroeconomic impact;
- homogeneity of market behavior is a threat to liquidity, particularly at times of high volatility when convention has broken down; it is therefore important to enhance heterogeneity wherever possible and to secure an effective lender of last resort;

- regulatory policies that increase homogeneity must be balanced by measures that mitigate the potentially destabilizing consequences; and
- financial markets are today international, and hence policy formation and policy implementation should be international in scope too.

On the basis of these principles it would be possible to combine the benefits of risk management with mitigation of systemic risk.

Notes

1. Two other factors considered are (a) weaknesses in infrastructure underpinning regulatory systems, and (b) government ownership of financial institutions. However, these are not *trends*, but characteristics influencing the success of prudential regulation.
2. Caballero and Krishnamurthy combine the concept of Knightian uncertainty with the Diamond and Dybvig (1983) model of bank runs and deposit insurance.
3. There are a number of other important market failures in the financial sector that attract the concerns of public policy, most notably the asymmetry of information between individual savers and market professionals that is the motivation of consumer protection. This paper deals solely with the market failure manifest in systemic risk.
4. The most powerful convention of all is that imposed by governments. When the exchange rates of the future Euroland currencies were declared prior to being irrevocably fixed on 1st January 1999, the markets rapidly converged on those rates.
5. '... there is a peculiar zest in making money quickly, and remoter gains are discounted by the average man at a very high rate ... It is the long-term investor ... who will in practice come in for most criticism, wherever investment funds are managed by committees or boards or banks' (Keynes, 1936, p.157).
6. 'With higher activity in risk transfer markets, financial market participants with traditional business lines could assume completely different roles as "virtual insurers" or "virtual bankers"' (OECD, 2002, p. 2).
7. The change in correlation is a market manifestation of what the individual agent cannot know prior to an 'abnormal' event.
8. Philippe Jorion (2002) has rejected this argument. However, his defence of risk management systems is not convincing: he claims that 'financial markets are no more unstable recently than over the past century', when the key comparison is with the 1950s and 1960s; he admits that the 'jury is still out' on herding and acknowledges pro-cyclical effects; he argues that VaR models should be smoothed, ignoring the impact of daily-earnings-at-risk systems.
9. Even at the most simple level these interactions undermine the calculation of MPIs. For example, not only is the value of capital, and hence the capital adequacy ratio, directly effected by the revaluation of assets consequent upon a change in the interest rate, but also declines in the level of activity can rapidly transform prudent investments into bad loans.
10. This does not mean that regulatory standards were abandoned entirely: '... money centre banks whose loans to heavily indebted countries exceeded their capital in the early 1980s were allowed several years to adjust – but there was no doubt that they would have to adjust' (Turner, 2000).

11. Of course, effective risk-management reduces the risk of shocks in normal times.
12. In addition the international surveillance of financial crime, particularly money laundering, is conducted by the Financial Action Task Force (see Alexander, 2000).

References

Alexander, K. (2000) Multi-national efforts to combat financial crime and financial action task force', *Journal of International Financial Markets*, 2(5).

Bank of England (2001) *Risk Transfer Between Banks, Insurance Companies and the Capital Market*; available at www.bankofengland.co.uk.

Basel Committee on Banking Supervision (BCBS) (2004) *Credit Risk Transfer* (Basel: Bank for International Settlements).

Bank for International Settlements (BIS) (1998) *68th Annual Report* (Basel: Bank for International Settlements).

Bank for International Settlements (BIS) (2001) 'Marrying the Macro- and Micro-Prudential Dimensions of Financial Stability', *BIS Papers*, 1.

Bank for International Settlements (BIS) (2005) *Credit Risk Transfer* (Basel: Committee on Banking Supervision, The Joint Forum).

Caballero, R.J. and A. Krishnamurthy (2006) 'Flight to quality and collective risk management', *NBER Working Paper*, 12136.

Davies, H. (2002) 'A toxic financial shock: general insurance companies may be taking on risks that are hard to quantify', *Financial Times*, 30 January.

Diamond, D.W. and P.H. Dybvig (1983) 'Bank runs, deposit insurance, and liquidity', *Journal of Political Economy*, 91, 401–19.

Eatwell, J. and L. Taylor (1998) *International Capital Markets and the Future of Economic Policy* (New York: Center for Economic Policy Analysis and London: IPPR).

Eatwell, J. and L. Taylor (2000) *Global Finance at Risk: the Case for International Regulation* (New York: New Press).

Evans, O., A. Leone, M. Gill and P. Hilbers (2000) 'Macroprudential indicators of financial system soundness', *IMF Occasional Paper*, 00/192.

Financial Services Authority (FSA) (2002) *Cross-sector risk 'transfer'* (London: Financial Services Authority).

Financial Services Authority (FSA) (2002) 'Operational risk systems and controls', *Financial Services Authority Consultation Paper*, 142.

Gilboa, I. and D. Schmeidler (1989) 'Maximum expected utility with non-unique priors', *Journal of Mathematical Economics*, 18 (2), 141–53.

Greenspan, A. (2004) *Risk and uncertainty in monetary policy*, remarks at the Meetings of the American Economic Association, San Diego, California; available at www.federalreserve.gov/BoardDocs/speeches/2004/20040103/default.htm.

Group of Ten (2001) *Report on Consolidation in the Financial Sector* (Basel: Bank for International Settlements).

Hendricks, D., J. Kambhu and P. Mosser (2006) *Systemic Risk and the Financial System* (New York: Federal Reserve Bank of New York).

Hilbers, P., R. Krueger and M. Moretti (2000) 'New tools for assessing financial system soundness', *Finance and Development*, 37 (3).

International Association of Insurance Supervisors (IAIS) (2004) *Credit Risk Transfer between Insurance, Banking and Other Financial Sector*.

International Monetary Fund (IMF) (2004a) *Financial Sector Regulation: Issues and Gaps* (Washington: IMF).

International Monetary Fund (IMF) (2004b) *Financial Sector Regulation: Issues and Gaps – Background Paper* (Washington: IMF).

Jackson, P. (1999) 'Capital requirements and bank behaviour: the impact of the Basle accord', *Basle Committee on Banking Supervision Working Paper*, no. 1.

Jorion, P. (2002) *Fallacies in the Effects of Market Risk Management Systems*, University of California at Irvine, mimeo.

Keynes, J.M. (1936) *The General Theory of Employment, Interest and Money* (London: Macmillan).

Organization for Economic Cooperation and Development (OECD) (2002) *Risk Transfer Mechanisms: Converging Insurance, Credit and Capital Markets;* available at www.oecd.org/dataoecd/30/9/1939376.pdf.

Persaud, A. (2000) *Sending the Herd off the Cliff Edge: The Disturbing Interaction Between Herding and Market-sensitive Risk Management Practices* (State Street Bank).

Persaud, A. (2001) *Liquidity Black Holes* (State Street Bank).

Robinson, J. (1951) *The Rate of Interest and Other Essays* (London: Macmillan).

Turner, P. (2000) *Procyclicality of Regulatory Ratios?*, paper prepared for the Ford Foundation project on 'A World Financial Authority', Centre for Business Research, Judge Institute of Management Studies, Cambridge, January.

Wagner, W. and I. Marsh (2004) *Credit Risk Transfer and Financial Sector Performance*, Working Paper 13, CERF, Cambridge; available at www.cerf.cam.ac.uk.

Ward, J. (2002) *The Supervisory Approach: A Critique.* mimeo, ESRC Centre for Business Research, Cambridge; available at www.cerf.cam.ac.uk.

White, W.R. (2006) 'Procyclicality in the financial system: do we need a new macrofinancial stabilisation framework?' *BIS Working Papers*, 193.

13
Optimal Transition Trajectories?

László Csaba

13.1 Introduction

The nature of analytical social science is such that the search for the right measure is one of its core elements. For this reason the two decades of transition from communist to market order has been revolving around the big question of whether it could have been done better. Once we reject the widespread and self-condoning *post hoc ergo propter hoc* type of argumentation, the question if and to what degree, things could have been better done, if costs were excessive, or results less than justified, must figure eminently on the agenda. In the present chapter we try to address some of these normative issues. Both descriptive and interpretative evaluations of this historic process abound, and a 'final word' is as much unlikely to be spoken as over the French Revolution, for that matter.[1]

At the onset of systemic change two trends of the literature attempted to raise these concerns. One was the debate over shock therapy versus gradualism, and the second was related to the social costs of transformation. The first strand of literature was rather emotional and loaded with immediate political misgivings about the nature any comprehensive change may trigger in an established and urbanized society, such as those in Central and Eastern Europe. While the fact that the collapse of the Soviet empire was not foreseen by most observers, nor the depth and multi-dimensionality of its crisis properly understood by most contemporaries hold, still the question remains of 'how far and how fast' socio-economic changes were bound to go.

Interestingly, as observed by contemporaries (Murrell, 1992), political conservatives were more in favor of social engineering, which is about the opposite of what we observe in the West. And by contrast social democrats, the successors of enlightenment with its belief of the inherently good features of human nature, were in favor of more cautious steps.

Whatever we think about the merits and de-merits of the discussion of the early years, it has become quite clear that certain measures take longer than others. For institutional reforms cannot be introduced by fiat, and nobody familiar with the nature of structural reforms has advocated it, even if coming from the radical camp. Furthermore it has become clear that the nature of changes is such that these must go much deeper than usual adjustment programs of the International Monetary Fund (IMF), including the more ambitious – though less successful (Krueger, 1998) – structural adjustment programs. Changing *informal institutions,* such as rule-abiding or rule-averting behavior, creating trust in the place of general distrust, gaining credibility for a previously non-existent system of financial intermediation, or bringing about conditions of the rule of law where lawlessness used to be the name of the game, are obviously challenges that cannot be mastered over a few months or even years. And even if we abstract away from the fallacy that dominated the Western literature of the first 4–5 years, when stabilization was equaled to institutional reforms, the depth and the time dimension of the required changes have only very gradually been understood, not only by policy-makers, but also by the guild of analysts.

13.2   The broader framework and its applications

By 1999–2001, a stage of overall reassessment had emerged. On the one hand, international agencies have also understood the imminent need to revise their conventional wisdom, for shorthand the Washington Consensus. Capitalizing on the failures and shortcomings of policy reforms across the globe, but not least in the post-communist world, the so-called Post-Washington Consensus emerged (Kolodko, 2000, pp. 119–40), where institutional features, social safety net, environmental and gender issues as well as overall sustainability considerations have come to the fore. Although the interpretation of the precise meaning of the new consensus has remained open to debate, for example on the relative importance of traditional components of solid policies *vis-à-vis* institution building, or about the complementarities versus concurring nature of both areas of change (Havrylyshin and van Roden, 2003), there seems to have been a relatively broad *common understanding* over what needs to be done and how. This convergence of views has been strengthened by the fact that frontrunners in transition were successfully applying for membership in the European Union (EU). Being a specific model of the market economy itself, the acquis of the EU has been playing a formative role for the acceding countries in a large number of policy areas, from monetary policy to environmental protection. Furthermore, since accession has been granted, to a large degree, on the basis of promises or further commitments, this role is unlikely to evaporate any time soon, notwithstanding the more recent erosion of the implementing capacity of the EU against its core member states.[2]

One of the underlying reasons for the appreciation of the role of institution building has been the insights stressing the importance of *sustainability* in all major policy areas, not only in fiscal and monetary policy. The more we care about the time dimension, the higher relevance we attribute to the precise and transparent formation of the rules of the repeated games, as well as to their implementation capacity (an aspect highlighted particularly by the last book of North, 2005). So if early debates tended to focus on macroeconomic policies and stabilization, later discussions focus on the quality and nature of new institutions, the quality and outcomes of privatization, the efficiency enhancing features of the regulatory framework and its components ensuring favorable outcomes. Judging by the convergence of previously polar positions, such as for example those of the Economic Commission for Europe on the one hand, and IMF and EBRD on the other, *at least at the level of the theory of economic policy*, a substantial amount of agreement has emerged over the basic question, what needs to be done. For instance, appreciating the role of competition, of independent regulatory agencies, standard reporting and transparency requirements, counted among the common insights. Likewise the renewed emphasis on the social side, in terms of employment and a social safety net alike, education and Research and Development (R&D) accounted for the rapprochement.

This consensus has been strengthened by the nature of *Europeanization*. For one, the regular and organized interactions with incumbent EU polity, from the level of cabinet members to more frequent encounters among scholars on a large number of occasions, has obviously contributed to the evolution of a common *language* of analysis, common *agendas* and a degree of commonality of *perceptions*. On a more practical level, both the stage of acquis screening and the process of accession has included a fair amount of *direct imitation and adaptation* of pre-existing arrangements, even monitoring and checking the sincerity and success of implementation 'on the ground'. This circumstance may be evaluated both as a plus and a minus. It has been a plus insofar as the substantive features of regulation could be implemented, and not only on paper. Thus a *higher quality institutional setup* emerged than in comparable cases, be that the New Independent States, Southeast Europe or the Mediterranean. On the other hand, the 'domestic ownership of reforms', to use the parlance of the Wolfensohn Presidency of the World Bank, has not always been ensured. For this reason the *identification* of domestic actors as a side condition for sustainability has not been secured. For example, the dodging of environmental regulations, or even watering down the new features of common agricultural policy favoring rural development against traditional production subsidies, has been anything but unusual.[3]

13.3 The derailment to populism

It is all the more puzzling against this background to find that *policies* that could have followed from the common insights *have not materialized*. Most conspicuously, a quick adoption of the single currency seems to have been one of the fundamental consensus points of the economic policy debates. For if there is consensus in terms of the desirability and feasibility of lastingly low inflation policies in catching up economies, the arguments in favor of joining in become overwhelming. The more we accept the bipolar view that has become dominant in the financial literature, namely that only the corner solutions in exchange regimes are sustainable in the long run, the more we would see as an imperative for any small open economy to bring about conditions for joining monetary integration.[4] If for no other reasons, the substantially decreased likelihood of a speculative attack on the local currency, the abolition of the exchange rate constraint, the probability – and in the longer run inevitability – of interest rate convergence, and not least the elimination of the balance of payments constraint on economic growth, together add up as a weighty package of arguments in theory and policy practice alike. It seemed, at least at the time of striking the accession deal at the Copenhagen Council of December 2002, that this was part and parcel of the common understanding. For this reason each applicant agreed to adopt the entire EU acquis including monetary union, though with a timely derogation. In other words, unlike Britain or Sweden, the new members accepted the implicit obligation to meet the criteria for European Monetary Union (EMU) entry as part of EU entry 'within foreseeable period of time'.[5]

But *reality has become quite different*. The commitment to sustainable public finances, of fiscal consolidations, and to accepting these as preconditions for lasting growth has become increasingly feeble in the period immediately following establishment of the EMU. This is not a theoretical nor a generally valid statement, but a politically weighty one, as it does relate to the three *core economies of the EU* – France, Germany and Italy. It is interesting to observe that it was the core EU economies where domestic developments have led to ebbing out of reforms, although EMU could, in theory, have called for their intensification. By contrast, Scandinavians outside the EMU framework have tended to adopt policies of reform and consolidation, even tougher than EMU membership would have required (Aiginger and Gugger, 2006).

It would require a separate analysis (de Haan *et al.*, 2003; Buti and Franco, 2005) to elaborate how the change in the domestic balance of forces in the core EU states has led to the previously unthinkable practice, of the very major players finding various pretenses and sideways to dodge the self-imposed fiscal discipline of the Stability and Growth Pact (SGP). Whatever we may think about the substance of the SGP, the fact of the matter remains that regular breaches have developed immediately before, during and following eastward enlargement. The reference to reform fatigue is customary, but less than fully convincing in view of the rather marginal changes that occurred in the major trespassing countries (as against the new members and Scandinavians alike).

What really matters from our perspective is the *negative synergy* that emerged in the two interrelated, though quite different, practices. At the immediate level, it has become crystal clear, especially following the November 2003 Council decision not to start excessive deficit procedure against France and Germany (later overruled by the European Court of Justice), that it is, indeed, *possible to get away with non-compliance.* It is not that imposing sanctions of last resort, such as the actual fining of the two with a penalty equaling to 0.5 per cent of GDP, as envisaged originally in the Treaty of Amsterdam, would have been required. However, the circumstance that governments obviously and openly flouting the letter and the spirit of the coordinated fiscal rules of the game could get away without even a formal reprimand has made the impression that the fiscal framework meant to support the EMU is a dead letter, which is not invoked if anybody of importance is involved.

Second, all new members, themselves struggling with the disequilibria owing to reforms and policies alike, have faced the *demonstration effect* of the major countries. Quite irrespective of the need to join the euro quickly or not so quickly, they could observe the locomotives of the EU to dodge reforms, basically for reasons of short-term political considerations. Under a competitive political system and facing the gradual disintegration of governing parties on the left and right alike, it seemed trivial for them to replicate the experience of the 'frontrunners'. The cost, in terms of power, of joining the single currency later, and not meeting the criteria now, that were seen as by and large arbitrary and irrelevant anyway, has not seemed to be prohibitive. For this reason the oft-invoked 'straightjacket' nature of Maastricht and the SGP has not been at work at all, since participation in the coordinated fiscal framework has not and could not exert any disciplinary influence over the new members.

This is not to put the entire blame for the populist derailment of frontrunner transition economies on any of the external factors, that included, inter alia, the historic low of *international interest rates.* The fact that in the last Greenspan years the FED prime was the lowest in 46 years was basically an outcome of an attempt to avoid a recession in the USA. But for the new member states this created an opportunity for, and a lure of, bridging domestic disequilibria from cheap external sources, irrespective of the sobering Polish and Hungarian experiences of the 1970s and 1980s.

Analyzing the Hungarian experience, Györffy (2007) points to the low institutionalization of the budgeting procedure, the lack of professional and political understanding, the perhaps too quick adoption of creative accounting of advanced economies, and the relatively low professionalism of public debate over public finances among the causes.[6] While these factors may and perhaps also do vary by the Visegrád countries, the overall feeling of economic issues becoming less pressing must have played a role.

Last but not at all least, it is worth noting that in the 1990s successful transition countries have, to some degree, transformed their economic problems into social ones. When wages grow slower than productivity, capital income and wealth emerge, and so does mass unemployment and open poverty, joined with conspicuous consumption at the other end of the social spectrum, so macrodata seem often irrelevant for the man in the street. While in terms of macroeconomic indicators it would be hard to dispute the primacy of Poland (in terms of increments over the 1989 levels in GDP per capita, consumption, and so on),[7] it was precisely that country where strains have become manifest already years before the rightist–populist turn of 2005.

On the base of established economic insights it is anything but surprising to see the deceleration of growth, the sustainingly low activity levels, and the ensuing phenomena of *jobless growth*. Since the growth of the Visegrád countries in the 2000s has increasingly been export- and FDI-led, while the latter evolved around a capital-intensive pattern, this implies limitations on the demand side. On the supply side of labor one could observe the extension of higher education in terms of quantity, irrespective of labor market demands (replication of the experience of the 1970s and 1980s in core EU). Meanwhile traditionally competitive secondary schooling and vocational training tended to be neglected. Cultivation of skills, particularly important for employability, such as foreign languages, computer literacy, the ability and willingness to cooperate (even under unusual circumstances and with persons from different cultures), have tended to be neglected. Thus the relatively favorable numbers on formal education, such as the next to general spread of secondary education, or the quantitative expansion of tertiary education, tell little about the actual outcomes in terms of economic potential. The production of degrees has become a rather poor reflection of the state of human capital (Polónyi and Tímár, 2001). The above sketched circumstances may account, at least in part, for the emergence of jobless growth by the 2000s in Central Europe.

13.4   The quality of institutions and policies matters

One of the possible answers that may be given as a partial solution to our puzzle may lie in the quality of policies and institutions. In short, the process of accelerated structural change in Central Europe has been externally imposed on the respective societies. This involves *a number of factors*, starting up with the collapse of the Soviet Empire, which has been *extraneous* to those societies.[8] When the largely unforeseen changes of 1989–91 occurred, analysts both inside and outside the region tended to be rather unprepared for the challenges. *Local economists* did have a lot of tacit knowledge of the system and experience with manipulating reforms, which included a fair amount of policy skills for timing and sequencing. External experts tended to have two types of knowledge, which remained largely disconnected in most of the cases. *Sovietological* knowledge was extensive in anthropological and cultural terms, but tended to be backward in analytical economic backing. By contrast, *mainstream* and also developmental economists, active in policy advise and in international financial organizations, tended to have very limited if any region-specific experience. Knowledge of the Soviet-type economy was limited and schematic, and this contributed to a tendency of underestimating the time dimension, as well as the complexity, of post-communist change.

True, with the passage of time, the *interaction* of the above listed different brands of knowledge tended to improve, inter alia by way of learning by doing, or *trial and error*. Several ideas have been tested on the transforming societies (for better or worse), and this experience has finally contributed to the improvement of global economic knowledge. The learning process has been accelerated by the spread of standard knowledge and business expertise in the region (Pleskovic, 2007) at the formal level, and via interaction with IMF, the World Bank and not least the EU and multinational corporations at a more practical level. From the point of view of social learning, the latter, more pedestrian, variant has been equally, or even more, important than formal knowledge transfer. The above listed institutions have contributed to the evolution of relevant *professional knowledge*, via assistance programs, involvement, conditionality and simple on the spot learning (which was mutual), both in the region and globally.

With all due respect for those involved on both sides, it should be observed that change in the region has remained to a large degree *externally determined*. Learning at the expert level has been much quicker than at *the social level*. And while one may bemoan the relatively slow and shallow acquisition of cutting edge knowledge, even this speed tended to be breathtakingly quick for the formerly closed and stagnant ex-communist societies.

Learning has been anchored to a large extent in the process of European-ization, that is, the interaction of EU and candidate country structures and policies. Ever since the signing of the trade and cooperation agreements in 1988 the EC/EU has been involved openly and deeply in the formation and restructuring of domestic institutions in Central Europe (Balázs, 1996, Part V). Since the accession to EU has been one of the very few consensual points among the divided local elites, the EU has gained an *unusually strong bargaining position* in the period leading up to accession. By the same token, technicalities stemming from the autochthonous development of the acquis communautaire and extraneous to domestic concerns, and the dynamics of transition, have played a major role. Perhaps the first and most conspicuous warning example of the mismatch was the White Book of the Commission of 1995, when it first listed the major tasks for candidates. The latter included, in the same order, such issues as the need to treat national minorities prop-erly, to ensure the independence of the monetary authority, and the qualities tea boilers have to meet. Whereas the latter was clearly a reflection of the nature of any bureaucracy, the outcome has remained the same.

These and other examples may explain why the adoption of Western, that is mostly EU norms, has been *rather formal*. In making the choices, the stick and the carrot of the EU, as represented by the Commission and a few major members, played a decisive role. Therefore, considerations of an appropriate fit to the acquis rather than coherence with national norms, even the Constitution, remained subordinate (on the latter, see Sajó, 2004). On the other hand, the limited administrative capacity of the Commission Directorate General (DG) for enlargement, and also the relatively marginal significance of enlargement issues in the overall agenda of the EU until 2002–04, together allowed for the acceptance of lastingly formal adaptation. Even if the EU experts Commission had its doubts, political and *strategic considerations* tended to sweep these under the carpet.

The best example of this approach has been the option for big bang rather than small group/incremental enlargement in 1999 in the Helsinki Council. By *de facto* giving up the principle of differentiated treatment, the EU has rejected an important bargaining chip in the process. By contrast, local politicians tended to adopt a minimalist approach. Rather than echoing the concerns of the founding fathers, they considered it necessary to deliver whatever was required, but not a penny/inch more. This approach, often dubbed in the more academic EU literature as the return to intergovernmentalism, has not caused the lapses, but it has undoubtedly contributed to them.

Let me list just the *major policy areas* where improvements have proven to be *formal and fragmentary!* The obvious starting point is *public finance* where, as discussed above, the incentive to joint the area of single currency (a technocratic argument) has become subordinate to redistributory concerns (a socio-political argument). While new member states have long been involved in the rituals of the EU aimed at ensuring compliance with the letter and spirit of EMU – such as the elaboration of Broad Economic Policy Guidelines, the Fiscal Convergence Programs, since 2004 even the Excessive Deficit Procedures (some of them), and moreover their representatives being present during the deliberations of Ecofin in elaborating the Financial Perspective and in the co-decisions of the European Parliament – all these exercises have obviously fallen short of preventing the new members from the derailments already immediately upon their accession.

Membership in the EU has not contributed, as many of us would have expected, to a qualitative *improvement of the system of financial intermediation*. The story starts with the monetary authority, whose independence in real terms has proven lower than the ECB would have liked. It follows with the limited role of the State Audit Offices in correcting fiscal malpractices. Competition agencies are active, but their role is more supplementary than formative in shaping decisions of macrostructural nature (Bara, 2006; Kravtsenniouk, 2002). The slow if any progress in EU-wide financial services sector liberalization has contributed to keep a large segment of the economy closed. This is only in part counteracted by the fact that the banking sector in the region is one of the most transnationalized by global standards (Gém, 2004). This had to do with the need to import professional knowledge and strategic investors, whose capital is sufficient to ensure the solidity of the local banking system.

But the shortcomings of similar sorts could be listed in a number of *non-economic areas*, such as rule of law. Here the discontinuity with the interwar period has been particularly manifest, though differing by the country. While many aspects of legal culture have survived the Communist period, or have been revived in the early years of transition, the substantive components of application remain fragmentary. Business surveys of various sorts continue to name red tape, corruption, clumsy and inefficient legal arrangements, among the major components limiting competitiveness of the new member states, over and above the respective levels of unit labor costs or statutory tax rates.

Microeconomic reforms have also slowed down in the years during and after EU accession. To list a few: tax reforms prevented the collapse of state revenues that could be observed in the New Independent States prior to the emergence of the oil windfall and centralization of power structures, but were of limited success. With the exception of Slovakia, the system of public dues has remained rather non-transparent, serving a multitude of ad hoc purposes. For these reasons most business surveys contain repeated complaints against the tax system, and even more against the arbitrariness of administration, despite the well established fact that the consolidated level of public dues of Visegrád countries is among the lower ones in the OECD area. In the administration of investment-related tax holidays, a strange development could also be observed. Following the competition policy guidelines of the EU, the Commission pressed the new members to abolish the lavish tax holidays granted to big investors. While these ceased to grant new benefits since the end of 2002, a competition for FDI has intensified. At least in some of the industries, notably in automobiles, the often prestige-driven race for new big investment did trigger a series of concessions granted to the big investors, contrary to the declared principles and contrary to commonsensical and elementary economics (as documented in Kolesár, 2006). The workings of courts has remained slow, inefficient and often insensitive to the needs and time considerations of business. Support for small and medium-sized enterprises (SMEs) has been vocal, but neither the money allocated, nor the institutions specifically tailored to their needs, were able to overcome the numerous obstacles to bottom-up entrepreneurship and its growth (Dallago and McIntyre (eds), 2003).

Also in the broader socio-political sphere, *the stagnation of reforms* has become observable once the formal requirements of the EU were, by and large, met. For instance in Hungary, the agency supervising the media worked for 4 years without involvement of the opposition, although the stipulations require their presence. In Poland and Hungary, the monetary policy board has been widened so as to enhance governmental influence. Corruption cases abound, most prominently in the Czech Republic, when prime ministers and other high officials had to resign due to involvement. In Slovakia, several of the reforms of the Dzurinda government could be easily reverted, such as the symbolic flat tax, showing the weak institutionalization of policies. The politicization of civil service has become manifest in all the four countries, with changes in the top triggering wholesale restructuring, reaching even the lowest levels. Most affected were the ministries of culture and foreign affairs, but these are by no means singular/exceptional cases.

The spread of populism in overall political approaches has paved the way to, what was once termed in the USA during the Reagan period, woodoo economics. Calls for tax cuts and parallel expenditure increase abounded in left and right wing parties or governments alike. The ballooning of deficits, most manifestly in Hungary, has been a clear indication of how dire the consequences of such policies can be. For if the government regularly overspends and crowds out private investment, the deceleration of growth rates is anything but surprising, especially in the medium run.

Lack of consensus, low credibility and insufficient commitment have made joining the eurozone illusory in each of the countries by the time of writing. While this step was seen around 2002 as a given, the nature of policies has evolved in such a way that the floating of the entry date is the adequate option, since nobody can make quantifiable and thus checkable commitments on macroeconomic targets, especially the ones enshrined in the Maastricht and the following Nice Treaty on the EU. This should not be a major problem per se, if only we had not considered two circumstances. For one, the above listed shortcomings reflect the weakness of new democracies. Furthermore, they also reflect *a missed opportunity* in the period of relatively high growth. Instead of implementing the painful but necessary third generation reforms, or at least paving the way for the latter, the policymakers of the region opted for short-sighted policies, despite the formal commitments made, explicitly and implicitly, during the accession process. On the other hand, at times of increased capital mobility, these small open economies – the Visegrád Four – who had also opened their capital markets by the early 2000s, are increasingly subject to the *volatility of international capital markets*. Under these circumstances sustaining a national currency becomes an expensive and dangerous luxury, as the potential number of targets for speculative attacks has been on the increase. Furthermore, in such small open economies the sovereignty of monetary policy has become by and large an illusion anyway, since room for conducting policies, other than accommodating the ups and downs of international markets, has become narrow or even next to nil. This can be tested any time they wish to follow a different line, for example in order to reflect domestic balance of power considerations, such as trying to keep the prime rate low in order to help finance the government deficit.[9]

13.5 What is the terminus?

The mere listing of the above-sketched issues may already justify our doubts about the uses of the term 'transition'. The semantics of the word would imply that we know by and large not only *the starting point*, which is the case with the benefit of hindsight, but also *the end point of the process*. Under this assumption, the real question is only that of the trajectory, in two planes. At one level we may ask if societies have indeed come closer to their production frontier, if they have rejoined the mainstream of human progress, or if they have entered the path of sustainable development, whether they allow for applying the concept of the World Bank and others that is broader than sheer quantitative growth (and includes environmental, social and financial equilibrium considerations). At the other level we may compare, at least *ex post*, actual policies with those that could, in theory, have been implemented. This second exercise is of course to a large degree speculative. However, it allows for identifying alternatives against which the self-congratulating tone of the official accounts can be replaced with analytically better elaborated insights.

The above list is by no means meant to be exhaustive, and could be extended perhaps at will, with further issues such as the problem of social exclusion, the major dilemmas of developing physical infrastructure, the need to turn education into a component of competitiveness, and many others. However, the mere enumeration of issues reflects a new reality: namely, that countries of Central Europe face by and large *the same type of challenges as the incumbent EU-15*. In other words, transition, as a specific set of tasks leading to EU maturity, is basically over. However, the EU itself has come to a certain stagnation in both policy and institutional planes. At the *policy level* major items of common or coordinated policies have been subject to doubts and disagreements, from common foreign and security policy (over Iraq) via the above-described flouting of the fiscal framework, to the open questioning of the *rationale* of common agricultural policy, in terms of size and funding alike, by the net contributors. Meanwhile, *at the institutional level*, the rejection of the Constitutional Treaty by the Dutch and French electorate, and the ensuing freezing of ratification in such major member countries as Britain and Poland, have sent a clear signal to policy-makers that the seclusive, elitist, non-responsive style of European governance has reached its clear limits.

In short, what seemed to be a safe haven for the new members only a few years ago has become a sea of rather troubled waters by the time they have arrived. The stagnation of the EU as an institution follows, by and large, from *the stagnation of domestic reforms* in some – though by no means all – core member states such as France, Italy and Germany. The challenges, such as reforming the welfare state model (broadly conceived), and introducing fiscal sustainability while regaining global competitiveness, bear considerable similarities between old and new members.

For this reason it is legitimate to ask, if and to what degree, the *Lisbon Strategy*, as re-launched in March 2005, is an adequate answer to these challenges.[10] The new agenda can be read at least in two ways. At a more narrow *technocratic* level, it is a collection of measures that are relatively loosely dovetailed. The two basic innovations at this level are the so-called open method of coordination, namely the rejection of previously predominant centralized methods, stemming from the French and German traditions in public administration. For this reason annual programs are decentralized to the national level, and this is where funding for most initiatives is being secured. This also is an important novelty, reminding the new members of the fact that the EU is decreasingly about redistribution. What used to be a British peculiarity (ever since the famous exclamation of Baroness Thatcher: 'I want my money back!') is by now general practice. Maximizing transfers from EU funds does not qualify as a meaningful, not even a feasible, integration strategy, as the coffers are basically empty. The Financial Guidelines for 2007–13 allow for a redistribution of a mere 1.045 per cent of Gross National Income (GNI) despite the joining of two poor countries, Bulgaria and Romania in 2007.

But seen in a *broader perspective,* the Lisbon Agenda is a call for rejuvenating Europe, for it contains a refocusing of priorities to the high tech industries, to education and competitiveness in general. The Lisbon Agenda does not contain big investment projects in physical infrastructure, but it calls attention to a number of major issues. It adopts a *back to basics* approach by calling for more growth, and for more growth deregulation of factor and product markets. It also stipulates the use – rather than the production – of information technology across the board, also in traditional industries and households. It conceives education as a strategic sector, one whose major function is not to keep entire cohorts of young people out of the labor market, but prepare them for more and better jobs, for non-traditional forms of employment, for life-long learning and for working with different corporate cultures. It sustains the previous concerns about gender equality and social protection, but the previous bureaucratic approach of plan indicators has been softened and even given up.

If we accept that this rather general agenda, just owing to its high level of abstraction, is perhaps best suited to address the *diverse concerns* of the member states, and that its reformist quest and focus on global competitiveness reflects the basic coordinates of strategy, this translates into a call for *further reforms within the member states, old and new.* The tasks of attaining fiscal sustainability as a side condition for a viable welfare state is a big challenge, but a manageable one, as the experience of the Scandinavian countries has convincingly demonstrated. The concept of 'flexsecurity', as the combination of flexibility with retraining and decent living conditions, coupled with the expressed willingness to work originating from Denmark, is perhaps a sign of what needs to be done.

One of the remarkable features of *international competitiveness studies,* such as those by the World Economic Forum in Geneva and the International Management Institute in Lausanne is clear evidence, at global scale, of the viability of distinctly different roads to success. For instance the leading players, such as Singapore, the USA, or Finland, Denmark and Switzerland, have markedly different arrangements at the macro- and microlevels alike. Similarly, if we look at labor market data, even the EU liberal arrangements, such as those in Ireland and Hungary, may be equally effective as more regulated arrangements, as in Denmark or Austria. In sum, the lasting diversity of the routes to success seems to be a sustaining feature of transition.

If this is the case, we cannot and *should not speak,* even at the more abstract level, about a well-defined terminus in the singular. Perhaps it makes sense to talk about termini, in plural, within the established traditions of Pryor, Montias and Bornstein, namely the defining figures in comparative economics. This non-mainstream approach has now in part been revived in comparative political science by the 'varieties of capitalism' approach (Iversen, 2005; Bohle and Greskovits, 2007). The message of all these – in part competing, in part complementary – approaches is that there is nothing wrong or surprising to see the end point of 'transition' being inherently different by the country and *even open-ended in historical perspective.*

If this is the case, the question mark in the title of this essay remains legitimate. For the past, we may still want and perhaps are obliged to ask, if the costs could have been lower and the gains higher. As in standard economic analysis, the answer is often[11] affirmative. For the future, however, *we have lost the standard, the rod of measure.* Most probably we can run the standard analyses to find the usual suspects in bringing about less than ideal outcomes. However, the lack of a clearly defined end-point, as well as allowing for *path dependence,* and even more for *public choices* that may differ by the country and the generation, will render the concept of optimality less than operational. Perhaps the difference between micro- and macroeconomic concepts and levels of interpretation is likely to remain a lasting feature in understanding real-world developments, such as the historic change from communism to the EU. Once we give up the implicit assumption that Georgia should as equally end up being a version of Sweden as Slovenia, there is nothing surprising about the divergent paths and also of the different end-stations. To judge the difference may remain, to a large degree, *a matter of value judgment,* not liable to quantitative checking.

Notes

1. For own reading of events, see Csaba (2007).
2. Not only the Stability and Growth Pact is recurrently flouted, but so are a number of other regulations, such as those envisaging the single market or environmental protection. The Commission produces regular monitoring reports, naming and shaming trespassers, which include not only and not primarily the new member states.
3. For instance, in the case of Hungary in 2004 and 2005, funds originally earmarked for regional development projects have been re-channeled by the Ministry of

Agriculture for production subsidies, in one case, for example, to support the notoriously crisis-ridden poultry sector.
4. It is a different issue that shortcut solutions such as unilateral euroization or the currency board option may be counterproductive (Nuti, 2002).
5. In this line of reasoning, meeting EMU criteria does not imply any additional burden, as it is a synthesis of stability and growth promoting tasks that need to be implemented anyway (Csaba, 2001).
6. According to an opinion poll of spring 2006, only 18 per cent of the voters of the governing Socialists believed that fiscal deficits constitute a problem (while the actual magnitude of the latter was above 10 per cent by the end of the year).
7. More on this issue in Kolodko (ed.) (2005).
8. Earlier attempts to modify the boundaries set by Moscow, such as the 1956 Polish and Hungarian uprisings, the 1968 Prague Spring, or the 1980–81 Solidarity movement, all foundered on the constraints set by the geopolitical situation. Changing of the latter was not entirely independent of what happened in Central Europe, but it would be an exaggeration to attribute the erosion of the system to factors within the satellite states.
9. This experience has perhaps been the most palpable in the 1980s when the Maroy Government in France and the Papandreu Government in Greece attempted to revitalize the economy following old-fashioned Keynesian recipes. The openness of the economies as well as the size and depth of international capital markets has only increased, and capital controls abolished.
10. A recent special issue of the monthly of the Hungarian Academy of Sciences has been devoted to elaborating various aspects of this set of issues from a number of disciplinary perspectives by articles written by leading authorities on the subject in *Magyar Tudomány*, 167 (2006), 9.
11. One of the first econometric analyses comparing the potential to the actual outcomes (de Melo *et al.*, 2001) has actually found a number of cases, for example Mongolia and Kyrgyzstan, which have outperformed their potential in terms of reforms of the 1990s.

References

Aiginger, K. and A. Guger (2006) 'The ability to adapt: why it differs between Scandinavian and continental European models?', *Intereconomics*, 41 (1), 14–25.
Balázs, P. (1996) *Az EU külpolitikája és Magyarország (CFSP of the EU and Hungary)* (Budapest: Közgazdasági és Jogi Könyvkiadó).
Bara, Z. (2006) 'Competition and Hungarian competition policy', *Public Finance Quarterly*, 2 (2), 213–35.
Buti, M. and D. Franco (2005) *Fiscal Policy in Economic and Monetary Union* (Cheltenham, UK and Northampton, Md, USA: Edward Elgar Publishing Co.).
Bohle, D. and B. Greskovits (2007) 'Neoliberalism, embedded neoliberalism and neocorporatism: paths toward tyransnational capitalism in central and eastern Europe', *West European Politics*, 59 (2), in print.
Csaba, L. (2001) 'The euro – a new entry barrier?', in B. Vènard (ed.) *Économie et Management dans les pays en Transition* (Paris-Angers: jointly published by CNRS and ESSCA), pp. 81–102.
Csaba, L. (2007) *The New Political Economy of Emerging Europe* (Budapest: Akadémiai Kiadó/W.Kluver), 2nd edition.

Dallago, B. and R. McIntyre (eds) (2003) *Small and Medium Enterprises in Transitional Economies* (New York: Palgrave).

De Melo, M., C. Denizer, A. Gelb and S. Tenev (2001) 'Circumstance and choice: the role of initial conditions and policies in transition economies', *World Bank Economic Review*, 13 (1), 1–32.

Gém, E. (2004) 'A kelet-európai bankrendszer átalakulása és fejlődése (Transformation and development of east European banking)', *Külgazdaság*, 48 (9), 23–48.

Györffy, D. (2007) 'Deficit bias and moral hazard on the road to EMU: the political dimension of fiscal policy in Hungary', *Post-Communist Economies*, 1 (1), in print.

Haan, J., H. Berger and D. Jansen (2003) 'The end of the stability and growth pact?', *Munich CES/ifo Working Paper*, no. 145.

Havrylyshin, O. and R. van Roden (2003) 'Institutions matter in transition, but so do policies', *Comparative Economic Studies*, 45 (1), 2–24.

Iversen, T. (2005) *Capitalism, Democracy and Welfare* (Cambridge and New York: Cambridge University Press).

Kolesár, P. (2006) *Race to the Bottom? The Role of Investment Incentives in Attracting Automotive Strategic FDI in CEE*, MA Theses defended at the IRES Department, CEU.

Kolodko, G. W. (2000) *From Shock to Therapy* (Oxford: Oxford University Press for WIDER UNU).

Kolodko, G. W. (2005) *The Polish Miracle: Lessons for Emerging Economies* (Aldershot, Hants, UK: Ashgate Publishers).

Kravtsenniouk, T. (2002) 'Merger regulation in CEE: evidence from Hungary, Romania and Slovenia', *Acta Oeconomica*, 52 (3), 327–46.

Krueger, A. O. (1998) 'Wither the IMF and the World Bank?', *Journal of Economic Literature*, 36 (4), 1983–2002.

Murrell, P. (1992) 'Conservative political philiosophy and the strategy of economic reform', *East European Politics and Societies*, 6 (1), 3–16.

North, D. (2005) *Understanding the Process of Economic Change* (Princeton, New Jersey: Princeton University Press).

Nuti, D. M. (2002) 'Unilateral euroization – an unnnecessary exercise?', *Economics of Transition*, 10 (2).

Polónyi, I. and J. Tímár (2001) *Tudásgyár vagy papírgyár?(Manufacturing knowledge or degrees?)* (Budapest: Új Mandátum Kiadó).

Pleskovic, B. (2007) *Scaling Up Progress in Economic Research and Higher Education in Eastern Europe* (Washington, The World Bank and Budapest: CEU Press), in print.

Sajó, A. (2004) 'Learning cooperative constitutionalism the hard way: the Hungarian Constitutional Court shying away from EU supremacy', *Zeitschrift für Staats- und Europawissenschaften*, 2 (3), 351–71.

14
The Great Post-Communist Change and Uncertain Future of the World

Grzegorz W. Kolodko

14.1 Introduction

Globalization is one of the buzzwords: continuously used and often abused, most often without making an intellectual effort to define this notion. When one is asked whether he or she is for or against globalization, one should try to find out what the inquirer has in mind. It is difficult to answer this question, because no universal definition of globalization exists. Authors define it in various ways. An historian, an anthropologist, a sociologist or an economist – each mean something different by globalization. It is possible to look at globalization as an intricate mechanism of interdependence. It has not only an economic dimension but also a political one, helping some states and their elites advance in the modern world, while pushing aside and marginalizing others. I perceive globalization mainly in economic terms, which I consider as basic, although I am aware of its cultural, ideological and political ramifications.

14.2 Disputes about the definition

From an economic point of view, globalization means the historical process of first liberalization and then progressive integration of the formerly somewhat isolated markets of capital, commodities and (with some delay and on a limited scale) labor into a single world market (see Kolodko, 2001). There are three key words here:

– it is an historical, and hence a long-lasting, process;
– initially, it manifests itself through liberalization;
– and then, through integration.

The scope of economic activity has also been widened in this modern phase of the scientific and technological revolution. This is not a result of what some philosophers dreamt about – space exploration – nor an outcome of the discovering of the Americas which have long been discovered, but a consequence of the creation of a virtual area. The IT revolution, the dissemination of the Internet, has caused the emergence of a virtual area into which a great part of economic activity has moved, mostly related to information flows, but also with the flow of capital, financial operations and banking, education, the multibillion-dollar entertainment business and many other areas. It is not possible to send material goods via the Internet, but it is possible to disseminate through its methods about ways to produce, or know-how, and sell things or bring them to the market. Everything that happens in the virtual area happens globally.

Given such a definition of globalization, it is possible to ask the questions: is this process advantageous or harmful? And to whom? Are we to like it or not, be afraid of it or happy about it, support it or fight it? There is not and never will be any clear-cut answer to these questions. It depends on our position in this global economic and political game and our ability to cope with its inherent risks and costs, as well as on how we can maximize the benefits and take advantage of the new, additional opportunities it brings. It is not possible to have access to the potential benefits from this game without being open to its potential costs. If we want access to other parts of the world economy, to the capital flow and to the technologies to be transferred, we need also to be open to international competition, to the risk of confrontation with companies from other corners of the world, to the penetration of speculative capital, whose only motive is to maximize profit by exploiting some structural weakness – institutional or political – in the place where it is invested.

It is not possible to globalize the world, because it *is* global in essence. Therefore, we should not speak – as many authors mistakenly still do – about 'globalization of the world economy', but simply – 'globalization of the economy'. The world economy *is* global by definition.

Because of the complexity of the ongoing process of globalization, it is necessary to approach the dilemmas of globalization in a methodologically correct and rational way, assessing this dynamic and complicated process in its entirety. It is necessary to know what is related to globalization and what is not: there are many phenomena and processes around, which do not result from globalization, but simply from the fact that we live and act in the present epoch. Therefore, a causal connection is often absent. If somebody has lost his or her job, he or she might (and indeed sometimes does) say: 'It's all because of globalization'. But, is it?

To demonstrate this, it is necessary to prove the existence of a specific cause-and-effect link. For example, that in the context of the free flow of labor, a repairman coming over from another part of the world has pushed a local one out of business. Arguments of this type were often heard, for example, in France during the campaign preceding the referendum on the European Constitution, referring to the 'Polish plumber' depriving his

French colleague of his job. These arguments are reused in Poland, where bricklayers from Ukraine allegedly squeeze Polish building workers out of the labor market. In these cases, we might see it as a consequence of globalization, because these movements are a result of one of its mechanisms – the free, yet only to certain extent, flow of labor on a worldwide scale.

A similar case involves, instead of competitive labor arriving at our place, the relocation of work from our part of the world to another region of the world economy. This often happens because of the disparity of costs, especially wages, among various countries. In this sense, for instance, the British or the Americans are right to claim that workers from India, China, Brazil or Central and Eastern Europe take over some production processes or provide specific types of services. It is interesting to note that this concerns not only the old, traditional industries, like textiles, but also the most modern services related to the functioning of the so-called new economy – the widely spreading sector of information and telecommunication technologies.

But if somebody was fired because he could not or would not perform his duties, failed to improve his skills or simply was a loafer, then it has nothing to do with globalization. Nor does it in the case when someone loses a job through the operation of the implacable mechanics of the capitalist market economy: its inherent and inalienable structural feature consisting in the occurrence of a surplus of workforce – that is, unemployment.

Therefore, we should not hold the new system, which emerges as a result of the globalization processes responsible for all the mounting difficulties. In fact, for some individuals, social or labor groups, trades or sectors, countries or regions, globalization opens up more opportunities, while to others it brings more threats *at the same time*. Certainly, in the present phase of global competition, rich countries which have attained a high level of development – both large economies like the USA or France, and small but highly developed and open economies like Finland or New Zealand – are better positioned than such countries as Chad, Moldova, Paraguay or Mongolia. Many factors contribute to this, including not only the level of development (namely the soundness of market economy institutions and sophistication of management skills), which is a function of various historical processes, but also geographic location. Location can facilitate taking advantage of the benefits of globalization, or interfere with this process, as it does in the case of the latter group of countries.

14.3   Post-communist transformation and the Polish Case

Over the time span of a thousand years, Poland's geopolitics were rather unfortunate: if we were not invaded from the east, then we were from the west, or when we were left alone on both flanks, the Swedes would flood our country from the north... Nowadays, we have an excellent geopolitical position, which we can and should use wisely in the global economic game. Poland occupies a central position in Europe, between the enlarging European Union of which we are already a member since May 2004, and the growing economies of the Commonwealth of Independent States (CIS), which is embracing the mechanisms of the market economy and political democracy, though in a particular post-Soviet style. This favorable geopolitical position offers Poland and some other countries of East Central Europe opportunities which are not given, for instance, to the post-Soviet countries of Central Asia, like Kyrgyzstan or Turkmenistan.

The favorable geographic location translates into better chances in global competition. But if this opportunity is not used properly – which is what Poland's eastern policy, especially towards Russia, unfortunately suggests[1] – this will only be attributable to the deficiencies of this policy and the lack of judgment. No matter what progress we make in the context of the globalization process in general, and the integration within the framework of the European Union in particular,[2] geographic location will never cease to be of importance. As soon as it is possible to develop favorable economic (technological, trade, financial, marketing, etc.) relations with our neighbors, we should do it.

Even if Russia's GDP (according to purchasing power parity) of about US $1.5 trillion is only about three times bigger than Poland's and accounts for merely about 2.5 per cent of total world output, the potential of this country is huge, and it will show in due time. Hence, we should take advantage of this chance for further expansion of the Polish economy and entrepreneurship under the circumstances of globalization – that is, liberalization, opening and integration. Regrettably, Poland's erroneous foreign policy makes that difficult, as a result of which we are wasting time and losing the potential possibility of penetrating this important (not only for us) part of the world economy. We should harbor no illusions that others will fail to make skilful use of this opportunity.

Therefore, it is also possible to interpret globalization as an economic game, in which additional opportunities and additional threats appear simultaneously. It follows that we are opening up ever more widely to business, financial, investment, cooperative, political and cultural relations with foreign countries – or, better still, 'with other parts of the more and more integrated world economy', part of which we have already become. Taking advantage of this situation, we remove successive psychological and political obstacles, but first of all, we eliminate the tariff and non-tariff barriers to trade and capital flows. We make direct capital investments in new economic capacity, implement new technologies and management and marketing abilities, and attract portfolio capital that can be invested in short-term money markets and long-term financial and capital endeavors. Foreign capital – that is, savings made in other parts of the world economy – invested in our government securities or on capital or commodity exchanges, influences the prices of goods and services (and hence also, indirectly, supply and demand), wages and currency exchange rates. All of this has far-reaching, direct and indirect consequences for the functioning of the economy and society, whose complexity eludes many participants in the economic life and actors in public discourses.

With regard to exchange rates – the peculiar point of contact between ones' national economy and the rest of the world – the question remains as valid as ever: what is the result of what? A strong Polish zloty – in a still relatively weak economy, which delivers merely 0.84 per cent of the world output – is a consequence of foreign capital inflow, which by increasing the demand for the Polish currency is also raising its price, that is, the exchange rate. These capital flows into Poland are, to a large degree, speculative in nature. They are encouraged by the interest rates set by the National Bank of Poland (NBP), which for several years, until recently, had been raised beyond an economically justified level and higher than in other parts of the world – that is, more profitable for short-term speculative capital. Such an interest rate differential is destructive for a substantial part of the national economy, primarily export-oriented enterprises, because the overvalued zloty renders exports unprofitable.

By the same token, imports become relatively cheap and the flood of foreign goods sweeps out many domestic producers and distributors (from shipyards to food processing factories to tailor shops to shoemakers) from the domestic market. In consequence, earnings obtained by enterprises from sales in other parts of the world economy are dwindling. The falling earnings also mean losses for the state and for the beneficiaries of the budget, because of smaller tax revenues. Subcontractors are losing, too, as the demand for the goods and services they deliver is falling. A chain reaction follows which further affects the general economic situation, as we saw clearly (for other reasons as well) in 1998–2001, after the departure from the program of structural reforms and social and economic development known as 'Strategy for Poland', and again since mid-2004.[3] The relatively sound growth of exports in recent years – 16.6 per cent in 2005 and about 21 per cent in 2006[4] – is mainly due to the integration with the European Union and would be much higher, exceeding a sustained 25 per cent annually on average, in the absence of the Central Bank's higher interest rate policy.

14.4 From shock to therapy

The phenomena in question are illustrated by the recurrent periods of decelerated growth[5] (or even a recession resulting from the 'shock without therapy' at the beginning of the 1990s) shown in Figure 14.1; or, in the context of the past few years, by a drastic drop in the rate of growth, almost to a stagnation at the turn of 2001, followed by an acceleration connected

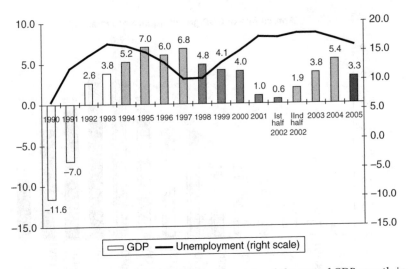

Figure 14.1 From Shock to Therapy. Unemployment and the rate of GDP growth in Poland, 1990–2005 (%)
Note: The periods: 1990–2003 – shock 'therapy'; 1994–97 – strategy for Poland; 1998–2001 – overcooling; 2002–04 – Program of Public Finance Reform
Source: Central Statistical Office (GUS), Warsaw. Unemployment rate according to the old methodology. The current actual rate, according to the ILO methodology, is about two points higher

with Poland's 'Public Finance Reform Program'[6] and, unfortunately, deceleration since mid-2004 (Figure 14.2).

What is important – and, unfortunately, socially painful – is the fact that the people are affected by the scarcity of jobs and, consequently, persistently high unemployment. Despite the fundamental acceleration of growth among 60,000 small- and medium-size enterprises (almost all of them private) in 2002–03, owing to the debt-relief anti-crisis package and the launching of the 'Public Finance Reform Program', which caused the economic growth rate to jump from 0.2 per cent in the fourth quarter of 2001 to 7.0 per cent in the first quarter of 2004, economic dynamics plunged afterwards again. Bringing down GDP growth to merely 2.1 per cent in the first quarter of 2005 was – apart from the inefficient government policies – caused by the overvalued exchange rate of the zloty.

Does it all relate to globalization? It does, yet the blame should not be attached to anonymous 'globalization', but to the country's fiscal and monetary authorities, that is the *sensu largo* government and the Central Bank. As a country, Poland could, if it chose, shape the exchange rate of its national currency to other currencies. This influence is not directly available to the government, but it is to the Central Bank, thanks to its constitutionally guaranteed independence from the government. The influence of the monetary authorities on exchange rates depends on the chosen

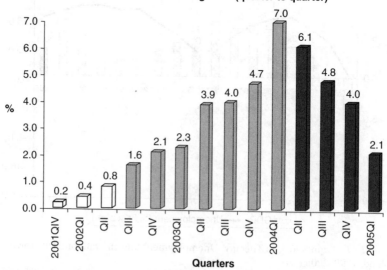

Annual rate of GDP growth (quarter to quarter)

Figure 14.2　Rate of growth fluctuations in Poland in 2001–05
Source: Central Statistical Office (GUS), Warsaw

currency system and on executed policies. Therefore, if exchange rates evolve adversely from the point of view of Polish enterprises and the entire economy, it is not globalization that is to blame, but the errors of this country's own policy, especially the monetary policy of the independent Central Bank. Other countries – including many of new European Union members being also involved in the systemic post-communist transformation to a market order and integration into the world economy – manage, in one way or another, to deal with this problem, as is the case, for example, with the large economies of China or India, as well as smaller ones, like Chile or Malaysia.

As a country, Poland does not have any influence on the exchange rate of the dollar to the euro, although its level – closely connected with the functioning of the global economy – is of great importance to the entire Polish economy. By a fluke of fortune – which is like fair weather for a farmer – we have been successful lately because of the appreciation of the euro to the dollar, being highly profitable for Poland in view of the geographic and currency structure of our exports, an increasing part of which is invoiced and booked in euros. In other words, the growing importance of exchange rates for our economy, which is becoming open and integrating with global economy, is an unavoidable consequence of globalization, and the appreciation or depreciation of zloty's rate to other currencies is an effect of a better or worse financial policy: the budget (fiscal) policy of the government and, especially, the monetary policy of the Central Bank.

Anyone can keep track of the exchange rate of the zloty and draw his own conclusions. For the same rate means different things for different economic actors, depending on whether one is an exporter or importer, producer or consumer, seller or buyer, a person who is about to leave the country or has just arrived. What is a great opportunity for one group of people may be an extra risk for some other group, for which it is likely to increase costs. The volatility of exchange rates, freedom and ease of travelling, open borders – all these have their consequences, which can act as a double-edged sword. Thus a person about to travel abroad can derive maximum profits from this opportunity when he or she pays before the rates go down; on the other hand, an exporter in this situation risks some extra costs which he or she may or may not be able to handle. In many cases, exporters are unable to face this risk and have to close down their business or go bankrupt, further increasing the level of country's poverty and unemployment. In this context, we can ask again: is it globalization that is responsible for that? It is, but not entirely, because – as we already know – we have no influence on the rate of the dollar to the euro, but we do have – or, rather, could have – an influence on the zloty's exchange rate to other currencies.

At this moment, the question arises: who is 'we'? 'We, Poland' do have such an influence, but 'we, the government' do not and neither do 'we, producers', that is the business sector. There exist various ways of shaping exchange rates in the short term and practically all of them are in the hands of the Central Bank, which is independent of the government. This is not to say that the Central Bank is immune to all kinds of influence, because it may be susceptible to lobbying from some groups of businesses, to certain types of views (if not even the ideologies), or to pressure from other global economic entities, not necessarily domestic ones, which foster their own interests and follow their own goals. It is always good to look at the complex mechanism of income redistribution – in this case, worldwide – and reflect on who is likely to gain and who to lose when the mutually related interest and exchange rates evolve as they do.

14.5 Apologists and opponents

There are many apologists of globalization, uncritical supporters of it; some of them may be seen as a kind of global market fundamentalists, and for some of them, it pays off well. And, obviously, globalization at the same time also has many opponents and disparagers. It happens that, sometimes, the same authors are acting in both roles, yet not as Dr Jekyll and Mr Hyde, but by attempting to balance the merits and drawbacks of the phenomenon and its implications for different agents. Books printed recently not only extol globalization[7] but also condemn it,[8] and are critical of free market and uncontrolled capital flows which result in greater inequalities in the contemporary world and a growing margin of social exclusion. Like in any debate, what some people praise, others criticize. It is not difficult to understand if only the potential, or better the real, conflict of economic interests is taken into account.

When there is a need for greater numbers of qualified nurses from Poland or other Slavic countries, or from former colonial and English speaking countries of Sub-Saharan Africa, like Malawi or Zambia, in rich European Union states, or (while the outsourcing is not sufficient to fill the gap) for the computer programmers from India or China in the USA, this kind of human flow is welcome by the receiving countries. When there is a need to have more unskilled workers from Haiti or Guatemala to work in the strawberry fields or orange orchards of Florida or California, this kind of human flow is seasonally accepted as well. The same is clearly to be seen in the Middle East where plenty of people from South Asian countries, like Pakistan or Bangladesh, work on construction sites in the Emirates or in Saudi Arabia, or in South Africa and Botswana where millions are trying to get in Mozambique, Swaziland and Zimbabwe.

Yet when a person wants to immigrate to another country, just because living standards are higher there, double standards very quickly come into play. 'We' want to travel to rich countries, but do not like it when 'they' come to our country from the poor ones. In our part of the global village, or rather the global city, we are expecting the European Union to abolish any limits concerning the transfer of the new EU members from East Central Europe workforce; but when a person from, say, Ukraine or Kazakhstan, wants to integrate, that is to immigrate and try his or her luck in our countries, we do not hesitate to apply many restrictions. And problems of this kind – opportunities or threats, depending on the vantage point – are widespread when it comes to opening, liberalization and integration, that is globalization.

Where does the influx of great supporters and fierce opponents come from? From the fact that one can look at globalization in yet another way, seeing it as nothing else than a great triumph of worldwide capitalism. Globalization *is* worldwide capitalism. It is not socialism or communism, it is not a planned economy and neither is it a social market economy in a social democratic, say Scandinavian meaning. It is quite a brutal, liberal, avaricious, aggressive capitalism, this time of a nearly worldwide scope. It operates on the global arena.

Of course, the situation is very dynamic and changes a lot and not only in one direction. It fluctuates. Globalization is a process, so it is logical that it evolves and develops, expands and ripens; it is on a track of permanent movement. Mostly, however, forward. Hence, another interesting question arises: looking from a strictly economic point of view, do we already have one integrated worldwide economy? This would imply that de facto we have one market in the world, with one curve of supply and one curve of demand, crossing at the point of world-economy equilibrium, in which way one worldwide price is set and the market is cleared. However, this is not the case. Let's take an example of the coffee thermos: in the real world, there are many local and regional markets for this product, and hence also many curves of supply and demand, and many equilibrating prices that can clear these local or regional markets and not the world markets.

In an ideal – yet, of course, unreal – 'world economy', there should be one market-clearing price and thus all coffee thermos flasks should cost the same (bar the costs of transport), because the perfect market mechanism would ensure that. Do such integrated markets at all exist? Indeed, there are some, but very few, because in general we still have to do with normal local markets where local customers declare their own demand, which determines the price of locally sold goods or locally provided services. Among the few existing worldwide markets are those of petroleum, which (simplifying things a bit) has one price (for products of the same quality, excluding transportation costs) all over the world,[9] as well as some very specific high-technology goods, such as aircrafts; there is one market for Boeings and Airbuses.

Globalization does not imply that everything has the same prices everywhere or that everything can be produced and sold everywhere. In a perfect 'globalized economy', it would be the case, if only a (global) company would:

- sell where clients get most value;
- get capital where it is most abundant;
- find resources in the most cost-effective location;
- organize production where it is most convenient.

That is not yet a reality, though some global firms already act according to these four principles, especially in motorcar and electronic appliances industries.[10]

Unlike such an 'ideal global economy', the real one, the one we act with and in, only concerns the operation of certain specific mechanisms of production and distribution. If it can be shown, for instance, that ther-moses – or one should say nowadays, an iPod or digital camera – are more expensive in Warsaw than in Beijing, yet to manufacture such items is less costly in the latter than the former, then they will be produced in the latter city and sold in the former. Free market, information flow, lowering costs of transport and convertible currencies make this possible and in the contemporary global economy unavoidable.

However, in the long run, this procedure will affect the costs and prices of the goods, as well as the profit margins and income relations, resulting also in capital flows alongside the flows of goods. And these are very often accompanied by the flows of people, with their abilities, cultures and – invariably – technologies. Instead of sending over the goods (thermoses, PCs, cars or aircrafts), the whole factory is being removed, which means that a new one (producing thermoses, PCs, cars, aircrafts) is built. Thus not all BMWs on American roads have been produced in Germany (Bavaria) as the name Bayerische Motoren Werke would imply, as the manufacturer has built factories also in America. Nowadays almost no Toyotas arrive in America by crossing the ocean like 25 years ago because, instead of transporting the cars, capital, technology, know-how, marketing skills, and some labor too, have been transferred to the USA or elsewhere. Nowadays, the Dell PC being sold in Massachusetts or England is assembled from parts manufactured by 400 companies on three continents. That would not be possible without the contemporary phase of globalization.

People who are caught in these processes and in the global division of labor – the proprietors of capital, manufacturers, distributors and consumers – are maximizing their own functions, their utility; capital returns grow, and so does the satisfaction of customers. Thus everyone concerned can be satisfied with the effects of globalization. But when someone else, facing the same opportunity, is losing capital, unable to deal with worldwide competition or to establish his products or services on a market, he or she has a real reason to be dissatisfied, and, well, to complain in this or another way.

Therefore, those who praise globalization while failing to penetrate the complexity of this process – in itself neither good nor bad, depending as it does on many different factors, the relative importance of which one cannot assess once and for all without first disentangling the mesh of contradictory social and economic interests – tend, in general, to be apologists or ideologues. In economics, we find no lack of people of this kind, who think that without any reservation capitalism is the best and the most efficient system of all, while whatever deviations or pathologies do occur result not from its very nature, but from inept policies (especially those leaning to the left or emphasizing social issues), external shocks or incompetent leadership.

That is not the case, since there are many built-in inefficiencies, negative externalities and defects in capitalism as such, that we know – or should have known for a long time. And that will cause in the future a great deal of social and political problems, since the global market economy, that is worldwide capitalism in its contemporary form, will prove unable to solve the mounting problems of still growing inequality and the widening scope of social exclusion, on the one hand, and coordinate on a global scale policy response to numerous economic challenges, on the other.

As Churchill once observed, democracy has disadvantages and may turn nasty because it is not easy to govern, but a better system has yet to be invented. Now we can say the same about capitalism: it has many disadvantages but so far no one has come up with anything better. It is not by accident that such opinions very often come from philosophers, economists, politicians and businessmen from countries which use the opportunities of global capitalism to their best advantage. Obviously, the greatest winners are the economically and politically strongest countries, whose capital resources and especially the quality of human capital are a source of huge competitive advantage in the global structure. The strength of the market economy institutions further reinforces this effect for them.

These countries are in a position to utilize more easily the extra opportunities that come from their openness, liberalization, privatization, access to new markets (called by them 'emerging') and new supplies of labor. And, of course, they can also take to their full advantage the ongoing IT revolution and immense technological progress. But even there, views, opinions and books can frequently be encountered which are extremely opposed to world capitalism and globalization. The word 'capitalism' itself was more readily used some time ago; today, we prefer to speak about a 'global market', contrasted to 'communism' or, less often, 'socialism'. Methodologically, we should be speaking about the opposition of 'market economy' versus 'planned economy', or 'capitalism' versus 'socialism'. We should already be aware of the fact that capitalism – which now becomes world capitalism – has different faces, which are going to change further and are already changing in the face of all that criticism. However, among justified criticism, there is also a lot of irrational disapproval, voiced, among others, by anti- and alter-globalists without a cause, or so often without any workable alternative agenda. The capitalist market economy is a system that so far has proved its higher efficiency compared to a socialist planned economy. However, in many aspects, it is still flawed. This is why the struggle for 'the human face' of (world) capitalism must and will continue.

14.6   Globalization with a human face or fierce capitalism?

Would globalization be able to survive, taking care not only of itself but also of efficiency and expansion, as well as showing justice and true human concern? Does a 'human face' of globalization exist?[11] Searching for it does make sense. It is necessary to keep searching for these very important social aspects in development processes through discussions and an adequate policy because, for sure, this is not the end of history; the most interesting part of history has just began, at least for us and a couple of following generations. Francis Fukuyama may have declared the end of history,[12] but in this respect, he was wrong (as he has known very well from the beginning himself). And so was Lenin when he said, already 90 years ago, that imperialism was the highest stage of capitalism.[13] If he lived nowadays, his work would probably have a title like: 'Globalization, the Highest Stage of Capitalism'. But he would be mistaken again, because this stage is not 'final', either.

Other stages will follow, as development goes on and contradictions are never in short supply, because the world is changing. So globalization is just the latest stage – and only a stage – in the permanently changing course of the evolving world. And even if we don't know a *priori* – and we do not – what the coming stages of mankind and economic orders will be like in the unforeseeable future, they will come. In due time, although we do not even know when such a time will arrive . . .

Thus globalization emerges as a historical outcome of development and a triumph of the world capitalist system – with all the consequences of this fact. What will be the consequences of this phenomenon? Is this system equitable or is it not? How do its performance and expansion affect the dynamics of production and the distribution of production capacity growth at the working place? It appears that the mechanisms triggered by the process of transformation, integration and globalization contribute to a higher growth dynamics than would otherwise be the case.[14] On average, output grows faster than it would without globalization.[15] It follows that all of us – all mankind, and not only the inhabitants of some region or country – on average, live a better life. However, the question immediately arises about who is included in this improvement: how many of us, where and in what ways live better lives – half of us or more? Who is in majority and who in minority? The answer we find is that in the last quarter of a century, so profoundly affected by globalization, the economic stratification of humanity has been increasing – for many different reasons.

A good example is provided by Botswana, an African country where the growth rate in the last 40 years amounted on average to 10 per cent per year, whereas in the neighboring Congo, where over 50 million people live in great poverty, a negative rate of growth was observed. In other words, the level of production and consumption is lower there today than it was in 1965, in the last years of brutal Belgian colonialism. Is this deplorable situation caused by globalization? Far from it,[16] it results – just as the progress in Botswana does – from regional, local and national factors, but mainly from the country leaders' economic policy followed for years. In Congo, the situation has severely deteriorated through the same mechanism, that is policy, this time dominated by years of corruption in government, macroeconomic mismanagement, and numerous military and ethnic conflicts, which unfortunately persist to this day, despite certain progress recently, and have little in common with globalization.

There are many more examples like this. Let me make a digression here: while discussing economics and, more importantly, implementing economic policy, it is always necessary to be able to distinguish results from reasons; manifestations from mechanisms; and, especially in politics and development policies, one must not confuse the means with the ends. Failure to understand this on the part of politicians hampers development, and on the part of scientists, it creates confusion. If somebody fails to grasp it, they tell the public that such problems result from some mysterious modern plagues rather than inept economic policy *vis-à-vis* the goals of counteracting joblessness, increasing competitiveness, gaining footholds in knowledge-based economies, improving hard infrastructure, constructing a pro-growth budget which at the same time restricts marginalization and social exclusion, or achieving monetary stabilization and pro-expansion exchange rates.

All this is necessary and possible to attain but has to be done under the circumstances of globalization. Thus a correct economic theory is essential for good economic practice, taking into account the global dimension of economic processes. In the last decades, when income disparities have been growing again, the question arises of whether it is really globalization that accounts for the fact that the rich are becoming richer and the poor are getting poorer? This is not the case and I think such an assumption is false. It is a claim put forward by some opponents of globalization who either do not know all the facts well enough and are not really qualified to take a stand, or do believe this claim to be false and yet make it for the sake of expediency.

And what is the truth? Globalization favours a situation where the allocation mechanisms of capital transfers, trade, liberalization and asset privatization in many countries cause the profits of the richest groups to grow faster than the gains of the poorest people and countries. There are certain exceptions, but they are not connected with globalization. The way things are, if one agent has capital in the amount of 100 units and somebody else has only 10 units, after a few production cycles, the first one will have achieved a profit of, for example, 80 per cent and now has 180 units, while the other – whatever it is, a country, a sector, an enterprise, a social group, a family – will have accrued an increase of about 20 per cent only. Thus the initial disparity, or inequality, of 10:1 will have grown to 15:1. This kind of outcome has been used so often in so many places to make a case against globalization, yet both agents have actually gained.

Although this is a win-win situation, the gainer of a smaller award in this game is keen to consider himself or herself as a loser. Yet he or she is not, especially if the growth of income by 20 per cent of the latter has, directly or indirectly, resulted from or was linked with, the growth of income by 80 per cent of the former.

Such an answer immediately suggests another question to be dealt with in a concrete context. We have to check whether higher growth is not achieved at the expense of slower growth at the lowest end of the spectrum, which would signify inequitable distribution. Or maybe the improvement of income by as much as 80 per cent was made possible by such a substantial increase of income in the first group, thanks, for instance, to boosting overall income through greater efficiency, entrepreneurship or innovation. Such a situation happens so often if entrepreneurs or good managers are contributing to economic expansion upon which employed labor is relying with growth of their individual incomes. Of course, in the long run, labor productivity must grow too, yet it is growing due to the very fact that sound entrepreneurship and management is at the foundation of this growth. If this is the case, such developments should be welcome, not because of the increasing disparities, but due to the accompanying increase of income and improvement in the living standards of many people. Unfortunately, this is not always the case. Worse still, entire large areas exist in the world where no improvement takes place, although – once again – globalization is not the sole culprit here, or, in many cases, has nothing to do with the existing state of affairs.

The situation of Africa calls for special attention in this context. We must not just leave that continent as it is, with its poverty and marginalization. Gradually and successively drawing Africa into the orbit of world economic exchange, along with care about its development, is a task of paramount importance in the modern world. The recent proposals of the British Prime Minister Tony Blair and Chancellor of the Exchequer Gordon Brown, introduced under the heading of 'Commission for Africa', are highly meaningful, especially in view of the British presidency of the G-8 group of the world's richest countries in 2005. The United Kingdom also held the presidency of the European Union in the second half of 2005. So if the British are saying that things cannot go on like that any more, and are indeed ready to write-off unsustainable debt of the poorest countries of the world, it appears to open up a chance to overcome a stalemate over structural assistance for Africa – a continent with over 800 million inhabitants, many of whom live in extreme poverty – and for other most miserable parts of the new brave world.

14.7   Things can go on like this much longer...

Although many people have been saying for a long time that 'things cannot go on like this any longer', there are still over a billion people around the world subsisting on less than a dollar a day, dozens of millions children in Africa and elsewhere go to sleep hungry and several million people die of hunger every year. This is not fiction. It happens for real – this is the way it is. The global economy emerges, but still lacks political arrangements that would address the creation of an autonomous development mechanism or, until such a mechanism is in place, provide redistribution of appropriate funding from the richer parts of the world to the poorer areas and lands. And the claim that the equivalent of half a bubble gum in London is enough to save a child's life in Africa has nothing to do with populism. It shows how great the distortions are in the world economy and how unfair the income distribution is if seen from the global perspective.

If, therefore, Great Britain has unilaterally suggested the cancellation of debt and done so for the benefit of the poorest countries, all others should follow suit. Then, increased investment spending must be directed in the coming years to infrastructure, without which no progress can be achieved in many backward parts of the world economy. Part of the spending from external sources should also be invested in human capital, particularly education and public health. At the same time, it is necessary to ensure such assistance because arguments of a humanitarian nature make a short-time impression, but yield few practical results. Likewise, African partners, and this is also true for Latin America, part of Asia and the poorest regions of post-communist countries in Eastern Europe and the former Soviet Union, must perform their part of the task and launch a vigorous fight against corruption, as well as put an end to military and ethnic conflicts, from Sri Lanka to Chechnya, from Middle East to Darfur, from Liberia to Columbia.

It will depend on our ability to deal with such massive problems as unpaid debts, excessive disparities in wealth, mass joblessness and poverty inherited from the colonial times and aggravated by bad governance, whether the world will look for a 'human face', or rather plunge into a revolution triggered by excessive social stress. I do not see any simple way of ensuring continued growth and sharing its results on a worldwide scale over the next generation or two by simply 'staying on the course'. After all, there is not a sound 'course' which deserves to be stayed on. It not only cannot, but even should not, succeed because the present neo-liberal (in the European meaning) 'development model', based on the naïve belief in the miraculous power of an invisible hand of markets and 'trickle down' economic policy, is economically inefficient, socially unfair and politically unsustainable. Such a situation turns against efficiency and economic growth. Simply, it is dangerous. Therefore, it must cause an explosion; it is only a matter of time. Such an explosion might take the form of uncontrolled waves of migration, which neither the poor nor the rich countries will be able to contain, and one fence here or another there will not stop; or of massive urban riots, economically motivated terrorism, and, of course, the energy and environmental crises. In what sequence and proportions will these maladies arise remains to be seen. Probably all of them, to some extent. And we will see it, since it will occur not too long into the future.

But there exist positive responses to these threats and challenges, too. In particular, better coordination of policy is essential on a worldwide scale, because, although a world economy is emerging, no 'world government' has emerged as yet. Does this mean that such a government is likely to evolve? Far from it. Expectations of this kind are unreal and there would be no point in calling for the establishment of a world minister of economy, world minister of finance, world minister of welfare, or a central bank of the world (even if there wouldn't be a shortage of applications for such positions...).

Because the world is too differentiated and disturbed, there is nobody able to rule it. Nevertheless, it is possible to understand it better and try to change it for the better. The world needs better policy coordination on a global scale. Do we have the proper organizations, institutions and instruments to handle this task yet? We can somehow coordinate common approaches to such different issues as the war against terrorism, money laundering, migration, greenhouse effect and climate warming, or defusing financial crises, when the need arises. However, it turns out that these political mechanisms often fail. Therefore, we are faced with new challenges in the era of globalization. If we do not handle them aptly, the world will be headed for a great crisis, and not only an economic one. Thus the main challenge for the years to come is a design and execution of a new world institutional order which will gradually and peacefully replace the existing world institutional chaos.

When we talk about globalization, we should bear in mind that we talk at the same time about conflicting economic interests and political priorities which are often on a collision course. This concerns not only the world at large but also our immediate surroundings. Here, too, it can be heard, that 'things cannot go on like this any longer', but we know that they will stay as they are for a long time to come.

Curiously, this all takes place in the conditions of functioning, at least nominally, parliamentary democracies in most countries. Indeed, democracy – as the market economy – is in full swing in most of the world. But democracy has not established a firm foothold in the entire world. Capitalism carries the day, the markets are more and more liberalized, but in the end democracy does not appear to be prevailing everywhere. And even if it does function in an ever increasing part of the planet, on the one hand, the world as a whole is not democratic, and on the other, quite often democracy is unable to deliver what it is supposed to do.

In many 'emerging markets' – where democracy is also emerging at the same historic time – the latter hardly helps and strengthens the former.[17] This would not be a cause for concern, if only the existing institutional arrangements of the world economy, undemocratic though they are, offered an opportunity to solve the above-mentioned major problems that afflict us. Unfortunately, they do not.

We do not vote in the world; we just do business – and wars are one of the ways to do business – although we say it is all for the sake of introducing democracy. A truly great policy should not rely on global control or on who sides with whom and for what reason, but only on solving great social problems on economic grounds. Therefore, in the years and decades to come, we must successively create mechanisms and instruments, and increase our ability to solve such problems on a worldwide scale, and not only on a regional level. Therefore, we now face the great challenges of the twenty-first century, completely different from those before, that stem from more advanced societies, liberalized and integrated markets, and great technological revolution related to the Internet, telecommunications, genetics or biotechnology, which puts the world in a completely different position.

Globalization will continue to be the subject of discussion and disputes for a very long time, if not forever. If there is anything 'forever' in the first place. Political struggle and intellectual wrestling should go on to find the best ways to understand the economic and political mechanisms that govern the whole business that we call 'our world'.[18] We should define correctly the values and find a way of putting into practice the adopted goal of development through dialogue. This is all very hard, but certainly not impossible. And even just trying to do so is worth an effort because it can help make the world better, although the future is not clear. For the economists this is good news, but for mankind not necessarily . . .

Notes

1. The same – going the other way around – can be said, for instance, about Belarusian policy towards the West.
2. On the many structural and institutional challenges prior to the formal accession of the post-communist economies to the European Union, see Nuti (2001).
3. For more information, see Kolodko and Nuti (1997) and Kolodko (2005).
4. Fob, in euro.
5. Concerning the political economy of the post-communist great change, see Kolodko and Nuti (1997) and Kolodko (2000).
6. 'Public Finance Reform Program' was executed, yet only to a limited degree because of the lack of political commitment of the then government, since the second half of 2002 until the beginning of 2004. For more extensive discussion, see Kolodko, (2004); see also Kolodko (2003). It must be stressed that during both of the most successful years of Poland's transformation to market economy, that is 1994–97 and 2002–03, during which the GDP per capita has increased altogether by about one third (in real terms) – the highest growth on such a scale in any post-communist country of East Central Europe and the former Soviet Union, Professor D. Mario Nuti was acting as my – then the deputy prime minister and minister of finance of Poland – chief economic advisor. A great part of the credit for such economic success, both towards structural reforms and fast social and economic development, is due to his wise and appropriate advice, based on reasonable economic theory.
7. See Wolf (2003).
8. See Hutton and Giddens (2005).
9. Certainly, this is a simplification too, because for various reasons of mostly political nature, petroleum can be cheaper for some buyers than on the so-called free global market. Thus some Arab states buy petroleum from other Arab states below the 'world price'; Venezuela sells petroleum considerably more cheaply to Cuba than to the USA; likewise, Russia supplies gas at lower prices to Belarus than to Ukraine.
10. On this subject see Friedman (2005).
11. The Institute of which I am the founder and director – Transformation, Integration and Globalization Economic Research – is well known by its acronym TIGER (www.tiger.edu.pl) and our slogan is 'Globalization with a human face'. Yet one must doubt that a tiger with a human face exists as much as one doubts that we'll ever find a unicorn . . .
12. See Fukuyama (1992).
13. Lenin's famous work, written 90 years ago, was called *Imperialism, the Highest Stage of Capitalism*; see www.marxists.org/archive/lenin/works/1916/imp-hsc.
14. On the implications of post-communist transformation for economic growth, see more in Nuti and Uvalic (eds) (2002).

15. This point is well argued in, inter alia (2002).
16. Yet the recent book by John le Carre may suggest so, see le Carre (2006).
17. This appears to be quite often the case of institutionally still weak post-communist market economies. Knowing very well both, the economic mechanism of emerging market economy and political nuances of emerging democracy in my own country, Poland, I must say that the market economy, with all its deficiencies, works a lot better than democracy. The latter, although being a value per se, hardly satisfies people's expectations and often does not at all help to implement necessary structural reforms.
18. On this subject see also North (2005).

References

Bhagwati, J. (2004) *In Defense of Globalizaton* (New York: Oxford University Press).
Friedman, T. L. (2005) *The World Is Flat. A Brief History of the Twenty-First Century* (New York: Farrar, Straus and Giroux).
Fukuyama, F. (1992) *The End of History and the Last Man* (London: Hamish Hamilton).
Hutton, W. and A. Giddens (eds) (2000) *Global Capitalism* (New York: The New Press).
Kolodko, G. W. (2000) *From Shock to Therapy. The Political Economy of Postsocialist Transformation* (Oxford and New York: Oxford University Press).
—— (2001) *Globalization and Catching-up In Transition Economies* (Rochester, New York: Rochester University Press).
—— (ed.) (2003) *Emerging Market Economies. Globalization and Development* (Aldershot, England and Burlington, VT, USA: Ashgate).
—— (2003) *Structural Reform and Economic Growth in 2002–2003*; available at www.tiger.edu.pl/english/aktualnosci/report_en.pdf, See also: *The World Economy and Great Post-Communist Change* (New York: Nova Science Publishers, 2006), Chapter 8, pp. 121–29.
—— (2004) *O Naprawie Naszych Finansów (On the Reform of Public Finance)* (Torun: TNOiK), in Polish, in English see: *Program for Restructuring of the Public Finance of Poland*, Warsaw 2003; available at www.tiger.edu.pl/english/index.htm.
—— (ed.) (2005) *Globalization and Social Stress* (New York: Nova Science Publishers).
—— (ed.) (2005) *The Polish Miracle. Lessons for the Emerging Markets* (Aldershot, England and Burlington, VT, USA: Ashgate).
—— (2006) *The World Economy and Great Post-Communist Change* (New York: Nova Science Publishers).
Kolodko, G. W. and D. M. Nuti (1997) *The Polish Alternative. Old Myths, Hard Facts and New Strategies in the Successful Transformation of the Polish Economy, Research for Action*, 33, The United Nations University World Institute for Development Economics Research, WIDER, Helsinki (reprinted in *Working Papers*, No. 55, Institute of Finance, Warsaw 1997, and by the Confederation of Indian Industry [CII] in: *On the Occasion of the Forth Partnership Summit*, Chennai, 8–10 January 1998).
le Carre, J. (2006) *The Mission Song* (Little Brown and Company).
Lenin, V. I. (1916) *Imperialism, the Highest Stage of Capitalism*; available at www.marxists.org/archive/lenin/works/1916/imp-hsc).
Norberg, J. (2003) *In Defense of Global Capitalism* (Washington DC: CATO Institute).
North, D. C. (2005) *Understanding the Process of Economic Change* (Princeton, NJ: Princeton University Press).
Nuti, D. M. (2001) 'Not "Just Another Accession" ', *Leon Kozminski Academy of Entrepreneurship and Management (WSPiZ) Distinguished Lectures Series*, No. 3; available at www.tiger.edu.pl/publikacje/dist/nuti.pdf.

Nuti, D. M. and M. Uvalic (eds) (2002) *Post-Communist Transition to a Market Economy. Lessons and Challenges* (Ravenna: Longo Editore).

Stiglitz, J. E. (2002) *Globalization and Its Discontents* (New York and London: W. W. Norton & Company).

Wolf, Martin (2004) *Why Globalization Works* (New Haven and London: Yale University Press).

World Bank (2002) *Globalization, Growth, and Poverty: Building an Inclusive World Economy* (New York: Oxford University Press for the World Bank).

Index